Comparing Democracies
Elections and Voting in Global Perspective

Lawrence LeDuc
Richard G. Niemi
Pippa Norris
editors

SAGE Publications
International Educational and Professional Publisher
Thousand Oaks   London   New Delhi

For information address:

SAGE Publications, Inc.
2455 Teller Road
Thousand Oaks, California 91320
E-mail: order@sagepub.com

SAGE Publications Ltd.
6 Bonhill Street
London EC2A 4PU
United Kingdom

SAGE Publications India Pvt. Ltd.
M-32 Market
Greater Kailash I
New Delhi 110048 India

Printed in the United States of America

Library of Congress Cataloging-in-Publication Data

Main entry under title:

Comparing democracies : Elections and voting in global perspective / editors, Lawrence LeDuc, Richard G. Niemi, Pippa Norris.
   p. cm.
  Includes bibliographical references and index.
  ISBN 0-8039-5835-8 (acid-free paper). — ISBN 0-8039-5836-6 (pbk.: acid-free paper)
  1. Democracy. 2. Comparative government. I. LeDuc, Lawrence.
II. Niemi, Richard G. III. Norris, Pippa.
JC423.C663 1996
321.8—dc20   96-10055

99 00 01 02 10 9 8 7 6 5 4

Sage Production Editor: Astrid Virding
Sage Typesetter: Danielle Dillahunt
Sage Cover Designer: Lesa Valdez

Contents

List of Tables

List of Figures

Acknowledgments

We would like to thank the National Science Foundation (SES-9410345) for making possible the conference that brought together the scholars who contributed to this volume. The conference was hosted by the Joan Shorenstein Center on the Press, Politics and Public Policy at the Kennedy School of Government, Harvard University; we are grateful to the Center for its services and to the School for the use of its fine facilities.

The conference was enhanced by the presentation of a number of papers on new democracies:

Vladimir Andreenkov and Anna Andreenkova, Institute for Comparative Social Research (CESSI), Moscow, "Different Ways to Democracy: A Comparative Analysis of the Electoral Systems of Russia, Ukraine, Lithuania, Latvia, and Estonia."

Roberto Espíndola, University of Bradford, Bradford, England, "Democracy and Elections in Latin America."

John Fuh-sheng Hsieh, National Chengchi University, Taipei, "Electoral Politics in New Democracies in the Asia-Pacific Area."

Shaheen Mozaffar, Bridgewater State College, Bridgewater, MA, "The Political Origins and Consequences of Electoral Systems in Africa: A Preliminary Analysis."

János Simon, Hungarian Academy of Science, "Electoral Systems and Democracy: Comparative Electoral Systems in Central Europe During the Transition (1990-1994)."

These papers and the insights espoused by the authors informed all of the participants about the ways in which present theories and generalizations might need to be modified in light of the experiences of countries that have recently undergone democratization or redemocratization. The papers are presently being prepared for publication, possibly as a unit. The conference also benefited from the contributions of other attendees, especially Ken Benoit, Jane Jenson, Cees van der Eijk, and Spencer Wellhofer.

We would like to thank Joanna ʿpear and Rory Austin for assistance in preparation of the tables, Rory Austin and Matthew Gardner for assistance in preparation of the manuscript, and Lynn Vavrek for preparing the index. We also thank Barbara Silveri for typing tables and other material, often on short notice.

Finally, we would like to thank Sage Publications for its support through all aspects of the project.

Introduction

The Present and Future
of Democratic Elections

LAWRENCE LeDUC
RICHARD G. NIEMI
PIPPA NORRIS

The final decade of the 20th century may be seen by future historians as a period of dramatic political change, a global surge toward democracy. Huntington (1991) refers to these developments as the "third wave" of democratization, following on earlier periods of expansion in the late 19th and early 20th centuries, and in the post-World War II period. The most significant changes have occurred in the republics of the former Soviet Union and in the nations of Central and Eastern Europe, where countries are attempting a triple transformation of their party systems, constitutional structures, and economic systems. The results, not surprisingly for such an ambitious venture, have thus far proved mixed. Some countries have moved rapidly down the path toward competitive party politics and free market economies. The Czech Republic and Hungary, for example, have developed strong trading links with the

European Union (EU) and are actively cultivating support for their eventual membership in the EU. Others have clung to reformed Communist parties and outmoded economic structures, and the process of change has been slower.

The expansion of democracy, however, has encompassed far more than the former Communist regimes, as important as the disintegration of the Soviet Union has been. The fall of communism was preceded in Europe by the collapse of authoritarian regimes in Greece, Spain, and Portugal, which are now fully functioning democratic political systems and members of the EU (Gunther, Diamandouros, and Puhle 1995). It was followed by the dramatic end of apartheid in South Africa and the holding of the first fully democratic election in that country in 1994 (Southall 1994). Throughout this period, the growth or reestablishment of democracy has extended to South American countries such as Brazil and Argentina, to Asian countries such as the Philippines and South Korea, and to African countries such as Mali and Zambia (Diamond, Linz, and Lipset 1995). Whether we choose to view this wave of democratization as a large global trend, or as a series of distinct but related developments in various parts of the world, the scope and pace of change have been impressive.

It is not yet known whether these global trends represent a sustainable shift toward democratization in countries that were formerly authoritarian, along with a revitalization of continuing democracies, or whether new and unforeseen obstacles lie ahead for both sets of countries. Huntington (1991) notes that previous waves of democratization have been followed by periods of reaction or "reverse waves" (chap. 1). The expansion of democracy in the early part of the 20th century eventually gave way to Mussolini and Stalin. The democratic revolutions that first accompanied the period of decolonization in Africa and Asia yielded many more authoritarian regimes than functioning democracies. The early growth of democracy throughout Latin America was followed by repressive military regimes in country after country. The global democratic revolution of the late 20th century is cause for optimism, but history suggests a more cautious outlook.[1]

Just as emerging democracies have been undergoing fundamental change, some long-established democracies have experienced major changes in their party systems, in the political attitudes and behavior of their citizens, and sometimes in the foundations of their representative institutions. In some Western nations, traditional patterns of party competition have become less stable and predictable, as Mair discusses in this volume (chap. 3). In France,

Austria, and Belgium, new antisystem parties of the extreme right have been fueled by the politics of race, immigration, and nationalism, further increasing the volatility of electoral politics. Green parties have become established in a number of countries, and the Greens are well-entrenched power brokers in German politics. European Communist and Fascist parties have attempted to reinvent themselves with varying degrees of success (Ware 1996). There has been a decline of traditional social cleavages, which as Dalton suggests (chap. 13), may be the root cause of increasing electoral volatility. And in response to new kinds of campaign opportunities, new forms of party organization are evolving (see Katz, chap. 4). Social movements have changed the political agenda, and "single issue" politics has become a commonplace phenomenon (Bashevkin, chap. 5). Similarly, as discussed by Semetko (chap. 10), Farrell (chap. 6), and Butler (chap. 9), the extensive growth of television and public opinion polling, along with recent technological changes, has changed the process of campaign communications. In some countries, cynicism about politicians and governments has become endemic, fueled by widely publicized cases of political corruption and perceptions of government failure, creating a crisis of legitimacy in its wake.

The cumulative effect of these developments has sometimes been dramatic. Japan, for many years a model of economic success and political stability, finds itself in the throes of political change. Italy, whose citizens have long expressed dissatisfaction with political institutions, has embarked on a long and complex odyssey of political reform. In Canada, voters turned down a sweeping set of constitutional proposals in a 1992 referendum, yet remain deeply dissatisfied with their political institutions and fear that the country might split apart.

Yet these changes should not be exaggerated. Most established democracies continue with relatively little fundamental change in their basic constitutional structures. Once established, an institutional framework acquires entrenched interests that benefit from the status quo, and large-scale constitutional reform becomes a difficult and complex enterprise with only a modest chance of success in most instances. Although some countries have engaged in minor tinkering with procedural regulations governing elections, the basic electoral system—the rules by which votes are cast and translated into seats—has generally persisted without much fundamental change. In countries such as Britain, the United States, Australia, and Mexico, despite pressures for change, the main parties on the ballot, and certainly the only parties in government, have been the same ones that dominated politics in those countries throughout the post-World War II period. The electoral system can present a formidable obstacle to new challengers.

In most industrialized societies, television has altered the conduct of national campaigns, but at the local level many of the traditional rituals of party campaigning continue. In countries such as India, traditional grassroots communication networks are especially important. Worldwide, there have been demands for an opening up of positions of political leadership, and women have made considerable strides in representative assemblies in the Scandinavian countries and elsewhere in Europe. Yet globally, women's parliamentary representation has fallen during the past decade, while the socioeconomic bias of political elites has actually increased over time (see Norris, chap. 7). A long-term assessment of elections and voting behavior in established democracies thus suggests a mixed picture: There are elements of both continuity and change.

The future of democracy in both established and emerging systems depends to a large extent on events related to the electoral process, because elections are the one political institution that both leads and reflects many of the social, political, and economic trends described here. Although elections and democracy are not synonymous concepts, the existence of free, competitive elections is invariably considered one of the critical features that define a nation as "democratic" (Inkeles 1991; Beetham 1994). Indeed, Schumpeter's (1942, 265) often-quoted definition equates democracy with a "competitive struggle for the people's vote." Although other writers (Braybrooke 1968; Barber 1984) would demand more stringent tests for a "true" democracy, it is nevertheless clear that elections are a central, if not *the* central, institution of democratic governance. Yet elections also reflect the conditions of democracy in as many ways as they define it. In countries with an established tradition of free, competitive elections, it is in the voting returns that social scientists and others can regularly discern the mood of the electorate. When U.S. voters elected Bill Clinton in 1992, they also gave 19 percent of their votes to independent candidate Ross Perot, an indication of dissatisfaction not only with the incumbent President George Bush but also with established patterns of party politics in America. Such indicators as the percentage of voter turnout, the votes obtained by extremist political parties, and the strength or weakness of incumbent parties or candidates are all routinely examined and analyzed in the aftermath of any election. Often, these can tell us a great deal about the state of the democracy in which they occur.

In addition to challenging citizens to rethink traditional modes of govern-ance, the new wave of democratization presents new challenges for political scientists. We have only begun to consider the many important theoretical questions stimulated by this global revolution. Much of our understanding of democratic political institutions and processes grew out of the experience of North America and Western Europe. Beginning with landmark works such as *The People's Choice* (Lazarsfeld, Berelson, and Gaudet 1944) and *The Ameri-can Voter* (Campbell et al. 1960), models of voting and elections that derived exclusively from the U.S. experience were widely accepted as providing a sound theoretical basis for understanding the democratic experience more generally. As the opportunity to test such models in political environments outside the United States increased, substantial revision of these theories was inevitable. Studies of voting and elections in Britain, Canada, Germany, the Netherlands, Sweden, Denmark, Japan, and Australia, among others, added to and refined an understanding of voting and elections as derived from the American experience alone. And in all of these countries, changes in the political, social, and economic environment over time allowed such theories to be tested and refined even further.

Now, with nearly 50 years of empirical study of voting behavior and electoral processes behind us, and with the ability to compare across time and across nations, we might conclude that the study of voting and elections has reached a plateau. But the challenges of the future are likely to be even greater. The explosion of democratic political institutions around the world provides many new opportunities to expand the universe of nations and theories on which our knowledge of democratic elections is based. We do not know if models of voting that seem satisfactory in Canada or Germany will prove as useful in Hungary or Brazil. We do not know if the changes that have taken place in the conduct of democratic politics in the United States or Britain will arise in new forms in Chile or Russia. In a similar way in the established democracies, the conduct of elections for the European Parliament now provides the ability to compare nations within the confines of a single political event—an occurrence that had no real parallel before 1979. Empirical studies of these multinational elections (e.g., van der Eijk, Franklin, et al. 1996) have the capability of enhancing our knowledge of voting behavior in a way that reaches beyond the confines of national politics.

Processes of electoral reform, undertaken with much fervor in Italy, Japan, and New Zealand, also contain the potential to push forward the boundaries of our knowledge of democratic institutions and performance. At the same time that newly emerging democracies implement new electoral systems and rules, established democracies have instituted reforms that provide the functional equivalent of experimental case studies. New Zealand's adoption of the additional-member system will generate comparisons not only with its own former system of single-member district elections but also with Germany. The move away from proportional representation with the 1994 election in Italy likewise provides students of elections with opportunities for both within-system and cross-system comparisons.

These developments have also created opportunities for innovative research designs. As the renewed interest of political scientists in political institutions, sometimes known as the "new institutionalism," has taken hold in the discipline, experimentation with different structural arrangements in both new and established democracies has the potential to greatly enhance our understanding of the efficacy of particular institutional characteristics and of the role of institutions in political life more generally (Sartori 1994). The new institutionalism has many different elements, but essentially it emphasizes the need to reintegrate different levels of analysis to understand how institutions shape, order, and modify individual choices (March and Olsen 1989; Taagepera and Shugart 1989). In contrast, a traditional approach to understanding election campaigns—exemplified by the "Nuffield" series of general election studies in Britain (see, e.g., Butler and Kavanagh 1992), the "Making of the President" books in the United States (e.g., White 1961), or the "At the Polls" series elsewhere (see note 3 below)—focused on describing the "high politics" of elections: an assessment of the government's record in office, the strategies and platforms of the major political parties, the campaign messages and media coverage of candidates and leaders, trends in the opinion polls, and the aggregate analysis of electoral outcomes. Traditional comparative research looked at how the rules and formal institutions, including electoral systems, party organizations, and communication structures, varied across countries. At the same time, the "behavioral" approach dominated the study of voting behavior at the level of the mass public. To explain electoral change, the behavioral approach focused on long-term trends in the social or economic structure, secularization, and generational change, as well as on short-term responses to campaign events, party leaders, and policy platforms. Today, in the comparative study of elections, a major challenge is to try to integrate results derived from these different levels of analysis. Sources such as the Eurobarometers (Reif and Inglehart 1991), the World Values Study (Abramson and Inglehart 1995), and the International Social Survey Program (Jowell, Witherspoon, and Brook 1989) have created invaluable comparative surveys of social and political attitudes. Building on these and other efforts, preliminary steps toward creating genuinely cross-national election data sets are starting to be taken by the International Committee for Research into Elections and Representative Democracy (ICORE; Thomassen 1994). Through adding contextual data about political systems to cross-national surveys of voting behavior, we are starting to explore how the attitudes, values, and behavior of individual voters interact with particular institutional contexts.

It should be evident from trends in democratization, political reform, and social and economic change that the context for the study of democratic elections has undergone a significant transformation in just the past decade. It is the magnitude and importance of these changes that have provided the impetus for this book. Most studies of democratic elections have been based on the experience of single countries, often drawing on survey and other data collected in studies of specific elections.[2] With the passage of time, the replication of new studies in the same countries, and the international exchange of researchers and research results, knowledge of those particular cases became more fully integrated. Comparative studies began to bring together research from several countries, often under a single theoretical framework (Dalton, Flanagan, and Beck 1984; Dalton 1988; Franklin et al. 1992). But few studies have attempted to integrate and synthesize our knowledge of democratic elections theoretically and empirically across a large stretch of time and a broad spectrum of nations. Daunting as this task may seem, it is the goal that we have set for this volume—to provide a broad thematic understanding of the study of democratic elections.

Butler, Penniman, and Ranney (1981) undertook a similar task in 1981, drawing on studies of elections in a number of countries that had been published during the 1970s in the "At the Polls" series.[3] A comparison of our work with theirs demonstrates how much the field has changed in a relatively short period of time. Many of the topics to be covered in this book are similar to those of *Democracy at the Polls*—electoral systems, political parties, candidate selection, public opinion polls, and political participation. But a closer examination reveals that each of these topics has taken on new meanings and that the literature on each of them has grown substantially. Electoral systems, which might have been considered a constant feature of the political landscape in 1981, are now actively debated in both newer and established democracies (Blais and Massicotte, chap. 2 in this volume). The role and function

TABLE 1.1 Major Democracies of the World, 1995

Country	Population (millions)[a]	DP or ES Lists[b]	Gastil PR Code[c]	Recent Election[d]
Argentina	33	E	2	93, 95P
Australia	18	DE	1	93
Austria	8	DE	1	92P, 95
Bangladesh	118		2	91R, 91
Belgium	10	DE	1	91
Bolivia	7		2	93P, 93
Brazil	146	E	2	93R, 94P, 94
Bulgaria	8	E	2	92P, 94
Canada	27	DE	1	92R, 93
Chile	13		2	93P, 93
Colombia	33	DE	3	94P, 94
Costa Rica	3	E	1	94P, 94
Czech Republic	10		1	92
Denmark	5	DE	1	92R, 93R, 94
Ecuador	11		2	92P, 94
Finland	5	DE	1	94P, 95R, 95
France	58	DE	1	92R, 93, 95P
Germany	80	DE	1	94
Greece	10	DE	1	93
Hungary	10	E	1	94
India	913	DE	4	91
Ireland	4	DE	1	90P, 92, 95R
Israel	5	DE	1	92
Italy	57	DE	1	93R, 94
Japan	125	DE	2	93
Madagascar	14		2	92R, 92P, 93
Malawi	10		2	93R, 94P, 94
Mali	10		2	92P, 92R, 92
Mexico	84	E	4	94P, 94
Mozambique	16		3	94P, 94
Nepal	19		3	94
Netherlands	15	DE	1	94
New Zealand	3	DE	1	93, 92R
Norway	4	DE	1	93, 95R
Pakistan	132		3	93
Philippines	65		3	92P, 92

TABLE 1.1 *Continued*

Country	Population (millions)[a]	DP or ES Lists[b]	Gastil PR Code[c]	Recent Election[d]
Poland	38	E	2	93, 95P
Portugal	10	DE	1	91P, 95
Russia	148	E	3	91P, 93R, 95
South Africa	40	E	2	94
South Korea	45		2	92P, 92
Spain	39	DE	1	93
Sweden	9	DE	1	94, 95R
Switzerland	7	DE	1	95
Taiwan	21		3	92, 95
Thailand	58	E	3	92
Turkey	61	D	5	95
Ukraine	52	E	3	91R, 94P, 94
United Kingdom	58	DE	1	92
United States	260	DE	1	92P, 94
Uruguay	3	E	2	94P, 94
Venezuela	20	DE	3	93P, 93
Zambia	9		3	91P, 91

NOTE: As of December 31, 1995.
a. *The Statesman's Year Book: 1995-96* 1995.
b. D = inclusion among the 28 countries listed in *Democracy at the Polls* (Butler, Penniman, and Ranney 1981, 12-8). E = coverage in *Electoral Studies* 14 (1995), 349.
c. *Freedom Review* 26 (1995), 16-17. The Gastil Political Rights Index varies from 1 (high) to 7 (low).
d. P = presidential election; R = significant referendum; year only indicates legislative election.

of political parties is often questioned. What were once unconventional behaviors have become standard forms of political participation (Franklin, chap. 8). Polling and the use of electronic media have become pervasive influences in the electoral process in many countries. The world of democratic politics in 1996 presents a different image than it did in 1981. We have learned a great deal about the conduct of democratic elections in the past 15 years, and the extension of democracy to new political environments holds out the promise of much more yet to come.

The 1981 volume surveyed 28 countries, most of which were in North America, Europe, or the English-speaking Pacific. Applying similar selection criteria, the present book includes information on up to 53 democracies (Table 1.1). Included are all countries with a population of 3 million or greater and a Gastil Political Rights score of 3 or less (Karatnycky 1995, 15-6).[4] However, India, Mexico, and Turkey were included in spite of their overly high Gastil Political Rights scores in the most recent Freedom House listing.[5]

Many of these new entrants—Argentina, Hungary, Russia, South Korea, the Philippines, South Africa—would not have been considered in a volume on democracy written even a few years ago. In some other countries—Japan and Israel, for example—both democracy and a tradition of electoral research were well established, but the research was often not well integrated into the Western literature. In short, the world of democracy as political scientists knew it a decade or so ago has changed in both scope and content.

Although the aims of this book are ambitious, we recognize its limitations. The topic of democracy is one on which many volumes have been written by social scientists and philosophers over many hundreds of years. We necessarily confine our attention here to the conduct of democratic elections, which is, of course, only one aspect of democratic governance. With few exceptions, the focus of our attention is on national elections, not on those that take place at other levels of the political system. And although our universe consists of the 53 democracies shown in Table 1.1, it is not possible to cover each of them in the depth that might be achieved in a study with narrower terms of reference. Our treatment is necessarily selective, drawing on examples of particular cases where they are most relevant and where empirical evidence can be found. Although we attempt to consider the experience of elections in the newer democracies of Asia, Africa, Latin America, and Central and Eastern Europe, we recognize that the vast majority of research that has been conducted to date is still drawn from the more established democracies of North America, Western Europe, Australia, and New Zealand. If the 21st century is truly the century of democracy, this too may change. We hope that this book will contribute in a modest way toward that end.

Comprehensive Tables

We provide here a number of general tables (Tables 1.2 to 1.7) with data from as many as possible of the 53 democracies covered in this book. In Table 1.2, we provide basic information on institutional features of electoral systems for all 53 countries. Together with the typology of electoral systems in chapter

2 (Blais and Massicotte), one has available a comprehensive compendium of electoral systems as they exist throughout the democratic world today.

Table 1.3 contains a variety of items about voting procedure and the franchise. In addition to information that is quite readily available—about voting age, for example—we include such information as whether elections are held on a workday or rest day. We hope that this larger set of information will make it possible to enlarge the scope of comparative studies of turnout.

Table 1.4 provides information on the most recent election (as of the end of 1995) and on an earlier election in those countries where appropriate. Although new elections are being held in some country virtually every week, so that any such list becomes outdated, this table provides a basis for understanding new results and the changes in party systems and governments that occur over time. In addition, the table introduces party names and commonly used abbreviations, providing a useful reference list for country- and party-specific examples given throughout the book.

Tables 1.5 and 1.6 provide information on the financing of parties and campaigns. This information is much less readily available, so the country coverage is less extensive. It is also more difficult to compile; it consists of a large number of regulations governing many details about contributions, expenditures, and reporting requirements. Its complexity, however, is precisely why it is valuable to have in a single place. We hope that its ready availability encourages its use in future analyses.

Table 1.7 contains information on media penetration and on political control of television. As with election financing, this information has not been readily available. We hope that the greater coverage provided here will allow this information to be incorporated into analyses not only of the media themselves but into studies of the relationship between the media and many other aspects of elections, including campaigning, turnout, and polling.

Notes

1. Pollack and Pollack (1993) provide a good overview that stresses the uncertainties facing new and revitalized democracies.

2. References to a large number of election surveys and resulting studies can be found in de Guchteneire, LeDuc, and Niemi (1985, 1991).

3. This series of studies, edited by Howard Penniman and others, was published by the American Enterprise Institute (Washington, DC). Full-length studies published between 1974 and 1981 included volumes on Australia, Britain, Canada, France, Germany, Greece, India, Israel, Ireland, Italy, Japan, New Zealand, Scandinavia, Switzerland, and Venezuela.

4. The population cutoff, which establishes a floor on size, excludes a number of cases among the smaller established democracies—Iceland, Malta, or Jamaica, for example—as well as several newly established or transitional democracies, notably the Baltic Republics (Estonia, Latvia, and Lithuania). The Freedom House categorization, on which our selection criteria are partly based, classified no fewer than 114 countries as "democracies" in 1994 (see Karatnycky 1995, 5-10). Political Rights scores range from 1 (most free) to 7 (least free).

5. For a discussion and comparison of the Gastil Political Rights score with other indicators of political democracy, see Bollen (1980, 1993).

TABLE 1.2 Electoral Systems of 53 Democracies (Mid-1990s)

Country	Electoral System in Lower House[a]	Formula for Lower House	Threshold for Lower House	Number of Seats in Lower House	Number of Constituencies in Lower House[b]	Closed, Preferential, or Panachage List for Lower House	Maximum Years Between Elections for Lower House	Popular Election of Upper House[c]	Popular Election of President and Frequency of Elections[d]	National Referendums Since 1945
Argentina	PR	D'Hondt	3% in district	259	24	Closed	2	No	Yes, 4 years	1
Australia	Alternative vote	N/A	N/A	148	148	N/A	3	Yes	N/A	23
Austria	PR	D'Hondt and Hagenbach-Bischoff	One local seat	183	9 + 2	Closed	4	No	Yes, 6 years	1
Bangladesh	FPTP	N/A	N/A	330	300	N/A	5	Unicameral	No	
Belgium	PR	D'Hondt	33% of the quota in at least one of the arrondissements	150	21	Preferential	4	Indirect	N/A	2
Bolivia	Mixed			130			4	Yes	Yes, 4 years	
Brazil	PR	D'Hondt	None	513	27	Preferential	4	Yes	Yes, 4 years	1
Bulgaria	PR	D'Hondt	4%	240		Closed	5	Unicameral	Yes, 5 years	4
Canada	FPTP	N/A	N/A	295	295	N/A	5	No	N/A	1
Chile	Dual majority	N/A	N/A	120	60	N/A	4	Yes	Yes, 6 years	4
Colombia	PR	LR-Hare	None	168	33	Closed	4	Yes	Yes, 4 years	2
Costa Rica	PR	LR-Double quota	None	57	7	Closed	4	Unicameral	Yes, 4 years	
Czech Republic	PR	LR-Droop	5%	200	8	Preferential	4	Yes	No	
Denmark	PR	LR-Hare and modified St. Laguë	One local seat or 2%	179	19 + 1	Preferential	4	Unicameral	N/A	13
Ecuador	Mixed			77	21 + 1	Closed	2	Unicameral	Yes, 4 years	2
Finland	PR	D'Hondt	None	200	15	Preferential	4	Unicameral	Yes, 6 years	1

continued

TABLE 1.2 Continued

Country	Electoral System in Lower House[a]	Formula for Lower House	Threshold for Lower House	Number of Seats in Lower House	Number of Constituencies in Lower House[b]	Closed, Preferential, or Panachage List for Lower House	Maximum Years Between Elections for Lower House	Popular Election of Upper House[c]	Popular Election of President and Frequency of Elections[d]	National Referendums Since 1945
France	Majority—plurality	N/A	N/A	577	577	N/A	5	Indirect	Yes, 7 years	12
Germany	Mixed		3%	656	328 + 1	Closed	4	No	No	0
Greece	PR	LR-Droop		300	56 + 13 + 1 + 1	Preferential	4	Unicameral	No	4
Hungary	Mixed			386	176 + 20 + 1	Closed	4	Unicameral	No	5
India	FPTP	N/A	N/A	545	543	N/A	5	Indirect	No	
Ireland	PR	Single transferable vote	None	166	41	Closed	5	Mixed	Yes, 7 years	20
Israel	PR	D'Hondt	1.5%	120	1	Closed	4	Unicameral	No	
Italy	Mixed			630	475 + 1	Closed	5	Yes	No	29
Japan	Mixed		None	500	300 + 11	Closed	4	Yes	N/A	
Madagascar	PR	LR-Hare		138	177	Closed	4	No	Yes, 5 years	
Malawi	FPTP	N/A	N/A	177	177	N/A	5	Unicameral	Yes, 5 years	
Mali	Majority—runoff	N/A	N/A	129	55	N/A	5	Unicameral	Yes, 5 years	
Mexico	Mixed			500	300 + 1	Closed	3	Yes	Yes, 6 years	0
Mozambique	PR	D'Hondt	5%	250	1	Closed	5	Unicameral	Yes, 5 years	
Nepal	FPTP	N/A	N/A	205	75	N/A	5	No	N/A	1
Netherlands	PR	D'Hondt	0.67%	150	1	Preferential	4	No	N/A	
New Zealand	Mixed	N/A	N/A	120	60 + 1	Closed	3	Unicameral	N/A	N/A10
Norway	PR	Modified St. Lague	None	165	19 + 1	Closed	4	Unicameral	N/A	1

Country	Electoral system	Formula	Threshold	Number of seats	Number of constituencies	List	Maximum years between elections	Popular election of upper house	Popular election of president	National referendums
Pakistan	FPTP	N/A	N/A	217	200	N/A	5	No	No	11
Philippines	FPTP	N/A	N/A	200	200	N/A	3	Yes	Yes, 6 years	5
Poland	PR	D'Hondt	7%	460	52 + 1	Preferential	4	Yes	Yes, 5 years	
Portugal	PR	D'Hondt	None	230	22	Closed	4	Unicameral	Yes, 5 years	
Russia	Mixed	LR-Hare	5%	450	225 + 1	Closed	5	Yes	Yes, 5 years	7
South Africa	PR	LR-Droop	None	400	9 + 1	Closed	4	No	No	6
South Korea	FPTP	N/A	N/A	299	237 + 1	Closed	4	Unicameral	Yes, 5 years	4
Spain	PR	D'Hondt	3%	350	50	Closed	4	Yes	N/A	
Sweden	PR	Modified St. Laguë	4% (national) or 12% (district)	349	28 + 1	Closed	4	Unicameral	N/A	
Switzerland	PR	D'Hondt	None	200	26	Panachage	4	Yes	No	3
Taiwan	Mixed	N/A	N/A	161	27 + 2	Closed	3	Unicameral	Yes (from 1996)	275
Thailand	FPTP	N/A	N/A	360	142	N/A	4	No	N/A	
Turkey	PR	D'Hondt	10%	550	79	Closed	5	Unicameral	No	4
Ukraine	Majority—runoff	N/A	N/A	450	450	N/A	5	Unicameral	Yes, 5 years	
United Kingdom	FPTP	N/A	N/A	651	651	N/A	5	No	N/A	1
United States	FPTP	N/A	N/A	435	435	N/A	2	Yes	Yes, 4 years	1
Uruguay	PR	D'Hondt	None	99	1	Closed	5	Yes	Yes, 5 years	8
Venezuela	Mixed	N/A	N/A	204	102 + 23 + 1	Closed	5	Yes	Yes, 5 years	1
Zambia	FPTP	N/A	N/A	159	150	N/A	5	Unicameral	Yes, 5 years	1

SOURCE: Blais and Massicotte in this volume (electoral system; formula; threshold; and closed, preferential, or panachage list); Inter-Parliamentary Union 1993 (number of seats, number of constituencies, maximum years between elections, and popular election of upper house); Banks 1995 (number of seats of upper house, and popular election of upper house); Europa World Yearbook 1994 (popular election of president and frequency of elections); Keesing's Record of World Events various years (updating national referendums since 1945); Butler and Ranney 1994 (national referendums since 1945); The Statesman's Year Book: 1995-96 1995.

NOTE: N/A = not applicable.

a. PR = proportional representation; FPTP = first-past-the-post. Mixed: For more detail, see Figure 2.2.

b. Two or more numbers indicates multiple tiers.

c. No = appointed upper house or delegated by provincial assemblies; indirect = there is a restricted electoral process.

d. Considered elected if there is any type of direct popular vote.

16

TABLE 1.3 Voting Procedures, the Franchise, and Turnout in 44 Democracies

Country	Voting Age	Number of Days Polling Booths Open	Workday or Rest Day	Voting Compulsory	Postal Voting	Proxy Voting	Polling Booths in Special Institutions	Constituency Transfer	Advance Voting	Turnout	Year, Election[a]
Argentina	18	1	Rest day	Yes	(ages 18-70)	No	No consulates	Embassies/	No	80.9	1995P
Australia	18	1	Rest day	Yes	Absentees, ill, pregnant	No	Embassies	Yes, within state	No	95.8	1993L
Austria	19	1	Rest day	In presidential elections and in some provinces for other elections	No	No	Hospitals, old age homes	By application in advance	No	81.9	1994L
Bangladesh	18	1	Workday	No		No	No	No	No		
Belgium	18	1	Rest day	Yes	Absentees, hospital patients, public service officials	Restricted to those abroad and in itinerant occupations	No	No	No	83.7	1995L
Brazil	16	1	Workday	Yes (ages 18-70)		No				82.9	1994P
Canada	18	1	Workday	No	No	Students, ill, those at sea, prospectors	No	Hospital patients, those absent through job, on religious grounds	For elderly, infirm, pregnant, armed forces,	71.3	1993L
Chile	18	1	Rest day	Yes	No	No	No	No	No	51.7	1993P
Colombia	18	1	Rest day	No	No	Embassies/ consulates	No	No	No	72.0	1994L
Costa Rica	18	1	Rest day	Yes	No	No	No	No	No	81.1	1994L

Country											
Denmark	18	1	Workday	No	Prisoners, hospital patients, diplomats, those on isolated residence and in national register offices	No	No	No	No	83.4	1994L
Ecuador	18	1	Rest day	Yes (ages 18-65)	No	Embassies/ consulates			No	70.0	1994L
Finland	18	2	Rest day and workday	No	No	No	Diplomatic missions abroad, ships, hospitals	No	Yes	72.2	1995L
France	18	1	Rest day	No	No	Sailors, some armed forces, civil servants, those abroad, invalids, disabled	No	No	No	69.3	1993L
Germany	18	1	Rest day	No	Absentees from country or constituency, ill and infirm	No	No	Yes	No	71.0	1994L
Greece	18	1	Rest day	Yes for ages 21-70 living within 200 miles of their constituency	No	No			No	78.2	1993L
India	21	5	Rest day and workday	No	Higher federal and state officials, armed forces, police serving in another state, election officials, prisoners, diplomats	No	No	No	No	50.0	1991L
Ireland	18	1	Workday	No	Obligatory for armed forces and police	No	No	No	No	68.5	1992L
Israel	18	1	Workday	No	No	No	Soldiers barracks	For nomads	For sailors	77.4	1992L
Italy	18	2	Rest day and workday	No	No	No	No	For armed forces	No	86.1	1994L

continued

17

TABLE 1.3 Continued

Country	Voting Age	Number of Polling Booths Open	Workday or Rest Day	Voting Compulsory	Postal Voting	Proxy Voting	Polling Booths in Special Institutions	Constituency Transfer	Advance Voting	Turnout	Year, Election[a]
Japan	20	1	Rest day	No	No	For illiterate and ill, two proxy voters required, appointed by election officer	No	No	For those away on business	67.3	1993L
Mali	21	1	Rest day	No	No					21.1	1992L
Mexico	18	1	Rest day	Yes	No	No	No		At special polling stations	77.7	1994P
Nepal	21	1	Workday	No	Government employees abroad	Yes, within strict limits				61.4	1994L
Netherlands	18	1	Workday	No			No	On advance application	No	78.3	1994L
New Zealand	18	1	Rest day	No	Yes	No	No	Yes	For all absentees, ill, infirm, pregnant, lighthouse keepers	85.2	1993L
Norway	18	2 (in most areas)	Rest day and workday	No	Yes	No	On ships and in diplomatic missions	No	For hospital patients and those absent through work	75.8	1993L
Philippines	15	1	Workday	No	No					70.6	1992P
Poland	18	1	Rest day	No	No					52.1	1993L
Portugal	18	1	Rest day	No	Yes	No		Yes		67.2	1995L
Russia	18	1	Rest day	No	Yes	No	Sick and handicapped vote at home			54.8	1993L
South Korea	20	1	Workday	No		No				71.9	1992L
Spain	18	1	Workday	No		No				77.2	1993L
Sweden	18	1	Rest day	No	Yes	Use of spouse and relatives as "messengers" before witness	Hospitals, ships, old age homes, embassies, prisons	No, but postal voting possible on election day	Yes, for any elector	87.3	1994L

Switzerland	20	2	Rest day	No	Automatic for armed forces, otherwise by application 4 days before voting: varies by canton	Varies by canton	No	No	No	46.0	1991L
Taiwan	20	1	Rest day	No			No		No	72.0	1992L
Thailand	20	1	Rest day	No	No		No		No	62.0	1995L
Turkey	20	1	Rest day	Yes	No	No	No	Special polling stations at border posts for citizens residing abroad	No	80.0	1991L
Ukraine	18	1	Rest day	No		On application:	No	No	No	71.6	1994P
United Kingdom	18	1	Workday	No	On application: disability, move to another seat, isolated residence, candidates, constables, returning officers, religious reasons, absence through job	armed forces, those working abroad and their spouses	No	No	No	77.8	1992L
United States	18	1	Workday	No	By application, rules vary across states	In some states for blind and disabled	No	No	No	51.5	1992P
Uruguay	18	1	Rest day	Yes	No	No	No	No	No	89.4	1994P
Venezuela	18	1	Rest day	Yes	No	"Assisted" voting for blind and disabled	Embassies/consulates; prisons, hospitals, old age homes	No	No	60.0	1993P
Zambia	18	1	Workday	No	No	No	No		No	50.0	1991P

SOURCE: Central Intelligence Agency 1994 (voting age); Butler, Penniman, and Ranney 1981, Ministerio del España 1992, supplemented by the editors (number of days polling booths open, workday or rest day, postal voting, proxy voting, polling booths in special institutions, constituency transfer, and advance voting); Inter-Parliamentary Union 1992 (voting compulsory); European Journal of Political Research Political Data Yearbook 1992-1994; Elections Today; Electoral Studies; Keesing's Contemporary Record; The Statesman's Year Book: 1995-96 1995 (turnout, year, election).
a. P = presidential elections; L = legislative elections.

TABLE 1.4 Most Recent and Mid-1960s Election Results for Lower House of National Legislature in 53 Democracies

Country	Year	Which Party(ies) Formed Government[a]	Number of Seats Won	Percentage of Vote Won	Political Parties Winning Seats in Lower House in Most Recent and Mid-1960s Election[b]	Year[c]	Number of Seats Won	Percentage of Vote Won	Effective Number of Parties in Parliament (ENPP), Most Recent Election[d]
	Most Recent Election					Mid-1960s Election			
Argentina	1995	Justicialist party President: PJ (95)	137 69 26 25	23 20 35 22	Justicialist party or Peronist party (PJ) Radical Civic Union (UCR) Frepaso Others	D			2.70
Australia	1993	Australian Labour party	80 49 16 2	45 37 7 11	Australian Labor party (ALP) Liberal party (LP) National party (NP) Others	1966	41 61 21 1	33 49 17 1	2.42
Austria	1995	Coalition of Socialist party and People's party President: ÖVP (92)	72 53 41 9 8	38 28 22 5 4	Socialist party (SPÖ) People's party (ÖVP) Freedom party (FPÖ) Liberal Forum Greens	1966	74 85 6	45 52 4	3.40
Bangladesh	1991	Coalition of Bangladesh National party, Jamaat-i Islami, and other small parties	140 95 35 18 12 3 3		Bangladesh National party (BNP) Awami League Jatiya party Jamaat-i Islami Communist party and allies to Awami League Other small parties Independents	N			3.59

Belgium	1995	Coalition of CVP, PS, SP, and PSC	Flemish Christian Democrats (CVP)	17	29	1965	77	34	7.95
			Flemish-speaking liberals (VLD) [was PVV]	13	21		48	22	
			French-speaking socialists (PS)	12	21				
			Flemish socialists (SP)	13	20		64	28	
			[Socialist party (PS and SP)]						
			Federation of French-speaking liberals and Francophone Democratic Front (PRL-FDF)	10	18				
			[Francophone Democratic Front (FDF)]						
			Francophone Christian Democrats (PSC)	8	12		3	1	
			Vlaams Blok (VIB)	8	11				
			ECOLO	4	6				
			Volksunie (VU)	5	5		12	6	
			AGALEV	4	5				
			National Front (FN)	1	2				
			[Communist party]				6	5	
			[Walloon Front]				1	1	
			[Walloon Workers party]				1	1	
Bolivia	1993	Coalition of MNR, USC, MBL; President: MNR (93)	Nationalist Revolutionary Movement (MNR)		52	D			3.71
			Patriotic Accord (AP)		35				
			Civic Solidarity Union (USC)		20				
			Conscience of the Fatherland (Condepa)		13				
			Free Bolivia Movement (MBL)		7				
			National Renewal Alliance (ARBOL)		1				
			Social Democratic Alliance (ASD)		1				
			National Convergence Axis—Patriotic (EJE—P)		1				
Brazil	1994	Coalition of PSDB, PFL, PTB, and PL; President: PSDB (94)	Party of the Brazilian Democratic Movement (PMDB)		107	D			7.86
			Liberal Front party (PFL)		90				
			Brazilian Social Democratic party (PSDB)		63				
			Progressive Reform party (PPR)		51				
			Party of the Workers (PT)		49				
			Democratic Labor party (PDT)		34				
			Other Cardosa coalition (PL and PTB)		77				
Bulgaria	1994	Coalition of BSP and NS; President: SDS (92)	Bulgarian Socialist party (BSP)		125	N			2.72
			Union of Democratic Forces (SDS)		69				
			Popular Union (NS)		18				
			Movement for Rights and Freedoms (DPS)		15				
			Bulgarian Business Bloc (BBB)		13				

continued

TABLE 1.4 *Continued*

Country	Year	Most Recent Election			Political Parties Winning Seats in Lower House in Most Recent and Mid-1960s Election^b	Mid-1960s Election			Effective Number of Parties in Parliament (ENPP), Most Recent Election^d
		Which Party(ies) Formed Government^a	*Number of Seats Won*	*Percentage of Vote Won*		*Year*^c	*Number of Seats Won*	*Percentage of Vote Won*	
Canada	1993	Liberal party	177	42	Liberal party	1965	131	40	2.35
			54	14	Bloc Québécois		21	18	
			52	18	Reform party		97	32	
			9	7	New Democratic party (NDP)		2	1	
			2	16	Progressive Conservative party (PC)		5	4	
			1	4	Others		9	5	
					[Social Credit]				
					[Ralliement des Créditistes]				
Chile	1993	Coalition of PDC, PR, PS, and PPD	37		Christian Democratic party (PDC)	D			4.92
			29		National Renewal party (RN)				
		President: PDC (93)	15		Socialist party (PS)				
			15		Party for Democracy (PPD)				
			15		Independent Democratic Union (UDI)				
			6		Center Union (UCC) and independent right-wingers				
			2		Radical party (PR)				
			1		Democratic Left party (PDI)				
Colombia	1994	Liberal party	89		Liberal party	1966	71		2.53
			56		Social Conservative party [was Conservative Union]		40		
		President: Liberal (94)	10		Democratic Alliance M-19				
			2		National Salvation Movement				
			2		Others and Independents				
Costa Rica	1994	National Liberation party	28	45	National Liberation party (PLN)	1966	29		2.30
			25	40	Social Christian Unity party (PUSC)		26		
		President: PLN (94)			[was National Unity party]				
			4	5	Independents		2		

Czech Republic 1992 — Coalition of ODS and KDS — N — 4.85

Party	Votes (%)	Seats
Civic Democratic party (ODS)	30	76
Left Block	14	35
Czechoslovak Social Democracy	7	16
Liberal Social Union	7	16
Christian Democratic Union—Czech People's Party (KDS)	6	15
Association for the Republic—Republican party of Czechoslovakia	6	14
Civic Democratic Alliance	6	14
Movement for Self-Administered Democracy—Society for Moravia and Silesia	6	14

Denmark 1994 — Coalition of SD, RV, and CD — 1966 — 4.70

Party	1994 Votes (%)	1994 Seats	1966 Votes (%)	1966 Seats
Social Democrats (SD)	35	62	38	69
Liberal party (V)	23	42	19	35
Conservative party (KF)	15	27	19	34
Socialist People's party (SF)	7	13	11	20
Progress party (FP)	6	11		
Social Liberal party (RV)	5	8	7	13
Unity List	3	6		
Center Democratic party (CD)	3	5		
Independent	1	1		
[Liberal Center]			3	4

Ecuador 1994 — Coalition of PUR and PC — President: PUR (92) — D — 5.92

Party	Seats
Christian Social party (PSC)	26
Roldosista party of Ecuador (PRE)	11
Popular Democratic Movement (MPD)	8
Democratic Left (ID)	8
Conservative party (PC)	6
Popular Democracy (DP)	4
United Republican party (PUR)	3
Socialist party (PSE)	2
Alfaroist Radical Front (FRA)	2
Ecuadorian Popular Revolutionary Alliance (APRE)	2
Independents	1
National Liberation (PLN)	1
Concentration of Popular Forces (CFP)	1
Radical Liberal party (PLR)	

continued

TABLE 1.4 *Continued*

Country	Year	Which Party(ies) Formed Government[a]	Political Parties Winning Seats in Lower House in Most Recent and Mid-1960s Election[b]	Most Recent Election — Number of Seats Won	Most Recent Election — Percentage of Vote Won	Mid-1960s Election — Year[c]	Mid-1960s Election — Seats Won	Mid-1960s Election — Percentage of Vote Won	Effective Number of Parties in Parliament (ENPP), Most Recent Election[d]
Finland	1995	Coalition of SSDP, KOK, SFP, and Greens	Finnish Social Democratic party (SSDP)	63	28	1966	55	27	4.88
			Centre party (KESK)	44	20		49	21	
			National Coalition party (KOK)	39	18		26	14	
			Left-Wing Alliance (VL) [was Finnish People's Democratic Union]	22	11		41	21	
		President: SSDP (94)	Swedish People's party (SFP)	12	5		12	6	
			Greens	9	7				
			Finnish Christian League (SKL)	7	3				
			Young Finns (NS)	2	3				
			Finnish Rural party (SMP)	1	1		1	1	
			Ecological party (EP)	1	<1				
			[Liberal Peoples party]				9	7	
			[Social Democratic League]				7	3	
France	1993	Coalition of RPR and UDF	Rally for the Republic (RPR) [was UNR]	247	20	1967	191	32	2.96
		President: RPR (95)	Union for French Democracy (UDF)	213	19				
			[Republican party]				41	6	
			[Democratic Center]				36	13	
			Socialist party (PS)	70	19		118	19	
			National Front (FN) and other right-wing parties	24	17		7	4	
			Communist party (PCF)	23	9		72	23	
			Other left parties	0	3		3	2	

Country	Year	Coalition	Party						
Germany	1994	Coalition of CDU/CSU, and FDP	Christian Democratic Union (BDU) and Christian Social Union (CSU)	294	41	1965	245	48	2.78
			Social Democratic party (SPD)	252	36		202	39	
			Greens	49	7				
			Free Democratic party (FDP)	47	7		49	10	
			Party of Democratic Socialism (PDS)	30	4				
Greece	1993	Panhellenic Socialist Movement	Panhellenic Socialist Movement (PASOK)	170	47	D			2.17
			New Democracy (ND)	111	39				
			Political Spring (POLA)	10	5				
			Communist party of Greece (KKE)	9	5				
Hungary	1994	Hungarian Socialist party	Hungarian Socialist party (MszP)	209	33	N			2.89
			Alliance of Free Democrats (SzDSz)	70	20				
			Hungarian Democratic Forum (MDF)	37	12				
			Independent Smallholders (FKGP)	26	9				
			Christian Democratic People's party (KDNP)	22	7				
			Federation of Young Democrats (FIDESz)	20	7				
			Agrarian Association	1	2				
			Liberal Civic Alliance	1	1				

continued

TABLE 1.4 Continued

| | Most Recent Election | | | | | Mid-1960s Election | | | Effective Number of Parties (ENPP), |
Country	Year	Which Party(ies) Formed Government[a]	Number of Seats Won	Percentage of Vote Won	Political Parties Winning Seats in Lower House in Most Recent and Mid-1960s Election[b]	Year[c]	Number of Seats Won	Percentage of Vote Won	Most Recent Election[c]
Italy	1994	Coalition of Northern League, National Alliance, and Forza Italia	118	9	Northern League (Lega Nord)	1963			7.45
			115	20	Democratic party of the Left (PDS)				
			109	14	National Alliance (AN)				
					[was Italian Social Movement (MSI)]		27	5	
			97	21	Forza Italia				
			40	6	Reconstructed Communists (RC)				
					[Communist (PCI)]		166	25	
			33	11	Popular party (PPI)				
			32	—[e]	Christian Democratic Center (CCD)				
					[Christian Democrats (DC)]		260	38	
			17	1	Democratic Alliance (AD)				
			15	2	Socialists (PSI)		87	14	
			13	5	Segni Pact				
			11	3	Greens				
			9	2	La Rete				
			6	—[e]	Christian Socialists				
			6	4	Pannella				
			5	4	Independents and others				
			4	—[e]	United Center (UC)				
					[Liberal party]		40	7	
					[Social Democrats]		32	6	
					[Monarchist party]		8	2	
					[Republican party]		6	1	
					[South Tyrol People's party]		3	<1	
					[Val d'Aosta Union]		1	<1	

Country	Year	Governing party / coalition	Seats	Party	%	1967 seats	1967 %	
Japan	1993	Coalition of JSP, RP, CGP, JNP, DSP, HP, and USDP	223	Liberal Democratic party (LDP)	37	277	50	3.95
			70	Japan Socialist party (JSP)	15	140	28	
			55	Renewal party (Shinseito) (RP)	10			
			51	Clean Government party (Komeito) (CGP)	8	25	6	
			35	Japan New party (JNP)	8			
			30	Independents and others	8	9	6	
			15	Japan Communist party (JCP)	4	5	5	
			15	Democratic Socialist party (DSP)	3	30	7	
			13	Harbinger party (Sakigake) (HP)	1			
			4	United Social Democratic party (Shaminren) (USDP)				
Madagascar	1993	Coalition of UNDD, Rasalama Active Forces Cartel, and others	46	Rasalama Active Forces Cartel		N		6.53
		President: Rasa. AFC (92)	15	Movement for Proletarian Power (MFM)				
			13	Fanilo				
			11	Famima				
			10	Others and independents				
			8	Fihaonana				
			8	Rally for Social Democracy (RPSD)				
			5	Congress party for Malagasy Independence (AKFM)				
			7	National Union for Development and Democracy (UNDD)				
			2	Fivoarana				
Malawi	1994	Coalition of UDF and AFORD	84	United Democratic Front (UDF)		N		2.75
		President: UDF (94)	55	Malawi Congress party (MCP)				
			36	Alliance for Democracy (AFORD)				
Mali	1992	Alliance for Democracy in Mali	76	Alliance for Democracy in Mali (ADEMA)		N		2.77
		President: ADEMA (92)	9	National Committee for Democratic Initiative (CNID)				
			8	Sudanese Union-African Democratic Rally (US-RDA)				
			6	Popular Movement for the Development of the Republic of West Africa (PMD)				
			4	Rally for Democracy and Progress (RDP)				
			4	Union for Democracy and Development (UDD)				
			3	Rally for Democracy and Work (RDT)				
			3	Union of Democratic Progressive Forces (UFDP)				
			2	Democracy and Progress party (PDP)				
			1	Malian Union for Democracy and Development (UMADD)				

continued

TABLE 1.4 *Continued*

| Country | Most Recent Election | | | | Political Parties Winning Seats in Lower House in Most Recent and Mid-1960s Election[b] | Mid-1960s Election | | | Effective Number of Parties in Parliament (ENPP), Most Recent Election[c] |
	Which Party(ies) Formed Government[a]	Year	Number of Seats Won	Percentage of Vote Won		Year[c]	Number of Seats Won	Percentage of Vote Won	
Mexico	Institutional Revolutionary party	1994			Institutional Revolutionary party (PRI)	1965	177		2.28
			300		National Action party (PAN)				
			119		Party of the Democratic Revolution (PRD)			33	
	President: PRI (94)		71		Labor party (PT)				
			10		Others				
Mozambique	Frelimo	1994	129	44	Frelimo	N			2.13
	President: Frelimo (94)		112	38	Mozambique National Resistance (MNR)				
			9	5	Democratic Union				
Nepal	Communist party	1994	88		United Nepal Communist party (UCPN)	N			2.33
			83		Nepali Congress				
			20		Rashtriya Prajakantra party (RPP)				
			7		Independents				
			4		Nepal Mazdoor Kisan party				
			3		Nepal Sadbhavana party				

28

TABLE 1.4 Continued

Country	Most Recent Election		Political Parties Winning Seats in Lower House in Most Recent and Mid-1960s Election[b]			Mid-1960s Election			Effective Number of Parties in Parliament (ENPP), Most Recent Election[c]
	Year	Which Party(ies) Formed Government[a]		Number of Seats Won	Percentage of Vote Won	Year[c]	Number Percentage of of Seats Won Vote Won		
Italy	1994	Coalition of Northern League, National Alliance, and Forza Italia	Northern League (Lega Nord)	118	9	1963			7.45
			Democratic party of the Left (PDS)	115	20				
			National Alliance (AN)	109	14				
			[was Italian Social Movement (MSI)]				27	5	
			Forza Italia	97	21				
			Reconstructed Communists (RC)	40	6				
			[Communist (PCI)]				166	25	
			Popular party (PPI)	33	11				
			Christian Democratic Center (CCD)	32	—[e]				
			[Christian Democrats (DC)]				260	38	
			Democratic Alliance (AD)	17	1				
			Socialists (PSI)	15	2		87	14	
			Segni Pact	13	5				
			Greens	11	3				
			La Rete	9	2				
			Christian Socialists	6	—[e]				
			Pannella	6	4				
			Independents and others	5	4				
			United Center (UC)	4	—[e]				
			[Liberal party]				40	7	
			[Social Democrats]				32	6	
			[Monarchist party]				8	2	
			[Republican party]				6	1	
			[South Tyrol People's party]				3	<1	
			[Val d'Aosta Union]				1	<1	

Country	Year	Governing coalition			Party	1965			
Ireland	1992	Coalition of Fine Gael, Labour, and DL	68	39	Fianna Fáil	1965	72	48	3.48
			45	25	Fine Gael		47	34	
			33	19	Labour party		22	15	
		President: DL (90)	10	5	Progressive Democrats				
			6	9	Independents and others		2	2	
			4	3	Democratic Left (DL)				
					[Republican party]		1	1	
Israel	1992	Coalition of Labour party, Meretz, and Shas	44	35	Labour party [Labour Alignment, including Mapam and Rafi]	1965	63	52	4.38
			32	25	Likud Bloc [was Herut]		26	21	
			12	10	Meretz				
			8	6	Tsomet				
			6	5	Shas				
			6	5	National Religious party		11	9	
			4	3	United Tora Judaism				
			3	2	Hadash				
			3	2	Moledet				
			2	2	Arab Democratic party				
			4	3	[Agudat Israel]		4	3	
			2	2	[Poalei Agudat Israel]		2	2	
			5	2	[Independent Liberal party]		5	2	
			4	2	[Communist parties and Rakah]		4	2	
			1	1	[New Force]		1	1	
			4	4	[Minority Lists]		4	4	

continued

TABLE 1.4 *Continued*

Country	Year	Which Party(ies) Formed Government[a]	Number of Seats Won	Percentage of Vote Won	Political Parties Winning Seats in Lower House in Most Recent and Mid-1960s Election[b]	Year[c]	Number of Seats Won	Percentage of Vote Won	Effective Number of Parties in Parliament (ENPP), Most Recent Election[c]
		Most Recent Election				*Mid-1960s Election*			
India	1991	Congress party	226	36	Congress (I)	1967	282	41	4.23
			119	20	Bharatiya Janata party (BJP)		19	4	
			55	12	Janata Dal				
			35	6	Communist party of India (Marxist)		23	5	
			14	3	Telegu Desam				
			13	3	Communist party of India (CPI)		25	4	
			11	2	All-India Anna Dravida Munnetra Kazhegam (ADMK)				
			6		Jhakhand Mukti Morcha				
			5		Samajwadi Janata Party				
			4		Shiv Sena				
			4		Revolutionary Socialist party (RSP)		1		
			3		Forward Bloc		2		
			2		Indian Union Moslem League		2		
			2		Asom Gana Parishad				
			1		Haryana Vikas party				
			1		Manipur People's party				
			1		Nagaland People's Council		1		
			1		Bahujan Samaj party				
			1		Kerela Congress (Mani)				
			1		Sikkim Sangram Parishad				
			1		Janata Dal (Gujerat)				
			1		Independents		29		
					[Jana Sangh]		35	9	
					[Swatantra]		44	9	
					[Samyukta Socialist]		23	5	
					[Praja Socialist party (PSP)]		13	3	

Country	Year		Party						
Germany	1994	Coalition of CDU/CSU, and FDP	Christian Democratic Union (BDU) and Christian Social Union (CSU)	294	41	1965	245	48	2.78
			Social Democratic party (SPD)	252	36		202	39	
			Greens	49	7				
			Free Democratic party (FDP)	47	7		49	10	
			Party of Democratic Socialism (PDS)	30	4				
Greece	1993	Panhellenic Socialist Movement	Panhellenic Socialist Movement (PASOK)	170	47	D			2.17
			New Democracy (ND)	111	39				
			Political Spring (POLA)	10	5				
			Communist party of Greece (KKE)	9	5				
Hungary	1994	Hungarian Socialist party	Hungarian Socialist party (MszP)	209	33	N			2.89
			Alliance of Free Democrats (SzDSz)	70	20				
			Hungarian Democratic Forum (MDF)	37	12				
			Independent Smallholders (FKGP)	26	9				
			Christian Democratic People's party (KDNP)	22	7				
			Federation of Young Democrats (FIDESz)	20	7				
			Agrarian Association	1	2				
			Liberal Civic Alliance	1	1				

continued

Country	Year	Notes			Party				
Japan	1993	Coalition of JSP, RP, CGP, JNP, DSP, HP, and USDP	223	37	Liberal Democratic party (LDP)	1967	277	50	3.95
			70	15	Japan Socialist party (JSP)		140	28	
			55	10	Renewal party (Shinseito) (RP)				
			51	8	Clean Government party (Komeito) (CGP)		25	6	
			35	8	Japan New party (JNP)				
			30	7	Independents and others		9	6	
			15	8	Japan Communist party (JCP)		5	5	
			15	4	Democratic Socialist party (DSP)		30	7	
			13	3	Harbinger party (Sakigake) (HP)				
			4	1	United Social Democratic party (Shaminren) (USDP)				
Madagascar	1993	Coalition of UNDD, Rasalama Active Forces Cartel, and others	46		Rasalama Active Forces Cartel	N			6.53
			15		Movement for Proletarian Power (MFM)				
			13		Fanilo				
			11		Famima				
		President: Rasa. AFC (92)	10		Others and independents				
			8		Fihaonana				
			8		Rally for Social Democracy (RPSD)				
			5		Congress party for Malagasy Independence (AKFM)				
			7		National Union for Development and Democracy (UNDD)				
			2		Fivoarana				
Malawi	1994	Coalition of UDF and AFORD	84		United Democratic Front (UDF)	N			2.75
			55		Malawi Congress party (MCP)				
		President: UDF (94)	36		Alliance for Democracy (AFORD)				
Mali	1992	Alliance for Democracy in Mali	76		Alliance for Democracy in Mali (ADEMA)	N			2.77
			9		National Committee for Democratic Initiative (CNID)				
		President: ADEMA (92)	8		Sudanese Union-African Democratic Rally (US-RDA)				
			6		Popular Movement for the Development of the Republic of West Africa (PMD)				
			4		Rally for Democracy and Progress (RDP)				
			4		Union for Democracy and Development (UDD)				
			3		Rally for Democracy and Work (RDT)				
			3		Union of Democratic Progressive Forces (UFDP)				
			2		Democracy and Progress party (PDP)				
			1		Malian Union for Democracy and Development (UMADD)				

continued

TABLE 1.4 *Continued*

		Most Recent Election				Mid-1960s Election			
Country	*Year*	*Which Party(ies) Formed Government*[a]	*Number of Seats Won*	*Percentage of Vote Won*	*Political Parties Winning Seats in Lower House in Most Recent and Mid-1960s Election*[b]	*Year*[c]	*Number of Seats Won*	*Percentage of Vote Won*	*Effective Number of Parties in Parliament (ENPP), Most Recent Election*[c]
Mexico	1994	Institutional Revolutionary party	300		Institutional Revolutionary party (PRI)	1965	177		2.28
			119		National Action party (PAN)				
			71		Party of the Democratic Revolution (PRD)				
		President: PRI (94)	10		Labor party (PT)				
					Others		33		
Mozambique	1994	Frelimo	129	44	Frelimo	N			2.13
			112	38	Mozambique National Resistance (MNR)				
		President: Frelimo (94)	9	5	Democratic Union				
Nepal	1994	Communist party	88		United Nepal Communist party (UCPN)	N			2.33
			83		Nepali Congress				
			20		Rashtriya Prajakantra party (RPP)				
			7		Independents				
			4		Nepal Mazdoor Kisan party				
			3		Nepal Sadbhavana party				

Country	Year	Government	Party	1994 / 1993 / 1993	1967 / 1966 / 1965		
Netherlands	1994	Coalition of PvdA, D66, and VVD	Labour party (PvdA)	37	37	24	5.38
			Christian Democratic Appeal (CDA)	34		27	
			[Catholic People's party]		42	10	
			[Anti-Revolutionary party]		15	8	
			[Christian Historical Union]		12	11	
			People's party for Freedom and Democracy (VVD)	31	17		
			Democrats '66 (D66)	24	7	5	
			Political Reformed party—Reformational				
			Political Federation—Reformed Political Association (SGP/RPF/GPV)				
			[SGP]	2	3	2	
			[GPV]	2	1	1	
			General League of the Elderly (AOV)	6		3	
			Green Left	5	4		
			Center Democrats	3			
			Socialist party	2		4	
			55+ Union	1		5	
			[Communist party]		5		
			[Farmers party]		7		
New Zealand	1993	National party	National party	50	44	44	2.16
			Labour party	45	35	41	
			Alliance	2		15	
			New Zealand First party (NZFP)	2			
			[Social Credit]		1		
Norway	1993	Labor party	Norwegian Labor party (DNA)	67	68	43	4.15
			Center party (SP)	32	18	9	
			Conservative party (Høyre)	28	31	20	
			Christian People's party (KrF)	13	13	8	
			Socialist Left party (SV)	13	2	6	
			Progress party (FrP)	10			
			Liberal party (Venstre)	1	18		
			Red Electoral Alliance (RV) (was Communists)	1		1	

continued

TABLE 1.4 Continued

		Most Recent Election				Mid-1960s Election			Effective Number of Parties in Parliament (ENPP), Most Recent Election[c]
Country	Year	Which Party(ies) Formed Government[a]	Number of Seats Won	Percentage of Vote Won	Political Parties Winning Seats in Lower House in Most Recent and Mid-1960s Election[b]	Year[c]	Number of Seats Won	Percentage of Vote Won	
Pakistan	1993	Pakistan People's party	86		Pakistan People's party	D			4.35
			72		Pakistan Muslim League (Nawaz)				
			15		Independents				
			6		Pakistan Muslim League (Junejo)				
			4		Islami Jamhoori Mahaz				
			3		Awami National party				
			3		Pakistan Islami Front				
			2		Pakhtoonkwa Milli Awami				
			2		Jamhoori Watan				
			1		Multahida Deeni Mahaz				
			1		Baluchista National Movement (Hai)				
			1		Baluchista National Movement (Mengal)				
			1		National Democratic Alliance				
			1		National People's party				
			1		Pakhtoonkwa Qaumi party				
Philippines	1992	Coalition of Lakas ng Edsa and NUCD	85		Laban ng Demokratikohg Pilipino (LDP)	D			3.30
			50		National Christian Democrats (NUCD) and Lakas ng Edsa				
		President: Lakas/NUCD (92)	48		Nationalist party				
			15		Liberal party				
			2		Others				

32

Country	Year	Notes	Party				
Poland	1993	Coalition of Democratic Left Alliance and Polish Peasant party President: SLD (95)	Democratic Left Alliance (SLD)	171	20	N	3.85
			Polish Peasant party (PSL)	132	15		
			Democratic Union (VD)	74	11		
			Labour Union (UP)	41	7		
			Confederation for an Independent Poland (KPN)	22	6		
			Non-Party Bloc in Support of Reforms (BBWR)	16	5		
			German minority organizations	4			
Portugal	1995	Socialist party President: PS (91)	Socialist party (PS)	112	44	N	2.55
			Social Democratic party (PSD)	88	34		
			People's party (PP)	15	9		
			United Democratic Coalition (CDU)	15	9		
			Others	0	4		
Russia	1995	Our Home Is Russia President: Yeltsin (91)	Communist party	151	22	N	6.89
			Liberal Democratic party of Russia (LDPR)	50	11		
			Our Home Is Russia	56	10		
			Yabloko	48	7		
			Agrarian party	21	4		
			Russia's Democratic Choice	10	4		
			Derzhava Movement	10	3		
			Congress of Russian Communities	5	4		
			Women of Russia	3			
			Others	20	< 3 ea.		
			Independents	76			
South Africa	1994	Coalition of ANC, NP, and Inkatha Freedom party	African National Congress (ANC)	252	63	N	2.21
			National party (NP)	82	20		
			Inkatha Freedom party	43	10		
			Freedom Front (FF)	9	2		
			Democratic party (DP)	7	2		
			Pan Africanist Congress (PAC)	5	1		
			African Christian Democratic party (ACDP)	2	1		
South Korea	1992	Democratic Liberal party President: DLP (92)	Democratic Liberal party (DLP)	149	39	N	2.70
			Democratic party (DP)	97	29		
			Unification National party	31	17		
			Independents	21			
			Party for New Political Reform (PNPR)	1			

continued

TABLE 1.4 Continued

Country	Most Recent Election — Year	Which Party(ies) Formed Government[a]	Number of Seats Won	Percentage of Vote Won	Political Parties Winning Seats in Lower House in Most Recent and Mid-1960s Election[b]	Mid-1960s Election — Year[c]	Number of Seats Won	Percentage of Vote Won	Effective Number of Parties in Parliament (ENPP), of Most Recent Election[c]
Spain	1993	Coalition of PSOE, CiU, and PNV	159	39	Socialist Workers' party (PSOE)	N			2.67
			141	35	Popular party (PP)				
			18	10	United Left (IU)				
			17	5	Convergence and Union (CiU)				
			5	1	Basque Nationalist party (PNV)				
			4	1	Canarian Coalition (CC)				
			2	1	Herri Batasuna (HB)				
			1	1	Catalan Republican party (ERC)				
			1	1	Aragon party (PAR)				
			1	1	Eusko Alkartasuna (EA)				
			1	<1	Valencia Union (UV)				
Sweden	1994	Social Democratic party	161	45	Social Democratic party (SDP)	1964	113	47	3.51
			80	22	Moderate party [was Conservatives]		32	14	
			27	8	Center party (C)		33	13	
			26	7	Liberals (FP)		42	17	
			22	6	Left party (VP) [was Communists]		8	5	
			18	5	Ecology party (MpG)				
			14	4	Christian Democrats (KdS)		3	2	
					[Citizens' Coalition]		2	2	
					Other				

34

Country	Year	Government	Party						
Switzerland	1995	Coalition of SP/PS, SVP/UDC, FDP/PRD, and CVP/PDC	Social Democratic party of Switzerland (SP/PS)	1967	54	22	51	24	5.60
			Radical Democratic party (FDP/PRD)		45	20	49	23	
			Christian Democratic People's party (CVP/PDC)		34	17	45	22	
			Swiss People's party (SVP/UDC)		29	15	21	11	
			Green party of Switzerland (GPS/PES)		9	5			
			Freedom party of Switzerland/ Automobile party (FPS/AP)		7	4			
			Liberal party of Switzerland (LPS/PLS)		7	3	6	2	
			Swiss Democrats (SD/DS)		3	3	3	2	
			Alliance of Independents (LdU/AdI)		3	2	16	9	
			Evangelical People's party (EVP/PEP)		2	2	2	2	
			[Party of Labour and Left Alternative [National Action]				5	3	
			Others		7	8	1	1	
Taiwan	1992	Kuomintang	Kuomintang (KMT)	N	96	53			2.17
			Democratic Progressive		50	31			
			Independents		14				
			Chinese Socialist Democratic		1				
Thailand	1994	Coalition of CT, NAP, PD, SAP, NT, and MC	Chart Thai (CT)	N	92				5.44
			Democrat party		86				
			New Aspiration party (NAP)		57				
			Chart Pattana		53				
			Palang Dharma (PD)		23				
			Social Action party (SAP)		22				
			Nam Thai (NT)		18				
			Prachakorn Thai		18				
			Seritham		11				
			Ekaparb		8				
			Muan Chon (MC)		3				

continued

TABLE 1.4 *Continued*

Country	Most Recent Election Year	Which Party(ies) Formed Government[a]	Number of Seats Won	Percentage of Vote Won	Political Parties Winning Seats in Lower House in Most Recent and Mid-1960s Election[b]	Mid-1960s Election Year[c]	Number of Seats Won	Percentage of Vote Won	Effective Number of Parties in Parliament (ENPP), Most Recent Election[c]
Turkey	1995				Welfare party (Rafah)	D			4.40
			158	21	Motherland party (ANAP)				
			132	20	True Path party (DYP)				
			135	19	Democratic Left party (DSP)				
			75	15	Republican People's party (CHP)				
			50	11	National Movement (MHP)				
			0	8	People's Democracy (HADEP)				
			0	4	Others				
			0	2					
Ukraine	1994	Coalition			Independents	N			23.06
		President: Kuchma (94)	215		Communist party				
			87		Rukh				
			20		Peasants party				
			18		Socialist party				
			14		Ukrainian Republican party				
			11		Congress of Ukrainian Nationalists				
			5		Inter-regional Bloc for Reform (IRBR)				
			4		Party of the Democratic Rebirth of Ukraine				
			4		Labour party				
			4		UNA-UNSO				
			3		Civic Congress				
			2		Social Democracy party				
			2		Democratic party of Ukraine				
			2		Ukrainian Conservative Republican party				
			2		Christian Democratic party				
			1		Party unknown				
			13						

Country	Year	Party	Seats	Votes (%)	Year	Seats	Votes (%)	Eff. N
United Kingdom	1992	Conservative party	336	42	1964	304	48	2.26
		Labour party	271	34		317	50	
		Liberal Democrats	20	18		9	1	
		Official Ulster Unionists	9	<1				
		Plaid Cymru	4	<1				
		Social Democratic and Labour party	4	1				
		Scottish National party	3	2				
		Democratic Unionists	3	<1				
		Ulster Popular Unionists	1	<1				
United States	1994	Republican party	230	51	1966	187	48	2.00
		Democrats	204	47		248	51	
		Other	1	2				
		President: Democrat (92)						
Uruguay	1994	Coalition of Colorado and Blanco			D			3.27
		Colorado party	43	32				
		Blanco party	41	31				
		Frente Amplio/Encuentro Progresista	40	31				
		Nuevo Espacio	6	5				
		President: Colorado (94)						
Venezuela	1993	Coalition of CN and other parties			1968			4.71
		Democratic Action (AD)	58			66		
		Social Christian party (COPEI)	52			50		
		Convergence Coalition (CN)	39					
		Radical Cause	32					
		Unreported	12					
		Minor Parties	8			4		
		[Peoples Electoral Movement]				26		
		[National Civic Crusade]				20		
		[Democratic Republican Union]				14		
		[Popular Democratic Front]				8		
		President: CN (93)						
Zambia	1991	Movement for Multiparty Democracy			D			1.38
		Movement for Multiparty Democracy (MMD)	125					
		United National Independence party (UNIP)	25					
		President: MMD (91)						

SOURCE: *Keesing's Record of World Events*, various issues (most recent election); *Electoral Studies*, various issues; Mackie and Rose 1982 (mid-1960s election); Stanley and Niemi 1995 (1964 U.S. election).

a. President's party and year of election also shown for all countries having direct presidential elections.

b. Parties in brackets held seats in mid-1960s only.

c. For countries having competitive democratic elections in 1963 (Banks and Textor 1963, 104). "N" denotes countries that were not classified as democratic as of that date or whose form of political or national organization was substantially different (e.g., Bangladesh). "D" denotes those countries that experienced a significant disruption of elections or democratic institutions after 1963.

d. Calculated by the editors based on the most recent election using the formula in Taakso and Taagepera (1978).

e. Seats won in the district vote; votes shown are PR votes.

TABLE 1.5 Public Subsidies to Parties and Candidates

| Country | Direct Subsidies | | | | Specific Grants or Services | Indirect Subsidies |
	Recipient	Interval	Basis	Eligibility		
Australia	Candidates, parties		Per vote	At least 4% of vote. Must be registered with electoral commission	Transportation, encouragement of voting, broadcasting	
Austria	Parties, parliamentary groups		per vote		Billposting, broadcasting, printing ballots, party foundations, press and publications, women's and youth organizations, education and information	
Belgium	No direct subsidies	N/A	N/A	N/A	Broadcasting, encouragement of voting	
Canada	Candidates, parliamentary groups	Election	Per vote	Candidate: 15% of votes in an electoral district. Party: must spend at least 10% of limit	Broadcasting, encouragement of voting	Tax credits
Denmark	Parliamentary groups	Annual	Per seat		Broadcasting, press and publications, women's and youth organizations	
Finland	Parties	Annual	Per seat		Billposting, broadcasting, press and publications, women's and youth organizations	
France	Presidential candidates	Election			Billposting, broadcasting, printing ballots, press and publications	Kickbacks of deputy salaries
Germany	Parties	Election	Per vote	0.5% of votes for national party lists of candidates, or 105 of first votes cast in a constituency if no regional list has been accepted	Broadcasting, subsidies to party foundations	Tax deductions

Country	Recipient	Frequency	Basis	Eligibility	In-kind support	Other benefits
Greece	Parties	Election	Equal distribution of 10% of flat rate, then per vote. If coalition, amount divided by agreement among parties involved.	Participated in last election and got at least 3% of votes. Has a list of candidates in at least 2/3 of the electoral districts. If a coalition: received at least 5%–6% of votes, depending on coalition status		
India	No direct subsidies	N/A	N/A	N/A	Broadcasting (by agreement)	
Ireland	No direct subsidies	N/A	N/A	N/A	Broadcasting	
Israel	Party groups	Annual, every election	Per seat	Had at least 1 MP in last parliament. Recognized as a group by Knesset Committee. Named representatives to deal with finances	Broadcasting, encouragement of voting, transportation	
Italy	Parties, parliamentary groups	Annual, every election	Per vote	Parties presenting candidate lists in more than 2/3 of constituencies and obtaining no less than 300,000 votes or 2% of total amount of votes	Broadcasting (according to guidelines of Parliamentary Committee), women's and youth organizations, education and information	Kickbacks of deputy salaries
Japan	Candidates	Every election			Transportation, publication, broadcasting, advertising, use of public halls, financing of election bulletins on candidates	Tax benefits
Mexico	Parties	Annual, every election	Per vote	Party should obtain more than 1.5% of the total ballot	Broadcasting	Tax exemptions
Netherlands	No direct subsidies	N/A	N/A	N/A	Broadcasting, encouragement of voting, party foundations, women's and youth organizations	Tax deductions

continued

TABLE 1.5 *Continued*

Country	Recipient	Direct Subsidies			Specific Grants or Services	Indirect Subsidies
		Interval	*Basis*	*Eligibility*		
Norway	Parties, parliamentary groups	Annual	Per seat		Broadcasting, nomination costs	
Poland	No direct subsidies	N/A	N/A	N/A	Broadcasting, use of public halls, printing and mailing, encouragement of the vote	Limited tax exemptions for political parties
Spain	Parties	Annual, every election	Per vote	Party must have won at least one parliamentary seat (which requires at least 3% of the national vote)	Broadcasting, free space for posters, use of public halls, reduced postal rate for campaign mail	
Sweden	Parties, parliamentary groups	Annual	Per seat, per vote	Party support: obtained at least 2.5% of votes in last two elections. Basic support: party obtained over 4% of the votes. Supplementary support: based on number of parliamentary seats won by each party	Publication, encouragement of voting, broadcasting, women's and youth organizations	
Switzerland	No direct subsidies	N/A	N/A	N/A		
Taiwan	Candidates		Per vote	Candidate should receive at least 3/4 of the number of votes needed to be elected to their constituency	Publication, encouragement of voting	Tax benefits
Thailand	No direct subsidies	N/A	N/A	N/A	Broadcasting, encouragement of voting	Tax benefits
Turkey	Parties	Annual	Per vote	Party must have obtained 7% of votes in last parliamentary election	Broadcasting, encouragement of voting	Tax benefits

United Kingdom	Parliamentary groups	Annual		Publications, mailing broadcasting, free use of public halls	Gifts to parties exempt from inheritance tax
United States	Candidates in presidential primaries and elections	Election	Matching grant in primary, fixed sum in election from funds earmarked by taxpayers	Nomination costs, mailing; most states pay for voter registration and ballots	Tax credits, tax deductions
Venezuela	Parties	Election	Per vote	Broadcasting, election advertising	

SOURCE: Levush et al. 1991 (Australia, Belgium, Canada, Germany, Greece, India, Israel, Italy, Japan, Mexico, the Netherlands, Turkey, and United Kingdom); Butler, Penniman, and Ranney 1981 (Australia, Austria, Canada, Denmark, Finland, France, Ireland, Israel, Italy, Japan, the Netherlands, Norway, Sweden, Switzerland, United Kingdom, United States, and Venezuela); Del Castillo 1989 (Spain).
NOTE: N/A = not applicable.

TABLE 1.6 Statutory Control of Campaign Finances

Country	Interval	By	Reporting To	Of	Disclosure	Audit of Reports	Publicity	Limits on Contributions	Limits on Expenditures
Australia	Every campaign	Candidate	Electoral commission	Expenditures	Details of expenditures, amount of contributions and donor's identity	Yes, if public funding sought	Public inspection	No	No
Austria	Annual and prior to every campaign	Parties	Government auditors	Expenditures	Details of income, sources, and expenditures	Yes	Annual public statements		
Canada	Annual and every campaign	Candidate and party	Chief electoral officer	Contributions and expenses	Amount of contributions, donor's identity, details of expenditures	Yes	Public inspection, daily press, reports to legislature	No	On total amount and by segment spent by candidates and parties
Germany	Annual and every campaign	Party	Speaker of the federal diet	Contributions, expenditures, assets, total campaign expenditures	Amount of contributions, donor's identity	Yes		No	No, but implicit because grants have to be matched by party's private income
Greece	Annual and every campaign	Candidate and party	President of parliament and minister of interior	Contributions and balance sheets, campaign expenditures	For donations greater than 200,000 drachmas, identity of contributor	Yes	Published in Athens newspapers	No	No
India	Every campaign	Candidate	District election officer	Election expenditures	Any corporate donations	No	Public inspection	Yes	On total amount spent by candidates
Israel	Annual and every campaign	Party group	State comptroller	Financial accounts	Amount of contributions, details of expenditures	Yes	State comptrollers report can be made public, report to legislature	On amount and source	On total amount spent by candidates and limits on parties relating to government funding

Country	Frequency	Who reports	To whom	What reported	Contributions	Disclosure required	Made public	Limits on contributions	Limits on expenditures
Italy	Annual and every campaign	Party	Minister or speaker of legislature	Contributions and expenses	Amount of contributions and donor's identity	Yes	Daily press, reports to legislature	No	No
Japan	Annual	Treasurer of political organization	Minister of Home Affairs or local Election Management Commission	Contributions and expenses	Amount, date, and source of contributions	Yes	Public inspection, published in official gazette	On amount and source	On total amount and by segment
Mexico	Every campaign	Political parties	General Council of the Federal Electoral Institute	Irregularities in *other* parties' finances	Contributions	Yes	Secretariat of Government informed of violations of law	Forbidden from abroad	
Netherlands	No reporting	N/A	N/A	N/A	N/A	N/A	N/A		
Poland	Every campaign	Minister of Finance (parliamentary and local elections); presidential candidates campaign (presidential election)	Public: Chair of State Electoral Committee	Report on expenditure funded from state budget; reports of expenditures	Sources of contributions		Public inspection	On sources	By segment
Spain	Every campaign	Parties	Election Commission	Contributions and expenses	Revenue and expenditures	No	Public inspection	On amount and source	On amount spent in each district
Sweden	Not mandatory	N/A	N/A	N/A	N/A	N/A	N/A	No	No
Taiwan	Every campaign	Candidates	Electoral Commission	Contributions and expenses		Yes		On amount and source	On total amount
Thailand	No reporting	N/A	N/A	N/A	N/A	N/A	N/A	On sources	On total amount

continued

43

TABLE 1.6 *Continued*

Country	Interval	By	Reporting To	Of	Disclosure	Audit of Reports	Publicity	Limits on Contributions	Limits on Expenditures
Turkey	Annual	Parties	Constitutional Court and attorney general	Financial statements	Any expenditure over 5,000 lira, contributions	Yes	Announcement of Constitutional Court decisions	On amount and source	No
United Kingdom	Every campaign	Candidate	Returning Officers	Contributions and expenses	Details of expenditures, contributions from corporations and trade unions	No	Public inspection, report to legislature	No	On total amount spent by candidates
United States	Annual and every campaign	Candidate, party, political committee	Federal Election Commission	Contributions, expenditures	Amount of expenditure, donor's identity, details of expenditures	Yes	Public inspection, reports to legislature	On amount and source	On total amount if candidate accepts public funds

SOURCE: Levush et al. 1991 (Australia, Canada, Germany, Greece, India, Israel, Italy, Japan, Mexico, the Netherlands, Poland, Sweden, Taiwan, Thailand, Turkey, and United Kingdom); Butler, Penniman, and Ranney 1981 (Australia, Canada, Israel, Italy, Japan, and United States); Del Castillo 1989 (Spain); Law Library of Congress 1979 (Austria).
NOTE: N/A = not applicable.

TABLE 1.7 Media Penetration and Political Controls on Television

Country	Ownership: Public or Commercial	Television and Radio				Campaign Regulations of Television Coverage				Newspapers			Press Freedom
		Year Regular TV Broadcasts Began	TV Sets per 1,000 People, 1970	TV Sets per 1,000 People, 1994	Radio Sets per 1,000 People, 1994	Paid Political Ads	Free Time to Parties	Fair Balance Rules	Leader Debate in Last Election	Number of National Dailies	Circulation per 1,000 People	Illiteracy Rates, 1992 (in %)	
Argentina	Public and commercial		146	219	673					197	82	5	Free
Australia	Public and commercial	1956	220	484	1,262	Yes	Yes	Yes	Yes	68	244	0	Free
Austria	Commercial	1956	254	475	622	Yes	Yes	Yes		34	358	0	Free
Bangladesh	Public and commercial	1956	0	4	41	No				72	9	65	Partly free
Belgium	Commercial	1959	285	447	776	No	Yes	Yes	Yes	23	221	0	Free
Brazil	Public and commercial		64	204	373	No	Yes	Yes	Yes	366	53	19	Free
Canada	Public and commercial	1952	333	626	1,023	Yes	Yes	Yes	Yes	107	226	0	Free
Chile	Public and commercial		53	201	340					39	67	7	Free
Colombia	Public and commercial		38	108	167	Yes	Yes		Yes	45	49	13	Partly free
Costa Rica	Public and commercial		58	136	259					4	106	7	Free
Denmark	Public	1954	372	528	1,012	No	No		Yes	46	359	0	Free
Ecuador	Commercial		25	82	314					26	84	14	Free
Finland	Commercial	1956	261	488	998	No	No	Yes	Yes	66	547	0	Free

continued

TABLE 1.7 Continued

Country	Ownership: Public or Commercial	Television and Radio				Campaign Regulations of Television Coverage				Newspapers		Illiteracy Rates, 1992 (in %)	Press Freedom
		Year Regular TV Broadcasts Began	TV Sets per 1,000 People, 1970	TV Sets per 1,000 People, 1994	Radio Sets per 1,000 People, 1994	Paid Political Ads	Free Time to Parties	Fair Balance Rules	Leader Debate in Last Election	Number of National Dailies	Circulation per 1,000 People		
France	Public and commercial	1935	236	400	895	No	Yes	Yes	Yes	96	166	0	Free
Germany	Public and commercial	1952	363 (FRG), 396 (GDR)	643	868	Yes (not on public broadcasters)	Yes	Yes	No	358	386	0	Free
Greece	Public and commercial		21	195	419	No (not on state owned-stations)	Yes	Yes		117		7	Free
Hungary	Public and commercial		205	409	592		Yes			28	273	1	Free
India	Public	1959	0	27	78	No	Yes			1,978	26	52	Partly free
Ireland	Commercial	1961	151	271	583	No	Yes	Yes	Yes	4	101	0	Free
Israel	Public and commercial		180	266	468	No	Yes	Yes		30	246	4	Free
Italy	Public and commercial	1954	223	423	794	Yes	Yes	Yes	No	73	105	3	Free
Japan	Commercial	1953	335	610	895	Yes (for party)	Yes (for candidates)	Yes	Yes	158	577	0	Free
Mali	Public		0	0	39					2	0.7	68	Partly free

Country	Ownership	Year											Status
Mexico	Public and commercial		536	127	242	Yes	No	No	Yes	286	119	13	Partly free
Nepal	Public and semipublic		0	2	33					28	6	74	Partly free
Netherlands	Commercial	1953	237	485	902	No	Yes	Yes	Yes	86	307	0	Free
New Zealand	Commercial		280	372	922	Yes	Yes	Yes	Yes	35	321	0	Free
Norway	Commercial	1957	264	423	796	No	No	Yes	Yes	83	548	0	Free
Philippines	Commercial		11	41	136					38	53	10	Partly free
Poland	Public and commercial		143	292	428		Yes	Yes		45	181	1	Free
Portugal	Public and commercial		56	176	216				Yes	28	83	15	Free
Russia	Public and commercial			323	1,003								Partly free
South Korea	Commercial		139	207	304					39	244	3	Free
Spain	Public and commercial	1956	122	389	885	No	Yes	Yes	Yes	102	82	4	Free
Sweden	Public and commercial	1956	458	471	851	Yes	Yes	Yes	Yes	107	520	0	Free
Switzerland	Commercial	1958	242	406	1,157	No	Yes	Yes	No	98	496	0	Free
Taiwan	Public and commercial	1962		411	182	No	No	Yes	No	192	269		Free
Thailand	Public and commercial		7	109						40	85	7	Partly free
Turkey	Public and commercial	1972	11	174	161	No	Yes	Yes	Yes	426	55	19	Partly free

continued

TABLE 1.7 Continued

Country	Television and Radio — Ownership: Public or Commercial	Year Regular TV Broadcasts Began	TV Sets per 1,000 People, 1970	TV Sets per 1,000 People, 1994	Radio Sets per 1,000 People, 1994	Campaign Regulations of Television Coverage — Paid Political Ads	Free Time to Parties	Fair Balance Rules	Leader Debate in Last Election	Newspapers — Number of National Dailies	Circulation per 1,000 People	Illiteracy Rates, 1992 (in %)	Press Freedom
Ukraine	Public and commercial		151	292	781							2	Partly free
United Kingdom	Public and commercial	1936	324	434	1,145	No	Yes	Yes	No	104	393	0	Free
United States	Public and commercial	1950	413	814	2,122	Yes	No	Yes	Yes	1,657	251	1	Free
Uruguay	Public and commercial		100	227	600					33	224	4	Free
Venezuela	Public and commercial		90	156	432	Yes	Yes		Yes	56	113	12	Partly free
Zambia	Public		4	25	74					3	12	27	Not free

SOURCE: United Nations Department of Public Information 1992 (television ownership, television sets 1994, radio ownership, radio sets 1994, number of national dailies, newspaper circulation, and illiteracy rates 1992); Butler, Penniman, and Ranney 1981 (year regular television broadcasts began, fair balance rules, and leader debate); United Nations 1994 (television sets 1970); Levush et al. 1991 (paid political ads, and free time to parties); Fletcher 1991 (updating leader debate); Banks 1995 (television, radio, and newspaper for Taiwan); Skidmore 1993 (updating paid political ads, free time to parties, fair balance rules, and leader debate); *Freedom Review* 26 (1995), 68 (press freedom).

2

Electoral Systems

ANDRÉ BLAIS
LOUIS MASSICOTTE

Electoral rules have fascinated politicians and political scientists for decades, because they are commonly assumed to condition the chances of success of competing parties or candidates. This chapter covers one important set of electoral rules, namely, the electoral system, which defines how votes are cast and seats are allocated. Other sets of rules, such as those concerning the financing of political parties, the control of election spending, and the regulation of political broadcasting, are dealt with in other chapters.

We first document the great diversity of electoral systems presently existing among democracies. This raises the question of whether electoral systems matter, of what concrete effect they have on political life. The second section thus examines the political consequences of electoral laws. Once these consequences are known, we are in a position to tackle the crucial normative question of which is the best electoral system. The third section reviews the debate and identifies the major trade-offs involved in the choice of an electoral system.

AUTHORS' NOTE: We thank the Social Sciences and Humanities Research Council of Canada for financial support and Agnieszka Dobrzynska for research assistance.

Diversity of Electoral Systems

Even scholars specialized in the field are amazed by the diversity and complexity of contemporary electoral systems. The rules that govern how votes are cast and seats allocated differ markedly from one country to another.

Selecting an electoral system is not a purely technical decision. It may have huge consequences for the operation of the political system. As discussed in the second section, applying two different formulas to the same distribution of votes will produce quite different outcomes in terms of members elected for each party.

To give a concrete example, let us look at the critical British election of 1983, the first election in a major nation where voters were passing judgment on the record of a neo-conservative government. As the ruling Tories were reelected with more seats than in the previous election, many observers concluded that Mrs. Thatcher's policies had been strongly endorsed. The fact is, however, that the actual vote for the Tories decreased slightly between 1979 and 1983, and the outcome of the election would have been quite different if Britain had had proportional representation.

The first necessary step for understanding the consequences of an electoral system is to have a good grasp of the kinds of electoral systems that exist, hence the need for classification.

Typologies of electoral systems can be based on the *electoral formula,* which determines how votes are to be counted to allocate seats, on *district magnitude,* which refers to the number of seats per district, or on *ballot structure,* which defines how voters express their choice (Rae 1967; Blais 1988). We follow the classical approach and describe electoral formulas first, while taking into account district magnitude and ballot structure.

There are three basic electoral formulas, corresponding to as many criteria of legitimacy as to what is required to be elected. Supporters of *plurality* are satisfied when a candidate gets more votes than each individual opponent, whereas others feel that one should be declared the winner only if he or she can muster more than half of the vote, that is, a *majority.* Advocates of *proportional representation* (PR) feel that political parties should be represented in Parliament in exact (or nearly exact) proportion to the vote they polled.

It is convenient to examine electoral formulas in chronological order (from the oldest to the more recent) and in the order of their complexity (from the simplest in its application to the most sophisticated). Although plurality in English parliamentary elections dates back to the Middle Ages and majority

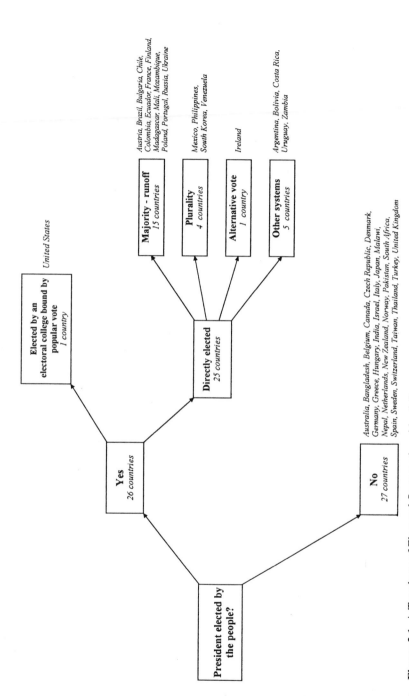

Figure 2.1. A Typology of Electoral Systems (presidential)

51

began to be applied to legislative elections in the early 19th century, PR was imagined during the first half of the 19th century and began to be used for national legislative elections at the end of that century.

Before the First World War, Joseph Barthélemy (1912) confidently predicted that the day would come when PR would become as widespread as universal suffrage. So far, he has not been vindicated. The proportion of democratic countries using PR has remained more or less constant since the early 1920s, hovering around 60 percent. The only significant trend is the increasing popularity, lately, of mixed systems, where different formulas are used simultaneously in the same election.

Figures 2.1 and 2.2 outline, in some detail, the electoral systems that exist in the 53 countries covered in this book, for presidential and legislative (first Chamber) elections.[1] Readers are advised to refer to those figures for a better understanding of the typology offered in this chapter.

Plurality Systems

Plurality, also known as *first past the post,* outperforms all other options in terms of its pristine simplicity. To be elected, a candidate needs simply to have more votes than any other challenger.

The plurality rule is usually applied in single-member districts. Indeed, this is so often the case that we sometimes forget or overlook that it can be used in multimember districts as well. For example, in U.S. presidential elections, members of the electoral college are elected within each state on a winner-take-all basis (also known as the *bloc vote*), as the party slate that gets the highest number of votes in the state gets all the votes of that state in the electoral college. Under plurality rule, even when voters cast as many individual votes as there are members to be elected (and thus can split their ballot between parties if they wish), party cohesion usually allows the majority party to sweep all, or almost all, seats.

As the bloc vote normally results in the elimination of minority parties within each district, variants were imagined in the 19th century to allow for some minority representation within multimember districts using the plurality rule. One is the now-extinct *cumulative vote,* used in the State of Illinois until 1980, whereby voters were granted as many votes as there were members to be elected but were allowed to cumulate two or more votes on a single candidate: It was expected that supporters of the minority party in each district would focus their voting power on a single candidate to enhance their chances of securing at least one seat. The *limited vote,* still used for elections to the Spanish Senate, aims at a similar objective, though by the different device of granting each voter *fewer* votes than there are members to be elected (e.g., most Spanish provinces elect four senators, with each elector casting up to three votes for different candidates). Here the expectation is that the majority party will not be able to carry all seats if the minority party presents a single candidate. A variant of the limited vote is the *single nontransferable vote* (SNTV) used in Japan until 1994, where electors cast a single vote in a district electing between three and five members.

Cruder procedures for ensuring minority representation while keeping the plurality rule were common in Latin America before PR was introduced, and they still can be found. Post-Pinochet Chile has two-member districts, where the leading party gets both seats only if it polls twice as many votes as the second party (i.e., two-thirds of the vote if there are two parties).[2] Otherwise, one seat goes to each of the two leading parties. In the recently reformed Mexican Senate, the leading party in each of the four-member districts gets three seats, and the remaining seat goes to the strongest minority party.

Out of the 53 democracies covered by this book, 4 use the plurality rule for presidential elections (Figure 2.1) and 13 for legislative elections (Figure 2.2).

Other countries have provided for presidential election systems that incorporate the plurality rule with some qualifications. Uruguay has an original system, known as the *double simultaneous vote,* whereby each faction (*sublema*) within a party (*lema*) may present its own presidential candidate. Voters vote for a single candidate and so, implicitly, for the lema he or she belongs to. Votes for all candidates under the label of each lema are added: The leading lema is proclaimed the "winner," and the elected president is the candidate who gets the highest number of votes within that lema. This system ensures the election of the candidate who gets a plurality within the party that secures a plurality of the vote. Costa Rica requires on the first ballot a plurality representing at least 40 percent of the vote. Failing that, a runoff election is held. In Argentina, which did away with the electoral college in 1994, the candidate with a plurality of the vote is elected, provided that plurality is equal to at least 45 percent of the vote, or exceeds 40 percent of the vote coupled with a lead of at least 10 points over the strongest challenger. Failing that, a runoff is held.

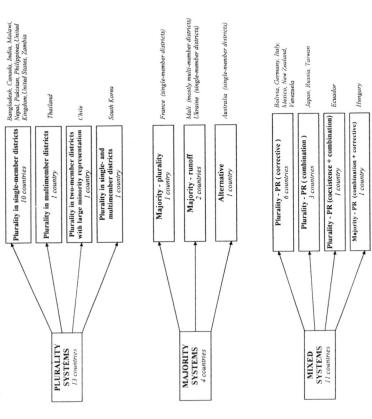

Figure 2.2. A Typology of Electoral Systems (legislative)
NOTE: PR = proportional representation; STV = single transferable vote.

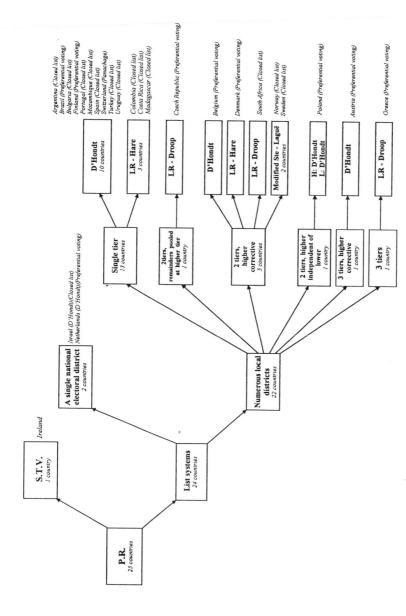

Figure 2.2. *Continued*

Majority Systems

With majority systems, we cross a small step toward greater complexity. Requiring a majority without further specification opens the possibility of having no winner at all if there is a single-round election, or to have a succession of indecisive ballots if no candidate is eliminated following each round. That problem is solved through one of the following three variants. In *majority-runoff* systems, a majority is required on the first ballot. If no candidate obtains a majority, a second and final ballot, known in the United States as a runoff, is held between the two candidates who got the highest number of votes in the first round.

This is the system used in 15 of the 25 countries with direct presidential elections (Figure 2.1); Mali and Ukraine use the same method for legislative elections (Figure 2.2). In *majority-plurality* systems (used for French legislative elections), there is no such drastic reduction in the number of contestants on the second ballot (although a threshold may be imposed for candidates to stand at the second ballot),[3] and the winner is the candidate who gets a plurality of the vote. Although one normally must have stood as a candidate on the first ballot to be allowed to compete at the second, there are past instances of major countries imposing no such requirement.[4]

As both formulas require the holding of a second round if no majority is reached on the first one, the *alternative vote* emerged as a less costly option whereby voters, instead of casting a vote for a single candidate, rank candidates in order of preference. First preferences are initially counted, and candidates winning a majority of these are declared elected. Second and lower preferences are taken into account only if no candidate secures a majority of first preferences. The candidate who got the smallest number of first preferences is eliminated, and second preferences expressed on his or her ballots are counted and "transferred" to other contestants. If this operation produces a winner, the contest is over. If not, the weakest candidate then remaining is eliminated and subsequent preferences on his or her ballots (which then means third preferences on transferred ballots and second preferences on untransferred ballots) are similarly transferred, and so on until eliminations and transfers produce a majority for one of the remaining candidates. As in all other majority systems, transfers may result in the final victory of a candidate who did not get the highest number of first preferences. The alternative vote is used in Ireland for presidential elections (Figure 2.1) and in Australia for elections to the House of Representatives (Figure 2.2).

Proportional Representation

By definition, PR can be used only in multimember districts, because it is obviously impossible to distribute a single seat among many parties, except on a chronological basis, an option that no legislature to our knowledge has adopted.

There are two major types of PR systems. With 24 countries, the *list system* is by far the most widely used type among the countries surveyed (Figure 2.2). The other type, the *single transferable vote*, is in force only in Ireland.

List Systems

Devising a PR list system involves making five major decisions as to districting, formula, tiers, thresholds, and preferences for candidates. There are many different ways of combining these variables, which explains why no PR systems are exactly alike.

Districts. The first choice to be made concerns district magnitude. One option, which is the most conducive to accuracy of representation, is to have the whole country as a single electoral district. Israel and the Netherlands both have a single national constituency electing 120 and 150 members, respectively (Figure 2.2).

The vast majority (22) of PR countries covered in this book have opted for smaller districts, the boundaries of which generally correspond to administrative subdivisions. For example, the 350 members of the Spanish Congress of Deputies are elected in 52 electoral districts: Each of the 50 provinces constitutes an electoral district, as well as the African enclaves of Ceuta and Melilla. The latter two are single-member districts in view of their small population. The number of seats in the provinces ranges from three in Soria to 34 in Madrid.[5] The resulting small district magnitude has repeatedly allowed the winning party to get a majority of seats with a plurality of votes.

The electoral formula. Second choice involves the method by which seats will be distributed *within each district*. The two basic options are *highest-averages* methods, which use a divisor, and the *largest-remainders* methods, which use quotas.

Highest-averages methods require the number of votes for each party to be divided successively by a series of divisors: Seats are allotted to the parties

TABLE 2.1 Distribution of Seats by the Three Highest-Averages Methods

Votes	Blues (57,000)	Whites (26,000)	Reds (25,950)	Greens (12,000)	Yellows (6,010)	Pinks (3,050)
			D'Hondt formula			
÷						
1	57,000 A	26,000 C	25,950 D	12,000 I	6,010	3,050
2	28,500 B	13,000 G	12,975 H	6,000		
3	19,000 E	8,667 L	8,650			
4	14,250 F	6,500				
5	11,400 J					
6	9,500 K					
7	8,143					
Seats won	6	3	2	1	0	0
			Modified Sainte-Laguë formula			
÷						
1.4	40,714 A	18,571 C	18,536 D	8,571 H	4,293	2,179
3	19,000 B	8,667 F	8,650 G	4,000		
5	11,400 E	5,200 K	5,190 L			
7	8,143 I	3,714	3,707			
9	6,333 J					
11	5,182					
Seats won	5	3	3	1	0	0
			Pure Sainte-Laguë formula			
÷						
1	57,000 A	26,000 B	25,950 C	12,000 E	6,010 K	3,050
3	19,000 D	8,667 G	8,650 H	4,000	2,000	
5	11,400 F	5,200 L	5,190			
7	8,143 I	3,714				
9	6,333 J					
11	5,182					
Seats won	5	3	2	1	1	0

NOTE: The letters indicate the order in which seats are awarded to parties in a 12-member district.

that secured the highest resulting quotients, up to the total number of seats available. There are three such methods currently in use,[6] which differ by the sequence of divisors. The most widely known and used (15 countries; see

TABLE 2.2 Distribution of Seats by the Two Largest-Remainders Methods

	Votes Quota Dividend	Seats Won
Hare quota		
Blues	$57,000 \div 10,834 = 5.260$	5
Whites	$26,000 \div 10,834 = 2.400\ (*)^a$	3
Reds	$25,950 \div 10,834 = 2.395$	2
Greens	$12,000 \div 10,834 = 1.110$	1
Yellows	$6,010 \div 10,834 = 0.550\ (*)$	1
Pinks	$3,050 \div 10,834 = \underline{0.280}$	0
Total	$10\ (2)^b$	12
Droop quota		
Blues	$57,000 \div 10,001 = 5.699\ (*)$	6
Whites	$26,000 \div 10,001 = 2.660\ (*)$	3
Reds	$25,950 \div 10,001 = 2.595$	2
Greens	$12,000 \div 10,001 = 1.200$	1
Yellows	$6,010 \div 10,001 = 0.601$	0
Pinks	$3,050 \div 10,001 = \underline{0.305}$	0
Total	$10\ (2)$	12

a. Seats going to the parties with the largest remainders.
b. Total number of seats allocated through largest remainders.

Figure 2.2) is the *d'Hondt* formula, with divisors being 1, 2, 3, 4, and so on. The logical alternative is the *"pure" Sainte-Laguë* formula (also known as the odd-integer number rule), where divisors are instead 1, 3, 5, 7, and so on. In this pure form (which can be found in the mixed system of New Zealand), Sainte-Laguë normally produces a highly proportional distribution of seats, a feature that may explain why a *"modified" Sainte-Laguë* formula was devised, the single difference being that the first divisor is raised to 1.4 (instead of 1), a move that makes it more difficult for smaller parties to get a seat. The modified Sainte-Laguë formula is used in Denmark (in local districts), Norway, and Sweden. Of the three highest-averages methods, d'Hondt is acknowledged to produce a bonus for larger parties and pure Sainte-Laguë the most likely to produce a proportional outcome, with modified Sainte-Laguë falling in between.

Table 2.1 shows how seats would be allocated in a 12-member district under each of the three methods among the six following parties: Blues, 57,000 votes;

Whites, 26,000 votes; Reds, 25,950 votes; Greens, 12,000 votes; Yellows, 6,010 votes; Pinks, 3,050 votes, for a total of 130,010 votes.

In this case, each formula produces a slightly different outcome. The strongest party, the Blues, are better off under d'Hondt, whereas the second weakest party, the Yellows, manage to secure a seat only under pure Sainte-Laguë.

Largest-remainders (LR) systems involve two successive operations. First, the number of votes for each party is divided by a quota, and the resulting whole number corresponds to the number of seats each party initially gets. Second, seats still unallocated are awarded to parties that had the largest surpluses of unused votes (known as remainders) following division.[7] The only variations within the LR system concern the computation of the quota. The total number of votes polled in the district may be divided either by the number of members to be elected (a *Hare quota*) or by the number of members to be elected *plus one* (a *Droop quota*).[8]

LR-Hare is used in Colombia, Denmark, Costa Rica, and Madagascar, and LR-Droop in South Africa, the Czech Republic, and Greece (Figure 2.2).[9] Raising the divisor by 1 unit gives a lower quota. As a result, fewer seats normally remain unallotted after division, which slightly reduces the proportionality of the outcome.

Table 2.2 uses the same example as in Table 2.1 to illustrate how LR-Hare and LR-Droop work. The first step is to obtain a quota, which corresponds to the total number of votes (130,010) divided by 12 in the case of Hare and by 13 for Droop. Each party's votes are divided by the quota (10,834 for Hare and 10,001 for Droop), and unallotted seats go to the parties with the largest remainders. LR-Hare yields more proportional results (in our example, they are identical to those obtained under pure Sainte-Laguë) than LR-Droop.

Tiers. Although most PR countries covered in our book have settled for a single tier of districts (whether national or local), quite a few have added a second tier of distribution, generally to reduce distortions resulting from the allocation of seats in the first tier (Figure 2.2).

There can be two or even three tiers. Belgium has 30 arrondissements within its nine provinces. The Greeks have been the fondest practitioners of multiple tiers, and they currently have 56 local districts, 13 regional districts, and a single national one.

The distribution of seats at the higher tier can proceed in three basic ways. The first approach, found in the Czech Republic, necessitates a pooling at the higher level of remainders from local districts. In the lower tier (i.e., in the basic electoral districts), party votes are divided by the quota. The higher tier is where the seats unallocated in each district following division by the quota are grouped and distributed among parties on the basis of the collected remainders from each district. This procedure normally works to the advantage of the smaller parties insofar as it allows them to offset the wastage effect produced by the dispersion of their vote in local districts.

One implication of this technique is that the number of seats that are allocated at the higher tier(s) are not predetermined by the law. Indeed, it may vary from one election to the next, depending on the extent of party fractionalization—the more fractionalized the electorate in districts, the smaller the number of seats awarded at this initial stage—and on the quota used. As noted above, a Hare quota normally results in a smaller number of seats being allotted at the lower level than a Droop quota.

The second approach uses the higher tier as a corrective. In this case, a fixed number of seats are reserved for correcting at the higher level the distortion between votes and seats generated by the use of local districts with small magnitudes. Sweden, for example, is divided into 28 basic districts, which together elect 310 members. There are also 39 seats to be awarded at the national level to correct imbalances. The distribution of those 39 seats involves the following operations. First, the total number of seats, 349 (310 + 39), is distributed among parties on the basis of their total vote as if Sweden were a single national constituency. Next, the resulting seat allotment is compared with the actual distribution of 310 district seats. Whenever a party wins fewer seats in districts than it would be entitled to under the national computation, it gets the difference as national seats. Thus, imbalances created at the district level are corrected at the national level. This kind of corrective higher tier is used in Denmark, Sweden, Norway, and South Africa. Belgium's *apparentement provincial,* through different procedures (which do not provide for a fixed number of corrective seats), and Austria's second and third tiers also have a corrective effect.

A third option is for members elected at the higher level to be selected independently of members elected in basic districts. Poland has 391 members elected in 52 districts under the d'Hondt rule. There is also a national constituency where 69 seats are distributed on the basis of national party totals under the d'Hondt formula, bringing the total size of the legislature to 460.

Multiple tiers normally reduce distortions, provided there is no threshold that prevents smaller parties from getting national seats. If such thresholds exist, a higher tier can serve to give a bonus to larger parties.

Thresholds. This brings us to a fourth dimension of PR, namely, the existence in quite a few PR countries of legal thresholds of exclusion. Politicians are rarely willing to follow a principle up to its full logical conclusion. As previous paragraphs make clear, there are plenty of ways, even in PR systems, to grant a "bonus" to stronger parties at the expense of the weakest. Whereas the effect of other techniques for dampening proportionality, like the d'Hondt rule or low district magnitude, is subtle and difficult to gauge except for trained electoral engineers, a threshold flatly states that political parties that fail to secure a given percentage of the vote, either in districts or nationally, are deprived of parliamentary representation or at least of some of the seats they would otherwise be entitled to.

Thresholds are fairly common. Only nine countries having list systems of PR do not impose any (Figure 2.3). Eight have local thresholds; five have national thresholds; and Greece, Poland, and Sweden combine local and national thresholds. The law may require a fixed percentage of the national or district vote, or a certain number of votes or seats at the district level, to be entitled to seats at the national level. Higher thresholds may be imposed on coalitions. The best-known threshold is the German rule, which excludes from the Bundestag any party that fails to obtain 5 percent of the national vote or to elect three members in single-member districts. Turkey goes the farthest by demanding 10 percent of the national vote to secure a local seat, followed by Poland with a national threshold of 7 percent for national seats.[10] All other countries require 5 percent or less of national or regional vote.

Thresholds send a clear and frank message that marginal parties are not considered suitable players in the parliamentary arena. As there is no logical reason to opt for a threshold of 1 percent rather than 10 percent, such thresholds are more vulnerable to constitutional and political challenges. When many parties fail by a hairbreath to reach the threshold, the total number of voters unrepresented may be as high as 51 percent, as occurred in the Russian elections of 1995.

Selection of candidates. Plurality and majority systems result in the election of an *individual,* whereas in PR, *seats* are distributed. This highlights the fact

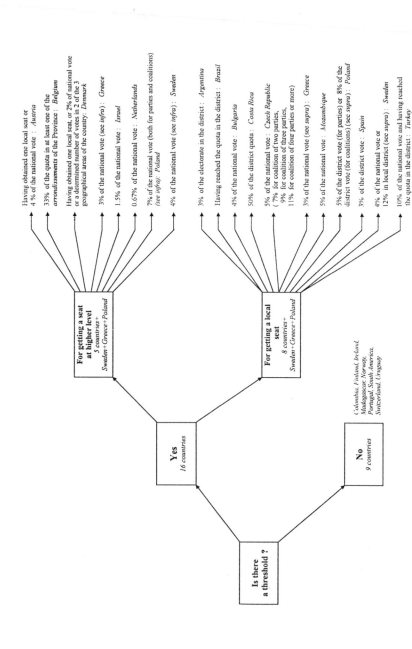

Figure 2.3. A Typology of Thresholds in Proportional Representation Systems

The following text appears as labels within the figure:

Is there a threshold ?

Yes *16 countries*

No *9 countries*

Colombia, Finland, Ireland, Madagascar, Norway, Portugal, South America, Switzerland, Uruguay

For getting a seat at higher level *5 countries+ Sweden+Greece+Poland*

Having obtained one local seat or 4 % of the national vote : *Austria*

33% of the quota in at least one of the *arrondissements* of the Province : *Belgium*

Having obtained one local seat, or 2% of national vote or a determined number of votes in 2 of the 3 geographical areas of the country: *Denmark*

3% of the national vote (see *infra*) : *Greece*

1.5% of the national vote : *Israel*

0.67% of the national vote : *Netherlands*

7% of the national vote (both for parties and coalitions) (see *infra*): *Poland*

4% of the national vote (see *infra*) : *Sweden*

For getting a local seat *8 countries+ Sweden+Greece+Poland*

3% of the electorate in the district : *Argentina*

Having reached the quota in the district : *Brazil*

4% of the national vote : *Bulgaria*

50% of the district quota : *Costa Rica*

5% of the national vote : *Czech Republic* (7% for coalition of two parties, 9% for coalition of three parties, 11% for coalition of four parties or more)

3% of the national vote (see *supra*) : *Greece*

5% of the national vote : *Mozambique*

5% of the district vote (for parties) or 8% of the district vote (for coalitions) (see *supra*) : *Poland*

3% of the district vote : *Spain*

4% of the national vote or 12% in local district (see *supra*) : *Sweden*

10% of the national voie and having reached the quota in the district : *Turkey*

63

that the chief preoccupation of proponents of PR is that each *party* gets a number of seats corresponding to the number of votes it polled. If election contests nowadays are basically fights between party organizations, PR certainly is the system that pushes this logic to its ultimate conclusion.

This can be seen by the prevalence in PR countries of the *closed list,* whereby voters are not allowed to express any preference for individual candidates and members are elected in the order specified on the party list. No less than 14 of our PR countries follow that method (Figure 2.2). In nine PR systems, voters may express a preference for one or more candidates within the party list they voted for. This can be done in various ways. Voters may vote for a party, and mark the name of one of its candidates (Belgium), or they may mark the name of a single candidate and have this vote counted as a party vote (Finland). *Panachage,* found in Switzerland, is the system that grants voters the highest degree of freedom, because they have as many votes as there are seats to be distributed in the district and may freely distribute those votes among candidates irrespective of the party they stand for.

The Single Transferable Vote

List systems of PR are frequently vilified for granting parties too much control over the selection of legislators. The single transferable vote (STV) is advocated as a form of PR that does away with party lists, thus giving voters more freedom. As in list systems, members are elected in multimember districts. However, candidates are grouped on a single ballot, to be rank ordered by voters as in the alternative vote. There is no obligation for voters to express preferences for the candidates of a single party, which makes it an instance of panachage.

Only first-preference votes are initially counted. A Droop quota is computed for the district. Candidates whose first-preference votes are equal to or greater than the quota are elected. Surplus votes cast for the winners (i.e., the number of votes in excess of the quota) are transferred to the other remaining candidates on the basis of second preferences. When all winners' surpluses have been transferred and seats remain unallotted, the weakest candidates are eliminated and their votes are similarly transferred to remaining candidates, until all seats are filled.

Although this system has been warmly advocated for over a century in Anglo-American circles (Lakeman 1974), Ireland is the single country covered in this book to use it for elections to the first chamber, and Australian senators are also elected by STV.

Mixed Systems

It is technically possible to mix together different electoral systems to devise a hybrid, or mixed system. The notion of a mixed system is not always defined very precisely in the literature. We define a mixed system as a system where different formulas (plurality and PR, majority and PR) are used simultaneously in a single election.[11]

Mixed systems were sometimes dismissed as eccentricities, transitional formulas, or instances of sheer manipulation doomed to disappear. It may be time to revise such generalizations, as 11 of our countries (including Germany, Japan, Italy, and Russia) have mixed systems.

There are at least three ways of mixing PR with either the plurality or majority rules. The simplest way (which we propose to call *coexistence*) is to apply PR in some parts of the national territory, and either plurality or majority everywhere else. In French Senate elections, a majority-plurality system is used in departments having four seats or less, whereas PR prevails in departments where five senators or more are to be elected.

A second type of mixed system involves having two sets of members for the same national territory. Following the 1994 electoral reform, Japan offers an example of this kind of mixed system, which we propose to call *combination*. Starting with the next election, 300 members of the House of Representatives will be elected in single-member constituencies under first past the post. The other 200 will be elected in 11 regional constituencies by PR. The Russian system is of the same broad type, except that PR members account for half of the total and are elected in a single national constituency. Taiwan combines 125 members elected by the single nontransferable vote in 27 constituencies, with 36 members elected nationally by PR.[12]

In the Japanese and Russian systems, PR seats are not distributed so as to correct party distortions created by the operation of the plurality rule in single-member districts. Each half of House membership is selected independently of the other. The German system is the best example of a third type of mixed system, where PR seats are distributed in a *corrective* way, so as to compensate weaker parties that did poorly in single-member seats and to produce a Parliament where each party gets its fair share of seats. Thus, the

Bundestag includes 328 members elected by plurality in single-member districts, plus 328 PR seats in a single national constituency. Electors cast two votes, first for a candidate in their single-member district, second for a party.

The allocation of seats requires first the distribution, on the basis of second or "party" votes cast by electors, of 656 seats by PR (LR-Hare method). The results of such computation are compared with the actual distribution of the 328 constituency seats among parties. The other 328 seats are then awarded so as to make the final distribution of 656 seats fully proportional. In 1993, New Zealanders opted for a formula close to the German one. The Italian system of 1994 reaches the same corrective goal through more complex procedures.[13] Mexico provides for PR seats so as to ensure the presence of some opposition members in its Chamber of Deputies, and the ruling party normally sweeps the vast majority of single-member districts. All these cases mix plurality with some form of PR.

Hungary's system *combines* 176 members elected by majority in single-member districts with 152 members elected by straight PR d'Hondt in 20 regional districts, but corrects somewhat the distortions that remain by providing for 58 national seats to be distributed by PR on the basis of votes cast for candidates defeated at the other two levels. Ecuador's 72-seat Parliament has two sets of members: 12 national members are elected by straight PR (LR-Double quota) in a single national district for a term of 4 years. In addition, there are 60 members elected in provincial districts for a shorter term: Plurality prevails in the five single-member districts, 8 members are elected in two-member districts by the plurality rule with some possible representation for minorities, and the remaining 47 are elected by PR in districts having three members or more. This complex system involves both coexistence and combination.

A country may use the same system for elections at all levels, but it may also resort to different formulas for different levels. France, for example, uses majority-runoff for presidential elections, majority-plurality in single-member districts for legislative and departmental elections, majority-plurality in multimember districts for senatorial elections in smaller departments and for municipal elections in smaller municipalities, and PR d'Hondt for European and regional elections as well as for senatorial elections in larger departments. Larger municipalities elect councillors, generally in a single constituency, through a unique procedure: Half the seats are allotted to the list that secures an absolute majority of the vote on the first ballot (or a simple plurality on the second), and the other half is distributed among all lists (including the leading) under PR d'Hondt.

Political Consequences
of Electoral Systems

We may distinguish two types of consequences: those that take place before the vote and those that occur after. Following Duverger (1951), we may call the former *psychological* and the latter *mechanical*. Mechanical effects are those that directly follow from electoral rules. Psychological effects pertain to how parties and voters react to these rules: They may change their behavior because of their expectations about the mechanical effects of electoral systems and about how other actors will react. Psychological effects affect the vote; mechanical effects affect the outcome of the election, given the vote (Blais and Carty 1991).[14]

Psychological Effect

Electoral rules can affect the behavior of parties and voters. Concerning parties, two questions may be raised. First, does the number of parties contesting an election depend on electoral rules?[15] Blais and Carty (1991) look at 509 elections in 20 countries over more than a century and compare the number of parties running in plurality, majority, and PR systems. The average number is five, seven, and eight parties, respectively.[16] Elites thus refrain from forming new parties in plurality systems because they know it is more difficult for small parties to win seats. On the other hand, there are almost as many parties running in majority as in PR elections. This underlines the fact that majority elections are quite different from plurality ones, a point to which we return below.

Party leaders respond to the incentives created by electoral rules. The response, however, is not automatic. This is clearly illustrated by Gunther's (1989) thorough analysis of the effect of the electoral law on party elites in Spain. Spain has a PR system, but it contains many correctives that make it strikingly unproportional. The system should serve as a deterrent to schisms and an inducement to mergers among parties. Yet little of this has happened, partly because party leaders miscalculate their likely level of support and partly because the maximization of parliamentary representation in the short run is less important than other political objectives. Gunther's analysis is a useful reminder that electoral rules only create incentives; they do not determine behavior. Over the long haul, however, these incentives do leave their imprint.

A second question is whether electoral rules affect party strategies. The question is examined by Katz (1980), who shows that PR and large district magnitude tend to make parties more ideologically oriented, whereas party cohesion tends to be weaker when voters are allowed to express preferences among candidates within the same party. In the latter case, as Katz explains, candidates must mount an independent campaign, and that weakens party attachments.

Turning to voters, the question that has attracted the most attention is the presence or absence of strategic or tactical voting in plurality systems.[17] Suppose there are three candidates in an election: A, B, and C. Consider voters who prefer C, then B, then A, and know C is not popular and has very little chance of winning. These voters have the choice of voting for their most-preferred candidate or of voting strategically for their second preferred, because that candidate has a better chance of defeating their least-liked candidate.

A number of studies have looked at how candidate viability affects the vote in plurality elections. Black (1978) and Cain (1978) have shown that the propensity to vote for a second choice is related to the closeness of the race (as indicated by the actual outcome of the election) in a district. Abramson et al. (1992) go a step further and show that the vote in American primaries reflects both preferences and perceptions of candidates' viability. Blais and Nadeau (1996) refine the analysis and apply a two-step procedure to the 1988 Canadian election. Around 20 percent of voters in that election were faced with the decision to vote sincerely or strategically, because they perceived their most-preferred party as less likely to win than their second-preferred one. Among these voters, around 30 percent did vote strategically for their second choice. The propensity to vote strategically increases as the intensity of preference for the first choice over the second decreases, as the perceived distance in the race between the first and second choices increases, and as the race between the second and third choices gets closer. Altogether, relatively few voters (around 6 percent) cast a strategic vote, but this is mainly because most of them do not face a strategic choice.

This raises the question as to whether strategic considerations play a role in PR or majority elections. We would expect thresholds in PR systems to induce some degree of strategic voting. If a voter's most-preferred party is expected to have fewer votes than the required threshold, he or she has to choose between voting for that party even though it has little or no chance of being represented in Parliament and supporting another party that is likely to meet that threshold. The only piece of evidence we have on this is provided by Gunther (1989), who shows that sympathizers of small parties are less likely to vote for those parties in smaller districts, with high effective thresholds.[18] An even more intriguing question, which has not been examined in the literature, is whether voters in PR systems hesitate to vote for parties that are perceived to have no chance of being part of the government.[19]

In two-ballot majority elections, the issue is whether voters express their pure preferences on the first ballot, knowing that they will be able to have another say in the second ballot. There is little doubt that the vote on the first ballot does not merely reflect preferences; strategic considerations play a role. In the French legislative election of 1978, for instance, a substantial number of RPR supporters voted UDF in those constituencies where the UDF had won in the previous election and was thus more likely to defeat the left (Capdevielle, Dupoirier, and Ysmal 1988, 29).[20] We should also note an intriguing pattern established by Parodi (1978): The electoral coalition that gets the more votes on the first ballot tends to lose votes on the second. The exact reason why this occurs has not been elucidated.[21] It is an interesting case of voters reacting to the collective signal given on the first ballot.

The Mechanical Effect

The electoral law determines how votes are to be translated into seats. The most direct issue regarding the mechanical effect of electoral systems thus pertains to the relationship between the proportion of votes a party gets and the proportion of seats it wins in the legislature. Two subsidiary questions concern the outcome of the election: the number of parties that get represented in the legislature and the presence or absence of a parliamentary majority.

Votes and Seats

Rae's (1967) seminal book is the starting point.[22] Rae regressed seat shares against vote shares under PR and under plurality-majority formulae. He finds the regression coefficient to be 1.07 for PR and 1.20 for plurality-majority. All systems give an advantage to stronger parties but that bias is much less pronounced in PR systems. The average bonus to the strongest party is 8 percentage points in plurality-majority systems, and only 1 point under PR.

Unfortunately, that specific line of inquiry has not been pursued in a cross-national perspective. Some studies have looked at specific countries and refined the analysis by incorporating other factors such as the concentration of the vote (Sankoff and Mellos 1972, 1973) and the relative performance of parties in constituencies of different sizes (Spafford 1970), but we do not have updated and revised estimates of the basic seat-vote relationship in various types of electoral systems.

Taagepera (1986) proposes a radically new perspective to the issue. His starting point is the cube law of plurality elections, formulated at the beginning of the century, according to which the ratio of seats won by two parties equals the cube of the ratio of their votes. Taagepera shows that the most appropriate exponential is not necessarily three but rather the logarithm of the total number of votes divided by the logarithm of the total number of seats. He extends the model to PR elections, in which case the exponential depends on district magnitude as well as on total numbers of votes and seats.

Taagepera's work constitutes a major improvement. It is elegant and has the great advantage of proposing a model that can be applied to all electoral systems. For plurality elections, Taagepera is very persuasive in showing that his model outperforms the cube law. It is not clear, however, that it does a better job than the models proposed by Spafford or Sankoff and Mellos. We still lack a systematic comparative evaluation of these various approaches.

With respect to PR elections, Taagepera and Shugart (1989, chap. 11) stress the decisive effect of district magnitude. Rae (1967) had already shown that district magnitude strongly affects the degree of proportionality of PR. He did not, however, take into account the presence of supradistrict adjustment seats or legal thresholds. Taagepera and Shugart devise a complex procedure for computing a measure of effective magnitude that incorporates all of these elements.

The Number of Parties in Parliament

Duverger (1951) claimed that the plurality rule favors a two-party system, and the majority rule (with second ballot) and PR are conducive to multipartyism. He also argued that only the relationship between plurality rule and a two-party system approached a true sociological law. Riker (1986) concludes that Duverger was basically right. There is an association, but only a probabilistic one, between PR and multipartyism. In Riker's view, the relationship between plurality and a two-party system is much stronger. He points out only two exceptions, India and Canada, and proposes a revised law accounting for these two exceptions. This is not very compelling, however, because the number of cases supporting the law is very small[23] and because Britain can hardly be characterized as a two-party system, at least as far as the distribution of votes is concerned.

This raises the question of how to count parties. One simple method is to count the number of parties represented in the legislature. Unfortunately, no study has compared electoral systems on that criterion. Attention has focused on measuring the "effective" number of parties, which weights parties according to their electoral strength.

The most popular measure is the one proposed by Laakso and Taagepera (1979), where N equals 1 divided by the sum of squared vote shares. Molinar (1991) proposes an index giving special weight to the largest party. As Lijphart (1994b, 69) shows, both measures have their merits and limits, and they yield similar results in most instances.

Lijphart (1994b) compares the effective number of parliamentary parties in various systems (see this volume, Table 1.4). The average is 2.0 in plurality, 2.8 in majority, and 3.6 in PR systems. Within PR systems, the only important factor is the effective threshold. Within the sample examined by Lijphart, the effective threshold varies from 1 to 13 percent; the number of effective parties is reduced by 1 when the threshold is over 8 percent.

Finally, Ordeshook and Shvetsova (1994) look at how electoral systems mediate the effect of ethnic heterogeneity on the number of parties. Ordeshook and Shvetsova use both a simple count of parties and the "effective" number of parties as their dependent variable and report that the former is "not only the more behaviorally meaningful . . . but also the more predictable measure" (1994, 121). They find that the relationship between number of parties and ethnic heterogeneity increases with district magnitude; however, "the superiority of the interactive model appears to derive solely from the fact that single-member district states not only have fewer parties on average but also are more heterogeneous than their PR counterparts" (1994, 119).

Is There a Parliamentary Majority?

The ultimate objective of an election is to determine who will govern. A crucial question in parliamentary systems is whether the election allows the formation of a one-party majority government. Clearly, parliamentary majorities are infrequent in PR systems. Blais and Carty (1987), in their study of 510 elections in 20 countries, report that 10 percent of PR elections produced such a majority. Lijphart (1994b), who examines elections in 27 countries between 1945 and 1990, finds a majority in 20 percent of the cases. He also shows that the probability of a one-party majority government in a PR system hinges very much on the effective threshold. It is about nil when that threshold is very small but reaches 30 percent when the effective threshold is 10 percent, as in Spain.

Parliamentary majorities, either natural or manufactured,[24] are much more frequent in plurality elections. Blais and Carty (1987) indicate that 69 percent of plurality elections in their sample produced one-party majority governments. Lijphart reports a much higher proportion—93 percent—partly because he includes India, which had many two-member districts in the 1950s.

What about majority elections? Lijphart (1994b) examines France and Australia; he finds a parliamentary majority in half of the cases. The same proportion is reported by Blais and Carty (1987), who consider many more cases. The latter study includes, however, multimember majority systems; the proportion drops to 27 percent when these are excluded. On this criterion, the single-member majority system is closer to PR than to plurality.

In plurality systems, one-party majorities are normally won by parties that secure a plurality or a majority of the votes. It is possible, however, for a party that comes second in terms of votes to obtain a majority of the seats. This was the case, for example, in two successive elections (1978 and 1981) in New Zealand. This may occur for two reasons. Either votes for the winning party are concentrated in less-populated districts, or votes for the losing party are too highly concentrated (and wasted) in some districts (Massicotte and Bernard 1985; Taylor and Johnston 1979).

The Debate Over Electoral Systems

Which is the best electoral system? Analysts and practitioners have debated the issue for more than a century. The debate has touched on every dimension of electoral systems—the ballot, the constituency, and the formula. As we have seen in the first section, there is a wide range of options available, especially if we take account of the possibility of combining these options in various ways.

The debate has focused mainly on the choice of an electoral formula, and it is thus logical to start with that dimension. We then turn to the debate over the constituency and the ballot. Our review is confined to the most important arguments advanced to support or oppose a given option.[25]

As we show, a good case can be made for almost any electoral system. This is so because there are alternative visions of democracy, and because electoral systems are meant to accomplish not one but many objectives, which entail trade-offs.[26] That the debate remains unsettled may account for the recent popularity of mixed systems.

The Formula

The dominant debate in the literature has been between plurality and PR systems. The basic argument in favor of the plurality rule is that it produces one-party majority government, whereas PR is advocated because it produces broad and fair representation.

Why is one-party majority government such a good thing, according to proponents of the plurality rule? For two main reasons. The first is stability. One-party majority governments are believed to be more stable, and government stability is perceived to enhance political stability. There is little doubt that one-party majority governments are more stable than coalition governments typically found in PR systems. At the same time, it must be acknowledged that most coalition governments in PR systems are reasonably stable (Laver and Schofield 1990, chap. 6). The most difficult question concerns the relationship between government and political stability. The jury is still out on this question. Powell (1982) finds no relationship, whereas Blais and Dion (1990) note that among nonindustrialized countries, democracy breaks down more often in PR systems with low government stability. More research is needed on this important topic to sort out the specific effect of electoral systems versus other factors such as presidentialism (Stefan and Skach 1993).

The second virtue that is claimed for one-party majority government is accountability. Accountability stems from decisiveness. An election is decisive when it has a direct and immediate effect on the formation of government (Powell 1989, 1993; Strøm 1990, 72-4). It is easier for voters in a plurality system to get rid of a government they do not like; they just throw the rascals out and replace them with a new government. In a PR system, the fate of a government is decided only partly and indirectly by voters. A party may lose support but still remain as a member of a coalition government, because the composition of government depends on deals among the parties.[27] One-party majority governments are more accountable than their coalition counterparts.

For advocates of PR, the two key words are fairness and responsiveness. Almost by definition, PR is fair because it is intended to give each party a share of seats more or less equal to its share of votes. That principle is, of course, qualified by the use of small districts and/or legal thresholds. Moreover, the distribution of seats in the legislature may be fair, but the distribution of cabinet seats in government is surely much less fair.[28] Nevertheless, it cannot be disputed that PR leads to fairer representation than the plurality rule.

PR also allows for a greater diversity of viewpoints to be expressed in the legislature and in government, because more parties are represented in both. Parties in plurality systems must, of course, be sensitive to different perspectives if they want to attract enough votes to win, but the mere fact that more parties get to argue their positions in a PR system should make governments more aware and concerned about the diversity of opinions.

PR is especially advocated for societies with deep ethnic or linguistic cleavages. The argument is that in such societies it is imperative that minority groups be fairly represented within political parties, in Parliament, and in Cabinet and that only under PR can that goal be achieved (see Cairns 1968; Lijphart 1977; Sisk 1994). Critics reply that PR can induce the formation of narrow ethnic parties that appeal to ethnic cleavages to maximize support (Tsebelis 1990).

The choice between plurality and PR is thus mostly about what is deemed to be more important: accountability and (perhaps) stability, on the one hand, fairness and responsiveness, on the other.

There is a third option—majority rule. The arguments in favor of majority rule have not been as systematically articulated.[29] There are, we believe, two basic reasons for advocating it. First, the majority principle is at the very heart of democracy (Spitz 1984). In a direct democracy, the majority wins, and in a representative democracy, most decisions are made by legislators through the majority rule. It would thus seem natural to apply the same logic to the selection of representatives.

The second argument in favor of majority rule is that it offers a reasonable degree of both responsiveness and accountability. It allows the presence of many parties, fewer than does PR but more than the plurality rule. It often leads to the formation of coalition governments, but the process of coalition building tends to be more open than under PR. Coalitions are more likely to be formed before the election, or at least before the second ballot, and to last well after the election, because of the electoral cost involved in abandoning government partners. Compared with the situation under PR, voters have a more direct say in which coalition will form the government, and parties and governments are more accountable, although less than under the plurality rule. The majority rule should thus appeal to those who wish to obtain a mixture of responsiveness and accountability. The majority rule is, however, much less satisfactory with respect to fairness. In fact, it is in majority systems that disproportionality between seat shares and vote shares can be the greatest.[30]

The Constituency

The main debate here is about the virtues and vices of single- and multi-member districts. That debate overlaps, to some extent, the one over plurality and PR systems, because the latter entail multimember districts and the former (as well as majority systems) usually resort to single-member districts.

Supporters of single-member districts claim that the single-member type gives voters a closer relationship with their representatives and maximize accountability, because district representatives can be held responsible for defending constituency interests. That responsibility is diluted among many representatives in multimember districts.

Single-member districts have at least one important drawback. They have to be modified on a regular basis to maintain populations of relatively equal size. This may make for artificial units of no particular relevance to citizens and raises all the problems involved in designing and redesigning districts (Baker 1986; Balinski and Young 1982). Multimember districts need not be of the same size. They can be made to correspond to sociological or administrative boundaries and are thus more congruent for voters (Niemi, Powell, and Bicknell 1986). Their boundaries can remain intact even if their population increases or decreases because it is possible to change the number of members to be elected in the district.

The alleged advantage of multimember districts is that they ensure a better representation of various groups, especially minority ones. There is much evidence, in particular, that women tend to be better represented in multimember districts, because parties strive for an overall balance (Welch and Studlar 1990; Rule 1992, 1994; Rule and Norris 1992; see also chap. 7 in this volume). The consequences of multimember districts are less certain, however, for groups that are territorially concentrated. In the United States, in particular, blacks and Hispanics do better under single-member districts (Rule 1992; Welch and Herrick 1992; Davidson and Grofman 1994), especially because the Voting Rights Act encourages the creation of districts where racial minorities predominate.

The choice between single- and multimember districts is thus one of competing values, mainly the advantage of having accountable individual representatives versus the benefit of having a more representative and responsive legislature.

The Ballot

How voters are allowed to express their preferences depends to a great extent on the kind of electoral formula that is used. Consequently, the debate over voting procedures takes different forms in plurality, majority, and PR systems. Before reviewing these debates, one general observation should be made. Everything else being equal, it seems likely that the more information the ballot reveals about voters' preferences, the more accurate the representation of preferences is likely to be. Thus, a system that allows voters to express degrees of preferences is preferable to one that does not. At the same time, however, such a system may be less simple for voters, and there may be a trade-off between simplicity and the amount of information that voters are asked to provide.

The Ballot in Plurality Systems:
One or Many Votes?

In single-member plurality systems,[31] voters are typically asked to indicate which candidate they prefer. There are other possibilities. Voters can be asked to rank order the candidates or to vote for as many candidates for which they approve. The latter approach, approval voting, has been advocated by Brams and Fishburn (1982).

There are two major reasons for supporting approval voting. First, it provides voters greater flexibility in expressing their preferences; voters are not forced to choose only one candidate. It thus yields a more accurate measure of preferences, without undue complexity. Second, it ensures the candidate with greatest overall support is elected. It makes it impossible, in particular, for an extremist to squeeze in as the winner when there are two moderate candidates, something that can occur in a standard plurality election (Brams and Fishburn 1988, 277-8).

The main objection to approval voting is that it may increase the number of parties and reduce the probability of a one-party majority government. The reason is that when voters have to vote for one candidate in a plurality election, they are induced to vote strategically for parties that have a chance of winning and not to support parties that appear to be weak. Although strategic voting may well occur under approval voting (Niemi 1984), the incentive for voters not to support weak candidates is not as strong: They may vote for both their preferred weak candidate and their second choice. As a consequence, more parties are likely to get votes and seats, and one-party majority government is likely to be less frequent.

For those who are firm believers in the virtues of one-party majority government, then, approval voting is not likely to be very popular. When such considerations are not crucial, for the election of a president, for instance, it has greater appeal. Approval voting can also be used for majority and PR elections, where it does not have the same disadvantage (one-party majority governments are unlikely anyway).

Majority Rule: The Alternative
Vote Versus Multiple Ballots

Under majority rule, a candidate must obtain more than 50 percent of the votes to win. It is possible that no candidate meets that condition and that no one is elected. As noted in the first section, there are two ways to proceed when this occurs. The first is to resort to multiple ballots. The second approach is to have voters rank order the candidates (the alternative vote).

The case for the alternative vote is that it provides richer information about voters' preferences; it conveys information about how they react to each candidate.[32] The procedure is somewhat more complex for voters but it is less costly because they vote only once. The case for two ballots is that it allows voters to reconsider their choice and to compare more systematically the two or three "serious" candidates that remain on the second ballot. Citizens are also faced with a simpler task, simply to choose one candidate on each ballot.

PR Systems: Can Voters Express
Their Preferences Among Candidates?

The basic principle of PR is that seats should be distributed among parties according to their vote shares. This assumes that people vote for parties or lists of candidates. The problem with closed-list PR is that voters are not allowed to express preferences among individual candidates. Critics claim that this is an important shortcoming. Proponents reply that it is preferences among parties that really matter. The bottom line here is the importance to be attached to the representation of opinions about candidates versus those about parties. It is possible, however, to allow voters to express their opinions about candidates in a PR system, through either panachage or preferential voting in a list system or the single transferable vote.

The single transferable vote allows voters to rank order candidates and thus grants them maximum freedom to express their preferences. It is a more complex procedure, but it provides richer information about voters' preferences. It has two drawbacks. First, it can be applied only if there are relatively few members to be elected in each district. Otherwise, there would be too many candidates to be rank ordered by voters. But small districts entail a lower degree of proportionality in party representation. Second, it induces candidates of the same parties to compete against each other, hindering party cohesion (Katz 1980). The single transferable vote is thus an appealing option only for those who are willing to accept only a modest degree of proportionality and relatively uncohesive parties.

The other approach is to keep the list system but to allow voters to indicate their opinions about candidates through panachage or preferential voting. This is a simpler procedure, and it can be used in large districts, thus ensuring a high degree of proportionality in party representation. However, panachage and preferential voting have the same detrimental effects on party unity. They entail the coexistence of two simultaneous contests, one among parties and one among candidates within the same party.

The debate over electoral systems highlights the role of competing values and trade-offs in deciding which rules best serve democracy. At least two basic questions need to be addressed. First, which preferences should be represented? The issue is the relative importance to be attached to preferences about parties and candidates. The case for list PR, in particular, rests very much on the assumption that top priority should be given to parties. The greater the importance given to individual candidates, the less appealing list PR becomes. Second, which is the best way to ensure that the elected follow public opinion? One approach is to focus on the make-up of legislatures and of governments. The assumption is that representatives are more likely to be in accordance with public opinion if they resemble those they represent. This is the fundamental belief underlying support for PR. A second view is to focus on legislators' and governments' incentives. The assumption is that representatives will follow public opinion if they think they will not be reelected if they do not and that we should devise a system that makes it easy to get rid of a government that does not do a good job. This is the reasoning of advocates of the plurality rule.

Notes

1. Data for this chapter are drawn from Blais and Massicotte (1996, Forthcoming). The main sources were Inter-Parliamentary Union (1993), updated by the annual *Chronicle of Parliamentary Elections and Developments,* published by the Inter-Parliamentary Union; *Keesing's Record of World Events*; and Blaustein and Flanz (n.d.). We also relied on the electoral laws of many countries as well as on many other sources, all of which are listed in Blais and Massicotte (1996, Forthcoming).

2. Some analysts (see, especially, Jones 1995; Cox 1995) characterize the Chilean system as PR d'Hondt. It is true that the system works exactly as PR d'Hondt would. It is also true, however, that the law does not refer to PR nor to d'Hondt nor to highest averages. Furthermore, the rule that applies in the great majority of instances is simple plurality: The two leading parties each get one seat. It seems to us that a system in which only one or two parties can get elected can hardly be described as PR.

3. The threshold for standing at the second ballot in French legislative elections is now 12.5 percent of the electorate.

4. The examples are German presidential elections under the Weimar Republic and French legislative elections in the 1930s (Lakeman 1974).

5. Those figures are from the 1996 election. See *El Pais* (Madrid), March 5, 1996.

6. There is a fourth highest-averages method, known as the Imperiali rule. In Belgian municipal elections (the only occasion where this method is used), the divisors are 1, 1.5, 2, 2.5, and so on. This rule works strongly in favor of larger parties (Van den Bergh 1955).

7. Largest-remainders and highest-averages methods are normally considered mutually exclusive. However, in South Africa, the first five seats unallotted after division are distributed to the parties with the largest remainders, whereas the d'Hondt highest-averages method is used for the remaining seats.

8. Strictly speaking, this should be called a *Hagenbach-Bischoff quota* rather than a Droop quota, as the latter is a Hagenbach-Bischoff quota increased by one. The difference is so minute that Lijphart (1992) has proposed to select the shortest name to refer to these two quotas. A few Latin American countries resort to a so-called double quota system, whereby the first quota serves

as a threshold, and the second is used for allocating seats among the parties that crossed the threshold. We classify those systems on the basis of the second quota.

9. We leave aside the Imperiali quota, where the total number of votes is divided by the number of seats *plus two.* This method was used in a single country (Italy) and was dropped in 1993.

10. In Turkey, in districts returning at least five members, the party getting the most votes is awarded a bonus seat, with the rest of the seats awarded under d'Hondt. The system not only disadvantages weak parties but also advantages the strongest of all.

11. Geographical conditions may necessitate, in a country where PR is the rule, the election of a handful of members in single-member constituencies. This occurs in Switzerland and Finland. In our view, such cases should not be considered as instances of mixed systems, a label that should be used only when the proportion of members elected under a different system is more than 5 percent of the total.

12. South Korea is sometimes erroneously considered a mixed system because it combines members elected by plurality in single-member districts with members elected at the national level. However, the latter are elected in proportion to the total of *seats* won by each party in local districts, not on the basis of votes. We consider that both sets of members are elected by plurality.

13. Three-quarters (475) of members of the Chamber of Deputies are elected by plurality in single-member districts, and the other 155 are elected by straight PR in a single national constituency and subsequently reallocated between 26 regional constituencies. However, PR seats are allocated to parties not on the basis of their total vote, but on the basis of "amended" party totals that include only votes cast for candidates defeated in single-member districts and for winning candidates in excess of what they needed to win—that is, a plurality of one over their strongest opponent. In other words, only votes wasted at the local level are considered for PR purposes, with the result that parties that do poorly in single-member districts are likely to get some correction under PR.

14. We focus, as does the literature, on legislative elections held in parliamentary systems. There have been few studies of the effect of electoral rules on presidential elections (see, however, Shugart and Carey 1992, and Shugart 1995). Little attention has been given to potential interaction effects between electoral systems and other institutional variables. It is quite possible, for instance, that the consequences of electoral rules are quite different in parliamentary and presidential systems.

15. Grumm (1958) has argued that the causal direction was reversed, that multipartyism caused PR. Riker (1986, 27) shows that the evidence refutes that hypothesis.

16. The numbers refer to single-member districts in the case of plurality and majority systems.

17. We leave aside the question of whether proportional representation fosters voter turnout, which is examined in chapter 8 in this volume.

18. The *legal* threshold is the minimum number of votes a party, at the national or district level, that is required by the law for a party to be entitled to seats.

19. The 1994 German election is quite interesting in that respect. As the FDP seemed not certain to get the 5 percent of the votes it needed to get represented in the Bundestag, a number of CDU-CSU supporters appear to have decided to vote for the FDP to help it reach the threshold. This is a rare instance of a party benefiting from its apparent weakness. But the reason CDU-CSU supporters voted strategically for the FDP is that the CDU-CSU needed the FDP to form a government. We may suppose that if the CDU-CSU could have formed a single-party majority government, such strategic voting would not have taken place. In this case, German voters voted at least partly on the basis of their perceptions of which parties were most likely to form the

government. In a PR election, then, voters may form expectations about which coalitions are likely to be formed after the election, may have preferences about these coalitions as such rather than about the various parties, and may vote partly on the basis of these expectations and preferences. Unfortunately, we know very little about these strategic calculations.

20. We should note that strategic voting is inferred here from the nonconcordance of party identification and vote. This inflates the amount of strategic voting because voters may vote for a party that is not the one they feel attached to because of the issues of the campaign, party leaders, or local candidates. The fact that the number of parties does not tend to diminish over time in France suggests that strategic voting on the first ballot is limited.

21. A similar pattern seems to take place in plurality elections. In Canada, at least, the front-runner at the beginning of a campaign tends to lose votes during the campaign (Johnston et al. 1992, 21).

22. Many authors dealt with this issue before Rae. Rae was the first to examine it in a systematic fashion.

23. Furthermore, one of the few cases supporting the law, the United States, has other institutional features, presidentialism and primaries, that could account for the presence of a two-party system.

24. A natural majority occurs when a party gets a majority of both votes and seats. A manufactured majority is one where a party obtains a majority of seats without having a majority of votes.

25. For a more elaborate review, see Blais (1991) and Dunleavy and Margetts (1995).

26. For a cogent exposition of the trade-offs, see Dunleavy and Margetts (1995).

27. As a Belgian party leader once put it, "Voters redistribute cards among players [parties], but it is the latter who play cards."

28. This problem is sometimes solved by a requirement that the executive mirrors party strength in the legislature (Austrian *Länder*) or by a decision to build government coalitions, including more parties than is mathematically necessary to command a majority in the legislature (Switzerland).

29. See, however, Fisichella (1984) and Blais (1993).

30. It is in France, for instance, that the index of proportionality tends to be the lowest (Rose 1984b, 75). This occurs, however, because only first-ballot votes are taken into account.

31. We confine ourselves here to single-member plurality systems and do not consider the single nontransferable or limited vote. Lijphart, Pintor, and Sone (1986) show that in their consequences these systems lie somewhere between single-member plurality and proportional representation.

32. This could also be obtained under multiple ballots through the use of approval voting.

their limits and possibilities when applied within comparative analysis. It then goes on in the second section to underline the importance of understanding the structure of competition in any given party system, because in many ways the whole notion of a party system is centered on the assumption that there exists a stable structure of competition. Structures of competition can be seen to be either closed (and predictable) or open (and unpredictable), depending on the patterns of alternation in government, the degree of innovation or persistence in processes of government formation, and the range of parties gaining access to government. The emphasis in the third section is on the need to distinguish between processes of electoral change, on the one hand, and changes in party systems and the structures of competition, on the other, a distinction that also allows us to conceive of situations in which electoral change is the consequence rather than the cause of party system change.

The most conventional and frequently adopted criterion for classifying party systems is also the most simple: the number of parties in competition. Moreover, the conventional distinction involved here has also proved appealingly straightforward: that between a two-party system, on the one hand, and a multiparty (i.e., more than two) system, on the other (see Duverger 1954). Nor was this just a casual categorization; on the contrary, it was believed to tap into a more fundamental distinction between more or less stable and consensual democracies, which were those normally associated with the two-party type, as opposed to more or less unstable and conflictual democracies, which were those associated with the multiparty type. Thus, two-party systems, which were typically characteristic of the United Kingdom and the United States and invariably involved single-party government, were assumed to enhance accountability, alternation in government, and moderate, center-seeking competition. Multiparty systems, on the other hand, which usually required coalition administrations and were typically characteristic of countries such as France or Italy, prevented voters from gaining a direct voice in the formation of governments, did not necessarily facilitate alternation in government, and sometimes favored extremist, ideological confrontations between narrowly based political parties. And although this simple association of party system types and political stability and efficacy was later challenged by research into the experiences of some of the smaller European democracies, which boasted both a multiplicity of parties and a strong commitment to consensual government (e.g., Daalder 1983) and thus led some early observers to attempt to elaborate a distinction between "working" multiparty systems (e.g., the Netherlands or Sweden) and "nonworking" or "immobilist" multiparty systems (e.g., Italy), the core categorization of two-party versus multiparty has nevertheless continued to command a great deal of support within the literature on comparative politics.[2]

This simple distinction is, of course, far from being the only possible approach, and since Duverger a number of attempts have been made to develop more sensitive and discriminating criteria (see Table 3.1).[3] In the conclusion to his classic *Oppositions* volume, for example, Robert Dahl (1966) sought to move away from an almost exclusive concern with simply the numbers of parties and built an alternative classification based around the competitive strategy adopted by the opposing parties, distinguishing between competitive, cooperative, and coalescent strategies, and distinguishing further between opposition in the electoral arena and opposition in the parliamentary arena (see also Laver 1989). This led Dahl to elaborate a fourfold typology, distinguishing between strictly competitive systems, cooperative-competitive systems, coalescent-competitive systems, and strictly coalescent systems. Shortly after this, in what proved subsequently a very influential study, Jean Blondel (1968) developed a typology that took account not only of the numbers of parties in competition but also their relative size (and, in a later refinement, their "place on the ideological spectrum"), distinguishing four types: two-party systems, two-and-a-half-party systems, multiparty systems with a dominant party, and multiparty systems without a dominant party. In practice, however, this new approach did little more than improve the traditional two-party versus multiparty distinction by disaggregating the otherwise overloaded multiparty category. Stein Rokkan's (1968) contemporaneous attempt to classify the party systems of the smaller European democracies also did little more than disaggregate the multiparty category, in this case by taking account of the likelihood of single-party majorities (akin to Blondel's dominant party) and the degree to which there was a fragmentation of minority party strengths. Using these criteria, Rokkan developed a threefold distinction involving a "British-German" type system, in which the system was dominated by the competition between two major parties, with a third, minor party also in contention; a "Scandinavian" type system in which one big party regularly confronted a more or less formalized alliance between three or four smaller parties; and an "even" multiparty system in which competition was dominated by three or more parties of equivalent size.

With the notable exception of Dahl, therefore, these early classifications have all remained closely tied to an emphasis on the numbers of parties, albeit sometimes supplemented by attention to the relative electoral weights of

TABLE 3.1 Types of Party Systems

Author	Principal Criteria for Classification	Principal Types of Party System Identified
Duverger (1954)	Numbers of parties	Two-party systems
		Multiparty systems
Dahl (1966)	Competitiveness of opposition	Strictly competitive
		Cooperative-competitive
		Coalescent-competitive
		Strictly coalescent
Blondel (1968)	Numbers of parties	Two-party system
	Relative size of parties	Two-and-a-half-party systems
		Multiparty systems with one dominant party
		Multiparty systems without dominant party
Rokkan (1968)	Numbers of parties	The British-German
	Likelihood of single-party majorities	"1 vs. 1 + 1" system
	Distribution of minority party strengths	The Scandinavian "1 vs. 3-4" system
		Even multiparty systems: "1 vs. 1 vs. 1 + 2-3"
Sartori (1976)	Numbers of parties	Two-party systems
	Ideological distance	Moderate pluralism
		Polarized pluralism
		Predominant-party systems

parties involved. In this sense, they can also be related to the importance attached to party numbers—or to the "format" of the party system—in the more comprehensive typology that was later developed by Sartori (1976, 117-323).[4] Although Sartori's approach emphasized the relevance of party numbers, it also went far beyond this by including a second principal criterion that had previously been largely disregarded, that is, the ideological distance separating the parties in the system. Sartori's typology, which was explicitly concerned with the interactions between the parties in any given system— what Sartori refers to as the "mechanics" of the system—and was therefore explicitly concerned with differential patterns of competition, drew on the combination of these two criteria. Party systems could therefore be classified according to the number of parties in the system, in which there was a distinction between formats with two parties, those with up to some five parties (limited pluralism) and those with some six parties or more (extreme pluralism); and according to the ideological distance separating the extreme parties in the system, which would either be small ("moderate") or large ("polarized"). The two criteria were not wholly independent, however, in that Sartori also argued that the format of the system, that is, the number of parties, contained mechanical predispositions (i.e., it could affect the degree of polarization), such that extreme pluralism could lead to polarization. The combination of both criteria then yielded three principal types of party system— *two-party systems,* characterized by an evidently limited format and a small ideological distance (e.g., the United Kingdom); *moderate pluralism,* characterized by limited pluralism and a relatively small ideological distance (e.g., Denmark); and, which was the most important for the typology, *polarized pluralism,* characterized by extreme pluralism and a large ideological distance (e.g., Italy in the 1960s and 1970s, and Chile prior to the 1973 coup). In addition, Sartori also allowed for the existence of a "predominant-party system," a system in which one particular party, such as, most notably, Congress in India or the Liberal Democrats in Japan, consistently (i.e., over at least four legislatures) won a majority of parliamentary seats. Although this is a useful category, it nevertheless fits rather uneasily into Sartori's framework, because it is defined by wholly different, ad hoc, criteria, such that a predominant-party system can by definition coexist with every possible category of party numbers (i.e., it can develop within a context of a formerly two-party system, a system of limited pluralism, and a system of extreme pluralism) and, at least theoretically, with every possible spread of the ideological distance.

There are a number of reasons why Sartori's typology can be regarded as the most important of those briefly reviewed here. In the first place, it is the most comprehensive of all the available typologies, in terms of the care with which it is developed, as well as in terms of the way in which it is applied to empirical cases. Second, notwithstanding the continued appeal of the simple two-party/multiparty distinction, it has subsequently been employed in a variety of sophisticated national and cross-national studies, yielding a degree of insight into the functioning of party systems that is simply incomparably better than that developed by any of the alternative typologies (e.g., Bartolini 1984; Bille 1990). Third, as noted, it is explicitly concerned with patterns of competition and with the interactions between parties, and in this sense it is much more directly concerned with the functioning of the party *system* itself.

Finally, it underlines the influence exerted by systemic properties, and by the party system, on electoral behavior and electoral outcomes. Unlike any of the other typologies, it therefore allows the party system to operate as an independent variable, constraining or even directing electoral preferences. This last aspect is particularly important in this context, and I will return to it at a later stage.

At the same time, however, and almost 20 years after the publication of Sartori's seminal volume, questions can be raised regarding the continued utility and discriminating capacity of the typology, not least because of what is now a potential overcrowding in the "moderate pluralism" category and a virtual emptying of the alternative types. For example, and this criticism can also be leveled against the traditional Duverger classification, it is now relatively difficult to find an unequivocal example of a real two-party system. The United States, which is often cited as a classic two-party model, might better be described as a "four-party" system, in which a presidential two-party system coexists with a separate congressional two-party system, or even as having 50 two-party systems, each functioning separately in each of the 50 states (e.g., Katz and Kolodny 1994). New Zealand, which also offered a classic example of two-partyism, is currently experiencing a strong pressure toward fragmentation, which is likely to be even further accentuated by the recent adoption of a proportional electoral formula. The United Kingdom, which was also always seen as the paramount case of a two-party system, currently, albeit perhaps temporarily, fulfills Sartori's conditions for a predominant-party system. Against this, of course, it might be argued that a number of the Latin American systems, and particularly Costa Rica and Venezuela, are now moving more closely toward a two-party model, which could restore the relevance of the category as a whole.

At the other extreme, and particularly given the recent decline and/or eclipse of traditional Communist parties, it has also become difficult to find an unambiguous example of polarized pluralism. Sartori's criteria for this latter system had been very carefully elaborated (1976, 131-73), but depended crucially on there being a "maximum spread of [ideological] opinion" (1976, 135), *bilateral* oppositions (1976, 134), and hence, necessarily so, on there being a relevant antisystem party, a party that "undermines the legitimacy of the regime it opposes" (1976, 133), at *each* end of the political spectrum. It follows from this that should either of these antisystem alternatives become irrelevant or disappear, there would then occur an inevitable attenuation of the spread of opinion and thus a reduction in the degree of polarization, so forcing the case out of the category. This is now certainly the case in France, for example, where the fading antisystem party of the left, the PCF, was sufficiently legitimated to be admitted to government office in 1981, and in Italy, where the PCI divided into the unequivocally moderate PDS and the smaller, more radical but certainly no longer antisystem alternative of the RC. In addition, with the advent of the AD-MSI to office in the Berlusconi government of 1994, Italy can also be seen to have shed its antisystem alternative of the right. This is not to suggest that antisystem oppositions have everywhere ceased to exist; on the contrary, despite the eclipse of the traditional antisystem parties of the Communist and Fascist variety, a number of European party systems are now confronted with the rise of new parties, particularly on the right, which might well be seen as antisystem in orientation, such as the National Front in France, the Flemish Block in Belgium, and possibly also the now-transformed Liberal party in Austria (Betz 1994; Ignazi 1992, 1994; Mudde 1995). But even if these parties do reflect an extreme of opinion on the right-wing side of the political spectrum, they tend not to be counter-balanced by an equivalent antisystem extreme on the left, and hence, by definition, the poles are no longer "two poles apart" (Sartori 1976, 135). In short, if two-party systems in a strict sense are hard to find, and if examples of polarized pluralism are also thin on the ground, then, perforce, most systems tend to crowd into the category of moderate pluralism,[5] which clearly reduces the discriminating power of the typology.

Party Systems and the Structure of Competition

That said, Sartori's approach remains particularly useful and important in that unlike the alternative approaches, it helps to focus attention directly on what is perhaps the most important aspect of party systems, and on what distinguishes most clearly between different party systems: the structure of interparty competition and, especially, the competition for government. To be sure, it might be argued that this is in fact the core variable underlying each of the other established classifications of party systems. Duverger's (1954) classic distinction between two-party systems and multiparty systems, for example, is ostensibly based on the numbers of parties in competition, but it can also be seen as differentiating systems in which two major parties compete with one another over the question of which will form a (single-party) government from those in which government usually involves some form of shifting coalition. In a similar vein, Rokkan's (1968) distinction between the British-German type ("1 vs. 1 + 1"), the Scandinavian type ("1 vs. 3-4"), and the even multiparty type ("1 vs. 1 vs. 1 + 2-3"), although ostensibly "purely numerical," is really an attempt to tap into the different patterns of coalition formation. But although some notion of the competition for government may well have informed these earlier classifications, they certainly did not confront the issue directly. Indeed, among alternative approaches, it is really only Dahl's (1966) distinctions that come anywhere close to addressing the question of government formation as a key defining feature, even though this is secondary to the more central question of identifying differences in party strategies in different competitive arenas.

Building from Sartori, then, how might differential patterns in the competition for government be understood? Three related factors are relevant here. First, there is the question of the prevailing pattern of alternation in government in any given party system, and the extent to which this is either wholesale, partial, or even nonexistent. Second, there is the question of the stability or consistency of the governing alternatives, and the extent to which innovative formulas are adopted. Finally, there is the simple question of who governs, and the extent to which access to government is either open to a wide range of diverse parties or limited to a smaller subset of parties. Let us now look at each of these factors in turn.

Alternation in Government

There are three conceivable patterns of alternation that can be considered here. The first and most obvious pattern might be termed *wholesale alternation,* in which a set of incumbents is wholly displaced by a former opposition. In other words, all of the parties in government at time t are removed from office and are replaced at time $t + 1$ by a new government made up of a party or coalition of parties that were previously in opposition. The British case offers the most obvious example of such wholesale alternation, with a single-party Labour government being replaced by a single-party Conservative government, or vice versa. A similar pattern has been evident in New Zealand, with the alternation between Labour and the National party. But although the classic two-party model offers the most obvious examples of wholesale alternation, the pattern can also be seen in more fragmented systems. In Norway, for example, wholesale alternation has regularly ensued on the basis of shifts between a single-party Labour government, on the one hand, and a multiparty bourgeois coalition, on the other, reflecting a pattern of competition similar to that which developed in Costa Rica in the 1960s and 1970s. More unusually, the recent French experience has witnessed wholesale alternation between competing coalitions, with the Socialists and various left-wing allies, including the PCF, alternating with a coalition of the RPR and UDF. This latter case is quite exceptional, however, in that even in fragmented systems, as was the case over extended periods of time in Ireland, Norway, and Sweden, and as was also the case in Japan in 1993, wholesale alternation usually involves at least one single-party alternative.

The second pattern, which is more common in fragmented systems, is *partial alternation,* in which a newly incumbent government includes at least one party that also formed part of the previous government. Germany provides the most obvious example here, in that all of the governments that have held office since 1969 have included the small FDP as a junior coalition partner, with the role of senior partner alternating sporadically between the SPD and the CDU-CSU. The Dutch system also approximates this pattern, with the CDA and, prior to 1977, the KVP tending to persist in office, albeit with alternating coalition partners.[6] Indeed, the major contrast between the German and Dutch patterns of alternation is simply that in the Dutch case, it has tended to be the biggest party that has remained in government, whereas it is usually the smaller party in the German case. Similar enduring patterns of partial alternation, albeit without involving such pronounced long-term continuity of one particular partner in office, can be seen in Belgium, Finland, and Luxembourg. However, the most striking example of partial alternation was that provided by the Italian case throughout most of the postwar period, with the DC holding office continually from 1946 to 1994, occasionally as a minority single-party government, and more often as the senior partner in a relatively variable multiparty coalition. In this sense, the Italian case also approximates to that of the Netherlands, the major difference being that prior to 1977, the core KVP was more often than not in a minority within the governing coalition, as was also the case with the CDA in 1981-1982.

The third pattern also borders closely on the Italian experience and is marked by a complete absence of alternation, or by *nonalternation,* in which the same party or parties remains in exclusive control of government over an extended period of time, being displaced neither wholly nor partially. Switzerland offers the clearest example of nonalternation over time, with the same four-party coalition holding office since 1959. A similar pattern of nonalternation clearly also characterizes what Sartori defined as predominant-party systems, as in the case of Japan from 1955 to 1993, with the Liberal Democrats holding office almost consistently alone over this 40-year period; in India, where the Congress party held continuous office until its first defeat in 1977; and in Mexico, where the PRI has held the dominant position since the 1920s.

Innovation and Familiarity

Party systems differ not only in their patterns of alternation but also in the degree to which the alternative governing formulas (i.e., the combinations of parties in government) are either familiar or innovative (see also Franklin and Mackie 1983). In the British case, for example, familiarity is everything, and no new governing formula has been experimented with since the broad coalition that held office during World War II. The formulas were also familiar and hence very predictable over a long period in the Irish case, with governments being made up of either Fianna Fáil, on the one hand, or a coalition of all the remaining parties, on the other, as well as in Germany, which has experimented with no new formula since the advent to office for the first time of the SPD-FDP coalition in 1969. Notwithstanding the German case, however, it is in systems of partial alternation that the greatest scope exists for innovation. In Italy, for example, despite the long-term dominance of the DC, there has been frequent experimentation with new coalition alliances. In the Netherlands, despite the continuity in office of the KVP and, later, the CDA, innovation has also been particularly marked, with differing and novel combinations of parties succeeding one another in office with remarkable frequency. It is important to note here that although innovative formulas are obviously involved when the party or parties concerned have never previously held office, they can also be deemed to occur even when the parties have governed before but never in that particular alliance. In the Irish case, for example, the first ever coalition between Fianna Fáil and Labour, which took office in 1993, can be defined as innovative, even though each of the parties involved had already had long experiences of government; similarly, both the ÖVP and SPÖ single-party governments in Austria (taking office for the first time in 1966 and 1970, respectively) can be treated as innovative, despite the fact that both parties had previously governed together in coalition.

Which Parties Govern?

The third factor involved here concerns the range of parties that gain access to government. Although not all possible parties can be expected to win a share of office, even with frequent alternation, party systems can nevertheless be distinguished in terms of the degree to which access to office is widely or narrowly dispersed. In other words, party systems can be distinguished in terms of whether all relevant parties eventually cross the threshold of government, as is more or less the case in the Netherlands, for example, or whether governing remains the privilege of just a limited subset of parties, as was the case in postwar Italy. Knowing the range of parties with access to office therefore allows us to distinguish between these latter cases, which otherwise tend to coincide in terms of both of the other criteria indicated above. That is, although both the Netherlands and Italy are similar in the sense of their pattern of partial alternation, in terms of the longevity in office of a core center party, and in terms of their resort to innovative formulas, they are nevertheless strikingly dissimilar when it comes to the range of parties gaining access to office. This particular distinction may also be related to what Sartori defines as polarized pluralism, which, as noted above, required the presence of antisystem parties at each end of the political spectrum, such parties being defined in part as those that were out of competition for government, thus forcing governments to be formed across the span of the center. Here, also, the concern is with whether certain parties are excluded as unacceptable partners in office. Where this criterion differs from that used in the definition of polarized pluralism, however, is that the question of whether such parties are genuinely and objectively antisystem, which has always been a point of dispute in the interpretations and criticisms of Sartori's model, becomes irrelevant. Rather, what matters is whether there are parties that are treated, in practice, as "outsiders" and that are regarded by the other parties in the system as unacceptable allies. In this sense, "antisystemness," like beauty, here lies in the eyes of the beholder. It is difficult, for example, to determine whether the Danish Progress party is genuinely antisystem; on the other hand, it is relatively easy to see that this party has been regarded by its potential allies as an outsider and, up to now, has always languished in opposition (unlike, say, the more ostensibly antisystem PCF in France).

Closed or Open?

The combination of these three criteria yields a fairly broad-brush distinction between two contrasting patterns in the structure of party competition (see Table 3.2). On the one hand, the structure of party competition can be relatively *closed,* and hence highly predictable, with little or no change over time in the range of governing alternatives or in the pattern of alternation, and with new parties and/or outsider parties finding it virtually impossible to break through the threshold of government. The British and New Zealand cases have afforded perhaps the best examples of such closed systems, with each being persistently characterized by wholesale alternation, by a complete absence of innovative formulae, and by the presence of just two governing, and governable, parties. On the other hand, the structure of party competition can prove relatively *open,* and hence quite unpredictable, with differing patterns of alternation, with frequent shifts in the make-up of the governing alternatives, and with new parties gaining relatively easy access to office. The postwar Dutch pattern comes quite close to this form, in that new parties have been relatively easily incorporated into government (such as DS 70 in 1971 and D 66 and the PPR in 1973) and in that innovative formulas have been adopted in almost half of the new governments formed since 1951. Where the Dutch system deviates from a wholly open pattern, however, is in the long-term presence in government of the KVP and, later, the CDA, and in the fact that alternation has always been partial. In this sense, at least prior to 1993 when the first ever "secular" government was formed, there was always a certain element of predictability involved, and to this extent the structure of competition was at least partially closed. Denmark in the postwar period also comes quite close to an open pattern, having experiences of both partial and wholesale alternation, having frequently adopted innovative formulas (almost one-third of all postwar governments), and having also proved to be relatively open to new parties, such as in 1982, when the Center Democrats and the Christian People's party were first admitted to government. On the other hand, even Denmark can be seen as partially closed and somewhat predictable as a result of the persistent exclusion from office of the Progress party and the Socialist People's party.

These examples also underline the extent to which the development of a closed structure of competition owes much to the strategies of the established parties, and in particular, their unwillingness to experiment with innovative formulas and their reluctance to admit new parties into government (Franklin

TABLE 3.2 Structure of Party Competition and the Pattern of Alternation in Government

	Structure of Competition Is	
	Closed	Open
Pattern of alternation in government	Wholesale alternation or nonalternation	Partial alternation
Types of governing formulas	Familiar	Innovative
Access to government office	Restricted to few parties	Open to many parties
Examples	United Kingdom	Netherlands
	New Zealand, to mid-1990s	Denmark
	Japan, 1955-1993	Newly emerging party
	Ireland, 1948-1989	systems

and Mackie 1983). In some instances, of course, the parties may feel themselves genuinely constrained in this respect, in that any new governing options might require the bridging of what are believed to be ineluctable divides in policy and/or ideology. The structure of competition may therefore be very predictable, and hence closed, as a result of the distances that separate the relevant parties along any one of a variety of different dimensions of competition. Such arguments might well have been used by Christian Democratic leaders in Italy, for example, to justify the persistent exclusion of the Communist party from office, and might equally be cited by a number of different party leaderships in Denmark to justify the persistent exclusion of the Progress party. In other instances, however, it is obvious that the maintenance of familiar and closed patterns of competition simply constitutes a strategy of self-preservation on the part of the established parties.[7] In Ireland, for example, the long-term refusal of the dominant Fianna Fáil party to even consider entering a coalition, a refusal that contributed substantially to the closure of competition in Ireland (see below), was clearly designed to maintain its status as the only party capable of offering single-party government and was thus intended to maintain its electoral credibility. A similar sense of self-preservation can be seen to characterize the long-term reluctance of the two major British parties to consider the possibilities of coalition with the smaller Liberal party, even though Labour did come strikingly close to such a path-breaking option during the Lib-Lab Pact in the late 1970s. To be sure, there are real limits on the capacity, and willingness, of the established parties to maintain a closed structure of competition. New parties might emerge that have to be taken on board, particular party leaders may have their own agendas and priorities, external crises might develop that force the adoption of new strategies, and so on; nonetheless, any explanation of the degree of closure of any given structure of competition must necessarily focus particular attention on the strategies of the parties themselves.

Closed structures of competition are also clearly characteristic of traditional two-party systems as well as, of course, of those systems that have experienced a real absence of alternation over time, such as Japan, the Stormont regime in Northern Ireland, Mexico, Singapore, or Switzerland. Conversely, openness, and a lack of predictability, tend to characterize more fragmented systems that experience partial alternation, and especially where there is no large, core party of government. Moreover, because closure necessarily requires the development of stable norms and conventions in the patterns of competition and in the processes of government formation, it is also clearly a function of time and, most crucially, is not something that can be seen to characterize newly emerging party "systems."

Indeed, what is most striking about new party systems, such as those that are currently emerging in post-Communist Europe, for example, is precisely their lack of closure and hence their lack of *systemness*, with systemness here understood to be the set of "*patterned* interactions" (Sartori 1976, 43, emphasis added) between the parties. Not only is the format of these new systems highly unstable, in that the parties as organizations are often inchoate and loosely constructed, but so too are the modes of competition and the nature of cross-party alliances and coalitions, a feature that also continues to characterize even many of the older party systems of Latin America. Seen from this perspective, the long-term process by which party systems may eventually become consolidated can also be seen as a long-term process by which the structure of competition becomes increasingly closed and predictable. Thus, although a more closed and predictable structure might well develop in a number of the post-Communist democracies in the next decade or so, this will, by definition, necessarily involve a relatively lengthy process.[8] Just such a long-term process of structural consolidation might now be seen to be reaching fruition in the relatively recently democratized Portuguese and Spanish systems, as well as in some of the Latin American systems, with perhaps the most notable examples being seen in the drift toward two-partyism in Costa Rica and Venezuela (McDonald and Ruhl 1989); in this latter region, however, as in the United States, the frequent combination of a presidential system of government, on the one hand, and the presence of largely undisciplined parties (e.g., Mainwaring and Shugart 1994), on the other, suggests that there remains a significant bias against the development of closed structures of competition, at least in the legislative electoral arena.[9]

Party Systems and Electoral Outcomes

The degree of closure therefore varies, being least pronounced in newly emerging party systems and being most pronounced in established systems in which there is little or no innovation in the processes of government formation and in which new parties rarely if ever break through the governing threshold.[10] What is also important about this notion is that it immediately allows us to move away from the conventional idea that party system change is largely, if not exclusively, a function of, or even a synonym for, electoral change,[11] and it affords a conception of changes in party systems that may owe their origin to other factors. For although party system stability/change and electoral stability/change may certainly be related to one another, they are nevertheless far from being mutually equivalent. Electoral alignments might shift, for example, even in quite a dramatic way, without necessarily impinging significantly on the structure of competition, and hence without necessarily altering the character of the party system itself. Conversely, the structure of party competition and hence the nature of the party system itself might suddenly be transformed, even without any significant prior electoral flux.

In Denmark, for example, the 1973 election witnessed one of the most substantial electoral shifts to have ever occurred in postwar Europe, resulting in an immediate doubling of the number of parties represented in Parliament. Prior to 1973, a total of five parties had been represented in the Danish Folketing, together accounting for some 93 percent of the total vote. As a result of the 1973 election, five new parties won representation, and the total vote won by the previously represented parties fell to less than 65 percent. This was a massive shift by any standards, and because the new entrants to the Parliament included both the long-established Communist party as well as the newly formed right-wing Progress party, it also resulted in a major increase in the level of polarization. In practice, however, it is certainly possible to question whether this change had any real systemic effect. To be sure, a new government had to be formed, which in fact was a minority, single-party Liberal government, the first such to take office since 1945. On the other hand, this novel government was then succeeded by a Social Democratic minority government, which was precisely the same form of government that had held office prior to the 1973 earthquake election, and then eventually by a center-right coalition, which was differently composed but otherwise essentially similar to the various other center-right coalitions that had governed Denmark in the early 1950s and late 1960s. To be sure, the increased fragmentation and the greater degree of polarization made governing more difficult after 1973— for a long time, no government won majority status in Parliament (although such a status had also been quite exceptional even prior to 1973), governments tended to collapse more frequently than before, and there was now a greater resort to elections, although this had also been not uncommon prior to 1973; moreover, as noted above, new parties had eventually to be accommodated into government, although the Progress party has not yet been accorded that privilege. But the question still remains as to whether this massive shift in electoral preferences has had any real effect whatsoever on the structure of party competition and on the party system itself. Denmark is now, but always has been, quite innovative in terms of governing formulas; it is now, and always has been, reasonably open to new parties coming into government; and now, as before, it experiences both wholesale and partial alternation in government on a regular basis. It had once, and still maintains, a relatively open structure of competition and hence a relatively unconstrained party system, and, in these terms at least, 1973 does not appear to have made any significant difference.[12]

The Italian case in 1994 might also offer a useful example, even though uncertainty still remains as to whether a genuine transformation of the party system is under way.[13] On the face of it, there is no other established Western party system that has undergone such a profound change. At the electoral level, for example, following decades of relative stability, the 1994 contest resulted in a level of volatility of some 37.2 percent, which is not only the highest figure recorded in Italian history but, even more strikingly, is substantially higher than that recorded in almost any election held in Western Europe between 1885 and 1989.[14] In terms of format, the system has also been totally transformed, with the emergence of new parties and the reconstitution of established parties leading to a situation in which virtually none of the parties currently represented in the new 1994 Parliament was represented under the same name or in the same form as recently as 1987. Finally, it can also be argued that there has also been a major change in the level of polarization, as a result of the transformation of the PCI into the PDS, on the one hand, and the transformation of the MSI into the AN and their incorporation into government, on the other, which, at least in Sartori's sense of the term, leaves Italy now with no relevant "antisystem" party. These are certainly profound changes. The most relevant question, however, is whether these changes will have any long-term effect on the structure of competition. The structure of competition in the old party system was certainly clear. Governments were formed from out of the center, were dominated by the DC, and involved shifting alliances with partial alternation across the center-left and center-right while excluding both the extreme left (PCI) and extreme right (MSI). Any fundamental change in this pattern would now require governments to be formed almost exclusively from the left or right (creating the potential for wholesale alternation), would require the incorporation (or disappearance) of the extremes, and, in this new bipolar world, would marginalize the independent position of the center. With the formation of the right-wing Berlusconi government in 1994, it certainly seemed possible that just such a pattern might emerge. Perhaps ironically, however, it quickly became clear that the new alliance was unable to maintain either its coherence or its majority and that any consolidation of its position would require the approval and incorporation of the now-reduced center, as represented by the successor to the DC, the PPI. At the same time, the PPI itself was divided, being particularly reluctant to share power with the old extreme right, the AN, and with some sections preferring to incorporate, or ally with, the new center-left, as represented by the PDS. As of now, of course, it is too soon to suggest what future patterns or alignments might yet emerge, and in this sense the structure of competition might be regarded as quite open and unpredictable, which, at least in the short term, does represent a fundamental change. Moreover, should the center split into left and right, as currently appears to be the pattern, then a wholly new bipolar structure might develop, and this would certainly transform the Italian party system. But should an independent center reconstitute itself, and should it prove capable of taking full advantage of its pivotal position by playing left against right in a way that would allow it to construct a broad alliance across the center, then, despite the different actors and their different weights in the system, it might well re-create more or less the same structure of competition as had prevailed prior to the 1990s (Bartolini and D'Alimonte 1995). As in Denmark, therefore, but more markedly so, massive shifts at the level of the electorate and at the level of the format of the party system could yet end up in a party system that reflected more continuity than change. The possibility certainly exists.

Question marks also hang over the real extent of change in the Canadian party system, notwithstanding the electoral earthquake of 1993. In this case, as in Italy, the level of volatility rose to an unprecedented high of 42 percent, almost five times that of the average level of volatility recorded in the 1970s and 1980s. The consequences were also very far reaching, with the once powerful Conservative party being reduced to just 16 percent of the vote (its lowest share since 1949) and, even more strikingly, to just 2 seats (as against 169 in the previous election), and with two new parties, the Reform party and Bloc Québécois, winning substantial representation in Parliament, the first parties outside the mainstream to do so since the effective demise of Social Credit in the mid-1970s.[15] Moreover, precisely because these two new parties are so evidently regional in character, they may also signal a potentially enduring shift in electoral alignments. This is substantial change by any standard. At the same time, however, there is also one striking continuity, in that the Liberal party, the traditional opponent of, and alternative to, the Conservatives, is now back in government with a powerful majority, and thus at least for now, and in terms of the patterns of alternation, the degree of innovation, and the extent of access to government of new parties, Canada remains as it has been for decades. At one level, the system has certainly changed: The Liberals now confront two major opposition parties instead of just one, and a regional divide has now erupted onto the federal stage in a manner that clearly damages Canada's prospects of maintaining its familiar, British style pattern of wholesale alternation in the future. Nevertheless, and much as in the Italian case, it is precisely because this potential for change still remains to be realized that it is as yet impossible to speak of any fundamental transformation in the structure of competition.

Finally, the Irish case offers a completely contrasting example (Mair 1987, 1993). Lacking a strong cleavage structure, and being characterized by quite marked institutional continuity, the party system had been stabilized largely by a very rigid structure of competition, in which the governments taking office for most of the postwar period were formed by either Fianna Fáil, on the one hand, or by a sometimes motley coalition of Fianna Fáil's opponents (principally Fine Gael and the Labour party), on the other. Indeed, in the more recent period, these alternatives also replaced one another in office with remarkable regularity, with each election from 1973 to 1987 resulting in a wholesale alternation in office. This enduring structure of competition had two principal effects. In the first place, it provided Fianna Fáil with one of the major foundations for its appeal, in that the party reaped a major electoral advantage from the fact that it was the only party that had the potential to provide single-party government, and for this reason, for example, it deliberately and very publicly eschewed the idea of coalescing with any other party, preferring to go into opposition on those occasions when it could not command a working majority. Second, this structure of competition helped to prevent Labour, the third party in the system, from mobilizing any independent and potentially realigning strategy. Indeed, the party was almost perpetually constrained by the choice of either languishing in opposition, or, regardless of the policy problems involved, joining with Fine Gael as the junior partner in a non-Fianna Fáil coalition. No other option was available. In 1989, however, all of this changed when for a variety of reasons, including the short-term ambition of the then party leader, Fianna Fáil performed an about-face and decided to enter coalition with a recently formed, right-wing liberal party, the Progressive Democrats (Laver and Arkins 1990). Four years later, following the collapse of that first experiment, the party formed a new coalition, this time with the Labour party. The result of both decisions was an effective transformation of the party system, with Fianna Fáil's coalition with the Progressive Democrats effectively undermining the foundations on which the postwar party system had been structured, and with its coalition with Labour then more or less destroying those old foundations in their entirety. Prior to 1989, the Irish party system had been structured around a bipolar pattern of competition—Fianna Fáil versus the rest. In entering coalition with a new, and ostensibly nonaligned party, Fianna Fáil had damaged the integrity of the first of those two poles. Later, by entering coalition with one of its traditional opponents, with one of "the rest," it forced the second pole to collapse. There was, in short, nothing that remained of the old order. But what is perhaps the most striking feature of this transformation was the fact that at least initially, and in contrast to the Danish, Italian, and Canadian cases, it occurred in a context on relatively little electoral change. The level of volatility in the 1989 election was just 7.8, which was below the postwar average in Ireland (Mair 1993, 164), with most of this being accounted for by the sharp drop in support for the Progressive Democrats since their first successful outing in 1987. Elsewhere in the system, and among the established parties, support for Fianna Fáil rose from 44.1 to 44.2 percent, support for Fine Gael rose from 27.1 to 29.3 percent, and support for Labour rose from 6.4 to 9.5 percent. Substantial electoral continuities therefore accompanied what was clearly to become a fundamental transformation of the party system.

What we see here, then, are one instance in which substantial electoral change does not appear to have led to significant party system change (Denmark); one instance in which there has been a major change in the party system change notwithstanding prior electoral stability (Ireland); and two instances in which, despite extraordinary electoral flux, question marks still remain as to whether a new type of party system might develop (Italy and Canada). Each of these instances therefore underlines the need to separate out the notion of party system stability/change, on the one hand, and electoral stability/change, on the other.

Not only that, however, for what may be most interesting about the separation of these two processes, and about the recognition that change in party systems may be due to factors other than electoral change—factors such as changes in elite behavior, in party strategy, in the patterns of competition, or whatever—is that it also allows us to *reverse* the conventional chain of influence and to probe the extent to which party system stability (or change) may itself lead to electoral stability (or change), rather than simply the other way around.

Electoral alignments are, of course, stabilized by a variety of factors, of which the cleavage structure is perhaps the most important (Lipset and Rokkan 1967; Bartolini and Mair 1990). At the same time, however, the long-term stabilization of electorates should not be seen simply as a function of the ties that bind distinct social groups (Catholics, workers, farmers, etc.) to parties or to blocs of parties. To be sure, social structure has certainly proved to be an important stabilizing element, especially in countries with strong social cleavages or subcultures, such as Italy, the Netherlands, and Sweden. But if social structure were the only freezing agent, then we would certainly have witnessed much greater change in European electoral alignments in the 1970s and 1980s than has actually been the case. The fact is that many of the old traditional parties in Europe remain alive and kicking despite the widespread weakening of religious and class identities, and despite the long-term processes of individualization.

There are in fact a variety of factors involved here, with party systems and electoral alignments being also frozen by the constraints imposed by institutional structures such as the electoral system, and by the organizational efforts of the parties themselves (Bartolini and Mair 1990). What is most relevant in this context, however, is that one additional freezing agent may well be the constraints imposed by the structure of party competition and by its relationship to processes of government formation.[16] A closed structure of competition clearly constrains voter preferences, in that it limits the choice of governing options in a way that is similar to the limits on the choice of parties in nonfragmented systems. A closed structure of competition therefore also clearly enhances party system stability and, indeed, helps to ensure that party systems generate their own momentum and thus freeze into place. In short, the stabilization of party systems is at least partly a function of the consolidation of a given structure of competition.

What this also implies, of course, and perhaps most interestingly, is that a *change* in that structure may then act to *de*stabilize the party system. In Italy, for example, the basis for a wholesale change in electoral preferences in 1992 and 1994 was at least partially laid by the legitimation of the PDS, which undermined the terms of reference by which Italian party competition had been structured since the late 1940s. Italian voters, as well as the Italian parties themselves, had long been constrained by the belief that there was no alternative to a Christian Democratic-dominated government. And once such an alternative finally did emerge through the transformation of the unacceptable PCI into the highly acceptable PDS, this particular anchor was cut loose, and voters began to shift in relatively great numbers. In Ireland also, following decades in which there had been no major changes in the electoral balance of the party system, the long-term basis for stability was finally undermined in 1989 when the dominant party, Fianna Fáil, decided for the first time ever to enter a coalition with another party. Prior to then, as noted above, party competition had been structured around the opposition between Fianna Fáil, on the one side, and all of the smaller parties, on the other, and this had severely constrained and stabilized voter preferences. From 1989 onward, however, when these constraints were removed, the potential for change was greatly enhanced, and hence although the level of volatility prior to Fianna Fáil's first coalition was relatively muted, the subsequent election witnessed a major upsurge in volatility that resulted in a doubling of the Labour vote to the highest level ever recorded—the result, quite simply, of the removal of what had been up to then the most powerful constraint on electoral mobility.

This is perhaps a roundabout way of saying that the structure of competition, and the structure of competition for government in particular, may impose a major constraint on voter choice and hence may act to stabilize electoral alignments. In this sense, voters are not simply expressing preferences for individual parties; rather, albeit not always to the same degree in different party systems, and this in itself is an important source of cross-national (and cross-institutional) variance, they are also expressing preferences for potential governments. And in much the same way that a shift in the range of parties on offer can act to undermine established preferences,[17] so too can a shift in the range of governing options, and hence a shift in the structure of competition, act to undermine established preferences and promote instability.

Just such a process might now be seen to be developing in many of the established party systems in Western Europe, in that the evidence suggests that we are now witnessing a major shift in the traditional patterns of government formation (Mair, 1995). There are two trends that are relevant here, each of which suggests that formerly closed structures of competition might now begin to open and hence might well promote greater electoral uncertainty in the future. In the first place, the past two decades have seen the opening up of government to an increasingly wide range of political parties. In other words, we have seen almost every established and substantial party in Western Europe winning at least one period in government, with the result that governing, even if only sporadically, is an increasingly standard experience for most parties. There remain nongoverning exceptions, of course, which include, first, the so-called new politics parties of the left, the Greens and the new left, most of which have gained access to office, if at all, only at the subnational level; second, the parties of the extreme right, many of which have begun to flourish in a number of Western democracies only in the past decade, and almost all of which have been excluded from government; and third, the "die-hard" opposition parties—the Italian PCI, which now no longer exists but has been transformed into the eminently coalitionable PDS (which actually joined a coalition government for one day in April 1993), and the British Liberal party, which although substantial in terms of electoral strength is nevertheless marginal in parliamentary terms. These few and relatively marginal exceptions apart, however, the opening up of government to more and more parties clearly has significant implications for the structures of competition in these established party systems.

Second, a related impression of developments at the level of government suggests that party systems are increasingly characterized by a gradual broadening of the range of coalition alternatives. In Germany, for example, all possible two-party coalitions between the three main parties have proved possible both in principle and in practice; in the Netherlands, each of the four main parties has by now coalesced with each of the others at various stages during the past 10 years; in Ireland, Labour has now had recent experience of joining governments with both Fianna Fáil and Fine Gael, whereas both Labour and Fine Gael have most recently been joined in coalition by the Democratic left; in Austria in the past 10 years the SPÖ has formed governments with both the FPÖ and the ÖVP; in Belgium, the Socialists, Liberals, and Christians have all recently worked with one another, and also, on occasion, with the Volksunie and the Rassemblement Walloon; even in Sweden, where a sharp two-bloc structure of competition has existed since the late 1950s, the run-up to the 1994 election witnessed a lengthy discussion of a possible coalition between the Social Democrats and the Liberals. The sense, therefore, is one of growing promiscuity in the process of coalition formation, which is also likely to affect structures of competition within party systems.

Should these trends continue, then, it is certainly possible that we might yet witness the progressive destruction of traditional patterns of party competition, with formerly closed patterns increasingly giving way to a style that is at once more open and less predictable, a development that has already become apparent in the 1990s in both Ireland and Italy. The result is likely to be the removal of one major constraint on voter choice and the potential, at least, for a significant destabilization of established electoral alignments. Other constraints on electoral mobility still remain, of course, including both institutional inertia and the cleavage structure itself, but should this particular anchor now begin to shift, and should structures of competition begin to open up, then, it will certainly enhance the scope of uncertainty.

Notes

1. For an overview of some recent cross-national studies in the field, and in addition to the various comparative and national studies that are cited elsewhere in this chapter, see, for example, Gallagher, Laver, and Mair (1995), Lawson and Merkl (1988), Mair and Smith (1990), Randall (1988), Ware (1987, 1996), and Wolinetz (1988).

2. See, for example, Almond, Powell, and Mundt (1993, 117-20), where this traditional distinction is recast as one of "majoritarian" versus multiparty systems; see also the influential study by Lijphart (1984) where one of the key distinctions between majoritarian and consensus democracies is defined as that between a two-party system and a multiparty system.

3. The approaches reviewed here are also summarized in the chapters included in Mair (1990, 285-349).

4. For earlier versions of Sartori's typology, see Sartori (1966, 1970).

5. The exception would be those systems that might be categorized as predominant-party systems, which, as noted above, do not easily fit into the criteria adopted for the typology as a whole.

6. In 1994, for the first time since the advent of full democracy, a government was formed in the Netherlands without the CDA/religious mainstream.

7. It is in this sense that closure also involves what Schattschneider (1960, 69, and passim) has termed *the mobilization of bias,* with the emphasis on particular conflicts and on distinct alternatives acting to preserve the interests of the various protagonists.

8. See Sartori (1994, 37): "When the electorate takes for granted a given set of political routes and alternatives very much as drivers take for granted a given system of highways, then a party system has reached the stage of structural consolidation qua system."

9. See Sartori (1994, 181, fn. 7); the lack of structuring is also reflected in the persistently high levels of electoral volatility that are strikingly and substantially higher than those occurring in the relatively structured West European systems (Coppedge 1992).

10. As noted, it is also probably least pronounced in the legislative electoral arena in presidential systems, notwithstanding any strong structuring that might be evident in the presidential electoral arena in these same systems.

11. See, for example, Rose and Urwin (1970), whose analysis of persistence and change "in party systems" was almost exclusively devoted to an analysis of persistence and change in patterns of electoral support. For an earlier discussion of this problem, see Mair (1989, 271-3).

12. On the Danish situation see Pedersen (1987, 1988) and Bille (1990).

13. See especially the analysis by Bartolini and D'Alimonte (1995).

14. The index of volatility measures the net aggregate shift in votes from one election to the next and is the equivalent of the total aggregate gains of all winning parties or the total aggregate losses of all losing parties (see Pedersen 1983). The average volatility in postwar Europe has been less than 9 percent, and apart from the 1994 election in Italy, only four other European elections in the past century have exceeded 35 percent: Germany in 1919 (47.5 percent), France in 1945 (36.4 percent), and Greece in 1950 (47.0 percent) and 1951 (45.1 percent)—see Bartolini and D'Alimonte (1995, 443-4); on electoral stability in Europe more generally, see Bartolini and Mair (1990).

15. For analyses of recent developments in the Canadian party system, see Bakvis (1988, 1991), Carty (1994), and MacIvor (1995).

16. This argument therefore echoes that by Bakvis (1988, 263), who seeks to explain the Canadian paradox of party system stability in the context of weakly anchored electoral alignments by pointing to the existence of "a more generalized loyalty to the party system as a whole." A similar argument might also be advanced for Ireland (see above), and perhaps even for the United States.

17. Note, for example, the strong relationship between the number of parties in competition, on the one hand, and the degree of electoral volatility, on the other (see Pedersen 1983, 48-55; Bartolini and Mair 1990, 130-45).

(4)

Party Organizations and Finance

RICHARD S. KATZ

Elections often are treated as contests among political parties. Bill Clinton is identified as "the Democrats' candidate for president"; it is reported that Forza Italia won 21 percent of the vote in the 1994 Italian parliamentary election; the Progressive Democrats are said to have called for more competition in the provision of health insurance in the 1992 Irish general election. Each of these statements, however, is problematic. Who are the "Democrats" who are said to have chosen Clinton as "their" candidate? In what sense should votes received by candidates endorsed by Forza Italia be regarded as votes for the party? And indeed should Forza Italia be regarded as a party in the first place? What of Progressive Democrats who did not emphasize health insurance?

Although no significant national elections are truly nonpartisan, elections vary in the degree to which they are contests among parties rather than contests among individuals who may (or, at least in form, may not) bear party labels. Elections vary in the degree to which party organizations recruit candidates and control access to the ballot; in the degree to which parties develop positions on issues to which all their candidates adhere; in the degree to which parties generate and channel the resources required for effective campaigning; in the degree to which voter choice is oriented toward party rather than individual candidate; and indeed in the degree to which it makes a practical difference which party wins. Where a system falls on this dimension depends on many things, including its political traditions, the structure of government (presidential or parliamentary, federal or unitary), and the electoral system (especially whether PR or plurality). The degree of "partyness" of elections also both depends on, and is reflected in, the nature of the parties and the way in which the state regulates the campaign activities of candidates, parties, and their supporters.

Place of Parties in a Democracy

Parties perform two classes of functions in modern democracies. Within government, they provide a regular structure for the organization of legislative chambers (e.g., the allocation of committee positions), for coalition building, and for coordination among individual officials both within and across branches of government. Externally, parties provide a forum for the debate of political ideas and a ready-made venue for political involvement by interested citizens. These two functions come together in the centrally defining activity of both parties and democracy, contested elections. The ways in which parties are organized and behave in elections fundamentally shape the nature of democracy, but party organizations also reflect differing conceptions of democracy and the role of elections in it.

In general terms, democratic elections serve two roles, which are only partially compatible. On the one hand, they allow groups of people (whether defined by residence, ethnicity, or opinion) to choose representatives who will articulate their views, protect their interests, and intercede with the government on their behalf. This "liberal" role can be contrasted, on the other hand, to a "populist" or "popular sovereignty" role of allowing the people to choose the government itself, and thus indirectly the policies it will pursue and interests it will serve (Riker 1982; Katz 1997). Although party organizations may facilitate the first role (e.g., by recruiting candidates, structuring the ballot, organizing campaigns), they are particularly crucial to the second, and indeed for some analysts they are defined by it.

All democratic elections serve both of these functions, but the relative emphasis given them differs considerably. In most democratic countries, relatively greater weight is given to elections as choices of governments. The most common institutionalization of this popular sovereignty ideal of democracy is "democratic party government" (Castles and Wildenmann 1986; Rose 1974a). Although not fully realized in any country, this model is approximated by the parliamentary systems of Western Europe. It assumes that elections are primarily contests among parties that are competing for the right to form a national government. Important political decisions are made first within parties, and public officials are elected primarily as representatives of their parties. If a single party wins an electoral majority, it should be able to form the government on its own and make all important decisions, and correspondingly the voters should be able to hold it fully accountable. If no party achieves a majority, there should be a coalition government or a minority government, with the parties negotiating and taking responsibility for the decisions they accept. All of this requires that parties be cohesive at the national level, so that voters are choosing among substantially the same alternatives throughout the country and so that votes for a party and votes for its particular candidates are substantively synonymous. It says nothing, however, about the way in which the party makes its decisions, how it generates its resources or recruits its candidates, or how, if at all, it is linked to other organizations or groups in society.

The United States is an important exception to this emphasis on "popular sovereignty" and competition between national parties, emphasizing instead liberal values and giving particular weight to the representation of individual constituencies. Voters are supposed to choose candidates rather than parties, and elected officials are supposed to be individually responsive and responsible to their constituents rather than being obedient to the dictates of their national parties. One result is a Congress that at least in some respects reflects the diversity of the country, in which a variety of interests and groups are given voice and in which it is difficult to muster majorities. But for precisely this reason, other results are that the people never have the opportunity to give or withhold an unambiguous mandate for particular actions; it is often unclear who is responsible for what, and when it is clear (as, e.g., when a congressional committee chair unilaterally blocks a piece of legislation) most voters, residing in other members' districts, have no way to reward or punish that person.

Although in some respects the American system is unique, it may also be seen as one extreme along a continuum, with the model of democratic party government at the other extreme. Questions about the organization and operation of parties are important all along the continuum. For example, notwithstanding its basic hostility to strong parties, American experience has shown some form of political party organization to be useful both for candidates and officeholders and for the functioning of the system as a whole. The same has proven true in other democracies with presidential systems and an emphasis on the representative functions of the legislature.

Elements of Party Organization

Although the party government model is based on parties as unitary actors, no party is or can be entirely monolithic. For one thing, there inevitably will be differences of opinion or emphasis, rooted in the backgrounds, values, and experiences of the individuals who collectively make up the party. As well, individuals with differing positions in the party structure have different responsibilities, experience different problems, and confront different patterns of incentives and opportunities. Moreover, these two aspects of the problem of party coherence are likely to be mutually reinforcing, as different kinds of people are channeled into different organizational roles.

Party actors may be classified in a number of ways: between amateurs and professionals; between those who hold or aspire to public office and those who hold positions in the party's extragovernmental organization; between those at the national level and those at the local level. All of these classifications are confused by the fact that an individual may occupy more than one position, for example, as a local party chair and a member of the party's national committee or as party official and elected officeholder. Looking particularly at parties as national organizations, and focusing on roles rather than individuals, many of these differences can be subsumed into a threefold classification (Katz and Mair 1993).

The first element of party organizations is the *party in public office*. These are the public officials who identify themselves, and expect to be identified by the electorate, as representing the party. Archetypically at the national level, this is the parliamentary party or *Fraktion*, but it may also include the national president and a variety of appointed officials. All these owe their positions either directly or indirectly to electoral success, and they potentially face a conflict between loyalty to their party and its program, on the one hand, and their responsibility to the electorate as a whole, on the other. Because they disproportionately enjoy the personal rewards of victory, the potential conflict between electoral expediency and principle can be especially acute for the party in public office.

Organizationally, this facet of party organization can vary in a number of respects. Most simply, there can be one national party in public office or several. The British Conservative party provides an example from one extreme, with a single leader elected by the Conservative members of both houses of Parliament, plus Conservative members of the European Parliament. The United States is at the other extreme, with completely separate party caucuses and leadership hierarchies in the two chambers of Congress, and with the presidential establishment excluded from both (Katz and Kolodny 1994). Several Latin American systems (e.g., Peru or pre-1993 Venezuela) occupy intermediate positions toward the American end of the continuum, with some separation of, and possible opposition between, presidential and congressional parties of the same denomination (Coppedge 1994); Italian parties, on the other hand, are near the British end, but still with separate party groups in the Senate and Chamber of Deputies. Parties in public office in parliamentary systems also differ in whether the party's members of the national cabinet (when it is in office) are included in the regular parliamentary party, or excluded from it; for example, in Canada members of the government attend the regular weekly meetings of their parliamentary party caucus, whereas in the British Conservative party the cabinet (and junior ministers) are excluded from the "1922 Committee" when the party is in office. Some parliamentary party organizations vote to make binding decisions, others provide an opportunity for members to express their views while deciding policy remains the prerogative of the party congress or leaders, while still others provide a structure for regular but purely voluntary cooperation with virtually no enforcement of party unity at all (e.g., the United States, Brazil, and Ecuador).

The second major element of party organizations is the *party on the ground,* consisting of the organized supporters of the party throughout the country. This element may employ some professional staff, and its leaders may include public officeholders, but it is made up primarily of volunteers. Thus, in contrast to the party in public office, the individuals making up this element of the party are motivated primarily by solidaristic and collective incentives, and so are less inclined to sacrifice policy consistency or party identity for electoral advantage (Panebianco 1988).

The most important organizational distinction here concerns the status of party members. Although in recent years a number of countries have enacted special party laws, most modern parties are structured like any private association. Individuals apply for membership and are accepted (or rejected). In joining a party, a member accepts certain obligations, most commonly the obligation to pay a membership fee, but sometimes also a commitment to attend meetings or do other party work. In return, members have rights and privileges within the organization, including the right to vote, either directly or through elected delegates, on the management of the party and the selection of its candidates. In most membership-based parties, the highest decision-making authority formally is the national congress, in which delegates (or in small parties, the members themselves) can decide major questions of party policy and elect the party's national executive. In reality, a variety of procedural devices, as well as deference to, and political skill by, the leadership may make the congress little more than a pep rally for the party's leaders. In some cases (e.g., the British Conservatives), there is a membership organization but it is explicitly an organization supporting the party, rather than being the party itself.

The American Democratic and Republican parties are highly unusual in having no members in the formal sense at all, although partisan registration is sometimes mistakenly taken to be the equivalent of party membership. Parties with formal memberships differ significantly, however, in the density of their memberships. Usually measured by the ratio of party membership to the party electorate, this "organizational density" tended in Europe in the last part of the 1980s to be well under 10 percent, although there were wide national and intranational variations (see Table 4.1). Even the peak of 55 percent achieved by KESK in Finland pales, however, in comparison to the claim of Acción Democrática in Venezuela that in 1985 it had card-carrying members equal to over 60 percent of the vote received by its presidential candidate in 1983 (Coppedge 1994, 29).

The final element of party organization is the *party central office* or national headquarters. It is composed of some mix of representatives of the two other elements of the party, often supplemented by representatives of various affiliated or ancillary organizations, plus the central party staff, generally headed by a national chairman or general secretary. Except in parties founded to support a charismatic leader or adhering to the principle of democratic centralism, the national headquarters tends formally to be in a dependent position. In reality, however, if it is able to maintain tight control over such "organizational uncertainties" as communication and resource allocation, it (or its head) may be the dominant element of the party (Michels [1911] 1962; Panebianco 1988). The presidents of the two Belgian Socialist parties are clear examples of a strong party central office.

The proper relationships between the party in public office and the rest of the party organization (especially the party on the ground), and between the party in public office and the electorate as a whole, have been a subject of continuing debate. From one side, it is argued that because parties are so important, true democracy can only be realized if the parties themselves are internally democratic. In practical terms, this would mean that the members (registrants or ordinary voters in the American case) would control the party in public office by controlling (re)nomination, and officials elected under the party's label would be expected loyally to support the program that the party congress, or the party executive as the agent of the congress, lays down. The other side, however, argues that the primary loyalty of public officials must be to the electorate rather than to their parties. In this view, democracy is realized by electoral choice between politicians who are free to pursue whatever policies they feel will meet with public approval or be in the public interest (Schumpeter 1942). Although of little practical effect, the constitutions of many countries reflect this position by asserting, for example, that "all binding instructions from outside bodies on members of Parliament shall be null and void" (Constitution of the Fifth French Republic, art. 27) or that "deputies . . . shall be representatives of the whole people, not bound by order and instructions, and shall be subject only to their conscience" (German Basic Law, art. 38).

Types of Parties

These three organizational "faces" may be balanced in various ways to produce different types of parties. These originated in response to social and political developments, and so there has been an identifiable evolutionary sequence. Many parties have retained characteristics associated with their genesis, however, and elements of earlier models have persisted even as new types emerge. Moreover, once a party type enters the menu of possibilities, it

TABLE 4.1 Party Membership as a Percentage of Party Vote for Selected Parties

Austria, 1990		Italy, 1987	
SPÖ	30	DP	1
ÖVP	32	PR	1
FPÖ	5	PCI	15
Greens	1	PSI	11
Belgium, 1987		PSDI	12
PCB/KPB	20	DC	14
PSB/BSP	13	PRI	8
PRL/PVV	12	PLI	5
VU	10	MSI	7
Ecolo/Agalev	1	**Netherlands, 1989**	
PSC/CVP	11	PvdA	3
Denmark, 1988		CDA	4
SF	2	D66	1
SD	10	VVD	5
RV	5	**Norway, 1989**	
KRF	13	SV	5
CD	1	DNA	14
V	21	V	13
KF	7	SP	28
FRP	2	KRF	26
Finland, 1987		H	27
SKDL	12	FRP	5
SDP	5	**Poland, 1994**	
KESK	55	PSL	9
SFP	30	UD	1
KOK	11	PC	2
Germany, 1987		PL	6
CDU	5	UPR	1
CSU	5	CEC	3
SDP	6	**Sweden, 1988**	
FDP	2	S	46[a]
Greens	1	VPK	4
		C	19
		FP	7
		M	8
		MP	3

continued

remains available to party organizers after "newer" types emerge. Even when parties face common pressures, their individual circumstances may lead to differing responses. Thus, although the various types developed in a historically determined sequence, this does not mean there is an inexorable pressure for all parties to follow a common path.

TABLE 4.1 *Continued*

SOURCE: Katz and Mair 1992; Millard 1994; Jasiewicz 1994.
NOTE: Party codes:
Austria—SPÖ: Sozialistische Partei Österreichs (Austrian Socialist Party); ÖVP: Österreiche Volkspartei (Austrian People's Party); FPÖ: Freiheitliche Partei Österreichs (Austrian Freedom Party).

Belgium—PCB/KPB: Parti Communiste de Belgique/Kommunistische Partij van Belgie (Communist Party of Belgium); PSB/BSP: Parti Socialiste Belge/Belgische Socialistische Partij (Belgian Socialist Party); PRL/PVV: Parti Réformateur Libéral/Partij voor Vrijheid en Vooruitgang (Liberal Reform Party/Party of Liberty and Progress); VU: Volksunie ([Flemish] People's Union); Ecolo/Agalev: Écologistes confederés pour l'organisation de luttes originales/Anders Gaan Leven (Ecologists); PSC/CVP: Parti Social Chrétien/Christelijke Volkspartei (Social Christian Party/Christian People's Party).

Denmark—SF: Socialistisk Folkeparti (Socialist People's party); SD: Socialdemokratiet (Social Democrats); RV: Radikale Venstre (Social Liberals); KRF: Kristeligt Folkeparti (Christian People's Party); CD: Centrum-Demokraterne (Center Democrats); V: Venstre (Liberal); KF: Konservative Folkeparti (Conservative People's Party); FRP: Fremkridspartiet (Progress Party).

Finland—SKDL: Suomen Kansandemokraattinen Liitto (Finnish People's Democratic League); SDP: Sosiaalidemokraattinen Puolue (Finnish Social Democratic Party); KESK: Keskustapuolue (Center Party); SFP: Svenska Folkpartiet (Swedish People's Party); KOK: Kansallinen Kokoomus (National Coalition).

Germany—CDU: Christlich Demokratische Union (Christian Democratic Union); CSU: Christlich Soziale Union (Christian Social Union); SDP: Socialdemokratische Partei Deutschlands (German Social Democratic Party); FDP: Freie Demokratische Partei (Free Democratic Party).

Italy—DP: Democrazia Proletaria (Proletarian Democracy); PR: Partito Radicale (Radical Party); PCI: Partito Comunista Italiano (Italian Communist Party); PSI: Partito Socialista Italiano (Italian Socialist Party); PSDI: Partito Socialista Democratico Italiano (Italian Social Democratic Party); DC: Democrazia Cristiana (Christian Democracy); PRI: Partito Repubblicano Italiano (Italian Republican Party); PLI: Partito Liberale Italiano (Italian Liberal Party); MSI: Movimento Sociale Italiano (Italian Social Movement).

The Netherlands—PvdA: Partij van de Arbeid (Labor Party); CDA: Christen Democratisch Appèl (Christian Democratic Appeal); D66: Democraten '66 (Democrats '66); VVD: Volkspartij voor Vrijheid en Democratie (People's Party for Freedom and Democracy).

Norway—SV: Sosialistisk Venstreparti (Left Socialist Party); DNA: Det Norske Arbeiderparti (Norwegian Labor Party); V: Venstre (Liberals); SP: Senterpartiet (Center Party); KRF: Kristelig Folkeparti (Christian People's Party); H: Høyre (Conservatives); FRP: Fremskrittspartiet (Progress Party).

Poland—PSL: Polskie Stronnictwo Ludowe (Polish Peasant Party); UD: Unia Demokratyczna (Democratic Union); PC: Porozumienie Centrum (Center Alliance); PL: Porozumienie Ludowe (Agrarian Alliance); UPR: Unia Politiyki Realnej (Union of Real Politics); CEC: Katolicki Komitet Wyborczy "Ojczyzna" (an alliance of the Christian National Union, Party of Christian Democrats, Christian Peasant Party, and Conservative Party).

Sweden—S: Sveriges Socialdemokratiska Arbetarparti (Swedish Social Democratic Party); VPK: Vänsterpartiet-kommunisterna (Left Party Communists); C: Centerpartiet (Center party); FP: Folkpartiet (Liberal Party); M: Moderata Samlingspartiet (Moderate Party); MP: Miljöpartiet (Green Party).
a. Includes corporate members.

Beyond reflecting social conditions at the time of its origin, each party type has also tended to be associated with a particular conception of democracy, which both reflects and legitimates the political interests of the dominant actors within the party. These differing conceptions of democracy then set up expectations that condition the parties' behavior.

Elite Parties

The earliest modern parties were of the caucus or elite type. These were based locally, in a quite restricted elite core that constitutes the party on the ground. The resources supporting an elite party, often primarily the personal clienteles of the core elites themselves, were generated locally, and consequently there was little need for deference to any central organization. Candidates, and hence ultimately those comprising the party in public office, were either the agents or among the leaders of the local caucus, obviating potential conflict between the party in public office and the party on the ground. Although there may have been an organized parliamentary party to coordinate activities in government or a rudimentary central office providing some services for both the party on the ground and the party in public office, these relied primarily on the voluntary cooperation of independent local actors. Particularly in the early days of elite parties, the rhetoric of politics tended to emphasize a single national interest, although different parties might have widely divergent views of where that interest lay, views that often coincided with the private interests of their own core groups.

This type of organization originated in Europe and Latin America under the predemocratic but liberal *régimes censitaires* of the 19th century, and it continues to typify many parties of the right. It also characterized the Japanese Liberal Democratic party, particularly in rural areas, well into the 1960s (Thayer 1969). The political situation in the United States was quite different, especially because universal manhood suffrage essentially was achieved for whites by the 1850s, and for citizens of all races in 1870 (although there was then substantial disenfranchisement of nonwhites, particularly in the South). Nonetheless, in important respects the European elite party and the American caucus party were similar. The caucus was dominated by a self-selecting and self-perpetuating group of leaders, generally nominating candidates from its own ranks. As with the European elite party, the party on the ground (really a collection of loosely allied parties on the ground) was central. National party organizations did little beyond nominating candidates for president and vice president and organizing Congress, without controlling the votes of its members (Ostrogorski [1902] 1964).

Mass Parties

The politics of elite parties was dominated by individuals with private wealth and position. The European mass party arose as the instrument of those groups that lacked these advantages. It was originally the party of those excluded from power, and in many cases, indeed, initially excluded from the vote altogether.

Although in some cases mass parties were organized by dissident members of parliament, in principle mass parties originated outside of government. Schematically, a group of founders organized a party central office, which then built a party on the ground with the ultimate aim of winning elections and thus building a party in public office as well. Because these founders were the leaders of the party on the ground, as well as constituting the party central office, they naturally privileged these elements of the party, casting the party in public office as the agents of the extraparliamentary party. But they also built hierarchical structures linking the party's local organizations into a single national unit (Duverger 1951).

The prototypical mass party represents groups that are individually weak but collectively numerous. It tries to substitute many small subscriptions for large individual patronage; collective action for individual influence; a party press and organizational networks for access to and sympathy from the commercial communications media. Structurally, its base is a number of card-carrying individual members organized into local units. Most generally, these are branches drawing their members from territories corresponding to local government units, but these might be supplemented or replaced by workplace-based cells (particularly Communist parties) or military style militia units (Fascist parties). Additionally, some socialist parties (e.g., the British Labour party and the Swedish Social Democratic Workers party[1]) have allowed other organizations, principally trade unions, to affiliate en masse, creating a class of indirect members. The branches and other local units then send delegates to higher levels of the organization, and ultimately to the national congress, which is in theory the supreme authority on all matters. In fact, real authority generally lies with the national executive elected by the congress, and possibly supplemented by representatives of affiliated or other organizations.

The basic political strategy of a mass party is one of mobilization rather than conversion. As an ideal type, the mass party is rooted in a particular segment of society. Most commonly, this is the working class, but religious subcultures also have been the basis for mass parties. Because it sees itself as speaking only for a particular group, it tries to mobilize and integrate the members of that group while insulating them from possible counter-pressures. This strategy leads the mass party to erect a panoply of ancillary organizations— trade unions, sporting clubs, insurance providers, and so on—that encapsulate the members of its *classe gardée*. Party loyalty is thus less a matter of policy preference or ideological commitment (although mass parties tend to espouse ideologies, be they socialism, Catholicism, Calvinism, fascism, etc.) than simply part of one's social identity.

In addition to a particular organizational form, the mass party model also introduced a distinctive view of democracy, and of the place of the party within it. The mass party specifically claims to represent a particular class or group. The party's claim to that role rests on its internally democratic nature. Elections are seen not as contests between individual candidates, but rather between parties, each representing a distinct social group and advancing a coherent program, legitimized by its congress. Candidates are representatives and agents of their parties, and the mandate won by victorious candidates is precisely a mandate to act cohesively in pursuit of that program. In contrast to the party in public office of the elite party, which may be united but is neither disciplined nor accountable to any central authority, the party in public office of the mass party in principle is supervised and disciplined by its party central office acting in the name of the party on the ground.

Catch-All Parties

Mass parties could organize the expanded electorates of the 20th century far more effectively than the informal networks of the old elite parties could do. Moreover, the idea of popular control of government through choice among unified parties was widely accepted, even among groups that did not support the mass parties themselves.

These successes forced the mass parties' competitors to adapt. Two further successes led to adaptation on the part of many mass parties as well. Electoral success altered the balance within the mass parties; particularly once they entered cabinets, or even formed governments on their own, members of the party in public office were far less willing to accept the subordinate position assigned to them by the mass party ideal. Furthermore, once in office the mass parties implemented policies that ameliorated the conditions of the groups they represented and transferred many of the social welfare functions that the parties and their ancillary groups had performed to the state. In doing so, however, they also undermined the social conditions that made a strategy of encapsulation possible.

The result was the emergence of what Kirchheimer (1966) described as the catch-all party, but which also has been described as the "electoral-professional" party (Panebianco 1988) and the "rational-efficient" party (Wright 1971a). On the surface, the catch-all party may look very much like a mass party, but several changes in orientation and practice mark it as a different type. Most fundamentally, the party in public office begins to think of itself as a potential government responsible to the nation as a whole, rather than as the agent of a particular sectional interest. Moreover, having personally experienced the rewards of office, it comes to value electoral victory over ideological or sociological purity. It comes to prefer a strategy of vote-mongering over one of encapsulation. All of these lead it to want to be free of the control of the party on the ground. (On the value of members, see Katz 1990; Scarrow 1996.)

The membership base of the party on the ground remains important in the catch-all party, at least initially, both as a font of political resources and as a legitimizing touchstone, but there is a tendency for the party central office to shift from being the agent of the party on the ground overseeing the party in public office to being the agent of the party in public office managing the party on the ground. In effect, the members become organized cheerleaders for the party leadership. Furthermore, as campaigning has changed to emphasize television and polling rather than rallies and personal canvassing, national campaigns and personalities rather than local activity and candidates, and professional consultants rather than party bureaucrats, money, which can come from many sources, has become relatively more important, whereas labor and local knowledge, two resources that the members were uniquely able to provide, have become less important (Bowler and Farrell 1992b; Butler and Ranney 1992).

The catch-all model entails its own conception of party democracy. Conflict is not about ends, which are agreed, or about ideologies, which have "ended" (Bell 1988), but rather about means. Parties are not the champions of particular interests, but brokers among interests and between interests and the state. The responsibility of the members of the party in public office to the people is direct, rather than being mediated by the external party organization, and therefore they are entitled to decide the line the party will take in government.

Cartel Parties

Developments contemporaneous with, and in some cases flowing from, the rise of the catch-all party, confronted nearly all major parties with a number of common problems. As shown in Table 4.2, the period since the late 1960s has seen a decline in party membership in nearly all European systems, if not in absolute terms then both relative to the size of the electorate and relative to the resources required for effective political competition (Katz, Mair et al. 1992). External and historical forces (accumulated debts, globalizing economies, etc.) have limited the freedom of action of any party in power (Rose and Davies 1994). Independent interest groups and citizen initiatives challenge the claim of parties uniquely to represent the people. The muting of conflict implicit in the catch-all strategy has lowered the policy stakes of party competition and has made it easier for politicians of all stripes to do business with one another. At the same time, the professionalization of politics has raised the personal costs of defeat, particularly for the party in public office. But even more than with policy compromise, the intensity and costs of competition over office can be contained by sharing, especially over a period of time. Thus, the situation is ripe for the formation of a cartel, in which no party definitively wins, but neither does any party definitively lose.

According to some interpreters (Katz and Mair 1995), this is what has been happening in most of the industrial democracies over the past three decades. The cartel, if there is one, is implicit, but nonetheless potentially very significant. Certainly, cartel-like behavior can be observed in many arenas. There has been a gradual inclusion of virtually all significant parties in national governments and a widening of the range of acceptable coalitions. (See chap. 3 in this volume.) Nearly all significant parties can expect to be in office at the national level some of the time, and at the subnational level virtually all of the time. Even at the national level, the distinction between government and opposition has become blurred, as all-party compromise and sharing of patronage become more common. Various provisions (restrictions on ballot access, artificial thresholds for representation) aimed at protecting the established parties from new competitors have been introduced into electoral laws.

Perhaps the most significant development, however, has been the introduction of state subventions. In their role as governors, the parties partially solved the problem of dependence on decreasingly adequate internally generated resources by providing themselves with subsidies from the state. Although these generally have been justified with reference to the essential role of parties in the maintenance of democratic government, they also have contributed to a change in the character of the parties and hence also of the

TABLE 4.2 Party Membership as a Percentage of the Total National Electorate

	First Election in the 1960s	Last Election in the 1980s
Austria	26.2	21.8
Belgium	7.8	9.2
Denmark	21.1	6.5
Finland	18.9	4.2
West Germany	2.5	4.2
Italy	12.7	9.7
Netherlands	9.4	2.8
Norway	15.5	13.5
Sweden	22.0	21.2
United Kingdom	9.4	3.3

SOURCE: Katz, Mair et al. 1992.

democracies supposedly being maintained. In particular, state subventions typically were given first and most generously to the party in public office, thus partially freeing it from dependence on, and control by, the party on the ground.

Often, state support has been accompanied by state regulations enforcing internal party democracy, but rather than allowing the party on the ground to control the party in public office, this may actually make the party in public office more independent. Previously, the party on the ground spoke through representative institutions, and this nurtured a class of activists and middle-level elites who could challenge and potentially control the party in public office. New technology, in particular allowing central, computerized membership records and direct mail, may allow the party in public office to appeal directly to the members and to be legitimated directly by them, without the intervention of the party apparatus. (See chap. 6 in this volume.) But because the ordinary members tend to be less extreme in their views and more deferential to leadership than the activists, this can be a way of marginalizing rather than empowering the party on the ground.

As with the other party models, the cartel model entails a particular vision of democracy. Competition is not about ideology or even issues, it is about managerial competence. Even the possibility of "turning the rascals out" is limited by the fact that no major party ever is definitively out. Democracy comes to be defined not by the capacity of citizens to direct government but merely by the fact of electoral choice. Choice requires parties, and so the state guarantees the provision of parties much as it guarantees the provision of hospitals or schools, and parties, rather than being the tools or leaders of civil society against the state, become part of the state apparatus. Elections may appear to some to have become, in Bagehot's (1966, 61) term, "dignified parts" of the government.

A number of the characteristics of these party types are summarized in Table 4.3. Although these models have been presented as separate types that result from a linear evolution, actual parties tend to involve elements of more than one type, and indeed many struggles internal to parties involve at least in part debate over which model the party should follow. Much of the politics of the British Labour party in the 1970s and 1980s, for example, may be characterized as a struggle over whether the party would adhere more to the mass party model (dominance by the generally more left-wing activist members) or the catch-all model (dominance by the professional politicians).

The Communist parties of Eastern Europe were structured as mass parties, although with some differences in both form and practice derived from their hegemonic position and their claim to represent the only legitimate class. In contrast to Western Europe, where the mass party model legitimized the idea of a party controlled by its members, the Communist experience tended to delegitimize not only a particular organizational form, but the idea of party altogether. Particularly after the breakup of the forum or consensus parties that led the transition from Communist rule, parties have tended to show many features of the cartel model. They tend to have the organizational structure of the mass or catch-all models (chairman, executive, geographically defined layers of organization, national congress), but given widespread antipathy toward the idea of party and the absence of the social basis for mass parties (a strongly differentiated society, strong organizations like trade unions, etc.), they generally have very small formal memberships (Olson 1993). They are heavily dependent on the state for their resources. And, of course, the realities of the world economic system constrain the degree to which fundamental questions can be disputed in domestic politics. On the other hand, the increased strength of the successor parties to the Communists, with their stronger infrastructure, and intensification of ethnic and other rivalries may lead parties to more closely approximate the mass party model in the medium term.

TABLE 4.3 Models of Party and Their Characteristics

Characteristics	Elite Party, 19th Century	Mass Party, 1880-1960	Catch-All Party, 1945-	Cartel Party, 1970-
Degree of inclusion	Restricted suffrage	Enfranchisement and mass suffrage	Mass suffrage	Mass suffrage
Distribution of political resources	Highly restricted	Relatively concentrated	Less concentrated	Relatively diffused
Basis for claims to support	Ascribed status	Representation of group	Policy effectiveness	Managerial skills, efficiency
Pattern of electoral competition	Managed	Mobilization	Competitive	Contained
Nature of party work and campaigning	Irrelevant	Labor intensive	(mixed)	Capital intensive
Principal source of party's resources	Personal contacts	Members' fees and contributions	Contributions from a wide variety of sources	State subventions
Relations between members and party elite	Elite are the "ordinary" members	Bottom up (pace Michels); elite accountable to members	Top down; members are organized cheerleaders for elite	Stratarchy; mutual autonomy
Character of membership	Small and elitist	Large and homogeneous; actively recruited and encapsulated; membership a logical consequence of identity; emphasis on rights and obligations	Membership open to all (heterogeneous) and encouraged; rights emphasized but not obligations; membership marginal to individual's identity	Neither rights nor obligations important (distinction between members and nonmembers blurred); emphasis on members as individuals rather than as organization; members valued for contribution to legitimizing myth
Party channels of communication	Inter-personal networks	Party provides its own channels of communication	Party competes for access to nonparty channels of communication	Party gains privileged access to state-regulated channels of communication

SOURCE: Katz and Mair 1995.

Parties, Candidates,
and Campaign Finance

The sources and uses of funds are among the key features distinguishing types of parties. These questions of finance, like the organization of parties, also relate strongly to the character of democracy.

Concern that elections will be tainted by disproportionate or inappropriate spending by or on behalf of candidates greatly predates modern conceptions of democracy. Candidates' offers of hospitality to prospective voters were limited in the Roman Republic, and an analogous prohibition of "treating" and excessive spending by candidates was introduced in Britain as early as 1695. As parties developed, and in many countries supplanted individual candidates as the primary organizers and financers of campaigns, they increasingly were subjected to regulation as well. In some countries, however, the myth that elections are contested by individual candidates rather than by parties continues to limit the effectiveness of campaign finance regulation.

Regulation of campaign spending and contributions necessarily limits freedom of speech; particularly in an era of mass electorates, the freedom to speak is far less significant than the freedom to disseminate one's speech, yet the means of effective dissemination—broadcasting, hiring a hall, displaying posters, advertising in the print media—all cost money. As the U.S. Supreme Court observed in striking down the expenditure limits of the Federal Election Campaign Act, "Expenditure ceilings impose direct and substantial restraints on the quantity of political speech" (*Buckley v. Valeo,* 424 U.S. 1, 57 [1976]). Where such limits have been accepted, it has been on the ground that unrestricted spending both gives unfair advantage to those interests with privileged access to money and makes elected officials excessively dependent on contributors at the expense of being responsive to the people at large (Alexander and Shiratori 1994).

Regulations concerning campaign (and other political) finance can be divided roughly into two categories: those concerning expenditure and those concerning contributions and other forms of income. Simplifying, the first are intended to prevent candidates or parties from buying elections, and the second are intended to prevent those with money from buying candidates. Each of these types of regulation then can be directed at any combination of candidates as individuals, parties, and other individuals or groups. Finally, the regulations can take the form of limitations or prohibitions on specific kinds or total amounts of expenditure or contribution, or they can merely require disclosure. (For extended discussions of these issues, see Seidle 1991; Alexander and Shiratori 1994.) Table 1.5 (chap. 1, this volume) summarizes the current variety of financial regulations in force in the major democracies.

Expenditure Controls

Expenditure limits can either restrict the total amount a candidate or party may spend, or they can limit the amount spent in particular ways, including the possibility that some forms of expenditure will be banned altogether. British and Canadian limits on spending by candidates (Britain) and both candidate and parties (Canada) based on constituency population illustrate the first type, and the French ban on paid broadcast advertising illustrates the second.

Three questions are central to the effectiveness of expenditure controls. The first is, to whom do the limits apply? As the British experience indicates, the entire exercise may be rendered nugatory if parties are excluded from the limitations; in 1983, for example, the Labour and Conservative parties spent more than three times the total amount allowed to their candidates (Butler and Butler 1986, 228, 248). Further complications are added by the possibility of spending on behalf of candidates or parties by individuals or groups that are not formally connected to either. The response in Britain and New Zealand has been to ban all spending supporting a particular candidate unless authorized by the candidate's agent and counted against the allowable limit. In India, on the other hand, such spending has (since 1974) been specifically excluded from control. Spending by candidates is not limited in the United States (except for presidential candidates who voluntarily accept spending limits in exchange for public finance), nor are "independent expenditures" made by nonparty groups without consultation with a candidate's own organization. Spending by parties on behalf of federal candidates, however, is treated as a contribution (see below) and is regulated under this guise.

One step beyond "independent expenditure" to support named candidates or parties is advertising in favor of specific policies. Even if no party or candidate is named, such advocacy advertising can have a significant effect on an election if it addresses questions on which the commitments of the candidates are particularly clear. This kind of activity may be used by interest groups, or by supporters of a party or candidate, to circumvent campaign spending limits, but it is virtually impossible to control without abandoning principles of free speech altogether.

The second central question is, what counts as an expenditure subject to control? One problem is the treatment of expenditures that are not directly related to the campaign of an identifiable candidate but that nonetheless may substantially contribute to it. British exclusion from control of spending on behalf of a party, rather than any of its particular candidates, is paralleled by American exclusion of "party building activities" like "get out the vote" campaigns or the 1980 "Vote Republican, for a Change" campaign. A second problem is the accounting of noncash or below-market-value transactions; in Canada, for example, if a self-employed individual donates services for which he or she normally would be paid, the value of those services must be counted as an expenditure by the candidate supported (Boyer 1983, 73). Because the most effective campaigning is likely to be that which looks like public service rather than self-aggrandizement, the use of the perquisites of office to benefit the reelection of the incumbent becomes a third problem. This is especially the case in the United States because of the scale of facilities that members of Congress have given themselves. Although the use of these facilities for overtly electoral purposes is illegal, the distinction is not always easy to draw. One answer is that constituent service becomes self-advertising if it comes too close to an election, for which reason congressional mass mailings, for example, are forbidden within 60 days of any election in which the member is a candidate.

As this suggests, the third central question is one of timing, when do the limits begin? This is particularly significant in the context of personal campaigning, because advertising for a private business (e.g., by a lawyer) can have significant spillover effects for a political campaign as well. In some systems, the applicability of spending limits is triggered by the calendar—either on a fixed date or a specified number of days before the election will be held. In others, the trigger is some action by the candidate or party. Thus, British parties avoid formally selecting candidates until an election is actually called (until then, they have "prospective candidates") to avoid the imposition of the strict limits applied to candidates.

Although it is easy to talk about a well-defined "formal" campaign period, the campaign for one election really begins almost immediately after the conclusion of the last election. The effectiveness of spending limits is seriously undermined if they are applied only to the few weeks before the election. Because New Zealand's controls only apply during the 3 months before an election, parties have been able to evade them simply by prepaying many expenses (Penniman 1980a, 90). Pre-1988 French restrictions applied only during the official 3-week campaign, making them largely irrelevant (Avril 1994, 90).

Control of Contributions

The other side of financial regulation is the control of contributions. These fall under three main headings: limits on the acceptable source of contributions, limits on the acceptable amounts, and requirements concerning disclosure.

In the United States and Canada, early limits on acceptable donors were introduced by agrarian interests deeply suspicious of the power of business. The Tilman Act (1907) prohibited contributions from federally chartered banks and corporations. A similar ban was introduced the next year in Canada, but it proved ineffective because it applied only to candidates and not to parties, the existence of which the law did not recognize. Unions were included in the prohibition in 1920 in Canada, and in 1943 in the United States. Other frequently prohibited donors include foreigners, public employees, and state or semistate agencies.

One justification for barring union contributions has been that the union's majority should not be able to use funds collected from all members to support candidates that the minority opposes. A similar argument might be raised with regard to minority shareholders in corporations. Whatever the merit of this argument, the problem can be solved with measures less extreme than total prohibition. For example, since 1913 British unions have been allowed to contribute to political campaigns provided that (a) they raise the funds contributed through a political levy that is kept separate from regular union funds, (b) the creation of the political fund be approved by ballot of the members, and (c) any member so desiring may "contract out" of the political levy without penalty. In the United States, the employees or members of an organization that is barred from making political contributions can form a political action committee (PAC), with substantially the same effect.

Even if acceptance of contributions from some groups is not prohibited, an attempt may be made to limit the concentration of influence in a few hands by limiting the *amount* that may be accepted from a single source. For such limits to be effective, however, total contributions from a single source must be limited as well. For example, the American Hatch Act's (1940) limit of $5,000 per year on individual contributions to a candidate or political committee was easily circumvented by multiplying the number of nominally separate committees all supporting the same candidate. After being modified several times and repealed in 1972, contribution limits were reimposed in the United States in 1974 in the wake of the Watergate scandal. Japan introduced similar, but apparently less effectively enforced, restrictions after the Lockheed scandal. Under the simpler circumstances of a party-oriented electoral system, Spain in 1985 limited individual contributions to a party to 1 million pesetas. With a candidate-oriented electoral system, French law limits contributions from individuals to FF 30,000 in a single election, and for corporate bodies (including parties) to 10 percent of the legal spending limit for the office.[2] Donations to parties by individuals and corporate bodies are limited to FF 50,000 and FF 500,000 per year, respectively.

Financial Reporting

Although a requirement that expenditures, contributions, or both be reported may supplement other restrictions, more often it is a substitute for them. Thus, when the Canada Elections Act of 1974 introduced the requirement that all contributions over C$100 be reported, it repealed the earlier bans on corporate and union contributions. In the United States, however, the Federal Election Campaign Act not only limits contributions but also requires federal candidates to list all contributors, and all recipients of expenditures, of over $200 in a single year.

The intention of reporting requirements is to fight potential corruption or influence buying and selling with the cold light of publicity. For this to be achieved, several things are necessary. First, the reports must be public and timely. Ideally, reports should be available in time to allow a candidate's opponents to publicize any questionable transactions before the election. Reports that can be delayed long after interest in the election has waned are unlikely to be of much deterrent value. American law, which requires quarterly reports, plus a report filed no later than 12 days and complete through the 20th day before the election and a report filed no more than 30 days and complete through the 20th day after the election, is particularly stringent in this regard. British candidates, who need only report expenditures, must do so within 35 days of announcement of the result. In Canada, on the other hand, candidates' agents have 4 months and parties have 6 months, and agents in Australia have 20 weeks. And indeed in some cases, such as Spain in 1989, it is not clear that the fact that reports are required implies that they must be made public.

Second, effective reports must be detailed and comprehensive. In the United States, Canada, and Spain, for example, even relatively modest contributions must be itemized; in Germany and Austria, on the other hand, only quite large contributions (roughly $6,000 and $10,000, respectively) need be listed individually; Italian reports simply list private donations as a single aggregate entry. Moreover, whereas American and Canadian reports are required from all entities attempting to influence the outcome of an election, Austrian, Italian, and Swedish party reports include only the finances of the central party, leaving local parties, ancillary enterprises, and independent factions to raise and spend funds without reporting. Conversely, only candidates, not the central parties, are required to report their expenditures in Britain. In either case, this opens the possibility that parties and politicians will be able to evade control by transferring questionable items from a budget that must be publicized to one that is not.

Third, reports are only likely to be effective if they are subject to independent audit, and the regulatory body must have the capacity to seek out violations. The Federal Election Commission in the United States provides an outstanding negative example in both respects. Although presidential campaign reports are audited, reports from other campaigns are audited only if the Commission receives a signed and notarized complaint and at least four Commissioners vote to pursue the investigation. Because the Commission consists of three Democrats and three Republicans, the chance that four votes will be mustered to investigate any but the most flagrant violations by major party candidates is slim. A further problem with Federal Election Commission enforcement is that the Commission has no investigators; although it once had them, they were eliminated, in part because of pressure from Congress (Jackson 1990, 7). In Canada, on the other hand, one reason why reports need not be filed immediately after the election is that they must be audited before filing.

Subsidies and the
Public Finance of Campaigns

The development of new campaign technologies has been associated with an explosion in the cost of political campaigns. According to Federal Election Commission reports, candidates for the U.S. House and Senate spent $459 million in the 1987-1988 elections cycle, more than double the figure from 10 years before. To this may be added the $250 million spent by candidates in presidential primaries and the $90 million spent by the major party presidential candidates. Similarly, campaign expenditures doubled in Austria between 1975 and 1990 (to Ös300 million), nearly doubled in Britain between 1983 and 1987 (to £ 22.4 million) and in Sweden between 1982 and 1988 (to SEK 70.4 million). The 1989 presidential campaign in Brazil is estimated to have cost in the neighborhood of $2 billion (Aguiar 1994). In the face of these dramatic increases in perceived need, and the failure of membership-generated income to keep pace, many parties have turned to the state for financial support, arguing that effective democracy requires vigorous parties and campaigns. Public support has also been justified by claiming that the alternative is excessive dependence of parties and politicians on contributors. The arguments against public support are essentially the same, as Koole (1989, 210) has summarized the debate in the Netherlands:

> First, public subsidies are thought to reinforce the status quo of the party system. Secondly, the danger of manipulation and control by the state would be enhanced. Thirdly, the distance between elite and grass roots would increase because the parties would no longer have to rely financially on their members.

That public support of parties and campaigns has become virtually universal among democracies is evidenced by Table 1.5 (chap. 1). In general terms, public support can take any or all of three forms. Least subject to objections of the sort that Koole cites are indirect supports, such as making political contributions deductible against income tax or maintaining artificially low prices for goods and services required by the parties or candidates (e.g., the requirement that American broadcasters charge candidates the lowest rates charged for comparable time). Second, candidates or parties can be provided with goods or services without charge directly by the state. The most common supports of this type are the provision of free broadcasting time, mailing of election addresses, and meeting halls. Finally, most controversial, and increasingly common, is the provision of cash.

One of the attractions of indirect supports is that they do not require the state to make overt decisions regarding allocation. The others, however, force the state to decide which candidates or parties are eligible to receive support in the first place, and then to choose between two criteria of allocation: equality and proportionality. Equality has the advantage of apparent fairness and neutrality, as well as reflecting the fact that the costs of many forms of campaign activity are independent of the level of a party's support. On the other hand, it encourages candidacies motivated only by the availability of resources (e.g., the candidate of the "Connoisseur Wine Party" who used the free mailing provided to British candidates to advertise his wine shop) and the splitting of parties (particularly in highly proportional systems) to multiply the resources provided. The alternative of providing resources in proportion to support, whether measured by vote shares (e.g., Austria, Denmark, Mexico, Turkey), seats in the legislature (Belgium, Finland, Germany, Sweden), or private contributions raised (in the case of matching funds, as provided for American presidential primary candidates), however, tends to entrench the already strong.

Resources such as free mailings and use of meeting facilities generally are allocated on the basis of equal shares for all. The formula for the allocation of broadcasting time is the most variable. In France, Denmark, Italy, and Norway (where a party must have been officially recognized for at least 6 months), the policy has been one of strict equality. This has, for example, precluded direct debates in the first round of French presidential elections. Sweden and Britain have adhered to equality with regard to the big parties, but have given smaller and new parties less time. Canada, on the other hand, has allocated time in proportion to the number of seats a party holds in the House of Commons, with some time allocated to any party nominating candidates (and paying a deposit) in at least one-fourth of the ridings (constituencies).

Where significant direct cash subsidies are provided, they are invariably allocated roughly in proportion to strength. American public finance of presidential campaigns provides a particularly egregious example of the way in which such subsidies can entrench the status quo. First, all parties are divided into three classes: major parties (those whose presidential candidate received at least 25 percent of the vote in the previous election—that is, always and only the Democrats and Republicans); minor parties (those whose presidential candidate received between 5 and 25 percent of the vote in the previous election—generally none); and new parties (all others). Candidates of major parties who agree to accept no other contributions and to spend no more than $50,000 in personal and family funds receive equal public support ($20 million adjusted for inflation since 1974—$55.24 million in 1992) in advance of the election. Candidates of minor parties who agree to limit their spending to the total allowed to major party candidates receive a subsidy that is proportional to their previous support; were Ross Perot to be a candidate in 1996, he would be entitled to just under half the support given to the Democratic and Republican candidates. New party candidates also receive support in proportion to their strength, but based on the current election and paid only after the election has taken place.

Subsidies can be restricted to election campaigns (Australia, France, Germany, the United States) or they can be given for general party maintenance (Brazil, Colombia, Denmark, Finland, Germany, Japan, Norway, Sweden, Turkey). In the former case, they still can be given to the parties as organizations, or they can be paid directly to the candidates' independent organizations. Giving support directly to candidates, of course, tends to undermine the authority of the parties.

Conclusion

Parties are becoming increasingly expensive, and yet with such major issues as whether to have universal suffrage, a welfare state, a market economy apparently resolved, and with the parties' freedom of action on the small issues increasingly constrained by decisions of prior governments and the international economic environment, parties apparently have less to do. Moreover, with increases in education, leisure time, disposable income, and so on, ordinary citizens have less need of parties to speak for them or to channel their political activity.

Whether or not the major parties effectively have established a cartel, the old epigram that "two deputies have more in common, one of whom is a Socialist, than two Socialists have in common, one of whom is a deputy" has seemed to many to ring ever truer. As politicians of all parties have become more similar sociologically (middle class) and politically (moderate), there may appear to be less point in electoral competition and less reason for involvement in parties. When all parties are moderate and responsible, there is little opportunity for the disaffected to use the ballot box either to protest or to call for fundamental reform.

One response has been the growth of new parties not only outside the cartel but explicitly opposed to it. These have taken three general forms. First, a variety of "left-libertarian" and ecologist parties, most notably the Greens in Germany, have sprouted on the left. Second, these have been complemented by a number of neo-populist parties, including the National Front in France, the Northern Leagues in Italy, and the Progress parties of Scandinavia. In both cases, the grassroots organizations are extremely important. These two groups of parties differ in their value orientations and organizational styles—those on the left emphasizing postmaterialist issues (Inglehart 1990a) and an organizational structure reflecting participatory values and a hostility to formal leadership (Kitschelt 1989), whereas those on the right generally emphasize lower taxes and traditional social values and have been characterized by strong, in some cases charismatic, leaders. Finally, Ross Perot's "United We Stand" movement and, most spectacularly of all, Silvio Berlusconi's Forza Italia represent a third type of anti-party-system party—effectively the personal organization (in many respects, effectively the employees) of a single wealthy individual prepared to mount a campaign funded by his own resources. Although organizationally quite different from the first two types, all three are united in their disdain for the complacency of the established parties, the degree to which they appear to conspire to keep significant questions off the political agenda, and the degree to which they "feed at the public trough." Whether their antiparty zeal can survive electoral success remains to be seen.

Notes

1. Indirect membership was abolished in the Swedish case in 1990.
2. These limits are FF 500,000 for Parliament, except in districts with fewer than 40,000 inhabitants where the limit is FF 400,000, and FF 120 million for the presidency.

Interest Groups and
Social Movements

SYLVIA BASHEVKIN

Organized groups are among the most controversial topics of 20th-century political debate. At the same time as they have been attacked by their critics as selfish and destructive of the democratic process, they continue to be celebrated by their supporters as crucial, constructive actors in that process. Many of the harshest accounts of groups are contained in the memoirs of modern conservative politicians, including Margaret Thatcher and Ronald Reagan. Both describe what they view as the scourges of collectivism, the "special interests" in Reagan's (1990, 337) words or "rule of the mob" in Thatcher's (1993, 353) terms that fundamentally weaken individual liberties. Collective rights have been defended, by way of contrast, by participants in interest groups and social movements, and by moderate and left politicians. According to the pro-group point of view, interests are organized and, in the

AUTHOR'S NOTE: I wish to thank Yan Peng for her research assistance and the Social Sciences and Humanities Research Council of Canada for its support of the larger project from which this chapter is drawn.

words of philosopher Charles Taylor (1992), demand to be "recognized" as part of healthy democratic life.

Rather than engaging in a normative debate on the subject, this chapter addresses a series of specific empirical questions on both interest groups and social movements. What are they? How do they operate? How do we explain the success of organized groups? What are the effects of institutional structures on interests? Although the bulk of scholarly inquiry on groups is drawn from North American and Western European systems, this chapter will also consider interests in other political environments.

Defining Groups

Many different terms have been used in studies of groups in politics. These range from pressure group, interest group, lobby, and organized interest to the more sociological concepts of social movement organization and new social movement. This chapter refers to all of the former as interest groups and the latter as social movements although, as discussed below, the two categories do overlap in some cases. What interest groups and social movements share is a set of norms, beliefs, or values that keep the "interest" intact. These shared orientations are the glue binding together the group constituency, leading it to act as a coherent entity. Not all groups of people with common views necessarily organize as either interest groups or social movements; many remain as latent or potential interests, outside the formal political realm, until some crucial event or mobilizing process transforms the latent interest into a collective force. Student, antiwar, feminist, and environmental interests arguably existed long before they made headlines, beginning in the late 1960s, in Western Europe and North America. It was the vocal group articulation of these shared views and, over time, the public recognition of group demands that made the period after about 1968 significantly different from that which preceded it.

Interest groups, like social movements, are collectivities that have as their basis a shared outlook, identity, or framework of reference. The classic definition was provided by an American scholar, David Truman, in his 1951 book titled *The Governmental Process*:

As used here, "interest group" refers to any group that, on the basis of one or more shared attitudes, makes certain claims upon other groups in the society for the

establishment, maintenance, or enhancement of forms of behavior that are implied
by the shared attitudes. . . . These afford the participants frames of reference for
interpreting and evaluating events and behavior. (P. 33)

Truman's emphasis on shared norms and values helps to explain the basic
question of how interests cohere; because they attract or recruit people of like
mind, they are able to bring individuals together for collective action (Moe
1980, 157-8; Olson 1965). And because organized interests, like political
parties, function as social networks as well as political organizations, they
provide numerous nonpolitical or selective benefits to their supporters. Leading environmental groups including the Sierra Club, for example, offer
recreational programs for their members. One of the largest and most effective
interest groups in the United States, the American Association of Retired
Persons, provides a wide range of travel discounts (Hardin 1982; Putnam
1995).

The basis of shared values tends to vary enormously. In less complex
Yet it is clear that some groups find it more difficult to organize than others.
Interests that themselves contain class, geographical, ideological, or linguistic
differences may find it difficult to cohere, because potential sources of
division are present at all times. In some cases, governments may actively
intervene to support the establishment of group organizations across these
divides to advance a particular agenda. Efforts by the Canadian federal
government in the Trudeau years to encourage a national women's organization represented one such attempt; in subsequent years, the same constitutional conflicts that divided Canadians generally also led to splits within the
group (Vickers, Rankin, and Appelle 1993).

The basis of shared values tends to vary enormously. In less complex
societies, as British sociologist Herbert Spencer (1851) noted, interests may
be few in number and based on direct primary, especially familial and
religious, ties; as societies become increasingly urban and industrial, groups
tend to proliferate based on a diverse range of secondary and often indirect
affiliations such as class or profession. Whereas business groups, trade union
organizations, and medical associations are among the most prominent in
industrial societies, the range of organizations defending agricultural, wild-
life, hunting, educational, consumer, cultural, and other interests has continued to grow (Moodie and Studdert-Kennedy 1970, 63). Yet this seeming
explosion of new interests has not meant the disappearance of older, more
established ones. The Catholic Church, for example, has continued to play a

central role in local, national, and international debates over abortion and family planning policies, often in opposition to the positions adopted by newer women's groups (Staggenborg 1991).

Political scientists have focused on group efforts to influence or pressure (hence the term *pressure groups*) government decision makers. Researchers thus distinguish between collectivities that seek to hold power in a political system—notably political parties—and others that seek to *affect* the decisions of elected officials, bureaucrats, and judges. Interest groups can be differentiated from parties in that the former try to shape government policy without seeking themselves to hold formal state power (Eckstein 1960, 9-10; Castles 1967, 1). Many organized interests focus their activities on the electoral process; they may evaluate competing candidates and fund the campaigns of those who hold sympathetic positions. Interest groups that operate within the electoral process can be characterized as institutional participants, even though they may not be active in the political system for an extended period of time. A group might have a clear, short-term purpose that encourages people to mobilize rapidly—for example, a neighborhood group could form to pressure for a traffic signal near a school, win municipal approval for the signal, and disband, all within months. Longer-term, less episodic interest groups tend to be far more formal in organizational terms. Like political parties, associational groups usually collect dues from affiliated members, have relatively broad issue agendas, and organize as permanent vehicles to advance their claims; overall, their purpose as interest groups is to influence or lobby other actors in the policy process. As Graham Wilson (1990, 1) writes, "Interest groups are generally defined as organizations, separate from government though often in close partnership with government, which attempt to influence public policy. As such, interest groups provide the institutionalized linkage between government or the state and major sectors of society." Interest groups across a wide variety of political systems reflect this basic focus on shaping policy decisions, whether their purpose is broad and long range or narrow and short term.

Social Movements

The objectives of social movements contrast quite directly with those of interest groups. Although they share the same kinds of attitudinal and identity bases, movements are more pro-change, more challenging, vis-à-vis the institutional status quo than are interest groups (Inglehart 1990b). Social movements can be described as protest groups that mobilize their adherents in a more system-challenging manner than do either interest groups or political parties.[1] Rarely do social movements target a narrow governmental policy area for action, because their claims tend to involve broader societal transformation than can be effected through a single political decision. Social movements are characterized by a shared sense of group consciousness, identity, and solidarity (Heberle 1951) and by a history of collective exclusion from established parties and interest groups. As Kitschelt (1993b, 14) maintains, movements tend to follow from the experience of marginalization. Examples of social movements emerging in the 1960s and following in Western Europe and North America included student, peace, civil rights, environmental, and women's movements; what linked these "new social movements" was their determination to break with older left/right conventions of political discourse and, in some cases, to redefine what constituted public issues (Dalton and Kuechler 1990).

Studies of social movements frequently refer to system-challenging and transformational themes. Herbert Blumer (1951, 199) defines a movement as "a collective enterprise to establish a new order of life," meaning a fundamental cultural shift that will either be pursued or, conversely, opposed by movement adherents. Social movement participants, brought together by shared collective beliefs and goals that may grow out of pre-existing networks, therefore act on their larger institutional environment in a more engaged, less passive manner than their interest group counterparts (Oberschall 1973, 125). Given this more intensive form of collective engagement or mobilization, "one of the most significant end-products of social movements is the emergence and stabilization of new institutions and new forms of social organization" (Evans 1973, 17). Because movements adopt sweeping change agendas, their participants do not necessarily hold formal membership in any group; moreover, activists can differ considerably in their goals and values (Castles 1967, 7; McLaughlin 1969).

Variation within social movements can be seen among environmental and women's groups. Whereas some environmentalists, notably in Germany, have explicitly organized along formal party lines and sought representation in legislatures and cabinets via a Green party, many elsewhere have rejected the partisan route (Dalton 1993a, 1993b). Environmentalists who do not choose to form a separate party have been further divided between those who employ standard interest group lobby techniques (such as the Sierra Club) and others that pursue more high-profile, high-stakes confrontations (notably Greenpeace). Compared with the German Greens or the Sierra Club, Greenpeace is generally less likely to engage in standard electoral and lobbyist activities—or politics as usual—than it is to reject these approaches in favor of a more challenging "politics by other means."

Similarly, enormous differences exist among women's organizations, both within and across nations. At the same time as some feminists in North America and Western Europe have devoted their energies to pressing issues *within* established political parties, others have attempted to establish separate women's parties that compete directly with traditional formations. The Icelandic Women's party is among the best-known of these independent parties, but less successful parallels have been attempted in France, Canada, and elsewhere (Dominelli and Jónsdóttir 1988). Yet another type of women's group rejects within-party and separate party organization in favor of targeted interest group activity. Sustained lobbies to ensure abortion access have occurred in virtually all Western industrial systems since the 1960s, involving meetings with civil servants and politicians, petitions and postcard campaigns, letters to the editor, and media advertising. In periods of particular threat on the abortion issue, however, many of these same groups have changed gears and organized marches, vigils, demonstrations, and other kinds of protest in the streets. This social movement type mobilization attracted as many as 300,000 supporters to one Washington, D.C., march in 1989 (Staggenborg 1991, 138).

If, in general terms, parties attempt to win power, interest groups try to influence government decision makers, and social movements work to "change the world," then can the three categories overlap (Kitschelt 1990; Tarrow 1991; Rochon 1990, 112-4; Dalton 1993a, 1993b)? Environmental and women's organizations offer useful evidence on this point, as do trade union groups. In Western Europe and Canada, left-of-center political parties, affiliated labor movements, and pro-union lobby groups have tended to coexist within systems (Heberle 1951, 278; Castles 1967, 8; Wilkinson 1971, 30-1). The most tense periods in terms of relations among these varied formations have occurred while left parties were in power, because union interests have tended to view compromises by pro-labor governments as a betrayal of their support. For example, wage control policies introduced as "social contract" legislation in Britain and Canada clearly damaged relations between unions and left governments (Panitch and Swartz 1993). To some extent, turmoil among left/labor interests in these systems helped to ensure the subsequent election of conservative, pro-business parties.

If any factor can be said to link differing manifestations of a single underlying interest, it would appear to be movement identity. Groups that are united by a transformative social agenda tend to develop more diverse organizational vehicles to advance their collective values than do groups that begin with a narrower institutional or interest group framework. As Jane Jenson argues (1985), it is the "identity work" of social movements that gives rise to group consciousness that, in turn, assumes varied collective forms (see also Melucci 1988). By creating new identities and challenging established ones, environmental and women's movements can be seen as not only defining shared values for their groups but also generating many different organizational vehicles to advance those values.

Groups tend to develop strategies based on their institutional and ideological settings. German Greens operating in a competitive, multiparty environment were far more likely to obtain influence via the party system than were U.S. environmentalists working in a narrow, two-party framework. American women's groups seeking to maintain abortion access were less likely to organize massive demonstrations in Washington during the Carter years, when a relatively sympathetic president and Congress held office, than during the Reagan and Bush years, when almost no channels of communication were available to feminists other than the streets. The closing off of congressional, presidential, and bureaucratic avenues for conventional lobbyist work, combined with a growing sense of threat to abortion access in the courts, meant that crucial group resources were shifted toward movement style protest (Bashevkin 1994b).

Why So Many Interests?

The growth over time of interest groups and social movements has been attributed to many factors. Political science explanations emphasize the decline of political parties, meaning that fewer and fewer citizens identify with parties in a consistent manner over time, and that fewer and fewer parties seem capable of organizing issues in a coherent way for voters (Wattenberg 1991; Meisel 1991). Clearly, the rise of groups and the decline of parties are related, because parties see groups as fragmenting the policy process, consulting on their own with legislators and bureaucrats, and diverting media attention (see Dalton, chap. 13 in this volume).

Yet factors unrelated to parties are probably at least as significant to the rise of organized interests. As levels of formal education increased in Western systems after the Second World War, more citizens enjoyed access to the resources necessary for political engagement. Higher income, occupational prestige, personal confidence, sense of political efficacy, and skill in public communication tend to be positively related to formal education; as Verba, Nie, and Kim (1978, 73) argue based on a seven-case study, "in all nations, citizens appear to convert socioeconomic resources into political involvement." The fact that organized interests proliferated in the same affluent postwar period as access to higher education widened is hardly surprising (Schmitter 1981, 308).

Finally, a technological explanation of group growth holds considerable merit. Modern systems of transportation and communications permit interests to develop and cohere across large geographical distances, so that the direct face-to-face interaction that was once required to reinforce group identity is replaced by interaction via mass mailings, conference calls, or electronic mail (Petracca 1992, 25-6). Groups raise money for their activities through targeted telephone and mail campaigns that would not have been possible earlier in the 20th century. When public debate involves a key group issue, organized interests can go into action within hours to solicit support. During the period of the Clarence Thomas confirmation hearings before the U.S. Senate Judiciary Committee in 1991, issues of sexual harassment in the workplace and women's absence from senior legislative positions received unprecedented attention. This same period saw a massive increase in contributions to feminist lobby groups in Washington, D.C. (Bashevkin 1994b, 694). Similarly, women's groups in Australia mobilized rapidly during the 1980s in support of antidiscrimination legislation and in opposition to a consumption tax proposal (Sawer 1994).

Moreover, the basic collection of dues, organization of membership lists, and production of interest group literature has been altered and, arguably, made considerably easier by computerization and access to desk-top publishing. Groups are able to communicate with their members more efficiently and present arguments to their target audiences more effectively than ever before. Interest groups prepare postcards and petitions, for example, that are signed by supporters and sent to politicians; those same politicians often receive stacks of questionnaires from interest groups at election time, as part of an effort by groups to ascertain where candidates stand on relevant issues. This information is often channeled back to group supporters in an effort to build bloc voting within the constituency (Petracca 1992, 16).

Obtaining Group Voice

How are group claims heard and responded to by their target audience? What strategies are most effective? The first part of this question involves what social scientists term *voice,* meaning the public statement of group demands (Hirschman 1970). It is in the act of staking out interest group claims that cross-system variations become clear. Historically, the U.S. congressional system has involved the most numerous, diverse, and wealthiest interest groups in the Western industrialized world; over time, however, interest groups have become increasingly important elsewhere (Almond and Verba 1963; Pross 1986; Dragnich and Rasmussen 1982). Marian Sawer (1994), for example, has documented the significant growth since the 1970s in women's organizations in Australia. In terms of density of group membership within systems, the United States tends to maintain an edge in terms of noneconomic interests, but not economic ones (Wilson 1990, 88). Comparative measures of feminist movement density in the United States versus the United Kingdom in 1980, for example, indicate that the percentage of active feminists in the U.S. female population was approximately three times greater than in the British female population (Gelb 1989, 188-90). Data on unions tell a very different story, however, because less than 20 percent of employed Americans held union membership in the late 1980s, versus more than 40 percent in Britain. In both of these cases, as elsewhere, union density tended to decline markedly over time (Putnam 1995; LaPalombara 1987, 39-40; Wilson 1990, 88; Zermano 1990, 167).

If there has been a diffusion of innovation from the United States to other systems, it has primarily involved the second issue, group strategies. Traditional American methods whereby paid lobbyists working in national and state capitals met with elected politicians have given way to far more diverse influence strategies in both the United States and elsewhere. Interest groups increasingly work in coalitions to lobby bureaucrats, present their arguments in court, and make their case directly to the public via media interviews and advertising (Conway et al. 1995; Esberey and Skogstad 1991). As has been the case in political party development, this resort to different forms of voice is linked to a professionalization of interest groups whereby increasingly specialized paid staff and, frequently, outside consultants dominate group operations (Sabato 1981). Skilled pollsters and public affairs consultants, for example, may be engaged by an organized interest to study the reelection prospects of a key legislator to obtain access to and, ultimately, influence with that legislator.[2] Clearly, this type of group activity is most productive in the candidate-centered American system, where individual legislators conduct comparatively autonomous electoral campaigns and, once elected, operate relatively free of party discipline. As Richard Katz (this volume, chap. 4) points out, limited controls on campaign spending by organized groups in the United States provide an additional incentive for electoral involvement.

Yet the professionalized approach to interest group operations is hardly exclusive to the U.S. system. Attempts by American women's groups, for example, to raise money specifically toward the election of feminist legislators have generated spin-offs elsewhere. EMILY's List, established in the United States in 1985 "as a donor network and political resource for pro-choice Democratic women," served as the model for a similar effort in the British Labour party beginning in 1993 (Bashevkin 1994b, 693). In both the United States and the United Kingdom, EMILY's List was established as a way to recruit and fund viable female candidates. By attracting these women to the Democratic and Labour parties, and by building networks of motivated contributors who might not otherwise support the parties, both EMILY's Lists became effective interest groups within established parties. In the U.S. case, research suggests that over time, EMILY's became the leading recruiter, trainer, and funder of Democratic women (Young 1996).

In a party-structured system like the French one, groups have increasingly lobbied bureaucrats rather than politicians to obtain results (Ehrmann and Schain 1992, 190). Groups in France are themselves organized into thousands of government advisory or consultative committees, where representatives of interests meet regularly with civil servants. This arrangement constitutes one of the most developed systems of group-bureaucratic consultation in the world. Generally, representatives of influential groups tend to view these consultations as more useful than do members of weak interests; French farmers, for example, report more enthusiasm than business and labor representatives (Wilson 1983). Whereas agricultural interests were involved in committees that met frequently and made important decisions, business and labor participated in discussions that were less frequent and less likely to formulate official policy.

The strategies used by social movements to obtain voice tend to differ from the largely institutional channels used by interest groups. As Paul Wilkinson (1971) notes, movements do not necessarily exclude lobbies and similar approaches from their repertoire of activities, but neither do they exclude illegal or violent acts to bring attention to their claims (see also LaPalombara 1987, 169-70). In Wilkinson's (1971, 27) words, "A social movement is a deliberate collective endeavour to promote change in any direction and by any means, not excluding violence, illegality, revolution or withdrawal into 'utopian' community." It is for this reason that movement activities may involve protest rallies, marches, demonstrations, sit-ins, takeovers of public buildings, and illegal acts (e.g., wildcat strikes or the burning of draft cards; see McAdam 1988).

The willingness of movement participants to engage in these kinds of acts can be explained by reference to their underlying commitment to social transformation. Whether the purpose has been to stop a war, halt pollution, extend rights to blacks and women—or, conversely, to oppose what conservatives saw as the unraveling of society because of the threat from pro-change groups—movement activists are linked by their frustration with the status quo. This "stirring among the people," as Rudolph Heberle (1951, 6) described it, is fostered and reinforced by the kind of mass action that social movements engage in; massive demonstrations, after all, can enhance movement solidarity far more effectively than would an arranged visit by a few paid lobbyists to a member of cabinet.

Although social movements may adopt interest group strategies from time to time, and vice versa, movements are usually more willing to exploit mass, spontaneous, and potentially unlawful avenues for gaining voice. In 1995, for example, the Greenpeace vessel *Rainbow Warrior* challenged a French government decision to resume nuclear testing in the South Pacific. By sailing inside a French-declared exclusion zone, Greenpeace knowingly risked seizure of the ship—just as it had in a long series of other environmental protests around the world. In terms of gaining media exposure and public support, Greenpeace was in many respects better off once the seizure occurred; as one activist in the group observed, "It's public pressure that makes change, and Greenpeace knows that."[3] In international terms, Greenpeace membership in the mid-1990s was about 3.1 million, with annual revenues of approximately $200 million (Matas 1995).

Overall, according to Tarrow (1983, 8), the broader and more flexible the "tactical repertory" of a movement, the more likely it is to be successful. Because feminists and environmentalists could adopt partisan and interest group as well as social protest strategies, they have been able to temper their message to suit specific settings. Moreover, the novelty of movement activities can prove significant in shaping media and governmental responses. Graham Wilson (1990, 82) argues that the long tradition of direct, publicly disruptive social action by groups in Italy and France meant that new movements of the late 1960s and following received less attention in those systems than in more quiescent cases like Scandinavia, Britain, and the Netherlands. One explanation of group militance in Mediterranean cases is the fragmentation of interests; bold action by an organization attracts attention and diverts it from competitors in the same sector—except that the strategy tends to be overworked (Ehrmann and Schain 1992; LaPalombara 1987). When challenging interests burst onto a scene where confrontation has been uncommon, public attention is immediately focused on the new claimants. During the Thatcher years in Britain, bitter conflict between the government and unionized miners led to a 1984 pro-union march by 10,000 women. Protests during 1982 at the Greenham Common peace camp attracted about 30,000 women (Bashevkin 1996). These mobilizations by a previously diffident group in a diffident political system were unprecedented, and they suggest why the peace camp was known to all but 6 percent of British survey respondents in 1983 (Rochon 1990, 107).

Models of Group Activity

Broader efforts to explain the ability of groups to capture public attention and win support for their claims often begin with the use of conceptual models. Many early theories of group influence evolved from a fundamental unease in the United States with what was called the "power elite" school. Represented by the postwar writings of C. Wright Mills (1956), Floyd Hunter (1953), and other sociologists, the power elite stream maintained that a small, cohesive, and at times covert elite controlled American government, thus limiting the opportunities available to citizens for political participation. The development of a competing conceptual framework began in full force during the 1950s and early 1960s, when David Truman (1951) and Robert Dahl (1961) published major statements of what became known as the pluralist perspective. In *The Governmental Process,* Truman argued that struggles among competing groups formed the essence of democratic politics; the major role of government, in his view, was to establish and maintain orderly relations among them. According to Truman, government regulated this interaction in such a way as to produce stable intergroup relations and social equilibrium. The existence of multiple points of access for diverse interests meant that group participation in public policy making was virtually assured. This pluralist notion of open competition among groups was advanced further by Dahl (1961). His pivotal study of local politics in New Haven argued that no single power elite but rather a set of influential groups shaped municipal decision making; government decisions were thus a balanced response to the demands of competing groups.

In explaining the extent to which collective demands were satisfied, both Truman and Dahl emphasized the importance of internal group charac- teristics, especially organizational resources. Dahl (1961), for example, noted that the socioeconomic status, media access, and education of group leaders played an important role in determining policy influence. Similarly, Truman (1951) maintained that the "strategic social position" of groups, as well as their internal organizational cohesion, helped to explain success in the policy arena. Although neither Truman nor Dahl developed a concrete model of the societal paradigm, their work and that of subsequent writers suggests that four basic variables determine policy success, namely, group resources, cohesion, expertise, and representativeness.[4] Each has a specific relationship to govern- mental action: group resources, in that the extent of financial and human resources controlled by a group would be positively associated with policy influence; group cohesion, in that the degree of organizational control, disci- pline, and unity would be positively related to policy success; group expertise, in that policy and administrative knowledge would be positively associated with organizational influence; and representativeness, in that a favorable "strategic position" or comprehensive group standing in a policy domain would be positively related to its success.

It must be noted that these propositions follow from a literature that for the most part assumes between-group competition to be open, fair, and ultimately resolved in favor of the interest with the highest measures on all four factors. In a pluralist environment, groups are seen as a crucial intermediary between individual citizens and a potentially overpowerful state; they are not viewed as a threat to the democratic process. It can thus be hypothesized that if Group A has extensive resources but only moderate cohesion, expertise, and representativeness, then it is less likely to achieve its policy objectives than a competing Group B that commands extensive resources as well as high cohesion, expertise, and representativeness. Group A, in turn, would be more likely to obtain policy success than a competing Group C that had only limited resources, cohesion, expertise, and representativeness.

Just as the pluralist view developed in reaction to power-elite studies, so too have subsequent approaches evolved in response to this societal model. In particular, critics have taken issue with its treatment of challenging or innovative issue areas that were not already on the public agenda. Peter Bachrach and Morton Baratz (1963), drawing on E. E. Schattschneider's (1960, 71) notion that "some issues are organized into politics while others are organized out," propose that the pluralist view overlooks "non-decisions," a realm beyond the status quo policy arena in which organized interests are unlikely to obtain open and unfettered access.

Following Schattschneider's (1960) observation, further questions have been raised about the extent to which intergroup competition is consistent with social equality. As neo- or postpluralist writers acknowledge, societal interests often compete in an unbalanced manner, just as the state frequently intervenes to accommodate groups in a manner that reinforces existing inequalities. Arguing that governmental and specifically bureaucratic actors can pursue their own interests in the policy process, proponents of a state-centered view maintain that institutional preferences shape policy outcomes more directly than do simple group attributes. Neo-pluralists emphasize the distinction between favored or insider groups versus disadvantaged or outsider interests. The fact that some groups are systematically excluded means that their messages are not generally heard by elites.

Theda Skocpol (1979, xiii), in advocating a state-centered approach, argues for greater attention to "the specific interrelations of class and state structures and the complex interplay over time of domestic and international developments." This plea for "bringing the state back in" to political analysis formed the pivot of Skocpol's contribution in 1985 to a text she edited with Peter Evans and Dietrich Rueschemeyer. Titled *Bringing the State Back In,* this collection helped to establish a counter-pluralist, essentially statist model.

Among researchers who had become frustrated with the societal paradigm, the emergence of an alternative theoretical framework provided a welcome change. As John Ikenberry, David Lake, and Michael Mastanduno (1988, 7) suggest in their study of U.S. trade policy, the pluralist approach was limited by its view of "policy outcomes on any particular issue [as] a function of the varying ability of groups to organize and give their interests prominence in the policy process. In this approach, government institutions essentially provide an arena for group competition, and do not exert a significant impact on the decisions that emerge." If pluralists claimed that policy success was determined by the outcome of open competition among competing groups, then critics in the statist stream maintained that institutional structures provided far more than a fixed landscape for group interaction. Instead, state actors often intervened to direct policy outcomes in a manner consistent with their own institutional interests and abilities.

The challenge of specifying the effects of institutional factors was taken up in a number of case studies. Work by Peter Katzenstein (1986), Stephen Krasner (1978), and others identified three key variables, namely, state preferences, capacity, and autonomy. The first of these factors was illustrated in research on U.S. national security policy by Krasner and by Graham Allison (1971). Both authors suggest that foreign policy elites can develop preferences that are distinct from and potentially at odds with those of group actors. Instead of viewing policy decisions as passively driven by organized interests, then, these analysts portray state actors as driving the process—wearing an identifiably institutional rather than societal set of lenses.

Second, the statist literature has elaborated a concept of institutional capacity, borrowing to some extent from the pluralist emphasis on resources. Capacity is defined as the ability of the bureaucratic state to execute its actions and, logically, depends on the ability to concentrate, coordinate, and exploit governmental resources. Finally, autonomy acts as a further brake on institutional action. State elites may be variously dependent on or independent of societal groups, such that those officials who possess extensive autonomy are likely to formulate goals and pursue them with little reference to organized interests.

As is the case with the pluralist view, authors who employ a statist approach have not produced a concrete model. What their work suggests is a framework within which bureaucratic elites hold preferences that may be distinct from those of group actors. The former are able to direct policy along paths congruent with their preferences to the extent that they are capable of mobilizing resources to execute actions, and to the degree that they are autonomous or independent of societal actors.

In terms of propositions, the statist approach suggests that a highly capable and autonomous state Unit A that possessed distinct preferences would be more effective in policy terms than a less capable and autonomous Unit B whose preferences were unclear. Moreover, in comparing interactions with societal groups, state Unit A would be more likely to dominate and to control organized interests than Unit B, because Unit A could be expected to direct its various strengths toward controlling the institutional environment, shaping policy issues, or mobilizing new groups in a manner not available to Unit B.

A third major stream in the theoretical literature on groups is the corporatist one, which views organized interests as subordinate to a dominant liberal state or, alternatively, to an authoritarian one in cases such as Mexico (Camp 1993; Wiarda 1974). As Philippe Schmitter (1979, 13) writes:

> Corporatism can be defined as a system of interest representation in which the constituent units are organized into a limited number of singular, compulsory, noncompetitive, hierarchically ordered and functionally differentiated categories, recognized or licensed (if not created) by the state and granted a deliberate representational monopoly within their respective categories in exchange for observing certain controls on their selection of leaders and articulation of demands and supports.

Corporatist formations are contingent on interest groups operating as integral parts of, rather than external influences on, government activity. As Claus Offe (1981, 71) argues, social movement organizations are generally not involved in these arrangements because, for the most part, they lack the requisite levels of internal cohesion and external policy standing.

The state constitutes the apex of the corporatist system; it organizes a hierarchy within which interests operate vis-à-vis government as well as other groups. Corporatist models describe the incorporation of insider groups, so that favored groups play a structured and significant role in policy making. Competition among groups is thus far more limited than in the pluralist model, whereas the role of the state is more assertive and sustained. Unlike the statist model, the corporatist view emphasizes structured interaction among dominant states and subordinate groups, rather than highlighting only bureaucratic actors.

Liberal, neo-, or societal (as opposed to state or authoritarian) corporatism involves interest groups developing a monopoly on representation in a particular policy sector, within a larger democratic environment. Liberal corporatism usually requires centralized or peak organizations representing labor and business, each of which is able to speak credibly as the uncontested voice of the interest, and each of which is able to carry through on its commitments to other corporatist partners. Societal corporatism tends to be most fully developed in social democratic environments where governing parties have effectively placed labor interests on a par with business ones. As Schmitter (1981, 292) notes, neo-corporatism evolves "from below," and state corporatism emerges "from above." The latter is not voluntary, because it relates to "a conscious effort by those in power to mold the type of interest intermediation system most congenial with their authoritarian mode of domination" (Schmitter 1981, 292).

Applying the Models

As the empirical literature summarized below suggests, distinct models of group activity become blurred when applied to actual systems. Most liberal democracies tend to reflect blends of pluralism, with direct competition among interests; statism, with government elites limiting the range of what groups do; and corporatism, with regimes directly coordinating or channeling group participants.

If existing systems, mixed as they are, can be said to approximate these three ideal types, then the United States is probably the closest to a pluralist model. Relatively weak patterns of party organization, decentralized power structures that have become even more fragmented over time (notably as a result of post-Watergate changes in the Congress), and a long tradition of distrust for government all characterize the American environment and contribute to multiple points of entry for group interests. The number of interest groups operating in Washington, D.C., reflects clear expansion over time: From about 1,100 registered lobbyists in the early 1960s, this figure rose to more than 23,000 by 1987 (Petracca 1992, 13). A veritable "cause industry" emerged in Washington, from membership-based groups and professional associations to corporations, foreign governments, and even pro-lobby lobbies devoted to protecting the industry. Political action committees (known as PACs) represent the most visible evidence of interest group growth in this period. Rather than using a traditional system of lobbying individual legislators who are already elected, PACs raise and spend money to ensure both the electoral success of sympathetic candidates and the defeat of unsympathetic ones. By the late 1980s, PACs in the United States numbered in the thousands and, on an annual basis, spent hundreds of millions of dollars (Petracca 1992, 20). As Richard Katz (this volume, chap. 4) points out, these increases over time directly parallel a generalized growth in campaign spending.

Accounts of the British and French systems suggest a mixture, involving dominant statist traditions with some liberal corporatist arrangements in individual policy fields. Compared with the U.S. case, both Britain and France are strong states with powerful, autonomous political executives that tend to limit open, pluralist group access. Economic policy making in Britain during the two world wars and through the late 1970s was based on an implicit form of neo-corporatism involving the state, business, and labor. Over time, labor was increasingly excluded from the system (Panitch 1977). French governments have recognized insider groups as opposed to excluded, outsider ones; they have subsidized some interests including trade unions. Yet the literature generally maintains that France is not a corporatist system at the national level (see review in Wilson 1983). French labor and business tend to be divided organizationally, meaning that varied groups compete to represent one constituency in a comprehensive and uncontested manner. This fragmentation of key interests outside the agricultural sector, government's own sense of being "above" politics, and the fierce independence of leading societal groups mean that macrolevel corporatism is simply not workable (Ehrmann and Schain 1992).

Japan can also be considered a hybrid form, in that it evolved in statist directions as well as neo-corporatist ones that excluded labor interests. Core economic departments including Finance as well as the Ministry of International Trade and Industry have high levels of administrative capacity and are able to maintain consultative ties with key interest representatives. Under the terms of limited corporatism, peak organizations speak for big business and have frequent and close contact with the government; generally, these groups are highly cohesive on matters of broad economic policy (Stockwin 1982). Purer examples of liberal corporatism include Austria, Sweden, and Germany, where a range of corporatist arrangements exists at both national and sectoral levels. In these cases, labor is included as a partner with the state and business and is less likely to be internally fragmented than in mixed environments (Cawson 1985).

Mexico is frequently cited as an example of authoritarian corporatism, in that the dominant state traditionally grants legal recognition to groups as official voices of a particular sector. Government thus stimulates the formation of, subsidizes, and controls groups. Camp (1993, 123) and Zermano

(1990, 178) argue that interests that do not conform experience harsh sanctions, as in the case of the petroleum workers' union in 1989. Union leaders who did not support Carlos Salinas's presidential candidacy were arrested, criminally charged, and replaced once he was inaugurated. Under the terms of state corporatism, government elites employ their resources "to disarm and co-opt dissidents" (Camp 1993, 126); the lure of power and money means that most group leaders comply by delivering their constituency to the dominant party in return for personal career ascendance. The state at that point essentially "owns" the interest and rewards the compliant group leadership for its behavior.

Over time, however, Mexican state corporatism may be in decline. A new generation of jobless, uneducated youths combined with lower levels of unionization and religious affiliation mean that top-down systems of collective organization are less and less effective. Despite the growth of new groups during the 1980s, Zermano (1990) argues, the vast majority of Mexicans remain excluded, marginalized, and not organized on their own; withdrawal into self or gangs is more common than group formation. In the case of Mexican peasant groups, Harvey (1990) claims that the state has increasingly intervened directly in the countryside, thus eliminating in many cases both the challenge of autonomous groups as well as the need to maintain older state-controlled ones.

Research Findings

Empirical studies indicate that among a myriad of interests variously organized, business groups are the most influential in most systems (Bauer, Pool, and Dexter 1963; Moe 1980, 191-9). As William Coleman (1988, 4) writes with reference to one case:

> There is a systematic bias in the Canadian system, which consistently gives the business community a better hearing and considers its demands and proposals more seriously when policies are being designed. This observation can be demonstrated in virtually any instance of public policy-making. And politicians should not necessarily be rebuked for this systematic bias: nothing could be more natural in a capitalist liberal democracy.

A long series of studies report that business groups retain a privileged position in that their claims are more likely to be heard, and subsequently acted upon in favorable terms, by decision makers.

Aside from finding pro-business bias, what other patterns have been noted by researchers? Elements of the literature confirm the importance of internal group factors. Studies of well-financed, cohesive, expert lobbies in policy areas where the organization in question virtually monopolizes the field tend to report positive outcomes from the perspective of group claims. For example, the literature on financial institutions indicates that banks are usually able to build effective, consistently influential sectoral associations (Coleman 1990, 102). In some instances, these associations have organized large public campaigns involving bank customers, as occurred in the United States over a 1983 tax amendment (Petracca 1992, 21). Conversely, research on groups with limited funds, significant internal divisions, minimal policy knowledge, and contested standing in a policy field suggests the reverse. Antipoverty organizations and child care lobbies in North America, for example, are usually less than effective lobbies (Piven and Cloward 1977; Norgren 1988; Haddow 1991; Phillips 1989).

Scholars in the neo-pluralist stream emphasize the importance of "political opportunity structure," or the attitudinal and institutional boundaries within which groups operate. Structural constraints, they argue, operate alongside internal organizational factors to shape group activity. Joyce Gelb's (1989, 2) analysis of women's movements in the United States, the United Kingdom, and Sweden maintains that differences "in the respective 'political opportunity structures' (i.e., institutions, alignments, and ideology), have patterned the development, goals, and values of feminist activists in each nation . . . movement structure and systemic differences have affected and constrained opportunities for movement impact within each nation." According to Gelb, British and Swedish women's groups after the late 1960s depended on close ties with existing trade union and party organizations, whereas American feminism developed as a far more autonomous and self-directed social movement—largely because of the differing opportunities for noneconomic interests in the United States versus elsewhere. This same set of factors has been employed to explain cross-national and cross-time patterns of environmental and worker protest (Dalton and Kuechler 1990; Tarrow 1991). Overall, this body of research indicates that to be influential, groups require a combination of favorable internal conditions combined with some degree of external access (Moe 1980, 158, 161).

Do federal arrangements (whereby jurisdiction is divided between national and subnational levels of government) constrain or enhance group activities? Truman (1951, 112) maintains that interests in federal systems tend to structure themselves in a manner that mirrors the broader federal arrangement. This decentralization limits group cohesion and effectiveness, because the organization is spread out geographically and, using dispersed resources, is forced to target multiple audiences for its message. Other authors propose the opposite argument, claiming that groups are advantaged by multiple access points in a decentralized as opposed to centralized system. The British unitary state, from this perspective, offers few opportunities for groups to influence decision makers; cabinet ministers and senior civil servants in a centralized system hold "a reliable power of veto" over group claims, whereas this veto is shared among many diverse actors in federal cases, especially the United States with its formal separation of powers (Moodie and Studdert-Kennedy 1970, 75).

If empirical research on this question presents any clear response, it is that groups adapt fairly rapidly to their institutional circumstances. Interest groups in the British system have traditionally worked to establish credibility where it matters, among state elites in London (Eckstein 1960; Beer 1982); newer social movements that face limited prospects for influence among these decision makers pursue their claims elsewhere, including in the British media and the European Court of Justice (Lovenduski and Randall 1993). In Japan, business and agriculture groups enjoy direct ties with politicians and bureaucrats, whereas outsider interests such as environmental groups have resorted to other avenues including the courts (Stockwin 1982, 161). Groups in federal systems have, quite pragmatically, recognized that the same divisions that gave rise to federalism in the first place will likely recur in organized groups; many focus attention on the level of government that is either more powerful in their policy area or, in cases of shared jurisdiction, more amenable to their demands (Coleman 1987).

One study comparing decisions on women's movement policy claims in unitary (U.K.) versus federal (U.S., Canada) systems concluded that state structures did not, by themselves, predict effectiveness. The Canadian women's movement in the Mulroney years appeared to have more influence over legislative and judicial decisions than the British movement in the Thatcher years, which, in turn, was considerably more effective than the U.S. movement in the Reagan years. Overall, constitutional provisions for women's rights combined with the orientation of the regime in question to the ideas of the movement appeared to be more significant explanatory factors than state structures (Bashevkin 1994a). A similar conclusion follows from Coleman's

(1987, 172) analysis of chemical and construction business associations in Canada, Switzerland, West Germany, and the United Kingdom, which reported that "within the same sectors, differences among association structures in all four countries are relatively small."

The empirical literature on corporatism indicates that logically enough, societal corporatism is positively correlated with the density of trade union membership. Following a large body of Scandinavian research dating back to Rokkan (1966), Schmitter (1981) reveals the high-corporatism/high-density linkage in Sweden, Finland, Norway, and Denmark, as well as Austria. Work on the Dutch peace movement indicates that members of its moderate wing were frequently integrated into discussions with high-ranking politicians and civil servants (Rochon 1990, 118), supporting Schmitter's (1981) description of the Netherlands as a case of high corporatism with low density. Observers of group politics in the United Kingdom have commented on the integration of some interests including business and medicine in the Westminster system; Eckstein (1960), for instance, referred to a "persistent corporatism." Exceptional policy cases in North America have also been described as corporatist; for example, Tuohy's (1990) account of occupational health and safety administration in Quebec suggests an emphasis on tripartite business/labor/state collaboration since the late 1970s. Researchers argue that the Scandinavian and Austrian versions of corporatism follow from a long and relatively consensual history of party-group relations, where collectivities of both types enjoy considerable internal cohesion and social legitimacy (Castles 1967, 12). The more individualized nature of politics in North America, and the relatively limited cohesion and representativeness of those organized groups that do exist, suggest that corporatist practices could only emerge in places like Quebec, with its countervailing tradition of both a strong state and high social solidarity (McRoberts 1988).

Transitional Systems

Do interests only exist in competitive democratic systems? The problem with studying other environments, such as single-party regimes, is that groups are usually denied public voice once their claims challenge the government in any manner—witness the case of the Mexican oil workers. Studies of groups in single-party cases can be helpful, however, in understanding what happens *within* the transition toward liberal democracy. Wolchik's (1994, 216) account of Czechoslovakia during the Communist period maintains that the leading women's organization "began to operate as an interest group in the Western sense of the word." After 1967, according to Wolchik (1994, 215), the official Union of Czechoslovak Women "began to defend women's interests vis-à-vis party and government officials"; ironically, after the 1989 fall of Communism, economic hardship brought on by market reforms combined with what Wolchik (1994, 219) terms a "postcommunist backlash against the goal of sexual equality" led to women's group demobilization.

Research on Hungary, Poland, and the USSR, by way of contrast, indicates virtually no autonomous women's organization prior to the late 1970s (Koncz 1994; Siemienska 1994; Voronina 1994). The first independent feminist group was established in the Soviet Union (in Leningrad) in 1979, and the tradition of independent organizing in Poland dates from the 1980 establishment of Solidarity in Gdansk—the same year as a feminist group was launched at the University of Warsaw. In both Poland and Russia, women's umbrella or Forum groups were launched in 1990, within a year of the formal collapse of Communist hegemony. Probably the most engaged of these nascent interests was the Polish movement, which mobilized unsuccessfully beginning in 1989 when a restrictive abortion law was proposed (Koncz 1994). Newer women's organizations in Russia and Hungary have tended to be isolated from each other, small in membership and, as in the Polish case, limited in public influence (Siemienska 1994; Voronina 1994). Perhaps the most telling comment on transitional systems was offered by Wolchik (1994, 223) in her explanation of mobilization in post-Communist Czechoslovakia. In her words, "the existence of democratic institutions alone does not automatically lead to equal participation by all groups in the exercise of political power or in equal access to policy makers."

South Africa provides a different example of group politics in transition, in this case from apartheid to majority rule. The banning and sustained repression of leading antiapartheid interests through the 1980s did not eliminate organized opposition groups by any means. Challenges to the then-governing National party reached a crescendo after a state of emergency was declared in 1985; at that time, a coalition known as the Mass Democratic Movement brought together the African National Congress as well as leading trade union and church interests under a broad oppositional banner. This persistence of group activism despite difficult conditions can also be identified in the history of the ANC itself, which developed influential women's sections within the movement during the long period in exile. After 1990, when the official ban on ANC organization was lifted, these women's sections pressured for effective equal rights provisions in the new South African constitution (Klugman 1994).

Overall, it is hard to assess the effect of groups in newly democratic systems. Formal political rights, including freedom of association and free speech, often figure less prominently in the daily lives of citizens than does the struggle for work, food, and shelter—particularly when the provision of these basics was less difficult in the past. For many citizens, the potential to organize freely in groups remains just that, a latent potential, as it does for many millions in established liberal democracies. If developments in transitional cases point toward any generalization, it is that pretransition traditions of independent group organization may provide a crucial foundation for democratic politics. The prospects for building a resilient democratic culture are likely improved by a history of autonomous group formation and a tolerance for intergroup competition (Putnam 1993). The future shape of democratic politics in South Africa as well as the Czech Republic can thus be evaluated along these lines and compared with developments in other transitional systems.

Challenges Facing Groups

As organized groups in transitional systems attempt to benefit from political freedom under conditions of considerable economic hardship, what challenges face interests in Western liberal democracies? Three problems can be identified, beginning with contradictory perceptions of groups. Longitudinal data suggest that public identification with organized interests has tended to grow at the same time as identification with parties has declined. Research by Martin Wattenberg (1991, 157-8) on the United States, for example, reports "a rise in identification with social groups is a major trend in American public opinion, encompassing greater psychological ties to religious, class, occupational, racial, gender, and age groups." Although it might be argued that this pattern is not by itself a problem, surveys indicate the general public in North America is increasingly convinced that power rests in the hands of "special interests" as opposed to average citizens and their elected representatives

(Petracca 1992, 10). The view that too much money and too much power are in the hands of too few interests, however, conflicts quite directly with the perceptions of many group activists. In particular, participants in social movements tend to view themselves as lacking both resources and influence (Bashevkin 1994b).

A second challenge follows from efforts to restrict, or at least expose to public view, group activities. Attempts to establish conflict of interest regulations, register lobbyists, limit the ability of groups to fund campaigns for public office, and monitor the activities of groups holding charitable tax status are in many ways a response to negative public attitudes (see Katz, chap. 4 in this volume). Although none of these efforts may do much to alter the way groups operate, they cumulatively represent a shift away from traditions of unfettered organizational activity. American groups have responded to this trend by creating their own associations of lobbyists and PACs to defend what they view as the vital role of organized interests in democratic politics.

Finally, despite the presumed threat posed by too many active groups in Western systems, one can argue that a far more significant trend is the *retreat* of individual citizens from community participation. Putnam's (1993) research on civic engagement, or what he terms social capital, links the effectiveness of governments with citizen involvement in group activities. In extending his earlier work on Italy to the United States, he argues that levels of voter turnout, protest participation, party involvement, and membership in voluntary associations (including trade unions) have declined considerably since the mid-1960s (Putnam 1995). Americans trust each other less and, according to Putnam, this measurable erosion in social capital holds direct negative consequences for the larger political system (see Dalton, chap. 13 in this volume). Organized groups thus benefit from the multiple affiliations of active individuals, but retain very limited legitimacy and organizational potential outside this group-attached minority of the population.

The decline of the social collectivity and the ascent of anomic individualism—whether attributable to the rise of television, increased family mobility, or changes in women's roles—constitute a significant challenge for groups on the edge of the 21st century. The weakening over time in key measures of social engagement in the United States may presage not just a decline of formal belonging in that system but also a broader crisis of citizenship in liberal democracies.

Notes

1. As defined by Oberschall (1973, 102), "mobilization refers to the process of forming crowds, groups, associations, and organizations for the pursuit of collective goals."

2. This particular strategy was employed by an abortion rights organization to influence U.S. senators during the Reagan years.

3. Michael M'Gonigle, cofounder of Greenpeace International, as quoted in Matas (1995, A7).

4. It should be noted that later work by Dahl (1982) and Lindblom (1977) tended to acknowledge the privileged role of business within the pluralist universe.

◀ 6 ▶

Campaign Strategies and Tactics

DAVID M. FARRELL

Campaign strategies and tactics have tended to attract a great deal of attention from journalists, personified by Theodore White's (e.g., 1961) classic studies, and contemporary historians, the classic exemplar being the "Nuffield" series (e.g., Butler and Kavanagh 1992). In the United States, it has been a long-held tradition for campaign strategists to publish their "how to win an election" guides (Agranoff 1976a; Bernays 1955; Chagall 1981; Chartrand 1972; Hiebert et al. 1975; Napolitan 1972; Shadegg 1964, 1972; Steinberg 1976a, 1976b; Woo 1980). For a long time, what was lacking was a similar level of interest among the political science community. Until recently, apart from a few notable exceptions (Agranoff 1976b; Nimmo 1970; Rose 1967), the basic situation remained that "the study of election campaigns, as opposed to elections, is a major gap [in the literature]" (Harrop and Miller 1987, 240).

There were understandable reasons for this gap, at least two of which are worth mentioning. First, for some time there was the belief that campaigns were of secondary importance. The "party identification" tradition was in the ascendancy and the conventional wisdom among political scientists through to at least the mid-1970s, was that long-term factors, such as social alignments and partisanship, were the primary explanations of voting behavior; short-term factors, such as campaigns and campaign issues, were of minimal influence. Second, there was a lack of appropriate research methods to deal with the question of campaign influences on the vote. The standard methods of studying voting behavior—single-shot, cross-section surveys—were inappropriate for examining campaign effects.

The research agenda changed in the 1980s, for three main reasons. First, the arrival of voter dealignment, with the concomitant factor of greater voter volatility, made it likely that campaigns may now matter after all. Second, the nature of campaigns changed, with the rise of professional campaigning attracting ever more interest from the academic community. Third, political scientists began to use research methods more appropriate for the types of analysis required to assess campaign effects. These include panels and rolling cross-sectional surveys, focus groups, experiments, and the content analysis of campaign messages.

Since the early 1980s, the study of election campaigning has become a growth industry, particularly in the United States, where a number of studies have been produced on campaigning American style (Godwin 1988; Luntz 1988; Mauser 1983; Newman 1994; Sabato 1981, 1989). There have also been several European studies (Farrell 1986; Lindon 1976; Mannelli and Cheli 1986; O'Shaughnessy 1990; Statera 1986; Wangen 1983). Seriously lacking have been cross-national studies that attempt to explore differing patterns of campaigning across two or more systems (exceptions are Bowler and Farrell 1992b; Butler and Ranney 1992; Farrell and Wortmann 1987; Swanson and Mancini 1996; Penniman 1981). And there has been very little attention to campaigning outside of the United States or Western Europe.

What is campaigning? How does it vary across different countries and why? How has campaigning changed in recent years? Does campaigning matter? We can start with a basic definition: Election campaigning is the process by which a campaign organization (be it a party, candidate, or special interest organization) seeks to maximize electoral gains.[1] It consists of all those efforts (promotional or financial) made by the campaign organization to meet that goal.

The exact nature of campaigning varies across different countries and over time, and it is the function of this chapter to set out some of the main variations

and possible reasons for them. Before we attempt any description and classification of campaigns, we need first to consider the context in which they
occur, because this plays an important role in determining the nature of the
party's campaign, for instance, as party centered or candidate centered, as
"defensive" or "offensive," and as reactive or proactive.

Factors Affecting Campaign Strategies

There is a series of environmental factors (across and within different
systems) that affects a party's campaign. First, campaigns vary across different political systems. As we shall see, presidentialism promotes candidate-
centered campaigning. In turn, federalism contributes to a high degree of
decentralism of party organizations and campaigns. Political systems differ
also in terms of basic sociocultural traits. Countries characterized by a localist,
clientelist emphasis, such as Ireland, are more likely to have lower degrees of
campaign centralism and cohesion.

Second, the electoral laws, such as those relating to the voting system or
rules over party finance, play an important role in influencing degrees of
campaign centralization and certain types of campaign practices. Proportional
representation list systems, where voters are choosing between parties and
their programs, tend to promote greater campaign centralization than do
plurality or single transferable vote electoral systems where voters are choosing among candidates (Katz 1980). And as the chapter in this volume by Katz
shows, the availability of campaign finance makes a major difference to the
nature of the campaign mounted by the parties and, in particular, to its degree
of professionalization. Third, there is a vital role for the media systems,
whether in terms of the nature of the media market, styles of media coverage,
rules of access to the broadcasting media, the regulation of election broadcasts, or the right to make use of television spots (Kaid and Holtz-Bacha
1995b; see below, and Semetko in this volume, chap. 10).

Fourth, a distinction can be drawn between types of party systems, where
the focus is on the number of parties in the system. In a two-party system,
such as in Great Britain, the parties "go for broke" in their election campaigns,
trying to "win" the election. By contrast, in the multiparty systems of most
everywhere else in Western Europe the parties have to make allowances for
possible coalition partners and so they temper their campaign messages

appropriately. A good example of this is provided by the Netherlands, where coalitions are the norm, so that in campaigns, "the attitude of the political parties towards each other is highly correct and positive; personal attacks on politicians are few and far between, and negative campaigning is nonexistent" (van Praag 1992, 144). In predominant-party systems (i.e., where government tends to rotate between single-party and coalition), there tends to be a mix of the two scenarios, with one large party going for broke and other, smaller parties seeking possible coalition deals. Ireland offers a good example of this mix of strategies, where the Fine Gael party has been conscious of the need to tread carefully with other parties like Labour or the Progressive Democrats because of the possibility that there may be a coalition government formed after the election (certainly, this was relevant in the 1989 campaign; see Farrell 1990). By contrast, the larger Fianna Fáil party, which traditionally eschews coalition arrangements, tends not to pull its punches.

Intrasystem comparisons can be grouped under two main headings: level of election and type of party. The election level concerns the distinction between campaigns for national elections and those for local or regional elections (although in federal systems such as the United States or Canada there can be a multiplicity of different levels of election). Local election campaigns are bound to be less coordinated than those for the national level. However, with the general process of campaign centralization, this distinction is breaking down (Elklit 1991), and in newer democracies it probably never had a chance to manifest itself (Robinson 1989). In Northern Ireland, where the parties have only a local forum in which to compete, there is a tendency to treat local elections as surrogate national elections.

Styles and modes of campaigning also vary across the different parties within each system (Bowler 1990). Incumbent parties are often constrained by their record, although in certain prominent cases (notably the British Conservatives in the 1980s; Webb 1992) this has not stopped incumbent parties from going on the offensive, making a virtue out of their position. The role of challenging parties may be complicated by the degree to which the party space is crowded, and, especially in multiparty systems, the challengers may spend as much time campaigning against other challenging parties as against the incumbent(s). Smaller parties are more concerned with attracting new support than larger parties, whose main aim is to maintain vote share. Right-wing parties and "catch-all" parties find the abandonment of ideological baggage and the switch to a greater reliance on leader image much easier to achieve than left-of-center parties, which tend to have more complex—and potentially more restrictive—organizational forms (Panebianco 1988; Wright 1971b).

We should also take note of the rise of new types of parties in many countries, parties that are as different from the established parties as they are from each other (Mair 1991). Research on Green parties has shown how different a party type they are from the norm in terms of organization, policies, and support groups (Poguntke 1989). In turn, this influences their approach to campaigning, with less emphasis on the party leadership, and a greater role for grassroots, local campaigning. Whereas the new Green parties stress factors like internal democracy and a decentralized party organization, the new parties on the right (antitax and neo-Fascist) place great emphasis on leader image, in some cases (notably Le Pen in France) to the point of demagoguery.

A survey of campaign practices among European and Australasian parties in the late 1980s and early 1990s found that in the bulk of cases, there was clear evidence of a shift toward greater emphasis on promoting the party leader in the election campaign. The few exceptions tended mostly to be among left-of-center parties, such as the Irish and New Zealand Labour parties, the Danish Social-Liberals, and among many of the Green parties (Bowler and Farrell 1992a).

It is clear from this brief discussion that campaign strategies can be greatly influenced by the context in which the campaign is occurring and by the types of parties carrying out the campaign. Many of these issues reemerge in later discussion.

Candidate-Centered Versus Party-Centered Campaigning

When comparing elections in the United States with elections in Europe, a distinction tends to be drawn between candidate- and party-centered campaigning. It is easy enough to see how the United States can be characterized as candidate centered. As David Broder puts it, the system

is run by 536 individual political entrepreneurs—one president, 100 senators and 435 members of the House—each of whom got here essentially on his own. Each chooses the office he seeks, raises his own money, hires his own pollster and ad-maker and recruits his own volunteers. (cited in Wattenberg 1991, 165; for the classic overview of U.S. candidate-centered campaigning, see Agranoff 1976b)

Contrast this with the West European situation where "the modern campaign is manifestly a party campaign" (Bowler and Farrell 1992a, 223). As Karvonen (1991, 195) points out, given the dominance of the American literature on campaigning, there has tended to be "a major imbalance" in that the focus has tended to be on campaigning as candidate centered. As a result, observers of new campaign styles in the European context (especially journalistic observers), following the standard thesis that developments in Europe are merely following American trends (Epstein 1980; Negrine and Papathanassopoulos 1996), have talked of European campaigns becoming candidate centered, pointing to such things as the growing significance of the party leaders' campaigns. The issue of campaign professionalization is dealt with later; for now the basic point is worth stressing that campaigns worldwide may be becoming more "presidential" (Mughan forthcoming) and more "personalized" (Butler and Ranney 1992), but this is far from saying that they are becoming candidate centered. The leading candidate in the West European context is generally the party leader who has been selected by the party and can be dropped by it, who campaigns on behalf of the party and is therefore associated with its standpoints and ideology. The party leader is constrained by his or her position in the sense that it is difficult to dramatically change established party policies or dogma; he or she is supported by the party machinery and organization.

But it would be wrong to draw the conclusion that all European campaigns are party centered. If we take just one aspect, namely, the degree of autonomy of organization and self-reliance of the individual candidates, we find a number of European cases that reveal distinct candidate-based activities. For instance, France has its own equivalent of political action committees (PACs), known as *comités de soutien* (support committees). These play a prominent role in presidential elections, particularly in the runoff between candidates from the same party. In 1988, the competition between Raymond Barre and Jacques Chirac was described as the *"bataille des comités de soutien"* (Legavre 1990; Lawson and Ysmal 1992). Similarly, Finland has its version of PACs in the form of "supporter groups," which are described by Sundberg and Högnabba (1992, 84) as a small active nucleus that attends to all the practical arrangements. Its members need not be party members because other qualifications are more important than formal membership. Formally they are run totally independent of the party organization. . . . In recent Finnish elections there has been a distinct trend towards the situation where the party organization, with the help of its advertising agencies, assists the individual candidates via their supporter groups and not *vice versa.*

The French and Finnish cases are consistent with the quasi-presidential nature of both systems and the effects of electoral systems that focus attention on individual candidates. There are some other European cases that appear to be moving in the direction of candidate-centered campaigning. In the Austrian 1990 election the SPÖ leader, Franz Vranitzky received the personal backing of an "above-party support group" that "tried to recruit VIPs in the main but also 'ordinary' people who were willing to give testimonials for Vranitzky. . . . [T]he group acted independently of the party; it did not hesitate to articulate discomfort with the SPÖ, implying that Vranitzky should be elected despite his party" (Müller and Plasser 1992, 33). Other European countries to have experienced a recent tendency for campaigns to become more candidate oriented include Denmark (Bille, Elklit, and Jakobsen 1992; Esaiasson 1992) and Italy (Gundle 1992).

Once we extend our focus outside of Western Europe, it soon becomes clear that candidate-centered campaign activities are a feature of a large number of other countries. To a large degree, this is because the United States is not alone in having a presidential system; it is the dominant form of government in Latin America (Mainwaring 1990); the list of presidential countries has been added to recently by the decision of a number of the fledgling democracies in central and Eastern Europe and the former Soviet Union to adopt (quasi) presidential systems. The combination of low party cohesion and high elements of personalism in presidential systems ensures that candidates make greater use of their own resources and personal campaign organizations. So we find that in Colombian elections, "the campaign is almost exclusively the handiwork of the candidate and his personal team rather than being, in any meaningful sense, a corporate product of party organization." Similarly in Ecuador, whereas "there are a few parties with a superstructure on which candidates can rely, . . . others function as the personal fiefdom of the candidate" (Martz 1990, 36). Even in Venezuela, which combines its presidentialism with a powerful "partyarchy" (Coppedge 1994), we find that in the case of one party,

Acción Democrática, "the most striking characteristic has been the existence of a separate mini-structure paralleling the formal party organization, but also directly linked to the candidate" (Martz 1990, 22).

Candidate-centered campaigning can also be a product of parties with few resources, where candidates are forced to rely on their own means, where, as the Malta case shows, "it is pretty much every candidate for himself" (Boissevain 1965, 24). Clearly, the single transferable vote electoral system is playing a role here, but the main cause appears to be finance.[2] In Turkey, not only do the candidates have to bear the costs of their own election, they are expected to help fund the party's campaign and to pay a fixed sum to the party to be nominated, making electoral politics something that "only the rich could afford" (Szyliowicz 1966). Contrast this with the party-centered situation in Zambia, where

> the party regards the parliamentary constituency as party property rather than as the domain of the MP representing it in the Assembly, and the interests of constituents are usually handled by the full-time party officials in the area. MPs do not visit their constituencies frequently and, where they have not emerged through the local organization, may have little or no personal political base. (Molteno and Scott 1974, 177)

Finally, candidate-centered campaigning may be associated with campaign practices that border on the politically corrupt. The South Korean 1988 election is an interesting example, described by one observer as a campaign where "money, violence, corruption, mudslinging, fraud and every other conceivable means were permitted to determine the outcome" (Lee 1990, 101). The candidates of the ruling DJP party averaged personal expenditure of $1.5 million; some spent over $7 million. The opposition parties, lacking the financial resources of the DJP, "resorted to selling legislative seats to the highest bidders." The location of the wealthy candidates on the party list was determined by how much money they were prepared to spend: "Numbers one through five were assured of their seats in the National Assembly; they paid up to $3 million to buy a seat. Numbers six through ten paid up to $2 million. From number ten on, the chance of securing a legislative seat diminished and so did the cost" (Lee 1990, 102).

Japan provides the most fascinating example of an electoral process that is both heavily regulated and corrupt. Until recently, the combination of an election system based around multimember districts; a static, nonchanging governmental system; fast economic growth; and technological developments has made the electoral process costly and the exclusive preserve of the wealthy (Curtis 1971, 1988, 1992). The system is heavily regulated, right down to the fine details of, for instance, the size and proportions of posters, where they can be hung, and what they can say.

A central feature of "election campaigning Japanese style" is the candidate-centered nature of campaigning, particularly the role of the candidates' personal support organizations, or *kōenkai*. The Japanese twist on this is that the kōenkai have to be supported financially by the Diet members, as they provide a vital vote-delivery service in elections: Their role is not as fundraisers in the U.S. PAC model, but rather as opinion leaders and "ward heelers." Despite the best efforts of the electoral reformers to encourage a shift from candidate-centered to party-centered campaigns and thereby, it is hoped, a reduction in corrupt practices, "the fundamental characteristic of Japanese election campaigning continues to be the centrality of the individual politician. Extremely weak, almost non-existent, party organization at the local level means that individual politicians must build their own electoral machines, raise their own money, and run their own campaigns" (Curtis 1992, 227-8).

The Professionalization
of Election Campaigns

Contemporary campaigning has come a long way from the campaign practices of old. Buzzwords abound when describing the contemporary situation: "political marketing," "Americanization," "candidate-centered campaigning," "the presidentialization of campaigns," "new political campaign technology." When we strip away the nuances of individual arguments—the varying emphases of the separate authors—the single theme that they all share in common is one of change, of campaigns becoming more professionalized.

The object of this section is to show how contemporary election campaigning in many countries is very different from that of 20, or even 10, years ago. It is useful to draw a distinction between campaigns that are "labor intensive" and those that are "capital intensive," the latter representing a higher degree of campaign professionalism. Labor-intensive campaigns are characterized by the following features: They are decentralized, there is a major role for party workers and volunteers, they are "amateur" campaigns, and there is a stress on canvassing and mass public meetings. Butler and Ranney provide a useful summary description of how campaigning used to be:

a. Circulating written documents—party manifestos, candidate biographies, position papers, and fly sheets [campaign literature].

b. Door-to-door canvassing by party volunteers, intended mainly to identify potential voters so that they could be reminded to vote on election day; secondary goals included soliciting contributions from the faithful.

c. Holding public meetings, at which party candidates and leaders spoke, and organizing rallies and parades at which partisans could demonstrate their enthusiasm for their side. . . . The party faithful also showed their colors in window stickers and campaign buttons.

d. Using billboards, posters and newspaper advertisements to reinforce the party appeal.

e. Door-knocking on election day to get known supporters to the polling booth. (Butler and Ranney 1992, 5-6)

There are two other aspects of the "premodern" campaign that should be added to this list: (1) in many cases the preparations for the campaign were ad hoc, last minute, and generally unstructured; and (2) there was little central control over the campaign, a lack of standardization in the literature, and little coordination across the country (Farrell forthcoming). The main features of premodern campaigning are summarized in the first column of Table 6.1.

A common picture that emerges from an examination of labor-intensive campaigns is a stress on individual contact with voters at the local level; extensive canvassing operations (often with paid canvassers); mass rallies (with busloads of supporters brought in to boost the "spontaneity");[3] and posters, billboards, and daubing of paint on walls (Bhambhri 1994; Boissevain 1965; Mirchandani 1977). Richard Clogg (1987, 89) provides a fascinating description of the "poster wars" in the Greek 1981 election, which "meant that much of urban and rural Greece was covered with posters, banners and painted slogans, with rival bands of poster stickers fighting (sometimes literally) not only to display the posters of their own party, but also to cover up those of their rivals." Often, there is also the provision of gifts and money to prospective voters (Lee 1990; Manor 1992). Any support from the central party is usually small and intended to help the local canvassing effort. For instance, in the Zambian 1968 election the ruling United National Independence Party supplied each of its regional organizations with one new Land Rover, 10

TABLE 6.1 Professionalization of Election Campaigning

	Premodern	Television Revolution	Telecommunications Revolution
Campaign organization	Decentralized Local party organization Little standardization Staffing: party/candidate based, voluntary	Nationalization, centralization Staffing: party based salaried professional	Decentralization of operation with central scrutiny Staffing: party/candidate based, professional, contract work(?)
Campaign preparations	Short term: ad hoc	Long term; specialist committee established 1-2 years in advance of election	"Permanent campaign": the establishment of specialist campaign departments
Agencies, consultants	Minimal use "Generalist" role Politicians in charge	Greater use Growing prominence of "specialist" consultants Politicians still in charge	Even greater use of consultants Consultants as campaign personalities International links ("Saatchi-ization") "Who is in charge?"
Sources of feedback	Impressionistic, "feel" Important role of canvassers, group leaders, and intuition	Large-scale opinion polls More scientific	Greater range of polling techniques Computer-aided telepolling Interactive capabilities of cable
Use of media	Direct and indirect Direct = party press, newspaper ads, billboards Indirect = newspaper coverage	Emphasis on indirect Direct = ad campaigns Indirect = public relations, media training, press conferences	Emphasis on direct Direct = targeted ads, direct mail, videomail, cable TV Indirect = as before
Campaign events	Public meetings Whistle-stop tours	TV debates Press conferences "Pseudo-events"	As before; events targeted more locally
Targeting of voters	Social class support base Object of maintaining vote of specific social categories	Catch-all Trying to mobilize voters across all categories	Market segmentation Targeting of specific categories of voters

170

bicycles, and in the lake and swamp parts of the country, six motorboats (Molteno and Scott 1974, 182).

In countries with low levels of literacy, there is a tendency to make use of symbols as a means of distinguishing parties and candidates. This is particularly prominent in African countries and in the Indian subcontinent. The usual requirement is that the symbols cannot have special political or religious significance. But this does not stop the parties from making imaginative use of them for campaigning purposes. For instance, in an Indian election in the early 1950s, the Congress party used a pair of bullocks as its symbol, suggesting "all kinds of favorable connotations. Many Indians could be persuaded that they should certainly not vote against bullocks, which symbolized the source of their livelihood, their main source of power and transportation, and perhaps even their religious faith as well" (Palmer 1971, 243).

An alternative to pictures and symbols is to use slogans and mottos, such as the practice in Uruguay, which operates the "*lema* electoral process," where "*lema* literally means 'motto,' and each recognized party is identified by a *lema*" (Alisky 1969, 34). At a greater level of distinction, factions and individual candidates can be identified by "*sublemas*" and "*distintivos*" respectively, described by Fitzgibbon (1956, 154) as "the names of party heroes, or . . . ringing calls to party loyalty and triumph."

There is clear evidence that campaigning has been changing in recent years. Capital-intensive campaigns tend to have the following features: They are centralized; the role of local workers and volunteers is supplemented or replaced by new professionals, consultants, and agencies working from the center; television, advertising, and the use of new technologies feature strongly; and the campaigns are expensive. The strategies of the parties and candidates place greater reliance than ever before on the three "Ts" of electioneering: technology, technocrats and techniques. Although there may be debates over the causes of the changes in campaigning, there can be little dispute that two factors have played probably the most important role in facilitating change, technological development, and the professionalization of the workplace, the first introducing the new campaign tools, the second providing the knowledge and means of using them. We start with an examination of the role of technology.

A Two-Stage Technological Revolution

Much has been made of the pervasive influence of television on election campaigns. The mark of virility, as it were, is the "first TV campaign," usually characterized as the first time television advertisements or party election broadcasts are aired, the first time there is "coverage" of the election by the medium, and sometimes the first time there are television debates between the leading candidates. Television's influence on campaigning attracts key attention in election studies and is generally at the center of debates over what exactly is "new" about the contemporary campaign. According to those scholars who argue that campaigns have changed, it is television, more than any other factor, that has marked that change. It has contributed to the "nationalization" of campaign strategies, reducing the emphasis on local campaigns and contributing to the centralization of interest, influence, and resources. Campaigns have become more standardized, marked in particular by a greater uniformity in the campaign message and in its presentation by the organization countrywide. Television has brought the politician closer to the people; for the first time all voters can actually see their candidates and hear them on the hustings.

Meanwhile, there are other scholars who argue that the issue of new campaign styles is little more than another myth about the influence of television. Here the argument is that little actually has changed (Bartels 1992). Historical examples are dredged up to show how campaigns have always focused on party leaders, how campaign advertising was just as sophisticated and the messages just as snappy as today. For all the furor about television, apparently there is evidence of much that the new medium has not changed: in particular, despite the television emphasis on the national campaigns of the leading candidates, local, district-level campaigning still continues apace (Dionne 1976).

Each of these two interpretations has its merits: Television has had an influence, but this should not be exaggerated. The point is that both sides are telling only part of the story (Benjamin 1982). It is almost as if technological change stopped with the development of television. In fact, although there has been a technological revolution, it has occurred in two stages: the first one characterized by the introduction of television, and a second, more dramatic telecommunications stage associated with developments in satellites, cabling, and computers. Although in some respects these successive stages have marked a consistent trend of campaign professionalization, in other respects there have been marked differences. In fact, whereas the first stage resulted in a "centralization," or perhaps a "massification," of campaigning, the second stage has, if anything, resulted in a "decentralization," or "demassification," of campaigning. This point needs further elaboration.

The Television Revolution

Undoubtedly, television had a major influence on election campaigns, eclipsing radio and competing strongly with newspapers. Candidates were presented with a new medium across which for the first time they could speak face-to-face with the bulk of voters. They went on television training courses and employed the services of media consultants. Specialist agencies were commissioned to design campaigns maximizing the potential of television. Campaigning was never the same after the invention of television. According to Smith (1981, 185): "In the 1970s most Western societies overcame the fundamental diffidence of politicians towards television and accepted the new medium as an essential element in electoral campaigning." Of the 21 democracies in his sample, the bulk operated free election broadcasts; in half of the cases there had been television debates. At that stage, the introduction of paid television advertising was still quite restricted, with just four countries permitting it—Australia, Canada, Japan, and the United States. However, by the 1990s the number of countries allowing television spots had increased to at least 13, the entrants including Austria, Colombia, France, Germany, Italy, Mexico, New Zealand, Sweden, and Venezuela (Figure 6.1).

The effects of television on the campaign process have been enormous by any standards; by implication its effects on the nature of party organization have been equally significant (Katz and Mair 1994). More than anything else, television has contributed to a nationalization of campaigning, in the sense that everything is focused on one leader, one party, one set of common themes. The degree to which this level of standardization is achieved becomes the central measure of success or failure of the campaign. Local issues and the activities of individual politicians are acceptable only insofar as they are not in conflict with the national campaign; nothing must allow the impression to be created of splits or differences in the campaign; nothing must detract from the image of campaign homogeneity.

Undoubtedly, television has played a key role in the transformation of election campaigns. As such, therefore, the usage of television provides a good indicator of the level of professionalization of campaigning in a country.

"Labor Intensive"			"Capital Intensive"
0-100	101-250	251-450	451+
Bangladesh	Argentina	Belgium	*Australia*
Ecuador	Brazil	*France*	*Austria*
India	Chile	Hungary	*Canada*
Mali	*Colombia*	Ireland	Denmark
Nepal	Costa Rica	Israel	Finland
Philippines	Greece	*Italy*	Germany
Zambia	South Korea	*New Zealand*	*Japan*
	Mexico	Norway	Netherlands
	Portugal	Poland	*Sweden*
	Thailand	Russia	*United States*
	Turkey	Spain	
	Uruguay	Switzerland	
	Venezuela	Ukraine	
		United Kingdom	

Figure 6.1. Television Penetration as an Indicator of "Capital Intensity": Television Sets per 1,000 People in 1994

SOURCE: This volume, Table 1.7; Butler and Ranney (1992, appendix).
NOTE: Cases where television spots are permitted are italicized.

In Figure 6.1, the countries are grouped pretty much as we would expect. Japan, North America, Australia, and certain European countries fit the highest capital-intensive category; most of the other European countries, Israel, and New Zealand fit the medium capital-intensive category; some Mediterranean European countries and the bulk of Latin American countries are in the medium labor-intensive category; and the poorest countries in the sample appear most labor intensive.

It should be noted that this dimension is more than merely tapping the distinction between richer and poorer countries. There is also the question of freedom of access to the airwaves. When we take account of those cases in which parties are permitted to purchase airtime for television spots (italicized in Figure 6.1), there is a clear relationship between television saturation and the use of television spots.

Of course, there are other factors that affect the degree to which a campaign may become more capital intensive, such as the size of the electoral districts (requiring more or less use of methods of mass communication) or (as discussed above) the nature of the electoral system. One other factor of undoubted importance is the strength of the local party organization. As research in the British context by Seyd and Whiteley (1992) shows, this is a factor that parties may underestimate at their peril. This relates to some of the discussion above, and, indeed, to the writings of scholars such as Duverger (1954) and Epstein (1980), who stress the importance of mass memberships, particularly as campaign activists, for certain categories of parties. It is a point that has recently been recognized by the British Labour party, whose new leader, Tony Blair, has embarked on a major membership drive. Systematic research on European parties reveals that in many cases, mass membership continues to be important for certain parties, notably in Belgium, Germany, Norway, and Sweden (chap. 4, Table 4.2; Katz, Mair, et al. 1992).

As Figure 6.1 shows, many of the Latin American cases fit into the intermediate group between capital-intensive and labor-intensive campaigns. It has been suggested that Latin American "campaigns are arguably much more Americanized now than in Europe" (Angell, Kinzo, and Urbaneja 1992, 43; on the exceptions of Colombia and Ecuador, see Martz 1990). This process has been influenced by the provision of funds by foreign parties (notably the German party foundations), by agencies promoting democracy (Grabendorff 1992; Pinto-Duschinsky 1991), and by the activities of foreign political consultants, particularly from the United States, Germany, and France (Angell et al. 1992; Napolitan 1972). It has reached such a level that Latin American scholars talk of the rise to prominence of a new elite referred to as *profesionales y técnicos* (Martz and Myers 1994). But it would be wrong to exaggerate the degree of professionalization of Latin American campaigns. On balance, they continue to be dominated by traditional techniques, such as the use of local supporters for canvassing, a heavy emphasis on the local campaign, use of the print media, and billboards.[4]

The Telecommunications Revolution

More recently—and very much still ongoing—there has been a new telecommunications revolution, prompted by two technological developments: computers, and cable and satellite television. According to Abramson and his colleagues (1988), this dates from as recently as 1988 in the United States. As we move into the 1990s, there is evidence of greater use of new technologies in other countries, perhaps most notably in Germany (Boll and Poguntke 1992). This stage of the technological revolution has contributed to a further professionalizing of the campaign process, making campaigning even more capital intensive; at the same time, it has started to raise the issue of whether campaigning actually needs to be centralized and standardized to be successful. We can characterize the differences between the two stages of technological development as follows:

Stage 1	*Stage 2*
Centralization	Decentralization of operation
Nationalization	Market segmentation
Standardization	Targeting
Campaign homogeneity	Demassification
Massification	Narrowcasting
Broadcasting	

Campaign organizations are making use of the opportunities provided by the new computer and broadcasting technologies. Instead of talking of one image and one set of themes, increasingly, attention is paid to "market segmentation" and "candidate positioning." The structure of campaign organizations is also changing and not only in terms of the growing influence of the campaign consultants. In some cases, there is evidence of campaigning becoming more candidate centered, where the role of party organizations is changing to one of service providers. The relationship with the media is also changing: Greater use is being made of local channels, and where possible, advantage is being taken of the new technologies to bypass the media outright and make greater use of "direct" forms of campaign communication.

Table 6.1 provides a summary of the main characteristics of change in campaigns from the traditional period through the two stages of technological change. Among the new techniques increasingly being employed in campaigns in the United States and elsewhere are

- Telebanks with computer-aided dialing for canvassing of specially selected target categories of voters
- On-line computer organizational links
- Toll-free numbers for instant feedback, fund-raising, and attracting volunteers
- New polling techniques, such as "moment-to-moment" research (used to track responses to commercials second by second) and "push polls" (using mass phone bank polls to influence the results of elections); a far greater reliance on polling generally
- Use of CD-ROMs, the "superhighway," and e-mail
- Direct mail, also, increasingly, of videocassettes

- Satellite teleconferencing
- Targeted infomercials and campaign literature
- Computerized opposition research

Political Consultants and
Specialized Campaign Agencies

Technological change has coincided with a greater use of campaign professionals. As Chagall (1981), Sabato (1981), and Luntz (1988) have shown, political consultancy has become big business in the United States. A major factor behind its rise is the inherent organizational weakness of U.S. political parties: "Since there was no existing body of party professionals possessing these skills, candidates began to employ professionals from other spheres, thus forming a new breed of political professions" (Agranoff 1976b, 5).

Outside the United States, the rise of political consultancy has been less dramatic largely because the political parties have managed to bring professionals into the machinery as members, as volunteer advisers, even as full-time employees (Panebianco 1988). Nevertheless, there are prominent examples of the employment of outside agencies to provide expert advice in specialist areas. In practice, the U.S. case is not as unique as it may appear. For instance, although the majority of U.S. consultants are not exactly supporters of the parties for whose candidates they are working, they tend nonetheless to remain very loyal (Luntz 1988; Napolitan 1972; Sabato 1981).

The impression is often given, not least by U.S. political consultants, that the politicians have little influence over the design, coordination, and control of a campaign. Much like movie directors "discover" starlets, there are stories of consultants deciding on who they think will be worthwhile marketing as a candidate (Sabato 1981). Jimmy Carter's consultant, Pat Cadell, was notorious in this respect (Luntz 1988). The corollary of consultants avoiding high-risk candidates for fear of ruining their reputation is offered by the attitude of the American consultancy community toward Ross Perot (Newman 1994).

In the United States, a "well-managed" campaign is seen as one in which the candidate leaves decision making to his or her consultant. As one consultant has put it: "On a scale of one to one hundred, zero is the level a candidate should be involved in setting his own strategy" (quoted in Luntz 1988, 57; see also Napolitan 1972). In European and Australasian campaigns, for the most part, the tendency appears to be that the politician remains firmly in control of the campaign organization (Bowler and Farrell 1992a). However, there may be exceptions. It is hard to believe that strategists as senior as Joe Napolitan (who worked on Giscard's 1974 French presidential campaign) or Elisabeth Noelle-Neumann (who has worked on Helmut Kohl's campaigns) do not have significant powers of independent decision making. It is clear that in the French 1988 presidential campaign, François Mitterrand's media adviser, Jacques Ségéula, played a dominant role (Lawson and Ysmal 1992), as did Peter Hiort for the Danish Liberals in their 1990 campaign (Bille et al. 1992).

Writing at the start of the 1980s, Larry Sabato (1981, 61) saw evidence of political consultancy becoming accepted "all around the world; the new campaign technology is one of the most highly prized exports of the United States." There are a number of examples of the informal and formal sharing of campaign ideas that goes on all the time from party to party and from country to country. The German party foundations are particularly active in this respect (Grabendorff 1992; Pinto-Duschinsky 1991). Examples of where agencies and political consultants have been employed abroad include Jacques Ségéula, Mitterrand's advertising adviser, employed in recent elections by the Austrian and Swedish Social Democrats, and also by the (late) Italian Christian Democrats; Philip Gould, a senior consultant for the British Labour party, used by the Danish and Swedish Social Democrats, and by Bill Clinton in 1992 (to counter the negative campaign of the Republicans who were being advised by British Conservative strategists); the work of consultants throughout Latin America who had been prominent in Margaret Thatcher's campaigns of the 1980s; the commissioning of work from the German CDU's advertising agency by the Austrian ÖVP; the commissioning of polling research by the New Zealand Labour party from a company used by its Australian counterpart; the doyen of U.S. consultants, Joe Napolitan— noted for his work for the Democrats—employed by Ferdinand Marcos in the 1969 election in the Philippines.

Most striking of all has been the use of Saatchi and Saatchi, the troubled advertising agency, by parties in a number of countries: the British Conservatives since 1979, the Danish Conservatives in 1990, the Dutch Social Democrats in 1989, and the Irish Fianna Fáil party since 1989. Saatchi and Saatchi has also played an active role in campaigns in Latin American countries. In 1989, it established a new division specializing in election campaign consultancy, Saatchi and Saatchi Government Communications Worldwide.

Over time, there has been the development of an international profession of political consultancy. In 1968, Joe Napolitan founded the International

Association of Political Consultants (IAPC) and its sister organization, the American Association of Political Consultants (AAPC). They were joined in the early 1990s by the Latin American Association of Political Consultants. Members pool their knowledge and experience and discuss various approaches to campaigns all around the world. They meet at regular conferences and newsletters are distributed widely. According to Napolitan (1995), the IAPC has about 100 members, and the AAPC has 600 members. The profession even has a monthly magazine devoted to its interests, *Campaigns and Elections,* which is now in its 15th year. Another international organization that facilitates the exchange of campaign ideas is the World Association of Public Opinion Research, which includes among its luminaries, Elisabeth Noelle-Neumann (prominent in German CDU campaigns) and Robert Worcester (prominent in British Labour party campaigns).

Do Campaigns Matter?

The study of campaign effects has come a long way in the past decade or so. A number of studies have shown that campaigns do indeed "matter," and not just to the politicians. Semetko's chapter in this book assesses the competing campaign agendas of the media and the politicians. In this section, we explore the relationship between the politicians and the voters. There have been three main streams of research: on the local campaign, on the national campaign (particularly focused on advertising), and on "campaign events" (such as television debates, party primaries, and campaign conventions).

Local Campaign Effects

Studies on local campaign effects have by far the longest pedigree, dating back to Harold Gosnell's (1927) pioneering research of the 1920s. Indeed, it is the title of Gosnell's book, *Getting Out the Vote,* that summarizes much of the findings of this predominantly U.S. research, that is, that the efforts of local party organizations affect voter turnout, but not voter persuasion. Therefore, local party organizations should focus their efforts only on those areas where their natural support levels are strong; on no account should any efforts be made in hostile areas. There have been two main research methods. First, a series of studies has sought to assess the effects of strong local party organizations on the vote (see references in Weir 1985; also Frendreis, Gibson, and Vertz 1990; Herrnson 1986; Howell and Oiler 1981). A prominent indicator of party organizational "strength" is the amount of money it has to spend in the district. Given the relative ease of access to data on campaign finance, this has spawned a large literature in the United States and the United Kingdom on the effects of campaign spending on the vote, which has found clear evidence of an effect (Copeland 1983; Jacobson 1978, 1980; Seyd and Whiteley 1994; Johnston and Pattie 1995).

Much more prominent have been the studies that specifically set out to explore the effects of local party canvassing (see references in Weir 1985; see also Huckfeldt and Sprague 1992). Some other countries have also been considered, including Britain (Bochel and Denver 1971, 1972; Denver and Hands 1993; Pattie et al. 1994); Canada (Black 1984; Clarke et al. 1979); and Norway (Katz and Valen 1964). Overall, however, it is difficult to dispute Weir's contention (1985, 125) that research in this area "is predominately an American scholarly pursuit."

The work on canvassing efforts has sought to distinguish between different forms of canvassing. In general, the findings of the earlier studies were that personal (i.e., door-to-door) canvassing has the greatest influence, followed by direct mail, followed by telephone canvassing (Weir 1985). Given recent technological developments—notably the introduction of computer-aided dialing technology—this ranking undoubtedly has shifted, as more and more campaigners have been moving over to telephone canvassing (e.g., Johnson-Parker and Parker 1994; Nienstedt 1994).

The Effects of Campaign Advertising

In the latter part of the 1970s, and reflecting the centralization of campaign practices, the academic community shifted its attention to the measurement of national-level campaign effects, particularly television advertising and party election broadcasts. The pioneering research was by Patterson and McClure (1976), who demonstrated how television spots have clear "cognitive" effects, contributing to a general increase in levels of awareness of the candidates and their policies. It has also been shown that advertisements can affect voters' opinions on candidates and issues (Johnston et al. 1992; Kaid 1981). In a cross-national analysis of the United States, France, Germany, and Italy, it was found that "political advertising exposure can significantly affect a leader's image rating" (Kaid and Holtz-Bacha 1995a, 220), although in two cases (France and Italy) the effect was negative. Indeed, advertisements do not always have the precise effect intended by their sponsors. For instance, there is evidence that negative advertising can have a backlash effect, harming the candidate the advertisement is intended to help (Garramone 1985; Kaid and Boydston 1987). The significance of campaign advertising has also been demonstrated in Australia (McAllister 1992), Britain (Scammell and Semetko 1995), and Canada (Johnston et al. 1992). (See chap. 10 in this volume.)

Campaign Events and Their Effect on the Vote

An alternative means of measuring the effect of campaign activities on the vote is to focus on specific campaign events—primaries, party conventions, debates—and assess opinion poll reactions to them. The assumption here is that because the campaign organizations are concentrating their resources on these events, they provide ideal campaign highpoints where it can be expected that voter reaction will be significant. Once again, the United States is the main focus of attention, reflecting trends in scholarship and the nature of the their electoral process.

The U.S. presidential primaries represent an interesting case for research, given that these represent an example of where party attachment is of little importance and where candidates are only beginning to become visible. So we should expect to find plenty of evidence of campaign effects. For the most part, the evidence points toward information effects rather than persuasion effects. Bartels (1988) shows how attitudes and opinions have been formed over the course of a presidential primary, so that after the 1984 New Hampshire primary, voters who had heard of Gary Hart were able to make a prediction on his likely success in the nomination stakes. Throughout the 1984 primaries, there was clear evidence of a growing awareness of the personal traits of all the candidates (Brady and Johnston 1987).

Another set of studies has examined the party selection conventions, finding evidence of significant "bumps" in level of support for the presidential candidate after the relevant convention. Typically, this bump consists of a 5%-7% increase in the poll rating of the candidate (Holbrook 1996). Furthermore, the first convention tends to produce the bigger effect. This is consistent with the findings on the effects of primaries, showing how when voters have lower levels of information on candidates they are more likely to be influenced. As the campaign progresses and the voters are better informed, their votes are less likely to be swayed. In his comprehensive review of the evidence, Holbrook (1996) suggests that given the right circumstances, convention bumps can play a "pivotal" role in the result of the election. This is affected by a range of factors, among them the nature and tone of media coverage of the convention, its timing, the quality of the message of the convention (e.g., whether there were any gaffes), the potential for actual improvement in the polls, and the magnitude of the bump.

It has long been felt that television debates are influential. Ever since the famous Nixon-Kennedy debates of 1960, politicians and the media have invested time, money, and resources in these events. The scholars have not been far behind (see chap. 10). The first studies showed how the presidential debates of 1960 and 1976 increased levels of voter awareness of candidates and the issues. But the only persuasive effect appeared to be of the form of reinforcing predispositions (Chaffee and Dennis 1979; Katz and Feldman 1962; Sears and Chaffee 1979). Research on more recent debates has demonstrated some persuasion effects, notably in terms of voter opinion change on major campaign issues (Abramowitz 1978; Lanoue and Schrott 1989) and also on the candidates (e.g., Carter 1962; Kraus and Smith 1962; Davis 1979; Lanoue and Schrott 1989). The link between performance in television debates and candidate evaluations has also been explored in Canada (Johnston et al. 1992; Lanoue 1991) and Germany (Schrott 1989).

As we have seen, much of the research in this area has tended to be focused on the United States, but there have been some studies on Australasia, Canada, and a number of European countries. For the most part, however, the bulk of the evidence to support the contention that campaigns matter is from studies of campaigns in single-member, plurality electoral systems. It would be worthwhile exploring the potential for even greater campaign effects under voting systems that allow more scope for strategic voting (e.g., Cohan, McKinlay, and Mughan 1975).

Is Campaign Professionalization
a Good or a Bad Thing?

According to some authors, the new campaign styles are not welcome; they entail a growing influence of the politicians over the voters; they contribute to an oversimplifying of political debate; they reflect a shift away from campaign "communication" and toward "party propaganda" (e.g., Lawson and Ysmal 1992). Are such charges fair? A problem with these negative interpretations is that (at least implicitly) they are dealing with campaign change in isolation. There is no allowance for the fact that the other two sets of actors in the electoral process—the media and the voters—have also been adapting.

As Semetko's chapter (chap. 10) shows, media coverage of elections has changed dramatically. There is a more competitive media environment: "Horserace" media coverage of campaign events, together with the growing prominence of investigative journalism, has resulted in a closer scrutiny of the politicians and their images and campaigns. This "feeding frenzy" of "pack journalism" (Sabato 1993) has coincided with a voter environment that is also becoming ever more competitive, characterized by declining levels of voter attachment, increased voter volatility, and the rise of issue (and image) voting (see this volume, chap. 13).

The implication of these media and voter developments is that the electoral process has become more competitive, so that the politicians have to work harder to win new votes and to maintain old ones (Miller et al. 1990). Therefore, rather than viewing campaign professionalization as an unwelcome development, as somehow involving a tightening of the politicians' hold over the electoral process, it is probably more accurate to characterize it as an attempt by politicians to preserve the status quo. The politicians are running harder to keep still.

Notes

1. I am assuming throughout that the principal goal of candidates and parties is to maximize the vote. Obviously, other goals are possible: a stress on traditional ideology or a particular set of issues even if at the cost of votes, an attempt to constrain electoral gains so as not to upset potential coalition partners, a desire for a particular result to deal with a faction inside the party, and so on.

2. For similar reasons, it is common for Irish candidates to rely on their own resources; the crucial difference, however, is that their efforts are just one part of a larger national campaign waged by party headquarters (Farrell, 1986, 1987, 1990, 1993).

3. In the South Korean 1988 election, tourism increased by 30% as a result of the busing of supporters by the DJP (Lee 1990, 101).

4. I am grateful to Roberto Espíndola for this observation.

(7)

Legislative Recruitment

PIPPA NORRIS

Recruitment into political leadership represents an essential function of the political system, with significant consequences for parties, legislative elites, and democratic representation.[1] The process influences the distribution of power within party organizations, determines the social composition of parliaments, and shapes the pool of leaders eligible for government office. Through recruitment, some groups are mobilized into politics, and some are mobilized out. One long-standing criticism of the process is that it produces socially unrepresentative parliamentary elites. The aim of this chapter is to compare the evidence for this claim and to consider how we can explain the common social bias of legislatures.

Elected bodies can be evaluated as representative according to widely differing principles based on alternative democratic theories (Thomassen 1994; Birch 1993; Eulau and Wahlke 1978; Pitkin 1967). In the responsible *party government* model, voters are given the choice of alternative party platforms or elections, and individual candidates are regarded as members of their collective organizations (Norris 1996a). In this regard *who* stands for election is less important than *what* their party stands for. This model predominates in parliamentary democracies characterized by a high degree of party discipline. In the *district delegate* model, which is more common in the Anglo-American democracies, elected members are seen primarily as agents of the geographic areas from which they are elected. Members of Congress are regarded as representative of all citizens in their constituency, rather than members of party organizations taking collective responsibility for government. In contrast *social representation*—the focus of this chapter—refers to whether the composition of legislatures reflects the society from which they are drawn, in terms of politically salient cleavages like gender, class, language, and ethnicity.

The concept of social representation has historic roots in class politics. Arguments for reform in early-19th century Britain stressed that a parliament composed of landed aristocrats could not represent the interests of the rising urban bourgeoisie. The creation of Labour and Social Democratic parties at the turn of the century rested on the belief that trade unionists needed to send working men to parliament. The rationale for regional parties rests on similar grounds: that only residents from particular areas can articulate the concerns of their citizens. In recent decades, ethnic minorities have expressed greater concern about the exclusion of their voice in the political process, and the growth of the women's movement has increased demands for female representation. The case for social representation can rest on the simple grounds of equity. It can be argued that an elected assembly that excludes a large proportion of its citizens may be perceived as lacking democratic legitimacy. The most common argument is that the background and experience that members bring to elected office will color their priorities, attitudes, and behavior. It is claimed that women or ethnic minority politicians will articulate different concerns, and will bring different issues, into the public arena. Systematic evidence supporting the claim that women will make a difference is starting to emerge in the United States, Europe, and Scandinavia (Thomas 1994; Dodson and Carroll 1991; Dahlerup 1988; Karvonen and Selle 1995; Norris 1996b).

The Class, Gender, and
Age Bias of Legislative Elites

Despite strong demands for inclusion, most elected bodies continue to remain strikingly unrepresentative in their social composition. In a worldwide pattern, legislative bodies are drawn from higher-status strata in society (Lovenduski and Norris 1993; Loewenberg and Patterson 1979, 69-75; Putnam 1976, chap. 2; Mezey 1979, 223-53). Once the legal barriers were demolished, with the establishment of the universal franchise, many believed parliaments would gradually reflect the diversity of the societies from which they were drawn. Instead, political minorities—whether based on cleavages of gender, class, ethnicity, religion, nationality, or language—continue to lag behind in elected office in most countries. Some assume political elites will gradually become more socially diverse, but trends suggest this is far from inevitable. Worldwide, the percentage of women members of parliament has *fallen* in 1988-1994, from 14.6 to 10.5 (Inter-Parliamentary Union 1994b). Class disparities have widened substantially over time. The iron law of social bias, while rusting in some countries, remains a global phenomenon.

Class. Tables 7.1 and 7.2 show the occupational class of legislators in democracies where recent information is available. These data need to be treated with caution, because it matters what classification scheme is used. Nevertheless, the pattern confirms the class bias found previously. Lawyers are the largest group of members (18 percent), with business executives and managers close behind (17 percent). Administrators, teachers, and journalists—the talking professions—are also overrepresented. The main avenues for working-class recruitment are Labour, Social Democratic, and Communist parties (Epstein 1980, 167-200). The decline in working-class candidates has been found cross-nationally. In the British Labour party, about three-quarters of all MPs were rank-and-file workers in 1918-1931, compared with about one fifth today. By 1992, about 10 percent of all British MPs were from manual occupations, compared with 48 percent of the population (Norris and Lovenduski 1995, 96-9). In Germany, only 1 percent of Bundestag members can be classified as "workers and employed craftsmen" (Von Beyme 1983, 104-16; Brauntual 1983, 62-6). In Denmark, despite the strength of Social Democratic parties, in the mid-1970s only 4.5 percent of Folketing members listed themselves as workers (Arter 1984, 8-12; Elder, Thomas, and Arter 1988, 151-8). In Australia, at the turn of the century Labour candidates were evenly balanced between manual and nonmanual occupations. By 1990, only 6 percent were manual workers (McAllister 1992, 205-6; Jupp 1982, 162-4). Japanese politics has rarely involved many blue-collar workers: In the postwar period 7.5 percent of members of the Diet were workers, or union officials from manual occupations (Ramsdell 1992, 25-38). In Chile, 1.7

percent of deputies were industrial workers (Caviedes 1991). Similar patterns have been found elsewhere (Putnam 1976; Loewenberg and Patterson 1979). In the 1994 European elections, only 2.7 percent of candidates were manual workers.

Gender. The position of women in legislative elites is well known (see Table 7.3). In recent years, women are relatively well represented in Scandinavian countries and the Netherlands, where they comprise over a third of all members of parliament, with substantial growth in their numbers since the mid-1970s. Women are about one fifth of elected politicians in Germany, New Zealand, and Austria. In contrast, women are poorly represented in countries such as Turkey, Mali, Japan, Ukraine, Thailand, and France. Western democracies have experienced a modest increase in women's representation in recent elections, on average about 2.3 percent from one election to the next. Yet there was a sharp fall in women legislators in the first democratic elections in Eastern and Central Europe, due to the abolition of party quotas. In the democracies under comparison, by 1994 women represented 13 percent of all legislators in the lower house, 10 percent in the upper chamber, and 9.2 percent of cabinet-level posts. The success of women in the lower house is a reliable indicator of their status in national politics. There is a strong relationship between the proportion of women in cabinet and the lower house ($r = .85, p = .01$), as well as between the lower and upper house ($r = .62, p = .01$).

Age. The age pattern of legislators shows little change over time. Most members are in their mid-40s, although there are some cross-national variations (see Table 7.4). The issues of class and gender have attracted more attention; nevertheless, the lack of younger members may also be important for political representation if there are, as Inglehart suggests (1977), significant generational differences in basic values. Many parties have youth organizations, aiming to attract new blood into the party. Age is one factor that party leaders may consider when balancing party lists. Political minorities based on linguistic, religious, or ethnic groups may be critical to the politics of representation in particular countries, such as Belgium, Canada, and Northern Ireland, but these factors are more difficult to compare because the salient cleavages vary cross-nationally. The social biases of legislative elites are therefore long-standing and well established. Less agreement concerns how to explain this phenomenon.

TABLE 7.1 Occupations of Parliamentarians in the Lower House

	Total	Australia	Canada	France	Greece	Israel	Japan	Malta	New Zealand	Portugal	Switzerland	U.S.	U.K.
Lawmaking professions													
Legal profession	18	11	19	6	38	18	6	27	14	21	17	35	13
Civil servants	11	8	10	20		5	33	6		8		11	11
Politicians and party officials	10	11	1				33			1	30	11	7
Business and finance													
Commercial and business	17	22	22	6		18	13	4	20	15	12	30	24
Accountants/finance	1		3					4	6				2
Talking professions													
Educational profession	14	18	15	26	11	14	2	4	12	19	13	11	16
Journalism/media/writers	3	2	5	3		3	1	3		1	7	5	7
Social scientists	2		2		6	10		3		6			1
Literary and artistic	1			2		4					3		
Other professions													
Medical profession	5	4	4	12	14	1	1	20	3	6		1	1
Agriculture and farmers	3		5	3		8	3		15		13	4	2
Engineering/architects	3	2	1	2	10	4		13	3	10	7	1	1
Other white collar	3	10	4	13				6					
Armed forces	1	1			3	4				1			2

	Total	Australia	Canada	France	Greece	Israel	Japan	Malta	New Zealand	Portugal	Switzerland	U.S.	U.K.
Manual Trades													
Manual workers	3	5	1	3		4				4			10
Trade unionists	1	5							5			1	
Not available	6	10	10	4	20	12	7	10	21	8		1	1
Total	100	100	100	100	100	100	100	100	100	100	100	100	100
Election year		1987	1988	1986	1990	1992	1990	1992	1990	1987	1991	1990	1992

SOURCE: Inter-Parliamentary Union (1990-1992).

TABLE 7.2 Summary of Occupations of Parliamentarians in the Lower House (in percentages)

	Total	Australia	Canada	France	Greece	Israel	Japan	Malta	New Zealand	Portugal	Switzerland	U.S.	U.K.
Lawmaking professions	39	31	30	26	38	23	73	33	14	30	47	47	32
Business and finance	17	22	25	6		18	13	9	26	15	12	30	26
Talking professions	20	20	21	31	17	32	3	10	12	26	22	16	24
Other professions	15	17	14	30	26	17	4	39	22	17	19	7	6
Manual workers	3	10		3					5	4		1	10
Not available	6		10	4	20	12	7	10	21	8		1	1
	100	100	100	100	100	100	100	100	100	100	100	100	100

SOURCE: Inter-Parliamentary Union (1990-1992).

190

TABLE 7.3 Women Legislators in the Lower House

Country	Year of Election	Women MPs (N)	Total MPs (N)	Women MPs (Percentage)	Electoral System
Sweden	1994	140	349	40.3	List
Norway	1993	65	165	39.4	List
Finland	1991	78	200	39.0	List
Denmark	1990	59	179	33.0	List
Netherlands	1994	47	150	31.3	List
Germany	1994	177	672	26.3	AMS
Austria	1990	39	183	21.3	List
New Zealand	1993	21	99	21.2	FPTP
Canada	1993	53	295	18.0	FPTP
Switzerland	1991	35	200	17.5	List
Argentina	1993	42	257	16.3	List
Spain	1993	56	350	16.0	List
Italy	1994	95	630	15.1	AMS
Costa Rica	1994	8	57	14.0	List
Poland	1993	60	460	13.0	FPTP
Ireland	1992	20	166	12.1	STV
Colombia	1994	18	163	11.0	List
Hungary	1994	42	386	10.9	AMS
United States	1994	47	435	10.8	FPTP
Philippines	1992	21	199	10.6	FPTP
Bangladesh	1991	34	330	10.3	FPTP
Czech Repuplic	1992	20	200	10.0	List
Russia	1993	43	448	9.6	List
Belgium	1991	20	212	9.4	List
Israel	1992	11	120	9.2	List
United Kingdom	1992	60	651	9.2	FPTP
Portugal	1991	20	230	8.7	List
Australia	1993	12	147	8.2	AV
Mexico	1991	38	500	7.6	AMS
Chile	1993	9	120	7.5	FPTP
India	1991	39	531	7.3	FPTP
Zambia	1991	10	150	6.7	FPTP
France	1993	35	577	6.1	2nd ballot
Uruguay	1989	6	99	6.1	List
Brazil	1990	30	503	6.0	List
Greece	1993	18	300	6.0	List

TABLE 7.3 *Continued*

Country	Year of Election	Women MPs (N)	Total MPs (N)	Women MPs (Percentage)	Electoral System
Venezuela	1993	12	203	5.9	AMS
Ecuador	1994	4	77	5.2	List
Thailand	1992	15	360	4.2	FPTP
Ukraine	1994	12	337	3.6	FPTP
Nepal	1991	7	205	3.4	FPTP
Japan	1993	14	511	2.7	STNV
Mali	1992	3	129	2.3	FPTP
Turkey	1991	8	450	1.8	List
Mean		36	295	13.0	

SOURCE: Inter-Parliamentary Union (1994a).
NOTE: AV = alternative vote; STV = single transferable vote; AMS = additional member system; STNV = single nontransferable vote; FPTP = first-past-the-post.

Explanations of Legislative Recruitment

To explain legislative recruitment, politics can be seen as a pyramid with grassroots activists at the base, legislative candidates in the middle strata, and government leaders at the top. At the base, studies of public participation focus on why people become politically involved through activities such as voting, campaigning, or lobbying. The extent of mass participation is largely determined by "supply-side" factors: Any volunteer who fits certain minimum eligibility requirements can normally take part. People are mobilized into activity by parties and social movements (Rosenstone and Hansen 1993), but there are few formal barriers to entry. In the same way, legislative recruitment involves the *supply* of activists willing to pursue office. But the critical distinction is that recruitment also involves the *demands* of gatekeepers who select some from among the pool of eligibles.

Recruitment operates at all levels, from local office to political leaders, although this chapter focuses primarily on legislative recruitment to national parliaments. Parties remain the primary gatekeepers to elected office, including national leaders and party managers, regional organizations, constituency officials, and grassroots members. But in some countries, non-party gatekeepers may play an important role, including interest groups, media commentators, financial supporters, and civic notables, although their role as selectors

TABLE 7.4 Age of Parliamentarians in the Lower House

	Under 30	30s	40s	50s	60+	Election
Austria	0	17	42	32	6	1990
Belgium	2	21	38	38	1	1991
Denmark	4	11	46	25	15	1988
Germany	2	25	50	22	1	1990
Greece	0	26	32	33	9	1990
Iceland	0	24	41	25	10	1991
Israel	0	14	37	33	16	1992
Japan	0	5	24	31	39	1990
Luxembourg	3	13	32	23	28	1989
Malta	2	27	30	24	16	1992
New Zealand	3	21	51	23	3	1990
Portugal	8	27	38	18	9	1987
United Kingdom	0	12	39	33	15	1992
United States	0	9	35	31	25	1990
Mean	3	18	38	28	14	

SOURCE: Inter-Parliamentary Union (1990-1992).

has been less commonly studied (Norris 1996c). The electorate determines the final winner in electoral systems with single-member districts or open party lists, although voters have the greatest effect in direct primaries. The decision-making process may be open or closed, public or private, centralized or dispersed. No matter the agency or level of office, by definition all recruitment involves the twin components of supply and demand: Someone has to be willing to come forward, and someone else determines whether they are selected.

Legislative recruitment largely shapes the pool of eligibles for the highest offices of state. The diverse routes to power in higher office have been studied elsewhere and will not be covered here (see this volume, chap. 11; Blondel 1985; Blondel and Thiebault 1991; Laver and Shepsle 1994).

Despite its importance, few studies have compared legislative recruitment in a wide range of countries (for a review of this literature, see Lovenduski and Norris 1993; Putnam 1976; Gallagher and Marsh 1988; Gallagher et al. 1995; Epstein 1980; Ranney 1981; Katz and Mair 1992, 1994). Existing research falls into two major categories. Most studies have focused on the process of recruitment within party organizations to understand their power structures. In Schattschneider's words (1942, 101), "The nominating process has become the crucial process of the party. He who can make the nominations is the owner of the party." The key question in this literature is *who* selects within parties, based on analyzing the constitutions, rules, and institutional structures that govern the process. Yet this neglects the informal decision-making process and the supply of candidates who come forward.

In contrast, the dominant approach in the American literature focuses on the motivation of individual candidates, particularly the incentives and costs that shape strategic decisions to run within a particular structure of opportunities (Schlesinger 1966, 1991). The rise of voter primaries has shifted attention toward the motivation of "political entrepreneurs" and the role of political ambition (Ehrenhalt 1992; Fowler and McClure 1989; Fowler 1993; Williams and Lascher 1993; Kazee 1994). This approach provides a useful counterpart to the party literature, but the emphasis on office-seekers neglects the gate-keeping role of key supporters, whether political action committees (PACs), local notables, or the media. The focus on the personal ambition of candidates also underemphasizes the way that this becomes manifest within a particular opportunity structures set by the political system. Politicians with identical drive in Norway, the United States, and Japan, for example, would each pursue office within extremely different institutional contexts.

Both the European and the American focus seem unduly limited by themselves. The most appropriate alternative is a "new institutionalism" approach blending individual and institutional factors (March and Olsen 1989; Powell and Dimaggio 1991). The recruitment process involves rules, norms, and structures that determine, order, and modify individual choices. The "new institutionalists" differ on many issues. Nevertheless there is a broad consensus on three fundamental points:

1. *Institutions shape politics.* The outcomes of recruitment processes are not simply reducible to individuals, nor the social system. Instead, the rules and procedures of institutions structure political behavior in predictable and orderly ways.

2. *Institutions have historical baggage.* The recruitment process can be reformed and changed; nevertheless, the way the process works has inertia from the weight of its past. Whether parties use voter primaries or whether party leaders chose, their successors may have been "accidental" when first established, but once implemented these rules condition what comes later. Reformers have to work with existing institutions when seeking change.

3. *Institutions have formal and informal dimensions.* Institutions are embodied in organizational structures, written constitutions, and rule books. But equally

important are informal norms, unofficial procedures, and traditional practices. To understand recruitment, we therefore need to analyze individual perceptions of the rules of the game, and how this influences strategic behavior.

Using this perspective, we can identify three levels of analysis (see Figure 7.1). First, the *political system* sets the recruitment environment, notably the legal, constitutional, and electoral frameworks. Second, the *recruitment structure* determines the rules of the game. In most countries, the locus of recruitment is almost wholly within particular parties—hence the need to understand their power structure, processes, and cultures. But interest groups, the media, and financial supporters, as well as voters, may influence judgments of credible contenders in more open systems. Within this institutional context, we can compare individual-level supply-and-demand factors: who comes forward, who gets selected, and why (see Norris and Lovenduski 1995). Let us consider the influence of each in turn.

The Recruitment Environment

The Legal and Constitutional System

The legal system specifies the criteria of eligibility for candidates in all democracies and regulates the detailed recruitment process in a few. The most common candidacy regulations concern age, nationality, residence, personal conduct, and holding public office (see Table 7.5). The age requirements vary: In most countries candidates must be at least 18, 21, or 25, although a few set the minimum age higher (30 for the U.S. Senate, Canadian Senate, and Japan House of Councilors; 35 for the French Senate; and 40 for the Belgian and Italian Senates) (Inter-Parliamentary Union 1986, 65). Citizenship is an almost universal requirement, sometimes for a long period, occasionally from birth. Residency requirements within the country, province, or state are fairly common (Inter-Parliamentary Union 1986, 66).

The law also establishes certain other standards for politicians. As shown in Table 7.5, candidates can often be disqualified on the grounds of insanity, criminal convictions, undischarged bankruptcy, and in some developing countries, educational and literacy criteria. Certain offices are commonly seen as incompatible with membership of parliament, to prevent a conflict of interest, secure the independence of MPs, and prevent threats to the separa-

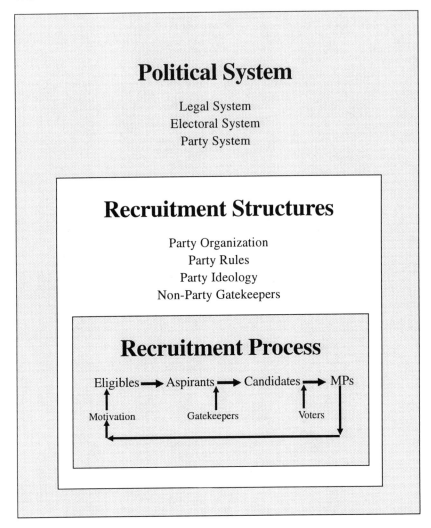

Figure 7.1. Three Levels of Analysis

tion of powers. Disqualified occupations include membership in other assemblies, public office, the armed forces, judiciary and police, and executives of public corporations (Inter-Parliamentary Union 1986, 70-101). Yet despite this lengthy list, these eligibility requirements mean that most citizens are legally qualified to run for office, should they so choose. After the

TABLE 7.5 Legal Eligibility for Legislative Candidates in the Lower House

	Minimum Age	Residency	Reasons for Disqualification				
			Criminal Record	Insanity	Election Offense	Bankrupt	Other
Australia	18	Country	Y		Y		
Austria	21	Country	Y				
Belgium	25	Country	Y	Y			
Canada	18	None	Y	Y	Y		
Denmark	18	Country					Y
Finland	18	None					
France	23	None					
Germany	18	None	Y				
Greece	25	None	Y				
Iceland							
Ireland	21	None	Y	Y		Y	
Israel	21	None	Y		Y		
Italy	25	None	Y	Y			
Japan	25	None	Y				
Luxembourg	21	Local	Y	Y	Y		
Malta	18	Country	Y	Y	Y	Y	
Netherlands	21	None	Y	Y			
New Zealand	18	Local	Y	Y	Y		Y
Norway	18	Country	Y	Y			
Portugal	18	None	Y	Y			Y
Spain	18	None					
Sweden	18	None					
Switzerland	20			Y			
United Kingdom	21	None	Y	Y	Y	Y	Y
United States	25	Local					
Mean/N	21		17	12	7	3	4

SOURCE: Inter-Parliamentary Union (1986).

universal enfranchisement of women, the legal system cannot explain who becomes a member of parliament, except perhaps for modest effects on the age of members.

The legal system regulates the recruitment process in detail only in the United States, Germany, Norway, Finland, Turkey, and Argentina. State laws in America closely regulate the selection of candidates for Congress and most other offices. Direct primaries became widespread during the 1960s, minimizing the selection powers of parties (Stanley and Niemi 1994, 148). Most primaries are closed (allowing only those registered for a party to vote in that contest), but some are open (allowing any citizen to participate).[2] In Germany, Article 21 of the 1949 Constitution provided public funding of parties and required them to select candidates for the Bundestag by a direct secret vote of all enrolled party members in each district, or by a district nominating committee (Kolinsky 1993). Finland's 1969 Party Act regulates the process in some detail and requires that every party member has the right to vote in party primaries for candidate nominations (Helander 1995). Norway's 1921 Nomination Act states that electoral lists must be decided by party conventions in each constituency, although this is interpreted quite flexibly (Valen 1988). Turkey's 1965 Political Parties Law requires that 95 percent of candidates are selected by the direct vote of dues-paying members in each district (Ranney 1981). Last, Argentina's 1991 Electoral Law established a compulsory 30 percent quota for female candidatures for all elective posts, which constrains the choice of parties (Inter-Parliamentary Union 1992, 97). Elsewhere, selection processes are regulated not by law but by the internal constitutions, rules, and informal practices governing recruitment structures.

The Electoral System

The comparison by Blais and Massicotte in chapter 2 outlines some of the main ways that the electoral system can influence candidate recruitment. In particular, these rules determine the nature of the voter's choice in party list elections. Systems with *preferential* (or open) voting, as used in Finland, Switzerland, and Luxembourg, let voters influence which candidates from within the party list get elected. In Switzerland, for example, voters may vote for the unaltered party list, or they may strike out some names on the list, vote twice for others, strike out some names from one party list and replace them with names from another list, or even compose their own party lists on the official blank ballot (Penniman 1983b). Systems that are *nonpreferential* (or closed), such as those in Germany, Portugal, and Spain, allow no choice to voters, and the rank order of candidates within the list is determined by party organizations with a fixed order of priorities. The last category of electoral systems offers preferential voting in theory, but in practice the order of candidates rarely changes, as in Belgium, the Netherlands, Austria, and Sweden (Gallagher et al. 1995, 285).

Previous studies by Czudnowski (1975, 221), among others, suggests that the electoral system can influence the centralization of the selection process: "Party selection seems to be closely related to the electoral system. When a candidate has to be elected by a local or regional constituency, he will tend to be selected by the local or regional party organization. In large multi-member constituencies central party organizations have a far greater influence, if not a monopoly, on candidate selection." Gallagher and Marsh (1988, 258) were more skeptical about this proposition on the grounds that national party leaders have more influence over recruitment decisions in plurality systems such as New Zealand and Japan than in countries with party lists such as Norway, Germany, and the Netherlands. More systematic evidence, however, confirms the relationship. The 1994 European Representation Study asked candidates for the European Parliament to estimate the power of different party bodies in their selection process. The results in Table 7.6 suggest that countries characterized by elections where the whole country forms one constituency have highly centralized recruitment processes. In contrast, Ireland and Britain had the most localized recruitment, and these countries use single transferable votes and simple plurality systems, respectively.

The effect of the electoral system on the representation of women is well established (Rule and Zimmerman 1992; Rule 1987; Norris 1985). The effects of the electoral system on working-class, ethnic, linguistic, or religious minorities is more complex, because this depends on the spatial distribution of group support, redistricting rules, reserved seats, and related issues. Chapter 2 in this book outlines the main alternative electoral systems. Women's representation may be affected by three factors in the electoral system: the ballot structure (whether party list, limited multimember, or single candidate); district magnitude (the number of seats per district); and the degree of proportionality (the allocation of votes to seats). All things being equal, ballot structure seems most significant: More women are elected under systems with a high number of seats per district. In a simple regression analysis, three factors—district magnitude, level of economic development, and the Nordic region—proved the most significant variables in predicting women's representation in all democracies (see Table 7.7).

We can compare the proportion of women MPs in the most recent election results (1989-1994) across all democracies (see Table 7.3). The average

TABLE 7.6 Powers of Selectorate

	National Party Leaders	Regional Party Leaders	Local Party Leaders	Local Party Members	National Party Factions	Party Officials
Ireland	1.4	1.4	1.4	1.4	1.4	3.1
Britain	1.7	2.5	3.9	6.8	1.7	2.5
Denmark	3.8	4.5	4.0	4.4	4.4	2.7
Germany	4.7	5.2	4.6	3.9	3.5	4.2
Netherlands	5.5	4.1	3.1	2.9	3.7	4.5
Belgium	5.6	3.9	2.6	2.6	3.9	3.3
Italy	5.8	5.3	4.4	3.9	4.0	3.2
Spain	6.1	5.4	3.6	3.1	4.5	5.2
France	6.3	4.0	3.2	3.1	3.6	3.0
Luxembourg	6.4	4.3	2.8	2.6	5.6	3.1

SOURCE: European Candidate Study (data file, 1994).
NOTE: Scaled from 1 = *not very important* to 7 = *very important*.

percentage of women representatives was 8.3 in majoritarian systems, 12.9 in semi-proportional systems, and 17.3 in proportional systems. All democracies where women are more than one-quarter of MPs use regional or national party lists with a high district magnitude. In contrast, most countries at the bottom of the table like Japan, Mali, and France use majoritarian systems. Yet there are two groups of outliers to this pattern. Some emerging democracies using proportional elections still have few women, such as Turkey, Ecuador, and Brazil. And women have made striking gains despite majoritarian systems, notably in New Zealand (with strong party quotas) and in Canada (with high incumbency turnover).

Moreover, in simultaneous elections in the same country, using different systems, more women succeed with party lists. Australia uses the alternative vote in single-member districts for the House of Representatives, and multimember state-level districts using proportional quotas for the Senate. In 1993, 8 percent of House members were women, but they were one-quarter of all senators. A similar pattern is evident in Germany. In federal elections to the Bundestag, half the seats are allocated by majoritarian single-member districts and half by proportional Land (regional) party lists. In 1990, 136 women entered the Bundestag, and the vast majority (109) won through Land

TABLE 7.7 Predictors of Women's Representation

	b	*Coding*
Electoral system		
District magnitude	.28*	Number of seats per district
Proportionality	.03	Gallagher least-squares index
Ballot structure	.08	Majoritarian (0), Semi-Prop (0.5), Proportional (1)
Number of parties	.09	ENPP[a]
Frequency of elections	.02	Number elections 1945-1994
Region		
Nordic	.68*	Yes (1), No (0)
Asia	.04	Yes (1), No (0)
Latin America	.04	Yes (1), No (0)
Western Europe	.11	Yes (1), No (0)
Central and Eastern Europe	.03	Yes (1), No (0)
Economic development	.26*	Per capita GNP
Adjusted R^2	.77	

NOTE: The model uses regression analysis with the percentage of women elected to the lower house in the most recent election (1989-1994) in 44 democracies as the dependent variable.
a. ENPP = effective number of parliamentary parties.
*$p \leq .05$.

lists. This pattern is further confirmed by countries like France that have changed their electoral system over time.[3]

Party list systems with a high district magnitude may facilitate women's entry for three reasons. First, there is the electoral argument. In single-member seats, local parties pick one standard bearer, and they may hesitate to choose candidates perceived as electorally risky. In contrast, there is a different "logic of choice" with long party lists where selectors have an electoral incentive to pick a "balanced ticket." With a lengthy list of names, it is unlikely that any votes will be lost by the presence of political minorities on the list. But their absence may cause offense, thereby narrowing the party's appeal. Second, there is the strategic argument. If parties want to help political minorities by affirmative action programs or selection quotas, this is easiest with longer lists. Last, there may be indirect effects. Greater proportionality can increase seat turnover, which may improve access for underrepresented groups.

Recruitment Structures

The political system sets the general context of recruitment within any country. But entry into elite positions is determined by certain procedures, rules, and practices set by recruitment structures. Political parties remain the main gatekeepers, although in more open systems interest groups, the media, and financial supporters may play a crucial role. The key selectors within parties may be grassroots party members, delegates at local party conventions, regional officers, factions, affiliated interest groups, or national party leaders, depending on the centralization of the system. Decisions by gatekeepers take place within the context of formal rules, and informal practices, which constrain choice. There is often considerable variance between parties within countries, depending on factors such as differences in party organizations, ideology, and power structures.

Identifying the key players is hindered by the complexities of the decision-making process within each party. Reviews have attempted to summarize the primary "selecting agency" in each country, such as the national executive or constituency committee (Ranney 1981; Gallagher et al. 1995, 254). But these summaries represent a considerable oversimplification: In practice many groups influence different stages of the recruitment process; a series of decisions produces the eventual outcome; practices vary substantially between different parties in a country; and formal constitutional powers may disguise de facto control.[4] There are many previous attempts to classify party organizations (see Katz in this volume, chap. 4). The increasingly stratarchical nature of parties makes it hard to generalize across different levels, because the party on the ground, the party in public office, and the party in central office may each have different functions, powers, and organizational structures (Katz and Mair 1994). The development of party policy, for example, may commonly be in the hands of the leadership, whereas members may retain the deciding vote over candidate selection. To develop a typology of recruitment, the process can be classified according to its degree of bureaucratization and centralization, producing four main categories (see Figure 7.2).

In this classification, the first dimension concerns the *bureaucratization* of the process. Following the classic Weberian notion, in highly institutionalized systems the application process is defined by internal party rules that are detailed, explicit, standardized, implemented by party officials, and authorized in party documents. The steps in the decision-making process are rela-

	Centralized decision making	Localized decision making
Bureaucratic	Examples: Austrian Socialists Greek PASOK	Examples: Swedish SDP British Labour party German SDP
Patronage	Examples: French UDF Mexican PRI Italian DC Japanese LDP	Examples: U.S. Democrats Canadian Liberals Swiss parties

Figure 7.2. Recruitment Structures

tively transparent to outside observers. There are formal appeal procedures. The significance of the rules for the distribution of internal party power may produce heated conflict over proposed changes. Financial supporters and other gatekeepers may use equally bureaucratic processes for evaluating which candidates to support. In contrast, in patronage systems the nomination procedure is relatively closed, gatekeepers have considerable discretion, the steps in the application process are familiar to participants but rarely made explicit, and procedure may vary from one selection to another. Guidelines and rules in official party regulations or constitutions tend to have de jure not de facto power. Because formal rules are rarely implemented, there are few effective courts of appeal. The process is less bureaucratic and more open to personal patronage by power brokers at different levels.

The second dimension of this typology concerns the *centralization* of decision making, an aspect that has been commonly emphasized in other comparisons (Gallagher and Marsh 1988; Gallagher et al. 1995). In centralized systems, the key players are national and regional party executives, affiliated groups, and faction leaders. In contrast, in highly localized systems the key players are located within constituencies,[5] districts, and ridings, including local officers, factions, groups, grassroots members, and voters. We can compare the powers of different bodies over the recruitment process as perceived by candidates for the European Parliament. As shown in Table 7.6, the most localized systems are those in Ireland and Britain, where national and regional party leaders played only a minimal role. In contrast in Spain, Luxembourg, Belgium, Italy, and France, grassroots members were seen to have relatively little influence. Differences between systems can be illustrated by examples of each type.

Central Patronage

Centralized patronage characterized the old Italian Christian Democrat (subsequently the Popular party) and the Italian Socialist party (PSI) (Guadagnini 1993). In these fragmented parties, selection was decided by a process of bargaining between the leadership of competing factions. Local officials tried to ensure their interests are heard, but they were often over-ruled.[6] In France, the UDF is a classic "caucus-cadre" organization, a loose network of like-minded followers coalesced around local and national nota-bles. In the UDF, the key gatekeepers are the leaders in party headquarters and regional notables who can "place" favored candidate in good positions, after taking account of proposals from departmental organizations. With no tradi-tion of internal party democracy, grassroots members play almost no role in the process. The French Socialist Party (PS), which developed a more organ-ized mass base, provides a weaker exemplar of this type. In the PS, candidate selection in principle is decentralized, with local constituencies choosing their own candidates by secret ballots of members. Yet in practice, as Appleton and Mazur (1993) suggest, the national party organization has very significant powers of supervision, which it has used to change nominations during the final stage of candidate ratification. The party has adopted quota requirements for candidate selection since the mid-1970s, but in practice these have not been implemented, except in recruitment to the European Parliament. Quota rules have proved rhetorical gestures rather than effective regulations. The proportion of women members, leaders, candidates, and elected officials in the PS is similar to that in the *Rassemblement pour la Republique* (RPR), which does not use quotas.

Centralized patronage is also common in Latin American parties where personalistic leaders retain power through acting as power brokers for clients seeking material rewards. Candidate selections are often determined by a small group of party chieftains. Some give the appearance of greater rank-and-file participation in decision making through party primaries but these contests are frequently manipulated (McDonald and Ruhl 1989, 7). In Vene-zuela, the party's national executive reserves for itself the prerogative of making the final decision concerning who is included on the list and their rank order (Hillman 1994, 59-66; Penniman 1980b, 41-5). In the predominant party

in Mexico, the PRI, candidates are formally chosen by an internally democratic procedure, but in practice the national leadership has all the power over
recruitment (Story 1992). Established leaders pick candidates, in a mentor-
disciple relationship. The political clique—or *camarilla*—determines who
gets to the top of the political ladder (Camp 1993).

Local Patronage

In contrast in systems with local patronage, it is difficult for the central
party leadership to play a major role—whether positive or negative—in the
recruitment process. The most extreme exemplar of this type is the United
States. Traditionally, American party organizations were relatively weak
caucus-cadre rather than "mass-branch" organizations. The decline of the
power of party bosses to choose their candidates in the proverbial smoke-filled
rooms, due to the introduction of primary elections by state law, produced the
rise of entrepreneurial candidates with their own independent funding, organization, and campaign. Any candidate who wishes to run in a party primary
can do so, once he or she fulfills the minimal legal requirements, although
parties in a few states retain a formal role. Far from being able to name, or
even veto, nominees, some state laws have even prohibited party organizations from endorsing particular candidates in the primaries (Katz and Mair
1994, 31).

The use of primaries in the United States has led many observers to stress
that "self-recruitment" is the norm (Ehrenhalt 1992; Kazee 1994). Yet this
overlooks the way all but self-financed candidates face other powerful "gatekeepers." PACs carefully scrutinize candidates before they offer funding.
Candidates may be interviewed by PACs in a formal process and may have to
provide documentation to support their application, or pledge certain policy
positions. Other actors who play a gatekeeping role include the local media,
individual financial contributors, campaign professionals, and local volunteers. Unless candidates are seen as strong and credible contenders by these
gatekeepers, they may be unable to run an effective campaign. Accordingly,
in the United States party organizations can no longer block, but neither can
they do much to promote, candidacies at the nomination stage (Burrell 1993,
1994). Elsewhere, few parties have ever used voter primaries, although in
Canada some ridings have occasionally opened the selection process to voter
meetings (Erickson 1993; Williams 1981). Primaries were also used by the
People's party in Austria in the early 1970s, and at the same time the Christian

Democrats experimented with them in Rhineland-Pfalz.[7] Nevertheless, voters have some role in legislative recruitment in all systems except those with closed party lists.

The local patronage system closest to the United States is probably Canada, which also has caucus-cadre parties. The extra parliamentary organization is pyramidal, with an executive body and small permanent office at the apex, and a wide and fluid body of voters at the foundation. Canadian parties are election machines not concerned with policy formulation. Between elections, virtually all the structure below the apex dissolves (Jackson, Jackson, and Baxter-Moore 1986). Yet within these weak parties, nominations remain the prerogative of the constituency associations, and most particularly the local party leaders. As a result, parties within ridings determine most of their own rules and practices for choosing their nominee (Erickson 1993; Landes 1983). Some constituency parties open the selection process to the whole membership, whereas others give a greater role to elected party officers. National leaders have formal veto power over the final choice of names, but in the past two decades this has only been used rarely by the major parties. The leaders of the major parties have encouraged women to run, assisted ridings searching for prospective candidates, provided some training conferences, and occasionally tried to parachute candidates into local ridings. Nevertheless, Erickson (1993) concludes that their hands are tied by the localized nature of the process. In the 1990s, following concern about possible abuse of the system, there have been moves to formalize the local selection rules in Canada, especially in the Liberal party.

Local Bureaucratic

The most common system in European parties is recruitment at local level governed by explicit bureaucratic rules that standardize the selection process throughout the party organization. Within the framework of rules, decisions about which individuals get chosen are taken largely at constituency level, although regional bodies may play a part. The major parties in Britain, Sweden, and Germany exemplify this category.

In Sweden, in the Social Democratic, Conservative, and Liberal parties, there are three stages: putting forward names, ranking nominees, and adopting the list. The middle stage is most critical. Here the nonsocialist parties often rely on meetings of activist members at the local and constituency level. In the Social Democrats, the local nominating committees and the constituency executives play a decisive role. The party lists are based on large multimember constituencies. In ranking the list, the party aims to produce a balanced ticket in terms of region, age, occupation, and gender. The Social Democrats recommend that at least 40 percent of all candidates should be women, and every other place on the party list should be allocated to the opposite sex.

In Britain, recruitment decisions are taken within constituencies, under strict formal rules that are established at national or region level. The precise steps in the process vary between parties, as described in detail elsewhere (Norris and Lovenduski 1995). In summary, the process can be seen like a game of musical chairs. All parties advertise vacancies widely to encourage applicants, then use a series of meetings involving party members within constituencies to shortlist, interview, and finally pick the local standard bearer. The process is highly bureaucratic; for example, in the Labour party there is a lengthy and detailed rule book establishing the correct procedure at every stage, monitored by regional officers, even recommending that the same questions should be asked of all candidates in the final constituency interview. The Conservative party has standardized the preliminary scrutiny of aspirants by introducing selection techniques derived from personnel management. The role of national party headquarters may be front-loaded, where they determine the overall pool of eligible applicants (in the Conservative, Liberal Democrat, and Scottish Nationalist parties). Or it may be back-ended, where they exercise veto control over the local nominee (in the Labour party, Plaid Cymru, and SNP). Despite this, key decisions are taken under formal, democratic procedures by grassroots members at the local level.

Last, Germany falls into this category, with the major parties based on formal mass-branch organizations. The process of candidate selection in constituencies, established by electoral law, follows two models. Either a meeting is held in a constituency where all party members may vote. Or party members elect delegates who in turn vote on candidates. The local parties determine recruitment for parliamentary elections, but regional party organizations influence the process, particularly in nominations on the Lander lists (Katz and Mair 1994, 189). Kolinsky (1993) notes that the regional and national party leaders have played a significant role in persuading local constituencies to accept more women. The names of nominees for constituencies and regional lists are compiled by the constituency and the regional executive, then passed to local parties for confirmation by party members. Gender quotas in the Social Democrats and Greens regulate the composition of party lists, whereas in other parties certain positions near the top of the list are reserved for women.

Central Bureaucratic

The decline of what Duverger termed caucus-cadre and "militant-cell" party organizations means that today few parties in liberal democracies use a centralized bureaucratic recruitment process. In this system, the party constitution and rules formally empower the national and factional leadership with the authority to decide which candidates are placed on the party ticket. In the past, this system operated most clearly in traditional Communist parties organized according to the principle of democratic centralism, such as the PCF in France and the PCI in Italy (Guadagnini 1993). Elsewhere in Europe, as Gallagher and Marsh (1988, 243-5) suggest, the national leadership or executive is the main selector of candidates in the Austrian Socialist Party, the Dutch Liberal party, the Greek PASOK, and several parties in Spain and Portugal. In the LDP in Japan, we find a similar pattern. Japanese parties tend to be highly centralized, exclusive in their membership patterns, and can be described as elite cadre parties (Hrebenar 1992). As parliamentary organizations, they have weak ties to the average citizen. Parties are internally divided between personality-led factions, which are well organized and cohesive, based on personal ties and fund-raising. These factions play the key role in the nomination of party candidates (Fukai and Fukui 1992). Recruitment structures therefore vary widely in who can select, and how far the process is bureaucratic or patronage based.

Individual Supply and Demand

Within recruitment structures, we also need to take account of factors that operate at the individual level. In the model discussed earlier, on the supply side, these factors include the motivation and resources of candidates, which determine who comes forward, and on the demand side, there are the attitudes of gatekeepers, which influence who is selected from the pool of aspirants (Norris and Lovenduski 1995).

The motivation of candidates has been stressed by many studies in the United States that suggest that political ambition distinguishes those who run for Congress from the pool of those who never consider public office (Kazee

1994; Fowler and McClure 1989). If political ambition is important, one reason why there may be fewer women in parliaments may be because they are not willing to campaign for elected office, whether because of traditional sex role stereotypes, lack of confidence, or lack of interest. Motivation is a highly complex issue to measure, in part because ambition may only be expressed within the context of the opportunities that are perceived as available. As a simple indicator to examine this proposition, we can compare the ambition of candidates for the European Parliament, when they were asked where they would most like to be "ten years from now." Candidates were presented with a list of possible careers, within the European Parliament, within their national parliament, and within the European bureaucracy, or retirement from public life. The results, in Table 7.8, suggest that women candidates expressed just as much ambition as men, if not more, for all these careers.

There are many resources that may help in the pursuit of elected office, including flexible brokerage careers, which allow time for politicking, financial resources, and security against electoral risks; social networks, which provide contacts; and political experience, which provides skills, knowledge, and credibility. One plausible explanation for the lack of women in higher office may be that they lack relevant experience at the lower levels within the party, local and state government, or affiliated organizations. There are fast routes into office (called *rampanti* or go-getters in Italy), but most accounts stress that political careers usually involve a lengthy series of incremental steps up the political ladder. To examine this possibility, we can compare the political experience of women and men running for the European Parliament, and whether they had held office in a variety of positions. The results in Table 7.9 reveal that contrary to this hypothesis, there were few major gender differences in political background. Women candidates for the European Parliament had slightly less experience than men as local government candidates and officers, but on the other hand, they had greater experience as national MPs, members of national governments, and officers for interest groups. The comparison suggests that women candidates for this body are equally well qualified by these measures and have moved up the lower levels of political careers.

Last, if supply-side measures fail to reveal any significant reason for the paucity of women politicians, we can turn to demand-side factors. Evidence that women are discriminated against by selectors is notoriously difficult to establish, although many believe that prejudice is the root of the problem if

TABLE 7.8 Political Ambition

	Men	*Women*	*Difference*
European parliamentary career			
Member European Parliament (EP)	43.1	48.3	5.2
Chair EP committee	12.5	17.7	5.2
Rapporteur EP committee	7.1	10.1	3.0
National parliamentary career			
Member national parliament	24.7	28.4	3.7
Member national government	19.9	17.0	–2.9
European leadership			
European commission	11.9	12.0	0.1
Head European agency	6.4	6.9	0.5
Chair parliamentary group	5.1	7.9	2.8
Retired from public life	22.9	25.2	2.3

SOURCE: European Candidate Study (data file, 1994).
NOTE: Entries are the percentage responding positively to the question, "Where would you most like to be ten years from now?"

gatekeepers favor traditional candidates. To assess this, candidates for the European Parliament were asked whether they thought that they had received opposition or support from a wide range of gatekeepers who play a role in different recruitment structures. The results, in Table 7.10, indicate that again contrary to expectations, women candidates reported receiving much the same or greater support than men reported across most categories of gatekeepers, including party officials, local party members, and national party leaders. This is a limited measure, but it casts doubt on the explanation that gatekeepers discriminate against women who come forward.

Conclusions:
Recruitment and Social Representation

We can conclude that the political system, recruitment structure, and individual factors interact within the recruitment process in complex ways that require further research to disentangle the effects. In particular, we understand little about how individual behavior is shaped by the structure of opportunities created by the political system and parties in different countries.

TABLE 7.9 Political Experience

	Men	Women	Difference
European parliament			
Been candidate	23.8	25.6	1.8
How often?	.4	.4	.0
Been elected	8.0	9.5	1.5
How often?	.2	.1	.0
Party office			
Local/regional party	33.3	32.5	−.8
National party office	30.9	30.6	−.3
Local government			
Candidate	59.7	55.2	−4.5
Elected	38.9	33.1	−5.8
National parliament			
Candidate	38.9	34.1	−4.8
Elected	7.7	12.3	4.6
Member of government	4.9	7.6	2.7
Public body			
Local	26.2	27.1	.9
National	20.3	18.0	−2.3
Group organizations			
Professional	22.5	21.8	−.7
Student	26.8	19.6	−7.2
Trade union	19.1	18.9	−.2
Women's organization	3.6	30.0	26.4
Local interest groups	28.6	34.1	5.5
National interest groups	20.4	24.3	3.9

SOURCE: European Candidate Study (data file, 1994).
NOTE: Entries are the percentage responding positively to the question, "Have you ever . . . ?"

Among other things, this discussion has implications for increasing the representation of political minorities, whether based on gender, ethnic, religious, regional, occupational, or linguistic groups. Fundamental constitutional reforms, such as the changes to the electoral system in New Zealand and Japan, are likely to have a significant effect on the opportunities facing candidates, but by their nature such reforms can also be expected to be relatively rare. Long-term changes in the motivation and resources of candidates, and the attitudes of gatekeepers, can also be expected to gradually shift the composi-

TABLE 7.10 Perceived Support by Gatekeepers

	Men	*Women*	*Difference*
Women's organizations	4.15	5.62	1.47
Party officials	5.49	5.77	.28
Other groups	4.53	4.80	.27
Local party members	6.06	6.23	.17
National party factions	5.07	5.24	.17
National party leaders	5.70	5.81	.11
Community groups	4.76	4.82	.06
Local party leaders	6.01	6.04	.03
Regional party leaders	5.93	5.86	−.07
Youth organizations	4.99	4.91	−.08
Trade unions	4.14	4.04	−.1
Business groups	4.02	3.82	−.2

SOURCE: European Candidate Study (data file, 1994).
NOTE: Scaled from 1 = *high opposition* to 7 = *high support.*

tion of legislatures. For example, as more women gradually enter the most common brokerage occupations, they may be expected to have a stronger springboard for legislative office. But in the short term, changes to recruitment structures seem likely to have the greatest practical effect.

In seeking greater social diversity, parties have implemented three types of recruitment policies (Lovenduski 1993). *Rhetorical strategies,* articulated in leadership speeches, official statements, and party platforms, aim to change the party ethos by affirming the need for social balance in the slate of candidates. *Affirmative action* programs aim to encourage groups to run by providing training sessions, advisory group targets, special conferences, financial assistance, and group monitoring. *Positive discrimination* sets mandatory group quotas, at a specific level—whether 20, 40, or 50 percent—applied to internal party bodies, shortlists of applicants, or lists of candidates. The distinction between advisory targets and mandatory quotas is often blurred in practice, particularly if quota rules are not implemented. The term quotas is often employed quite loosely and may have different cross-cultural connotations. But this does not invalidate the basic distinction between formal regulation and informal guidelines.

The analysis suggests that each type of party can employ rhetorical and affirmative action strategies, but positive discrimination operates most effectively in local-bureaucratic systems. It makes little sense to think about using positive discrimination for recruitment rules *within* the major parties in the United States or Canada. In local patronage systems, opportunities for candidates are not restricted by the central party leadership. At the same time, it is difficult to see what steps, beyond rhetorical encouragement, these parties could take to improve the social balance of legislatures. If the final decision rests in the hands of different local power brokers, and there are no standardized party rules concerning the nomination process, this seems to exclude effective positive action guidelines, financial assistance, or shortlisting targets for nominees.

Even if rules are passed, they are not likely to be implemented in the French UDF or the Mexican PRI. In centralized patronage systems, if the leadership decides to promote certain groups or individuals to balance the ticket, they have considerable power to do so. Through patronage, party leaders can improve the position of candidates on party lists, or place them in good constituencies. As a result, under this system of "benevolent autocracy" change can be implemented relatively quickly, although without institutional safeguards the gains can be quickly reversed. On the other hand, if the leadership resists change to the status quo, they can block opportunities for challengers. Under this system, positive discrimination strategies to increase social diversity will probably prove ineffective, because any regulations or guidelines will not be implemented. Because the process is not rule governed, changing the rules will not alter the outcome.

Positive discrimination quotas are taken most seriously in a rule-bound and bureaucratic culture, like the major German, Swedish, or British mass-branch parties, where decisions by different bodies within an organization are standardized. In particular, Social Democratic and Green parties are more likely to use positive discrimination strategies to bring about short-term change because this is compatible with their party cultures. Parties of the right are more likely to rely on rhetorical strategies, and possibly affirmative action, in the belief that political minorities should be encouraged to stand, and party members should be encouraged to select them, but the recruitment process has to involve "fair" and open competition. Just as right-wing parties favor a minimal role for government in the free market economy, so they prefer nonintervention in the recruitment process. This generalization needs one major qualification: Once positive discrimination is successfully implemented by left-wing and Green parties, in a competitive electoral environment other parties within the political system may follow suit.

We can conclude that the recruitment process can be understood to represent a central component of the political system, which may have significant consequences for democratic representation. Legislative recruitment determines the choice of candidates running in general elections and therefore the composition of elected assemblies. Ultimately, it can shape the pool of political leaders eligible for government office, the character of the nation's polity, and the linkages between citizens and representatives. As discussed earlier, there is a growing body of evidence that *who* gets into legislative elites has a significant effect on what concerns are prioritized, what legislation is passed, and what style of politics predominates. The focus on the responsible party government model of representative democracy, where politicians are held collectively accountable to the electorate through party platforms, should not blind us to the fact that candidates matter as well. Politicians create manifestos, manifestos do not create politicians. The background and experience of politicians may well be one factor, among many, that shapes which policy issues are prioritized, passed, and implemented. Therefore, the structure of opportunities for candidates may have significant effects on the social composition of legislatures, and thus the nature of representative democracy.

Notes

1. Different terms can be used to describe legislative recruitment, including "selection," "preselection," and "nomination," but all refer to the pursuit of elected office.

2. There are certain variations. Some states such as Michigan continue to employ conventions of party delegates for some state offices, and sometimes (as in Connecticut) conventions are used as a preliminary step to endorse candidates before primaries. Other variations include runoff majoritarian (second ballot) primary elections in Louisiana, Georgia, and South Dakota. For details on a state-by-state basis, see Smolka (1992, Table 5.3).

3. Between 1945 and 1956, and again in 1986, the French used proportional representation with department party lists without preference voting in the National Assembly. In contrast in the national elections from 1958 to 1981, and again in 1988, the system was changed so that candidates were elected by a single-member first ballot majority system, with a second runoff plurality ballot. As a result, more women were elected each term to the National Assembly by proportional representation than to any Assembly using the majoritarian system, with the exceptions of elections in 1981 and 1988.

4. For a summary of the rules and party agencies controlling candidate selection in 12 Western democracies, see Katz and Mair (1992).

5. Constituency (i.e., district, riding, or branch) meetings may be called selection conferences or conventions.

6. It remains to be seen how the move toward single-member plurality constituencies under the new electoral system will change the selection process within Italian parties.

7. For the use of voter primaries, see Gallagher and Marsh (1988, 238-9). It should be noted that other political systems, such as Norway, Canada and Israel, use "primaries," but these are elections where party members are enfranchised. These will be referred to as membership primaries. In the United States, party "membership" is a much looser concept, and "open" primaries allow any voter to participate, irrespective of party affiliation.

8

Electoral Participation

MARK N. FRANKLIN

Participation is the lifeblood of democracy, involving different numbers of people in different activities at different times. Maintaining viable party organizations requires the commitment of a few people over a considerable period. Campaigning, lobbying, or protesting require a rather greater commitment by rather more people, but over a shorter period. Voting requires a minimum commitment for a brief period, but involves the greatest number of people. In a book about elections, it seems natural to focus on voting. Indeed, the health of a democracy is often seen in terms of its level of turnout, and this will be our primary concern. However, low turnout may, as we shall see, be associated with the widespread use of alternative avenues for participatory activities; so those alternatives are not irrelevant even when we take a perspective that is primarily electoral.

This chapter starts by examining variations in voting turnout by country and by various social characteristics. In seeking to explain these variations, we consider three theories that have dominated research in this area ever since the start of behavioral political studies—one based on individual resources, one based on political mobilization, and the third based on instrumental motivation. The central argument in this chapter is that *instrumental motivation,* largely determined by the context in which elections are held, has been unduly neglected yet plays a critical role in driving electoral turnout. The salience of elections, the use of compulsory voting, a highly proportional electoral system, postal voting, and weekend polling provide the most plausible explanations of cross-national differences in voting turnout because these influence the costs and benefits of casting a ballot. The last section of the chapter considers cross-national variations in other types of political participation and the implications of these variations for democracy and democratization.

Turnout in Democracies

We can start by comparing turnout in 37 democracies.[1] Table 8.1 shows average turnout at free elections for the lower house in these countries, conducted between 1960 and 1995, along with the number of elections on which each average is based.[2] Countries marked with an [a] in this table are countries for which systemic characteristics have been compiled by Katz (1996). These countries are used in the country-level analyses reported later in this chapter.[3] Countries flagged with a [b] in this table are countries for which we have obtained survey data from the early 1990s. These countries are used in the individual-level analyses reported later in this chapter.[4] These overlapping data sets provide a snapshot of electoral participation across a wide variety of political systems, including those with emerging and established democratic institutions, parliamentary and presidential systems, and very different electoral and party systems.

When we turn to other types of participation, these are compared on the basis of studies conducted in seven countries by Verba et al. (1978), in five countries by Barnes et al. (1979), in Western Europe by Fuchs and Klingemann (1995), and in the United States by Rosenstone and Hansen (1993) and by Verba, Schlozman, and Brady (1995).

Who Participates?

Tables 8.1 and 8.2 show turnout variations between countries and across the social characteristics of individuals. The most striking message is that

TABLE 8.1 Average Turnout in Free Elections to the Lower House in 37
Countries, 1960-1995 (in percentages)

Australia[a] (14)	95	Costa Rica[a] (8)	81
Malta[a] (6)	94	Norway[a] (9)	81
Austria[a] (9)	92	Israel[a] (9)	80
Belgium[a, b] (12)	91	Portugal[a, b] (9)	79
Italy[a, b] (9)	90	Finland[a] (10)	78
Luxembourg[a, b] (7)	90	Canada[a] (11)	76
Iceland[a, b] (10)	89	France[a, b] (9)	76
New Zealand[a] (12)	88	United Kingdom[a, b] (9)	75
Denmark[a, b] (14)	87	Ireland[a, b] (11)	74
Venezuela[a] (7)	85	Spain[a, b] (6)	73
Bulgaria[b] (2)	80	Japan[a] (12)	71
Germany[a, b] (9)	86	Estonia[b] (2)	69
Sweden[a] (14)	86	Hungary[b] (2)	66
Greece[a, b] (10)	86	Russia[b] (2)	61
Lithuania[b] (1)	86	India[a] (6)	58
Latvia[b] (1)	86	United States[a, b] (9)	54
Czech Republic[b] (2)	85	Switzerland[a] (8)	54
Brazil[a] (3)	83	Poland[b] (2)	51
Netherlands[a, b] (7)	83		

SOURCE: Mackie and Rose (1991), Katz (1996), and *Electoral Studies* (vols. 5-14).
NOTE: Numbers in parentheses are the number of elections included in each average. For the United States,
only "on year" congressional elections are included (i.e., elections held in conjunction with presidential
elections). U.S. midterm elections do not respond to the same forces as elections elsewhere, because
executive power is not at stake. For the Netherlands, the series starts in 1968, after the abolition of
compulsory voting there.
a. Included in country-level analysis (29 countries).
b. Included in individual-level analysis. Romania (86 percent turnout) is included in these analyses (for a
total of 22 countries), but it does not qualify as a democracy according to the criteria established in chapter 1.

turnout varies much more from country to country than it does between
different types of individuals. It matters whether one is rich or poor, educated
or uneducated, interested in politics or not, but none of these things matter
nearly as much as whether one is an Australian or an American. Five countries
show turnout averaging over 90 percent (one shows turnout of 95 percent),
whereas four show turnout averaging under 60 percent (one shows turnout of
51 percent)—an average difference across these nine countries of nearly 40
percent. No difference in turnout levels across categories of individuals
averages more than two-thirds that. The strongest individual-level effect that
might be subject to manipulation—political discussion—averages only 13
percent (83.1 less 69.7 in Table 8.2). Individual-level differences are very
similar across Eastern and Western Europe, although rather greater in the
United States where education accounts for a 41 percent difference in turnout
levels, whereas age, income, and political discussion have effects that exceed

30 percent. But only the first of these differences even comes close to matching the difference between the United States and the high-turnout countries.

To make it clear that within-country effects never approach between-country effects, the final columns of Table 8.2 compare the variance explained by individual variables with that explained by country differences in a two-way analysis of variance. Only three variables have more than a tenth of the explanatory power of country differences, and only one has more than a fifth (that one being age, a variable hardly subject to manipulation).

This suggests that if one wants to increase electoral participation in a low-turnout country, the answer lies not in increasing levels of education or political interest of the citizens of that country—the only individual-level characteristics that appear amenable to manipulation. Even if everyone in the United States were college educated, for example, this would not bring turnout there even to levels found in medium-turnout countries such as Britain.[5] Of course, the effect of education might be additive with effects of political interest, party identification, and other variables so as to cumulatively raise turnout considerably, or the effects of those other variables might be largely subsumed by education. This question can only be evaluated by means of multivariate analysis (see below). In the meantime, our preliminary findings clearly imply that to increase the level of turnout in the United States, India, or Switzerland, we need to establish what factors make people more likely to participate in some countries than in others, and then see whether these factors can be imported by the low-turnout countries (cf. Powell 1986).

Why Participate?

Although a great many theories have been proposed to explain variations in political participation, these essentially boil down to explanations involving three different features that distinguish people from one another: *resources, mobilization,* and the desire to affect the course of public policy (what we shall call "*instrumental motivation*"). Resources are what people individually bring to the democratic process: knowledge, wealth, and time. Mobilization is the heightened awareness of their role that can be inculcated in people through the operations of the media, parties, and groups. Instrumental motivation is the sense that individuals may have that their actions (at least taken in concert with the actions of other individuals who share the same concerns) might affect an election outcome.[6]

TABLE 8.2 Turnout for Different Groups of Individuals in 22 Countries (in percentages)

Variable	Turnout in Group With		Variance Explained by	
	Lowest	Highest	Individual Effects	Country Effects
Age	58.8	88.9	6.3	9.9
Strength of party identification	70.1	89.2	1.6	9.9
Political discussion	69.7	83.1	2.1	9.9
Education	73.8	86.1	0.6	9.9
Religious participation	76.3	83.0	0.7	9.9
Union membership	76.8	81.6	0.3	9.9
Income	75.4	89.2	0.3	9.9
N	21,601	21,601	21,601	21,601

SOURCE: Based on Eurobarometer 41a; U.S. National Election Study, 1988; East European Barometer 2.
NOTE: Number of categories—age (5); strength of party identification (4); political discussions (2); education (2); religious participation (3); union member (2); income (5). The 22 countries are those marked [b] in Table 8.1 (see Table 8.1, note b).

Of these, the resource theory of political participation has been most widely studied. According to this theory, people participate who have the time and money to do so. The classic formulation of this approach was by Verba and Nie (1972), who proposed what they called a "baseline model" of political participation that generated an expected level of participation from education, income, and occupational variables.[7] This baseline produced expectations that might be modified by other individual characteristics, but generally not by much. The trouble with this approach is that it cannot explain the large differences in turnout that exist between countries. We have already seen that differences in turnout by levels of education and income are less than differences in turnout by country. Moreover, high-turnout countries do not have richer or more educated people than low-turnout countries. Indeed, two of the richest and most highly educated countries (Switzerland and the United States) are among the lowest in terms of turnout.

Taking account of the activities of groups and organizations (especially political parties) has recently gained prominence in studies of political participation (Rosenstone and Hansen 1993; Verba et al. 1995).[8] However, variations in mobilizing activities do not go far toward remedying the problems of the resource approach. According to Rosenstone and Hansen (1993), citizens (even those with most resources) are more likely to participate if encouraged to do so, and one source of encouragement comes from efforts made to "get out the vote." Yet in countries for which we have measured these effects (in the context of the European elections of 1989), country differences in mobilizing activities are smaller even than country differences in education or political interest.[9]

Both the resource and the mobilization theories indirectly address the instrumental motivations of citizens to affect the course of public policy. Those whose education and experience lead them to feel politically efficacious will vote because they are motivated to do so, and those who are mobilized to vote are evidently motivated as a consequence of involvement and persuasion (Verba et al. 1995). The role of the election *contest* as a source of instrumental motivation, however, has often been neglected by scholars who focus on the behavior of individuals. Among scholars who study differences between countries, on the other hand, the importance of institutional and contextual differences in affecting turnout has been a major theme in the literature of political participation since the earliest studies (Tingsten 1937; Crewe 1981; Powell 1980, 1986; Jackman 1987; Jackman and Miller 1995), and a link can be made between institutions and motivations if we consider differences between elections in how much is at stake (van der Eijk, Franklin, et al. 1996, chap. 19; van der Eijk, Franklin, and Marsh 1996). An election that does not decide the disposition of executive power (e.g., an election for the European Parliament or a U.S. midterm election) can be expected to prove less important (and therefore less likely to motivate voter turnout) than a national election in Europe or an American presidential election. If executive power is at stake, then we would expect that more people will turn out— especially if the election is a close one, the outcome seems likely to determine the course of public policy, and there are large perceived differences between policy alternatives. For example, the unprecedentedly high turnout in the 1992 Louisiana gubernatorial primary contested by the ex-Ku Klux Klan member David Duke shows the possible consequences in terms of turnout of an election whose outcome is expected to be close and whose protagonists arouse strong feelings.

This also means that an electoral system that ensures no votes are wasted will presumably motivate more people to vote and that a country like Switzerland, where the outcome of parliamentary elections has no discernible policy implications (because the same coalition will take office whatever the outcome and all important policies are in any case subject to referendum), will probably see lower turnout than a country like Malta, where every important political decision is going to be affected by the outcome of a single electoral contest (Hirczy 1995). Of course, the mobilization approach can also to some extent take account of differing electoral contexts because important elections will stimulate more electoral activity by parties and candidates, but the instrumental approach subsumes such activities. An electoral contest that stimulates voters to turn out in large numbers will evidently also stimulate parties and candidates to redouble their efforts to obtain the participation of those who might still stay at home.

In brief, the instrumental approach to understanding political participation is superior to the other two common approaches because it subsumes them both while explaining additional aspects of political participation that neither of the other approaches can address. Indeed, this approach is the only one that makes sense when we focus on the importance of the electoral context in conditioning people's motivations, and only differences in context show promise of explaining country differences in turnout.

Nevertheless, the fact that instrumental motivation has mainly to do with the benefits of voting should not blind us to the fact that voting also involves costs. Countries may differ not only in how important elections seem to voters but also in how difficult it is to vote. Later, we will describe some relevant ways in which countries differ from each other in these respects, but first we need to validate what so far has been merely suggested: that what matters in explaining turnout are differences between countries not differences between individuals.

Effects on Individual-Level Electoral Participation

We saw earlier that the differences between types of individual in terms of turnout were generally much less than differences between countries. The implication of that finding was that individual-level differences have less effect than country-level differences. This implication can be more formally confirmed if we conduct a multivariate analysis that attempts to explain individual-level electoral participation on the basis of demographic and other characteristics of individuals, and contrast the effects with those that can be seen when the country contexts in which individuals find themselves are taken into account. Such an analysis can assess the cumulative effects of many attributes at once, in contrast to our earlier descriptive approach.

A great many variables have been suggested as determining the resources that individuals bring to the participatory context and the success of parties in mobilizing these voters to turn out. In the data available to us for 22 countries (those of Western and Eastern Europe, together with the United States), relatively few variables are available that are relevant to electoral mobilization—only strength of party identification might be construed as a variable that would make voters responsive to mobilizing efforts. However, other analyses of specifically West European data (van der Eijk, Franklin, et al. 1996) has shown that campaign mobilization contributed less than one eighth of total individual-level effects on electoral participation, and the resource variables at our disposal do include virtually all those ever suggested in past research (cf. van der Eijk, Franklin, et al. 1996; Oppenhuis 1995).

Table 8.3 shows the effects of variables found to have statistically significant (at the .001 level) influences on individual-level electoral participation in three separate models: the first where only individual-level influences are considered,[10] the second where these effects are considered within their national contexts,[11] and the third where missing data indicators are taken into account.[12] As can be seen, individual-level characteristics explain only 5.2 percent of variance in electoral participation. Taking account of national context (in the central column of the table) multiplies this variance explained virtually fourfold. Taking account of missing data adds trivially (but significantly) to variance explained.[13] Effects (b) of the various variables included in the table are readily interpretable. The important finding is the extent to which national context exceeds in importance the effects of individual-level variables.[14] This is shown not only in terms of variance explained but also in the magnitude of the average country effect. Explicating these country differences is the purpose of the next section.

Country Differences in the Costs and Benefits of Voting

We have already suggested that the extent to which policy outputs are expected to depend on an election outcome will be important in determining

TABLE 8.3 Effects on Individual-Level Electoral Participation in 22 Countries

Variable	Individual Level Only		With National Effects Considered		With Missing Data Indicators	
	b	SE	b	SE	b	SE
Constant	.636	.017*	.065	.022	.069	.022
Age	.064	.002*	.063	.002*	.062	.002*
Strength of party identification	.010	.004	.040	.004*	.039	.004*
Political discussion	.097	.006*	.091	.006*	.093	.006*
Education	.005	.003	.025	.003*	.025	.003*
Religious participation	.008	.004	.024	.005*	.030	.004*
Union member	−.081	.006*	−.023	.006*	−.024	.006*
Income	.001	.001	.004	.009*	.004	.001*
Average country effect			.478	.017*	.489	.017*
Missing religious participation					−.041	.009*
Adjusted R^2	.055		.195		.195	
N	21,601		21,601		21,601	

SOURCE: See Table 8.2.
NOTE: For number of categories, see Table 8.2
*$p < .001$.

both the costs of failing to vote and the benefits of voting. Our example was Switzerland—a country where election results for the lower house are hardly linked to the political complexion of the executive. Another country with tenuous linkage between legislative election outcomes and government complexion is the United States. In these two countries, public policy outputs evidently rest on many imponderables apart from the outcome of legislative elections (cf. Hirczy, 1992), reducing the stakes of such elections (and hence the benefits of voting) compared to what they would be in systems where the linkage was tighter. A second feature of the electoral context that we have suggested will differentiate low-turnout countries from others is the number of electoral contests that are held. A country with federal as well as state elections, and frequent referenda (or propositions), is likely to see lower turnout than other countries. This feature will be hard for us to separate in practice from poor legislative-executive linkage, because the two countries in our data with least evident linkage between legislative electoral outcomes and government complexion are the same two countries (the United States and Switzerland) that have the largest number by far of electoral contests.[15] Because of the coincidence that these two countries are the only ones with both these reasons for low turnout, we cannot readily disentangle the two influences, and in the analyses conducted in this chapter we thus take both effects together, indicating their presence by means of dummy variable (which we refer to as "electoral salience" in the tables that follow) that picks out these two countries in contradistinction to all others.[16]

Another variable already mentioned as contributing to the benefits of voting is the proportionality of the electoral system. A country with single-member districts and a winner-takes-all electoral system will be one in which a large number of electoral contests have foregone conclusions because one candidate is known to be virtually certain of winning. People are less likely to vote in such contests, so overall turnout will be lower than in countries where a proportional electoral system ensures that fewer votes are wasted. In this research, we measure proportionality according to the votes/seats ratio (calculated over all parties in each country) observed in the last election held in each country during the 1980s (data from Mackie and Rose 1991).

Several potentially important variables have not yet been mentioned. Whether voter registration is automatic (as in most countries) or voluntary (as in the United States and some Latin American countries) will make a difference in the number of people registered to vote and hence able to respond to a late awareness of an election's importance. Voluntary voter registration is the reason customarily given for low turnout in U.S. elections (Piven and Cloward 1977; Wolfinger and Rosenstone 1980; Crewe 1981).[17] Whether the election occurs on a weekend or workday will evidently affect the ease with which working people can vote (Crewe 1981). In many countries, compulsory voting provides an incentive to vote (even if the penalties for not voting are nominal), and in some countries advance voting or postal voting will make it easier to obtain the participation of those away from their homes due to employment and other reasons. Finally, the number of days the polls are open might be thought to increase the opportunity to vote—except that it is also possible that having the polls open for more than a day will only happen in countries where there is some reason to suppose that the population will find it hard to get to the polls.[18] In that case, it is an empirical question whether the additional days the polls are open actually compensate for the additional difficulties of voting in such countries.

Effects of Country
Differences on Turnout

Across the 29 countries for which we have adequate data (this analysis excludes East European countries because of a lack of sufficient electoral contests), the country characteristics we have posited as being important prove somewhat sensitive to precisely which countries are included.[19] This can be seen in Table 8.4, which displays the findings from three different analyses. The first focuses on the 25 countries included in Mackie and Rose's *International Almanac of Electoral History* (1991), the only countries for which we have complete data on all the variables. The second adds another four countries for which we have most (but not all) of the relevant data. The third repeats this analysis with Switzerland and the United States omitted.[20]

The first two models explain a highly respectable 88 percent of variance in turnout, but the number of polling days only proves significant in the second of these two models. Five other variables are significant in both models. Of these, by far the most potent is electoral salience. Salient elections give rise to some 27 percent greater turnout than nonsalient elections. Because of the nature of this variable, our findings are driven by the low turnout in Switzerland and the United States, together with a plausible but unproven supposition about the reason for the anomalous turnout in these countries. These countries are omitted from the third model, with the consequence that salience plays no role in explaining turnout there, but the remaining coefficients are little changed; variance explained remains high at 80 percent. In the next section, we will report the results of an independent test of the importance of electoral salience in determining turnout, but first we should list the other variables that help to distinguish one country from another.

Compulsory voting, postal voting, and the proportionality of the electoral system between them can have an effect approaching that of electoral salience. Compulsory voting apparently increases turnout by about 7 percent in countries that make voting obligatory. Postal voting is worth about 4 percent. Proportionality is worth about six tenths of a percentage point in turnout for every percent by which the distribution of seats in the legislature approaches proportionality with the distribution of votes. Because countries vary in terms of the proportionality of their electoral systems from a low of 79 in Britain to a high of 99 in Germany, that is a 20-point difference, which (multiplied by 0.6) translates into a difference of about 12 percent in turnout. Sunday voting is worth 5-6 percent, and the effect of keeping polls open, in the second and

TABLE 8.4 Three Models Explaining Turnout in 29 Countries[a]

Variable	Mackie-Rose		29 Countries		Switzerland and U.S. Deleted	
	b	SE	b	SE	b	SE
Constant	21.94	14.78	26.46	13.53*	26.26	13.82*
Proportionality	0.62	0.15*	0.59	0.15*	0.60	0.15*
Compulsory voting	7.29	2.12*	7.30	1.74*	7.34	1.78*
Postal voting	4.06	1.99*	4.43	1.74*	4.42	1.78*
Sunday voting	5.29	1.20*	6.48	1.74*	6.32	1.84*
Number of polling days	−1.86	2.43	−5.02	1.02*	−5.04	1.05*
Electoral salience	−28.19	3.24*	−26.93	3.02*		
Adjusted R^2	0.866		0.881		0.797	
N	25		29		27	

SOURCE: Analysis of data is from Mackie and Rose (1991), and Katz (1996, Table 13.3).
NOTE: Number of categories—proportionality (numerical, range is from 79-99); compulsory voting (2); postal voting (2); Sunday voting (2); number of polling days (numerical, 1-5) electoral salience (2).
a. The 29 countries are those marked [a] in Table 8.1.
*$p < .5$.

third models, is actually negative—suggesting that countries where people have difficulty getting to the polls (such as India, Norway, and Finland) do not adequately compensate by means of additional polling days for the difficulties that lead such countries to extend their elections in this way.[21] In India, which keeps its polls open 4 days more than normal, this corresponds to a turnout that is 20 percent lower than in countries with only a single day of polling.[22] On the basis of these findings, we can assert (as we have in other work; see van der Eijk, Franklin, et al. 1996) that there are different routes to high turnout. Electoral salience is most important, but even in a country with low-salience elections, the use of compulsory voting, a highly proportional electoral system, postal voting, and weekend polling could apparently still raise turnout to 80 percent or more.

One proposed variable did not yield significant effects in any of the three analyses. Voluntary voter registration does not appear to reduce turnout when other effects are controlled.[23] This finding will come as something of a surprise to those who have assumed that low turnout in the United States can be largely attributed to this factor. Yet it is not possible that the factor has simply been included within the effects of low salience. Not only does Switzerland not have voluntary voter registration, but several other countries do have this attribute. So the research design we have adopted should have succeeded in detecting any general effect of voluntary voter registration. It failed to do so, reinforcing suggestions made elsewhere that the effects of this variable, even in the United States, may be less than had been supposed (see note 17).

Effects of the Nature of
the Electoral Contest on Turnout

We have pointed out that the most powerful influence reported in Table 8.4 has not been unambiguously identified. Switzerland and the United States may indeed be low-turnout countries because of low electoral salience. But there might be other reasons for the poor turnout in those countries.[24] One way to validate our assumption about the centrality of electoral salience is to establish its operation in a different context. Although there might be some question as to whether elections in Switzerland and the United States are of lower salience than elsewhere, there is little dispute among scholars that elections to the European Parliament are of lower salience than national elections in European countries. The difference between the two types of election is supposedly due to the fact that national executive power is not at stake in elections to the European Parliament (Reif and Schmitt 1980; Reif 1985; van der Eijk, Franklin, et al. 1996) any more than it is in Swiss or U.S. legislative elections. But European Parliament elections have an additional feature that makes them particularly suited to investigating the importance of electoral salience: They occur at different times in relation to elections in which national political power is at stake.

Careful analysis of votes cast in European elections held at different points in the national election cycle has validated the assumption that time until the next national election can be employed as a surrogate for electoral salience (van der Eijk, Franklin, et al. 1996, 301-2). The validation did not involve a study of turnout variations. Instead, it looked at the parties voters chose to support. The theory was that in elections of lowest salience—those occurring immediately after national elections—voters would have no reason to vote other than for their most-favored party. Such elections have no role as barometers of opinion, because better indicators of the standing of political parties already exist in the results of the recent national elections. However, as those most recent elections fade into the past, commentators and politicians become interested in the outcome even of elections that do not decide the allocation of political power—simply as markers of what might happen in real elections. The additional salience of these elections in such circumstances is attested to by the increasing tendency of voters to vote other than for their preferred party: indeed, to vote tactically in such a way as to signal their displeasure (if any) with the performance of the party they really prefer, or to signal their approval of parties they would never support in real elections (cf. Franklin, Niemi, and Whitten 1994).

In other words, even European elections become useful as vehicles for transmitting information from voters to leaders as they occur later in the electoral cycle. At such times, turnout should be higher because the elections have greater salience. Table 8.5 shows that in European elections held at the start of the electoral cycle (as much as 5 years before the next national elections in some countries) turnout will be 18 percent lower (30 percent of 60 months) than turnout in European elections held on the same day as national elections (such a conjunction occurred in three countries in 1989). This finding does not prove that electoral salience is the variable that chiefly accounts for low turnout in the United States and Switzerland, but it does confirm the importance of electoral salience—a necessary condition for our assumption to hold. So it adds plausibility to our assumption about the distinctiveness of Switzerland and the United States, without definitively ruling out possible alternative explanations.[25]

Other Types of Political Participation

When it comes to forms of political participation other than voting, differences between countries are again generally found to be greater than differences between social categories of voters, although the disparity is not as notable as in the case of voting (Verba et al. 1978, 57-62; Barnes et al. 1979, 541-2).[26] Moreover, the same studies show that the United States, in contrast to its relative position as lowest in voting turnout, is highest of all countries investigated in these volumes in terms of other forms of conventional political participation—particularly being active in community problem-solving organizations, and contacting officials about community and other social problems (Verba et al. 1978, 58).

TABLE 8.5 Regression of Electoral Participation on Systemic Characteristics
(European Union Elections, 1989)

Independent Variable	Aggregate Level b	Individual Level b
Systemic		
Compulsory voting	26.08	0.264
Sunday voting	9.35	0.093
Proportionality of electoral system	0.46	0.005
Political		
Electoral salience[a]	−0.30	−0.003
Constant	17.77	0.180
R^2	0.918	0.142
N[b]	14	10,500

SOURCE: Adapted from van der Eijk, Franklin et al. (1996, 318). The source does not give standard errors.
a. Time until next national election in months, coded 0 in the case of concurrent national elections.
b. In 1989, the EC had 12 members; however, the analysis was run separately for Britain and Northern Ireland and for Flanders and Wallonia.

Another marked difference between voting and other forms of participation is that (except in the United States) whether people vote is hardly at all affected by their socioeconomic status (SES) and hence the resources they bring to the political world. By contrast, other forms of participation are strongly affected by socioeconomic resources in all countries—some to an even greater extent than in the United States (Verba et al. 1978, 419-31). With our new perspective on the importance of contextual factors in turnout, we can shed light both on the different role of SES in the United States than elsewhere and on the different role of SES for different modes of participation.

Where turnout is virtually perfect, there is little room for individual-level factors to play a part (and it is notable that in the Verba et al. 1978 tables, SES plays the least part in explaining turnout in Austria and the Netherlands—the two countries with highest turnout of the seven they investigate). By contrast, where turnout is low there is space for other factors to play a role, as resources do in determining turnout in the United States (Verba et al. 1978, 122-3). The point about other forms of participation is that in no country does everyone work for a party or everyone contact government officials. These and other nonvoting activities are unevenly spread across the population, so there is room for individual characteristics to play a role in determining who participates and who does not. In such circumstances, differences in resources and the mobilizing efforts of parties and other political players can play a role unattenuated by systemic effects (cf. Verba et al. 1978, 6-7; Verba et al. 1995, 358).

The fact that Americans participate more than people in other nations in nonvoting activities has an additional implication. Evidently, Americans are not apathetic when it comes to politics. When we consider acts that citizens of other countries find difficult or unrewarding, Americans perform those acts in large numbers. In general, among countries for which we have relevant data, there appears to be a slight but significant inverse relationship between electoral and other forms of political participation, with low-turnout democratic countries showing greater participation of other types than high-turnout countries. Unfortunately, we do not have data for Switzerland on political participation other than voting—data that would provide a critical test of this tendency. For the moment, the hypothesis rests largely on contrasting one idiosyncratic country (the United States) with all others. Nevertheless, even in terms of an untested hypothesis, the relationship still is worth elaborating on. One reason for such an apparent inverse relationship between turnout and other kinds of political participation might be the fact that people who have exhausted themselves in other participatory acts do not have energy left for voting, but this seems unlikely—particularly because Verba and Nie (1972) showed that those who participate in other ways are likely also to be voters.

A much more likely reason for the relationship would provide indirect confirmation of our assumption that low turnout in the United States is partly due to the perceived lack of connection in that country between election outcomes and public policy. People who wish to determine the course of public policy may find the electoral route particularly unrewarding in the United States and Switzerland and hence be more inclined than in other countries to employ supplementary measures.

Conclusions

In this chapter, we have shown that going to the polls is an activity motivated primarily by the desire to affect the course of public policy. It is true that the stick of compulsory voting and the carrots of weekend polling and postal votes do lead more people to vote than otherwise would do so, but the major factors determining turnout—the importance of the electoral contest (what we have called electoral salience) and the likelihood that one's vote will not be wasted (encapsulated by the proportionality of the electoral system)—could only operate if people were motived to use their votes to achieve a political goal.

A country with low-salience elections and an electoral system that was not very proportional could easily show turnout levels 40 percent below a country with high-salience elections and a highly proportional electoral system. Such differences arise purely from differences in the institutional context within which elections are conducted—differences affecting the extent to which a political system will be responsive to the electoral choices made by voters.[27] Voters are not fools, and an unresponsive system will motivate many fewer of them to vote.

The fact that voters are not fools is also suggested by the extent to which they bypass electoral routes where those routes prove unresponsive. The United States suffers much from the unresponsive nature of its institutional character,[28] but the United States is the country (among those for which we have relevant data) in which citizens most frequently turn to nonelectoral modes of political participation. This concomitant of low turnout is no more than hypothesized on the basis of analyses reported in this chapter, but the hypothesis is highly consonant with the instrumental basis of political action that seems so clear in our findings.

Notes

1. These are the only countries for which adequate information could readily be obtained for use in the analyses conducted in this chapter—see notes to Table 8.1.

2. This number may be less than the total number of elections actually conducted in certain countries, due to missing data. Countries of Eastern Europe did not have free elections before 1989, so for them the table contains average turnout for elections held during the 1990s.

3. Because the systemic characteristics are available only for the period 1960-1985, turnout in the country-level analyses is also restricted to this period (see Katz 1996, Table 13.3).

4. See notes to Table 8.2. In addition, Romania is included even though it is not a democracy.

5. The 41 percent increment mentioned above would only apply to those who would not otherwise have completed high school (11 percent of the sample). For 37 percent of the sample, there would be no gain, because they already have a college-level education. The remaining half of the population might find its turnout increased by about 30 percent if everyone were college educated—an overall gain in turnout of 16 percent. Add the 4 percent (one tenth of 40) from those who now do not even have a high school education, and turnout in the United States might be raised 20 percent by this stratagem, bringing it to 74 percent—still 4 percent lower than in Britain and 20 percent below the level found in high-turnout countries.

6. Essentially, the instrumental approach views voters as social beings who see their vote not individually but as one of many. No individual vote, of course, has much chance of affecting the course of political events, but voters can take satisfaction in affirming their solidarity with others who feel the same way, knowing that together they might be able to affect the course of events (cf. Hirczy 1992).

7. Variations on this approach characterize much of the work on political participation. See, in particular, Milbrath and Goel (1977); Verba et al. (1978); Barnes et al. (1979); Wolfinger and Rosenstone (1980); Parry, Moiser, and Day (1990); Teixeira (1992); Rosenstone and Hansen (1993); and Verba et al. (1995).

8. This approach does, however, have a long pedigree. For earlier examples, see Huckfeldt (1979, 1986), Giles and Dantico (1982), Leighley (1990), and Kenny (1992).

9. Powell (1986) found significant effects from a variable he termed "group-party link-ages," but his data came from the 1960s. By the 1970s, such linkages had declined in many countries (Franklin et al. 1992), and analysis of turnout in the late 1980s found no remaining trace of this effect (van der Eijk, Franklin, et al. 1996, chap. 19). Other work has shown that the declining importance of group-party linkages can explain some part of the decline in turnout in European countries since the 1960s (Franklin, van der Eijk, and Oppenhuis 1995; but see Topf 1995 for evidence that this decline was from a historically high point in electoral turnout). In the analyses conducted for Table 8.4 (in which turnout is averaged for the period 1960 to 1985), we do find (barely) significant effects of group-party linkage across those countries for which the extent of this linkage can be measured—the countries of the (then) European Community. Fuchs and Klingemann (1995) also find significant effects from a similar variable (which they call "political linkage") over the same countries in a slightly later period. However, the extent of missing data costs the relationship significance even in the smallest subset of countries employed in Table 8.4.

10. Because the dependent variable in this analysis is a dichotomy (voted or not) many scholars consider regression analysis to be an inappropriate statistical method. In other work with identical variables (but whose case base was restricted to West European countries), logistic regression effects were calculated along with the OLS regression effects shown here (van der Eijk, Franklin, et al. 1996, chap. 19). That analysis did not indicate any way in which researchers would have been misled by relying on OLS regression, which, because of the interpretability of its results, is the method employed here.

11. To measure the maximum possible effect of national context, 21 dummy variables were included in the analysis whose results are reported in the second column of Table 8.3, one for each country less one for the base country (the United States in this instance). These variables will encapsulate differences between countries that go beyond anything that can specifically be measured at the national level, but we will see that in practice we can account for some 90 percent of the variance explained by these variables. By employing country dummies at this point in our investigations, we avoid the need to specify the variables we will use to explain country differences, which are introduced in the next section. We are also able to employ all the countries for which we have individual-level data, regardless of the fact that for some of them we do not have corresponding country-level data (see below).

12. In the analyses reported in this chapter, data missing on any variable have been replaced by mean values of that variable. Dummy variables were then defined that indicated the presence or absence of missing data for the corresponding substantive variable, as recommended by Cohen and Cohen (1983, 275-300). In all analyses, these dummy variables were included along with the corresponding substantive variables. However, this is the only analysis where any such missing data indicators proved significant.

13. Respondents who fail to disclose their extent of religious participation are 4 percent less likely to vote than those who are willing to disclose this information. The same was found over

Western European countries taken alone. See van der Eijk, Franklin, et al. (1996, chap. 19) for a discussion of this point.

14. Note that "national context," as used in this chapter, excludes social context variables. If education, for example, had proved to have large individual-level effects, some of these effects might properly have been attributed to the country level if people were more educated in some countries than in others. In this chapter, we ascribe all such effects to the individual level to give that level the greatest chance of showing its importance. Other research (van der Eijk, Franklin, et al. 1996) has shown that social context has no discernible effects, at least in countries of the European Union. More highly educated populations or wealthier populations, for example, are not more likely to show high turnout.

15. The Swiss are called to the polls on average seven times a year, mainly to render referendum verdicts (see chap. 1, Table 1.2, this volume). Americans face federal, state, or local elections more than twice a year on average (Boyd 1981, 45), less often than the Swiss, but many times more often than anyone else.

16. Finding that this variable has significant effects will not, of course, validate our assumption about its substantive meaning. That requires other analyses (see below).

17. But see Ayres (1995) and Mitchell and Wlezien (1995) for suggestions that the effects of this variable might have been overstated even in the United States. Hirczy (1992) suggests that its effects might actually be nil, based on comparison of North Dakota (which has no registration requirement) and adjacent states (cf. Erikson 1989).

18. For example, this occurs in large countries with widely separated polling places. In fact, not all large countries have multiple days of voting, but it is not implausible to assume that even large countries vary in the difficulty found in getting to the polls. The suggestion here is that multiple polling days may serve as an indicator of otherwise unmeasured difficulties in achieving adequate turnout, whatever the reason for those difficulties.

19. Including East European countries would greatly increase this sensitivity because of the noise introduced by idiosyncratic factors that cannot be averaged out over a short sequence of elections.

20. Missing data indicators were included in the analyses but did not prove significant. See note 12.

21. The number of polling days has to meet a more stringent requirement for significance than other variables because we were prepared to accept either a positive or a negative relationship in the case of this variable. Thus, the appropriate test is two tailed, unlike the tests for other variables in the table.

22. The finding regarding polling days is essentially driven by India. Excluding it (or including a dummy variable that picks out that one country) leaves polling days insignificant, as in the first model. Substantively it makes no difference which course is taken, because we do not know why Indians find it harder than others to go to the polls. If India is omitted from the analysis, we explain 89.5 percent of variance in turnout, with all effects but that of polling days retaining virtually the same values and remaining highly significant. Indeed, if we had sufficient contextual information we might be able to code India as a "low electoral salience" country, along with Switzerland and the United States—removing the need for special treatment. Doing so leaves all coefficients except for polling days virtually the same as in the second model in Table 8.4, with variance explained of 90.5 percent.

23. Countries without automatic voter registration that did have compulsory voting were coded as though registration was automatic. If this was not done, the effect of the variable proved significant *and negative*. That is, countries with automatic voter registration saw *lower* turnout than countries with voluntary registration if voluntarism was not deemed to be vitiated by a legal requirement to vote.

24. It can be argued that our use of legislative elections treats U.S. turnout unfairly, because congressional elections are, of course, less salient than presidential elections there. However, even in presidential elections turnout in the United States averages less than 58 percent. So, even had we employed presidential voting, the United States would still have been one of the three countries in our data with lowest turnout. Another problem with treating U.S. elections as low-salience elections arises from the fact that in the 19th century turnout was much higher—yet presumably elections had no greater salience then. In fact, even in the 19th century turnout was no higher than the level found today in medium-turnout countries, leaving plenty of room for low salience to have played a role—especially because one reason generally given for the higher turnout prior to wide-ranging reforms, conducted around the turn of the century, was the prevalence of electoral fraud (Converse 1974; Rusk 1974; but see Burnham 1965).

25. The effect of electoral salience on turnout in countries of the European Union appears to be less (at 18 percent) than the 27 percent measured in a wider universe. The effect of compulsory voting is also greater than in that wider universe. The differences are partly attributable to the different countries employed in the two analyses and partly to the fact that Table 8.4 contains a more fully specified model than Table 8.5. Note that in Table 8.5, an analysis conducted at the individual level yields findings that are identical (to within rounding error) with those found in an analysis conducted at the aggregate level. Moreover, the variance explained at the individual level is very similar to the additional variance explained by country differences in Table 8.3. See van der Eijk, Franklin, et al. 1996, chap. 19) for further discussion of these points.

26. Barnes et al. (1979) studied political participation in Austria, Britain, Germany, the Netherlands, and the United States. Verba et al. (1978) focused on Austria, India, Japan, the Netherlands, Nigeria, the United States, and Yugoslavia.

27. Again, it must be stressed that our attribution of responsiveness (or lack thereof) to Switzerland and the United States drives over half of this effect. Effects of electoral salience are lower in countries of the European Union, where they can be measured without the need for heroic assumptions. But even if we take the estimate generated from Table 8.5, of effects reaching 18 percent from electoral salience (when added to the maximum effect of proportionality), we still get total effects of some 35 percent attributable to institutional variations that affect government responsiveness to electoral behavior.

28. To say it "suffers" from its institutions is to look at things purely from the perspective of electoral turnout. The founding fathers, of course, designed a system that would be unresponsive to the popular will, and their system works pretty much as intended. Our findings suggest that low turnout is an inevitable concomitant.

(9)

Polls and Elections

DAVID BUTLER

From the earliest beginnings of representative democracy, those who fought in elections—as well as those who wrote about them—have striven to understand the voters. But campaigning and campaign coverage had to be based on unproven assumptions about the mood and motives of the public. Until sample surveys became established, an enormous amount of guesswork (and, often, self-deception) was involved.

Over the past 60 years, opinion polls have changed the nature of electioneering. Only the advent of television has had a greater effect. In every democratic country, those managing campaigns, as well as those reporting on them, have had their task transformed by the information and the expectations that sample surveys have made possible. At the same time, the voters have been given a mirror to their own attitudes and conduct, a mirror that has influenced the very phenomena it was reflecting.

The literature on election polls is now vast, but most of it is devoted to survey reports and methodological questions. It tends to be pragmatic and to be set in narrowly national contexts. Very little has been written that is comparative (but see Worcester 1983; Kavanagh 1995; Taylor 1995). It eschews history—pollsters, like natural scientists with their ever-advancing frontiers, are busy looking forward not back. It also eschews general theory—there is little mapping of survey research and its consequences.

Opinion polls are very diverse in quality and in purpose. Some obvious categorizations can be made. There are the broad differentiations between public polls and private polls, and between commercial surveys and academic surveys. There are the technical distinctions between random surveys and quota surveys; between one-shot and panel surveys; and among face-to-face, telephone, and postal surveys.

On a larger scale, the effect of polling has been divided by target. How have polls shaped party strategy? How have they shaped media coverage? How have they shaped voter behavior? But the distinction among these three questions is not, in the end, very useful. In the real world, the three elements are hopelessly intermingled. Evidence, or assumptions, about voter behavior lies at the heart of party strategy and, to a lesser extent, of media coverage. The electoral role of opinion polls has to be treated descriptively. Polls provide ever more detailed information about the voters and their actual or possible response to the stimuli offered by the politicians and the media; all the actors on the political scene are affected by the findings. This chapter offers a comparative summary of the volume and nature of that information and of the reactions to it.

Sample surveys have been developed primarily for commercial market research. All the big polling companies have made the bulk of their money exploring the marketplace for goods and services; they are employed to give guidance on how products ranging from canned beans to newspapers are perceived by their consumers and on how best they can be sold. At times, this basic approach can distort the way in which the pollsters set about research for their political customers. On the academic side, it is sociologists and social psychologists who have contributed most to the evolution of surveys, and this too has molded the style of research.

Background

Polls have many functions in politics, but from the outset, they have attracted attention primarily as devices to predict the outcome of elections. Pollsters' reputations—although, oddly, not their income as market researchers—

depend substantially on their success as forecasters. Dr. Gallup made his name into an international byword in 1936 when, using interviews with a small but randomly chosen sample of the electorate, he predicted Roosevelt's victory and pointed to the disaster that the long-established *Literary Digest* poll was facing (because it based its vast mail sample on telephone ownership and auto registration at a time when partisanship was being repolarized in terms of wealth and class).

Gallup's forecast was substantially in error (55-45 as opposed to the actual 62-38), but in contrast to the *Literary Digest,* he got the right winner and thereby gave his name to an industry (Smith 1990). Twelve years later, with a much smaller error (4.5 percent, not 7 percent), he met disaster when he predicted that Dewey would trounce Truman (Smith 1990). However, that setback—and a number of others elsewhere in the world—has not prevented the steady growth in influence of political polls. They may err at times, but politicians and journalists, eager to read the public mood, have found no satisfactory substitute. They want to position themselves to take advantage of whatever may be going to happen, and they find that polls, with all their weaknesses, provide the best available source.

Sample surveys have provided the opening for a large academic industry, researching into electoral behavior. In the United States, Lazarsfeld's first study (Lazarsfeld et al. 1944) in Erie County, Ohio, was succeeded by the University of Michigan's National Election Studies, which provide widely disseminated evidence about every presidential and midterm contest since 1952 (Thomassen 1994). The Michigan studies have been copied in modified form in many other countries. Since the 1960s, there have been regular series of surveys in the United Kingdom, in the Netherlands, the Scandinavian countries, and in Germany. Studies of particular elections in other countries have also provided valuable comparative material (de Guchteneire et al. 1985, 1991). This research, coupled with the data provided by the commercial polls, tells a great deal about the changing patterns and explanations of voting allegiance. It has been drawn on heavily by the more sophisticated political operators.

Since Gallup's first venture in 1936, election polls have spread worldwide. Some of the initial efforts were very amateurish and unchecked by competition. But all major democracies now have several rival survey organizations with good professional standards. Table 9.1 sets out in summary form the spread of election polling.

TABLE 9.1 The Spread of Election Polling

Country	First Prediction	Ban on Polls	Notable Failures
Australia	1946	No	1980
Belgium	1957	No	1995
Canada	1945	2 days	1957
Denmark	1945	No	No
Finland	1954	No	No
France	1945	7 days	1995
Germany	1957	No	1994
Greece	1956	No	No
India	1984	No	No
Ireland	1977	No	No
Italy	1948	7 days	No
Japan	1963	No	No
Netherlands	1946	No	1986
New Zealand	1946	No	No
Norway	1949	No	No
Portugal	1976	2 weeks	No
South Africa	1993	3 weeks	No
Spain	1977	5 days	No
Sweden	1944	No	1948
United Kingdom	1945	No	1970, 1974, 1992
United States	1936	No	1948

SOURCE: Rohme (1992).
NOTE: Between 1985 and 1991, the publication of polls was banned in Belgium. In 1969, the publication of polls was banned in Germany.

Polling is an art as much as a science. It is an instrument that demands constant tuning to increase its precision. Its practitioners have to assume that the future will broadly resemble the past and that the sample design and the adjustments that they have been using will continue to be valid. But sea changes can suddenly occur that make their methods inappropriate.

In election prediction, a very high degree of accuracy is required. In Britain in the 1950s and 1960s, a 3 percent error in the division of the major party vote could make a difference of 100 seats in the parliament. Yet, in their health warnings, the pollsters frequently suggest that a 3 percent error is possible based on standard mathematical theory.

In most areas of attitude research, accuracy to within 3 percent is adequate for most clients. Because of this, market researchers in general are naturally anxious about the extent to which the reputation of their trade turns on the performance of the polls in that most publicized of activities—the report of voting intentions. Those who actually conduct such surveys are uneasy too, because they get only a modest amount of their revenue but most of their publicity from election polling.

Effect

Sample surveys now have a decisive influence on the timing, the personnel, the issues, the language, the strategy, and perhaps, the outcome of elections.

Election timing. Except in countries where the election date is irrevocably fixed, the party in power looks eagerly at the pattern of poll findings before deciding when to go to the country. There is no doubt that in timing the 1970, 1979, and 1992 British elections, the prime minister of the day was powerfully influenced by the see-sawing indications that the polls provided. Australia, Canada, and India offer further examples of elections being called or delayed at the national or state level because of public or private poll findings.

Candidates. The personnel of elections can also be powerfully shaped by poll findings. At every level of government in the United States, measures of name recognition and trial heats (with hypothetical questioning about the outcome on different assumptions about the adversaries) have a key role in candidates' decisions on whether to run and in donors' decisions on whether to spend money in support of a particular candidate. Elsewhere in the world, the fortunes of aspirants to the French presidency have turned on their early ratings in public and private polls. In Britain, thinking on whether to challenge or change a party leader, be it the prime minister or the leader of the opposition, has been powerfully influenced by what the polls were saying about the party's prospects under him or her at the next election; when Mrs. Thatcher left, the instant polls testing how the Conservatives would fare against Labour under each of her three possible successors undoubtedly affected the ways in which some Tory MPs cast their ballots (*Sunday Times,* November 18, November 25, 1990). In Australia, poll findings contributed heavily to successive leadership changes in the Liberal party after 1983.

Issues. Although the issues on which elections are fought are partly determined by events and traditional loyalties, the special emphases, the leading themes are much shaped by increasingly sophisticated pretesting, sometimes with the public at large, but more often with small focus groups, carefully chosen to represent either the whole electorate or particular segments that constitute key targets (Kavanagh 1995).

Language. The words and slogans used to convey the main messages of a campaign are, in a similar way, increasingly pretested for their comprehensibility and their effect on various groups. Phrases can have very different significance to different regions or social classes.

In the days before opinion polls, there were, of course, journalists and party agents with a great flair for sensing the public's mood; wordsmiths and politicians developed high expertise in relevant and persuasive communication. But the increasingly sophisticated techniques of market research can help greatly in identifying the words and images that have the greatest appeal. The Republican campaign that demolished the Dukakis candidacy in 1988 owed much to the pretesting of themes.

Strategy and tactics. In the planning of campaigns and in their day-to-day management, the decisions on where a candidate should go and what media opportunities should be seized, as well as on what themes to pursue òr abandon or whether to engage in positive or negative campaigning, are more and more affected by the findings first of advance surveys and then of tracking polls, measuring from day to day the detailed effect of the campaign. The Canadian election of 1993 provides a notable example.

Forecasts. Polls too can have their own direct effect on the voters. The predictions about the likely outcome can deter people from casting their ballots for no-hopers and help those who are minded to vote tactically. It is clear that in majoritarian electoral systems polls can act almost as an alternative vote or an eliminating ballot, showing which third- or fourth-party candidates are "also-rans," thus enabling electors to cast a *vote utile* for the less objectionable of the two leading candidates.

Polls may also induce either a "bandwagon" or an "underdog" effect. Some temperaments may want to be on the successful side; others, suspicious of the arrogance of elected persons, may decide to reduce the scale of the predicted winner's victory. The evidence for either phenomenon is limited and contradictory. There is certainly no systematic pattern—although in seven of the last eight British elections the party shown to be in the lead has not done as well as predicted, suggesting that the British at least have a weakness for underdogs (Mann and Orren 1992, 136-40).

There is, however, no doubt that poll forecasts affect campaigners. The prospect of a tight race draws in extra funds and encourages extra effort. The evidence that the race is already decided can cool it down, with tough (and sometimes dirty) final advertisements being abandoned as unnecessary and, perhaps, likely to leave a bad taste. In Britain's 1975 referendum on staying within the European Community, the "yes" campaigners canceled some exceedingly abrasive advertisements when it became plain that they were going to win easily; there was nothing to be gained by embittering the vanquished (Butler and Kitzinger 1976).

Errors

Polls start with a necessary mathematical margin of error; to this is added a further fallibility due to human misjudgment, misguided sampling strategy, and last-minute changes of mind. In every country, there have been misleading polls. Sometimes their predictions have been spectacularly far from reality.

The most notable of recent errors in election forecasting was provided by Great Britain in 1992. In the contest of that year, four well-established polls, each with a good track record, agreed in suggesting on the morning of the vote that Labour had a lead over the Conservatives of around 1 percent. When the votes were counted that night, the Conservatives emerged 7.5 percent ahead.

The Market Research Society (1994) sponsored a detailed study of that debacle. They found three main causes of error.

1. *Late swing.* The most convenient reason for a pollster who proves to be in error must always lie in solid evidence that there was a movement of opinion between the time of the final interviews and the actual vote. This does, indeed, seem to have been the main cause of the celebrated failure of Gallup, Roper, and Crossley in 1948—but they stopped interviewing days or weeks early. In Britain in 1992, the fieldwork continued until the evening before the booths opened; indeed, there does appear to have been a small switch toward the Conservatives in the final hours—but it was not enough to explain much more than a quarter of the error.

2. *Poor sampling.* It is clear that the pollsters had not been as rigorous as they might have been in selecting and checking their demographic controls and in updating their selection of constituencies. But this too could not explain much more than a quarter of the error.

3. *Refusals and "don't knows."* It appears that a disproportionate number of those who refused or said "don't know" to the "How will you vote?" question were Conservatives. It is suggested that a "spiral of silence" (Noelle-Neumann 1984) made a significant number deny their support for the seemingly unpopular Conservatives. That may explain why the exit polls (which were not subject to late swing or poor sampling) still erred, although by less than half as much as the predictive polls.

4. *Residue.* The Market Research Society (1994) report concluded that there was no significant effect from differences in interview techniques (e.g., conducting the interviews on the doorstep or in the street, on weekdays or at the weekends, by telephone or face to face, or putting the voting question at the start of the interrogation or later on). They found no evidence whatever of deliberate lying. However, selective turnout could have had a minor effect, in part caused by the imperfections of the electoral register, with poll tax protesters keeping their names off it.

One consequence of the 1992 disaster has been to make British pollsters review their techniques and their presentation. During 1994, experiments with weighting by past voting and other characteristics produced remarkable results; there were sharp reductions (varying between 6 percent and 14 percent) in the Labour party's lead over the Conservatives compared with the figure given by the unadjusted answers to the "How would you vote?" question.

Disasters are good for pollsters and their followers. They have offered a reminder of the necessary fallibility of the survey-based predictions, and they have encouraged everyone concerned to reexamine their techniques. In every advanced democracy, an election is followed by elaborate postmortems on the performance of the polls (e.g., Ladd 1995).

Seats and Votes

Opinion polls indicate percentage divisions within the population. But, except under a few strictly proportional systems, party representation in the legislature is not correlated exactly with the division of public support. What the world usually wants to hear is evidence about the likelihood of victory or defeat, the outcome in seats, not in votes. What sort of parliamentary majority will the contest produce?

Even in strictly proportional Germany, the major parties know that their representation in the Bundestag depends on whether one or more smaller parties manages to cross the minimum 5 percent threshold. Thresholds and regional factors too have distorted the relation between votes and seats in Scandinavia, in Belgium, and in pre-1994 Italy. In Ireland and in Malta, the single-transferable vote system has produced significant deviations from pure proportionality. But these distortions are trivial compared with the situation in countries with single-member constituencies where outcomes can be wildly disproportionate and where, moreover, the disproportion is not consistent. Table 9.2 illustrates this phenomenon.

The relation between seats and votes has not been random in any of these countries but established patterns have changed as the advantage of incumbency has changed, as the number of third and fourth parties has grown, and as the geographic distribution of support has evolved.

To arrive at an accurate prediction of how, in any forthcoming election, votes will divide is difficult. But in places with single-member district systems the difficulty is redoubled when it comes to translating that prediction into the actual parliamentary outcome. This is a cross that pollsters, sensitive about their reputation for being right, have to bear.

Banning

Fears that the outcome of elections could be influenced by polls have led to pressures for banning their publication in the final stages of the campaign. Some countries have yielded to these anxieties. Because of the First Amendment, such demands have never been seriously voiced in the United States, but West Germany in 1969 (voluntarily) and France since 1977 (statutorily) have banned any publication of poll findings in the final week of the campaign. Belgium had a formal ban from 1985 to 1991, but this was defied because of a freedom-of-information clause in the Belgian Constitution and was then abandoned. Italy, Spain, and Portugal, together with most of the new democracies in Eastern Europe, have bans, and so do several Latin American countries (Rohme 1992). A 1995 ban in British Columbia is being challenged in the courts.

TABLE 9.2 Examples of Disproportionality in Votes and Seats in Plurality
Electoral Systems

Country	Election Year	Largest Party	% of Votes	% of Seats
Australia	1980	Liberal-NCP	50	60
(House of Representatives)	1987	ALP	51	58
	1990	ALP	50	53
	1993	ALP	49	54
Canada	1974	Liberal	43	53
(House of Commons)	1984	PC	50	75
	1988	PC	43	59
	1993	Liberal	41	60
India	1977	Janata	43	55
(Lok Sabha)	1980	Congress (I)	43	65
	1989	Congress (I)	40	36
	1991	Congress (I)	36	44
South Korea				
(National Assembly)	1993	DLP	39	63
New Zealand	1984	Labour	43	55
(House of Representatives)	1987	Labour	48	59
	1990	National	48	69
	1993	National	35	50
United Kingdom	1951	Labour	49	47
(House of Commons)	1966	Labour	48	58
	1987	Conservative	42	58
	1992	Conservative	42	52
United States	1978	Democrat	53	63
(House of Representatives)	1986	Democrat	52	59
	1990	Democrat	53	61
	1994	Republican	51	53

a. Percentage of two-party preferred vote (Bean and Butler 1991).

The case for the banning of polls rests on a straightforward desire to leave
a fair field for the rival arguments, unaffected by "scientific" predictions that
could, in theory, be manipulated for party purposes. The objections to the
banning of polls are many. First, there is the simple ideological objection to
the curtailing of free speech. How in an open society can one justify prevent-

ing a citizen or a company from asking people their views or from publishing the result?

Second, there is the difficulty of defining a poll. If a journalist talks to a dozen voters about their intentions, is that a poll? a hundred voters? a thousand?

Third, there is the difficulty of enforcement. When West German pollsters agreed on a voluntary ban on publication just before the 1969 election, the *Times* in London sponsored a poll, which was then reported in Germany as a foreign news story. The Sunday *Times* did the same during the 1993 French referendum on the Maastricht Treaty, publishing on the Sunday of the vote.

Fourth, there is the danger of a black market in rumor: "Private polls are showing a late trend to . . . " Such stories could spread, perhaps with malice aforethought, and have as much effect as any genuine poll published by a reputable source. There are instances from America of candidates citing totally fictitious private surveys to show that they were still in with a chance.

Fifth, despite any ban on publication, private polling would undoubtedly continue. In a period where the outcome of any national election can have worldwide stock market repercussions, dealers on the exchanges, deprived of the evidence of public polls, would certainly sponsor private polls to help them to decide their forward positions. It is surely desirable that such private sources should have open rivals available to the general public. In France, there was wide leaking of private polls during the banned 7 days before the presidential vote in 1995, not least by the French government itself.

Exit Polls

Exit polls have grown in prominence as a journalistic device designed to enhance the excitement of election night broadcasts, or, as some would say, to destroy the anticipation of the long hours of the count. They have also been used by brokers eager for early news of an event that is bound to have a heavy influence on the markets.

Exit polls, based on interviews outside the booths with those who have just voted, have an advantage over predictive polls in that two of their main problems—late switches and nonvoting—are eliminated because only people who have actually cast a ballot are interviewed. The problem posed by those who refuse to answer remains but it is possible to categorize the age, sex, and locality of such people and to make deductions about any systematic bias. Exit polls make special demands on sampling, especially in countries such as the United Kingdom or India where past voting data are not available for individual wards or precincts. But the record of accuracy from exit polls has been reasonably good—although in Britain in 1992 all three nationwide exit polls underestimated the margin of Conservative victory by about 3 percent (Market Research Society 1994).

There is, of course, the problem of exit polls having a distorting effect if their findings are released before the close of voting. This hazard matches the time-zone problem in Canada and the United States where early reports from the actual count on the East Coast may, in the final hours, deter people from bothering to go to the booths in the West. In most countries, the sponsors of exit polls accept a self-denying ordinance not to release their figures until the last vote has been cast.

To anticipate by a few minutes, or a few hours, the authoritative result from the actual counting of votes may not be very important, except for networks battling for viewers and reputation. But exit polls have great academic and practical value. They offer as accurate a picture as is anywhere available of who votes how and of the elector's immediate self-account of his or her reasons. Exit polls tend to be based on very large samples; they therefore make possible detailed breakdowns of the voting behavior of subsections of the population. The voters' opinions on issues, together with their immediate recollections of their exposure to the campaign, provide different and, in some ways, better evidence of mood than any earlier or later surveys.

World Comparisons

Polling techniques are not standardized across the world. Rohme (1985, 1992), in two studies for WAPOR (World Association for Public Opinion Research), collected evidence on general practice worldwide. Humphrey Taylor, in a 1994 survey of major polling firms in 13 democracies, found a wide diversity of approach. He commented, "Survey methods which are standard practice in some countries would be regarded as gross malpractice in others" (Taylor 1995). In particular, he found the world divided into areas that almost exclusively use telephone surveys based on random-digit dialing (e.g., United States and Canada), those that rely on personal interviews based on probability sampling (e.g., Australia and South Africa), and those that concentrate on personal interviews based on quota sampling (e.g., Britain and

Mexico). Taylor also noted a cleavage between those who favor weighting by claimed past voting (e.g., France and Germany) and those who tend to believe that this makes their forecasts worse.

In each country, there may be exceptions to these classifications, but there remain clear national differences. Some of these differences are necessary and inevitable. To give one obvious example, there has to be very high telephone penetration before great reliance can be placed on random direct dialing. Moreover, differences in political culture, with varying stability of party loyalty, can make weighting by past voting helpful or misleading. Similarly, the value of using ballot boxes or other techniques for reducing "don't knows" and refusals may vary greatly depending on local tradition.

What Taylor makes plain, however, is that pollsters have often become fixed in their ways and slow to adopt alternative approaches. Despite regular international conferences, they do not draw very extensively on what is being done abroad. Although some diversity is desirable, some current practices should be unacceptable anywhere. Taylor points to a few: nonrandom direct dialing in selecting telephone samples, failure to use weighting to compensate for patently imperfect samples, and completing interviewing too long before the day of the vote.

Media Coverage

Election polls are an important commodity in the media world. A nation-wide survey costs perhaps $30,000 in the United States; in the United Kingdom a figure of £10,000 is currently quoted. It is a very expensive way for a newspaper to get a headline plus a few column inches of print. As a major lead to a television news bulletin, it is still a costly buy. But if it is sufficiently talked about, it may be a cheap way of advertising the newspaper or the network. In the United States and Britain, polls were originally commissioned as exclusive scoops. But in time it was recognized that it was more profitable to leak the findings as an advertising device, so that rival media outlets would quote "a poll in the *Gazette* tomorrow will show . . . ."

This secondary use of polls has meant that during election campaigns in many of the major democracies, readers and viewers have a continuous diet of polls, often with four or five surveys hitting the front pages every week. There are, indeed, complaints that polls have helped to turn elections from a reasoned debate into a sporting event, with speculation about the outcome drowning the essential argument. This may be a romanticization of the past nature of campaigns. There is, however, no doubt that polls have changed the public perception of what constitutes a campaign.

Journalists, indeed, can become the slave of the polls. E. J. Dionne has discussed eloquently the distorting effect that survey findings can have on the strategy and content of election coverage (Mann and Orren 1992) and on the way in which the media treat the election results. Outcomes are always set against expectations. The strength of the mandate given to successful candidates or parties depends to a significant degree on whether the margin is seen as surprisingly large or surprisingly small. Poll forecasts contribute more than anything else to such impressions.

Politicians have a love-hate relationship with polling. They used to prize their personal empathy with the public and its moods as their own special skill; the intrusion of professionals who claimed to know better was resented. "You are taking the poetry out of politics," cried the British politician, Aneurin Bevan, when the Labour party first sponsored survey research. But survey research is now accepted as an indispensable political tool. Unfortunately, it often yields embarrassing findings that campaigners have, publicly at least, to dismiss as a "blip" or as "just wrong" or even as fraudulent. Explaining away unfavorable ratings or awkward percentages on issue questions is a developing art among campaign staffers—and the media have learned to dissect their sophisticated glosses.

One criticism of media coverage of polls lies in the overwhelming focus on voting intentions and the neglect of the evidence offered about public attitudes to the issues. How far do the voters agree with each specific item in the policies of the party they are supporting? Because the outcome of an election is so often cited as a "mandate" for the victor's program, polls can offer a powerful corrective, to be exploited in the coming sessions of the legislature.[1]

Publication practice varies widely. Editorial partisanship, as well as genuine news values, can determine the prominence given to a poll story. The pollsters do not control the headlines put over their findings. Because editors want sensation, every sampling fluctuation is in danger of being publicized as a new trend. A blip in the polls makes a better headline than a "no change" finding. Researchers can despair at the misuse of their work. In many countries, the pollsters have codes of conduct, insisting that reports of their findings should contain a statement of the dates of interviewing and the size and form of their sample. But even when their direct clients observe this condition, they have no control over the secondary reporting that occurs when rival media reduce the story to a sound bite or a sentence about the latest change in lead. They also have no control over the placing of their reports. Partisanship as much as news values may decide whether a story appears as the lead headline on the front page or as a snippet in the local news section.

In some countries, a few newspapers offer as a valuable safeguard regular and expert columns, reporting and dissecting the rival poll findings. Good polling, like good theater, benefits from good criticism.

Bad Polls

The polling scene is everywhere liable to be confused by unprofessional polls or by polls that are not polls. Amateurs with little understanding of sampling and untrained in interviewing can still get publicity for their find-ings—as indeed can polls conducted by party workers. The media sometimes publicize the results of phone-in polls or *vox pop* interviews as though they were representative samples. Even with serious surveys, the evidence about timing, method, and sample size, by which the quality of the research can be judged, is often missing.

However, the reputable competitors in the polling industry in almost every major democracy have been able to demonstrate their own credibility and to shrug off the embarrassing tail of shoddy operators. Unfortunately, it has proved more difficult to educate even sophisticated consumers of polls about the hazards of "polls of polls," the averaging of the findings of rival organi-zations—which may vary widely in date, in sample size, and in question wording. Polls of polls offer an antidote to a single rogue finding and provide a broad guide to long-term trends—but, like rolling polls (the averaging of successive small samples), they can be seriously misleading about the latest development (Worcester 1994).

One other aspect of polls and the media should be mentioned. Television and the press are, of course, the main channel for transmitting campaign messages, and in a circular way, polls provide the principal means of moni-toring the reach of the media. With good surveys of audiences and of page-traffic, it is possible to measure how far the electorate is paying attention to particular parts of the candidates' messages—and even to the opinion poll reports.

Polls and Campaign Managers

Campaign managers and party agents go back as far as competitive elections. For parties, as well as for politicians, it has become a status symbol, almost as much as a practical advantage, to have one's own private pollster. Even though most significant findings are readily available, free, from published polls, it seems to be a comfort—even a weapon—to have one's own secret source of information. But, since the 1950s, pollsters in some countries have moved into the advisory field. From providing campaigners with evidence about voters' attitudes and intentions drawn from straightforward market research, they have often moved on to political strategy. In the United States, Louis Harris became known as "Jack Kennedy's pollster," just as later Dick Wirthlin became "Ronald Reagan's pollster." They and their successors have had constant access to their candidates and have, at times, played a major role in giving campaign advice. In Britain, pollsters have been kept more at arm's length, but in the 1970s Humphrey Taylor of Harris UK attended the Conservative party's daily strategy meetings and Bob Worcester of MORI attended those of the Labour party. Pollsters may claim to be scientists, honest gatherers of data. But inevitably their clients turn to them for advice on how to translate their findings into action—and, in the hothouse world of Westminster and Washington, such advice is necessarily controversial. Harsh words are said about the pollsters' findings and about the pollsters themselves. Sometimes the pollsters have exaggerated the centrality of their role to advertise their firms; others have played it down lest they get too partisan a reputation, damaging to the objectivity of their research (Kavanagh 1995).

The nature and frontiers of opinion polling are not exactly defined. In the developing profession of campaign consultant, a wide range of skills is involved. Large-scale surveys are needed to get an idea of the likely outcome of an election or to distinguish differences in attitudes by class, ethnicity, religion, region, age, or sex. But much less expensive research can tell the campaigner what he or she needs to know about the issues that concern the electorate as a whole, about the policy stands that will be popular, and about the best language with which to convey a given message. Extensive interviews with focus groups or individuals, using open-ended questions, may tell a campaigner as much as the statistically precise answers to a nationwide questionnaire—and at much less expense. Politicians need to know who votes for them—and why. They need to know how solid is their own support—and that of their opponents. For this polls have no rival.

Cooperation

In some countries, the competition between polls has become very adversarial. In others, there is extensive cooperation. Those involved recognize that the failure of one poll brings discredit on all polls. In the United Kingdom, the five main pollsters unite in APOPO (Association of Political Opinion Pollsters), which seeks agreement on ethical standards and tries to present a common front to critics within and without the market research industry. In the United States and in France, the situation is often more secretive and competitive.

Internationally, for the past 40 years WAPOR has met regularly and tried to foster intellectual exchanges and to promote high technical standards. Its membership covers more than 50 countries. It has set out a code of practice and trained pollsters in developing countries. In some new democracies, polls have been used as an aid in monitoring the integrity of elections.

Conclusion

Larry Bartels (1992), in a perverse but insightful piece, has argued that the essence of electoral campaigning has not changed much since Ostrogorski ([1902] 1964) penned his great study of democracy. Most of the art and technique of winning votes has its roots deep in history, in ways established long before Dr. Gallup came on the scene. But, nowadays, the content of discussion in party headquarters and indeed in ordinary homes is greatly influenced by the existence of opinion surveys. A modern campaign manager, who had no polling evidence at his disposal, would feel very naked indeed. Every journalist would feel thoroughly uneasy. Polls are now an established part of the fabric of electioneering. They lie at the heart of all modern understanding of electoral behavior.

Note

1. In the early days, George Gallup saw in opinion polls a way to achieve the dream of direct democracy. He pointed out that for the first time since the Greek city-states, it was possible to gather together evidence on what the people really want. Certainly, polls have been important in showing legislators how far their mailbags reflect the views of the wider population and how far they have to believe the exaggerated claims of lobbyists. But in no country have the findings of opinion polls been given the recognition as a mandatory force. However, in places where referendums are used, politicians and issue enthusiasts have obviously been much influenced by polls when they have had to decide whether to launch a formal appeal to the people. Recently, Fishkin (1991) has energetically pursued the idea of assemblying a representative sample of the electorate during the campaign, exposing them to balanced seminars on the issues, and recording their opinions as a guide to those of the whole population.

The Media

HOLLI A. SEMETKO

Media Systems and Election Campaigns

For the vast majority of people living in democratic societies, election campaigns are experienced through the media. Politicians gear their daily campaign activities to meet the constraints and deadlines of the news. They know that far more people turn to print or broadcast sources for information than turn out for political rallies in the town square. The centrality of the media to election campaigns goes without question. But the way elections are presented in the news, the range and quality of information available to electors via the news media, and the effects of the media on political elites and the public may vary considerably from country to country. In this chapter, I begin with a discussion of the structural characteristics of media systems that help to explain such variation. I then discuss examples of some develop-

AUTHOR'S NOTE: I would like to thank the Global Affairs Institute at the Maxwell School of Citizenship and Public Affairs, and the S. I. Newhouse School for Public Communications at Syracuse University, for providing research support during the 1994-1995 academic year when the bulk of the writing was completed.

ments in a number of regions around the world, before turning to address questions of media effects.

What do we mean by "the media"? This catch-all term masks the point that some media are more important than others. For most people in most democracies, television is the primary source of information at election time. But the printed press is not unimportant. In Sweden, Germany, or Britain, for example, where newspaper readership is comparatively high, the press may have stronger effects on public opinion than in Spain, where newspaper penetration is comparatively low. But circulation figures alone are not an adequate measure of potential effect of the press. Spain's *El Mundo,* for example, a relatively new national newspaper known for its investigative journalism, has set the agenda for other news outlets and helped to focus public attention on the issue of corruption in government. Radio is also a major source of political information for different segments of the population, although it is too often overlooked in election research simply because of the difficulties presented by data collection. It has long been one of the most important sources for political information for residents of rural areas, particularly in less developed countries. Key characteristics of the penetration of various media and the general structure of media systems in democracies around the world are displayed in Table 1.7 in the first chapter of this volume.

Table 1.7 is also helpful in thinking about some of the macrolevel aspects of the media system that could have a bearing on the way in which elections are presented in the news. Four in particular are relevant here: (a) the balance between public and commercial (private) broadcasting, (b) the political autonomy of broadcasting from government and political parties, (c) the rules and traditions surrounding party access to broadcasting, and (d) the extent of partisanship in the printed press.

Balance Between Public and Commercial Broadcasting

The balance between public and commercial broadcasting has changed in most countries over the past decade as new channels have entered the marketplace and competition has intensified. In the late 1970s and up into the early 1980s, we could still speak of broadcasting systems that were entirely public service. A number of these public service broadcasting systems in Europe were financed entirely by the state via license fees (Belgium, Denmark, Norway, Sweden), described as "pure public" systems, whereas others were financed by a mixture of state funds and advertising revenue (Austria, Finland, France, Germany, Greece, Ireland, the Netherlands, Portugal, Spain, Switzerland), described as "mixed revenue" public broadcasting systems (Brants and Siune 1992, 104). Commercial or private broadcasting was well established by this time in the United Kingdom and Italy, described as "dual" systems, in which the public service channel(s) were competing with commercial or private channels. Other long-standing dual systems include Australia, Japan, and the United States, the last of which has always had a very small public service component (see Smith 1981), as well as many Latin American countries in which the broadcasting systems developed from a U.S. model. By the 1990s, however, the handful of these pure public systems had introduced competition and/or shifted to an advertising-based form of finance and thus became mixed revenue or dual systems.

The general path in Europe and Canada has been away from pure public systems to mixed revenue public service systems reliant on advertising. The introduction of private or independent commercial channels is the next step, and in such systems the public service channel may still dominate for a time in terms of overall audience ratings and revenues. As audiences shift from public to commercial broadcasters, and as advertisers put more revenue into the private channels, the dominance of the public service channel diminishes as the commercial channels become increasingly popular. The dual systems may therefore be (a) public service dominant, (b) genuinely mixed, or (c) commercial dominant. Between 1970 and 1990, Canada moved from a pure public service system to a mixed system to where it is today, a dual system in which the public service channel remains dominant in terms of audience ratings and revenue. Germany, to take another example, began as a mixed public service system in which advertising revenue partially funded the public service channels until the mid-1980s when private channels were introduced. Today, as audience ratings and advertising revenue for these newer channels threaten the public service channels, Germany might be described as a dual system of the genuinely mixed kind. In Spain, too, new private channels financed entirely by commercial advertising came into existence only in the mid- to late 1980s and are rapidly taking audiences from the old public service channels (Lopez-Escobar 1992; Lopez-Escobar and Faus-Belau 1985). Competition has forever changed European broadcasting systems (*European Journal of Communication* 1992).

This hypothetical trajectory from pure public or mixed to some form of dual broadcasting systems does not apply to many Latin American countries, however, where the public service channels are often small and attached to universities or the government and large independent commercial channels have long dominated the scene. The public service channels often also rely on advertising as a source of revenue; this is an additional pressure because their ratings can be very low in comparison with the big commercial channels. TV Globo in Brazil is one example of a long-standing successful and dominant commercial channel, as are the big commercial channels in Argentina.

In the new democracies such as Russia, the post-Soviet republics, and the former Eastern bloc countries, the shift has been a rapid one from one or two state-run and state-funded channels to a multitude of commercial channels (Paletz, Jakubowicz, and Novosel 1995). Broadcast advertising in these countries provides an educational service, as citizens are confronted daily with a multitude of choices, such as luxury goods and insurance policies. Audiences are shifting from public to private channels in these countries much faster than, say, in India, where the government-run public service channel remains the choice of most viewers.

The form of financing the broadcasting systems has important implications for the range and quality of political programming on offer, with public-service-dominant systems providing a considerably heavier fare (Blumler and Nossiter 1990). On a continuum ranging from entirely state owned at one end to entirely market driven on the other, the United States is perhaps the most well known example of a market-driven system, with many European countries having moved recently from entirely state owned to the center of the continuum. The more public service dominant the system, the more likely it is that prime-time television will include a broad range of political news and current affairs programming; the more commercially driven the system, the more market pressure for ratings and hence the more reluctant prime-time television will be to replace popular entertainment programming for political information programming (Blumler, Brynin, and Nossiter 1986). This predisposition for more or less political programming, stemming from the balance of public service versus commercial in the broadcasting systems, is likely to also be reflected in the amount of election-related programming during campaigns. In Britain, for example, a dual system with a very strong public service component, during the 1983 general election the BBC and ITV carried more evening prime-time political news and current affairs programming about the campaign in 4 weeks than all three U.S. networks over the 2 months before voting day in the 1984 presidential campaign (Semetko et al. 1991). There are, of course, exceptions such as Israel, where special rules ban regular news and current affairs programs from showing politicians on television in the final weeks before the vote, apart from debates and special party-produced broadcasts (Cohen and Wolfsfeld 1995; Caspi 1996).

Political Autonomy of Broadcasting

An important, related characteristic is the political autonomy of broadcasting from government and political parties (see Smith 1979, 1981). The more "pure public" the broadcasting system, the more likely it is that government or political parties exert influence over the main public broadcasting organizations. But as competition increases and the number of channels increases, there is also a diversification of income sources and a corresponding lessening of control by political authorities (see Brants and Siune 1992). The more "pure commercial" the broadcasting system, the less opportunity for government or political parties to exert direct influence over broadcasting organizations.

Public service channels in Germany, for example, are subject to oversight by state-level boards composed of "socially relevant groups" including representatives of the political parties in each state-level parliament, although no such oversight applies to the private channels (Schoenbach 1987). German public broadcasters' concerns over possible repercussions in the advisory boards could have consequences for the quantity and quality of election-related programming (Semetko and Schoenbach 1994). These are concerns that commercial or independent broadcasters need not share. That said, the process of opening up the television marketplace in Europe has meant a major role for national governments in designing the rules and regulations for awarding and renewing licenses to independent broadcasting companies, and when licenses come up for renewal these companies have an economic interest in not offending the government of the day.

The loosening of the grip of politicians over broadcasting is most notable when one looks back at the study of the first European Parliament elections in 1979, in which Kelly (1983, 73) identifies a continuum along which the extent of political intervention in European public service broadcasting systems varies from " 'formally autonomous' broadcasting systems, through 'politics in broadcasting' systems, to 'politics over broadcasting' (or relatively subordinate) systems." In regard to the policy positions taken by the public service broadcasters in covering the campaign, Britain and Ireland displayed elements of the "formally autonomous" systems, with Italy and France closer to the "politics over broadcasting" end of the continuum, and Denmark and

Belgium in between. The "subordinate" systems of 1979 can no longer be classified as such because of the range of independent commercial channels now available in these countries.

That said, in countries where there continues to be a substantial public service component to the broadcasting system, the forms of control exerted by the political parties or government over the public service channel(s) varies. Public service broadcasting is not always equated with a pro-government stance. In Germany, as already noted, there are advisory boards for the two public service channels in which political parties participate. In France, Greece, and Spain, however, the party in power appoints the key people in the public service broadcasting organizations, and many of the appointees are known partisans. Spain's TVE1 is by popular assumption pro-government (Rospir 1996). In Britain, however, even though Mrs. Thatcher arguably ended the tradition of appointing nonpartisans to the BBC's Board of Governors, there is no popular impression that the BBC is pro-government. On the contrary, the BBC has distinguished itself by often being on the receiving end of government criticism.

Party Access to Broadcasting

The rules, traditions, and practices surrounding party access to broadcasting during election campaigns also vary in important ways cross-nationally. Although it is probably difficult for citizens living in most democracies to imagine, there is at least one democracy in which television is prohibited from broadcasting news about the politicians or parties in the weeks preceding the vote. Israel's restrictions on the visual appearance of politicians in news and current affairs programs in the 4 (officially, but about 10 in practice) weeks before election day stem from the country's unique historical circumstances. As a consequence, viewers in Israel have witnessed some rather bizarre news clips in which the most important person in the story is missing—Egypt's Anwar Sadat meeting with Menachem Begin's empty chair in the 1981 campaign is just one example (Cohen and Wolfsfeld 1995, 113). Politicians are not entirely invisible on Israeli television at election time, however. They are given some free time to broadcast "election propaganda" as well as debates during the final 3 weeks; this material is prepared by the parties but must be approved by an Election Commission, with a prohibition on using any footage shown previously on Israel television (Cohen and Wolfsfeld 1995, 114). Other examples of restrictions on broadcasting during elections include the ban on reporting the campaign the day before or the day of voting in a number of European countries; restrictions on the publication of opinion polls, which is less common; and restrictions on the content of political advertising, which are also rare (Kaid and Holtz-Bacha 1995a; see also chap. 9 in this volume).

In the United States, we often distinguish between "free" media (e.g., being seen in a television news program or in a newspaper article) and "paid" media (television or print advertising). But in countries with strong public service broadcasting traditions, free air time for political parties to speak directly to the electorate is often made available with a corresponding prohibition on the purchase of air time. The situation has been in flux in many of these countries in regard to political advertising on television, with question marks over whether, and if so, how much time, parties can purchase to broadcast ads on the commercial channels. Britain answered both questions with a firm no in the 1990 Broadcasting Act, but most other European countries have said yes, and as a result the wealthier parties can have an advantage. Table 1.7 shows whether paid political ads, and free or subsidized air time, are available during election campaigns in each country.

Table 1.7 also indicates whether there are rules concerning "fairness" or "balance" in political broadcasting during election campaigns. In theory, television (whether public or private) is expected to provide impartial coverage of politics, and this is deemed of particular importance at election time. In practice, the meaning of balance in election news varies not only cross-nationally but also within countries across news organizations (Semetko, 1996). The length of the "official" campaign in each country, during which time such rules or traditions apply, is understandably quite important.

There is often a visibility bonus for the parties of government during the "precampaign" period. It is also not unique to public service channels that are accountable to government. It was documented by Miller et al. (1990) in Britain in advance of the 1987 general election. It was also found in Spain in 1993 (Diez-Nicolas and Semetko 1995) and in Germany during the "official" campaign on both the public service and private channels—the final 8 weeks before election day when the parties air their ads—in the historic Bundestag election of December 1990 (Semetko and Schoenbach 1994) although this was not the case in the Bundestag election of 1994 (Semetko and Schoenbach 1995). Research from Latin America also suggests that preelection campaign news can play a major role in shaping a candidate's future (de Lima 1993). But visibility is not always a bonus. There can be more news but it can be negative, as it was for incumbent George Bush during the U.S. 1992 presidential campaign (Patterson 1993).

Parties of government and the president or prime minister continue to conduct the business of government during the official election campaign as well as in the weeks preceding it. The so-called long campaign is the period of a year or so where governments are using the media to prepare for an election (see chap. 11 in this volume; Miller et al. 1990, 59-82). Often, certain events are orchestrated to enhance the leader's image. It is up to reporters and journalists, as well as political partisans, to label such an event or activity as "campaigning." U.S. television reporters are and have been quick to label as campaigning any incumbent activity at any time during the election year, regardless of the gravity of the event or situation—hence Jimmy Carter's "Rose Garden strategy" in the final weeks of the 1980 election during the U.S. hostage crisis; George Bush's visit to Florida, a key state in the presidential campaign, to provide government relief to the victims of Hurricane Andrew; or Richard Nixon's speech to the National Association of Broadcasters in spring 1974 (Paletz and Vinegar 1977-1978). British TV reporters, let alone "Spitting Image" satirists, did not let Mrs. Thatcher's scheduling of the 1983 general election around her appearance at the Venice Summit go without mention, and in subsequent years they have been quick to identify the possible electoral motives behind government or leader actions. But in Germany in the final days before the 1990 election, television news reporters were reluctant to refer to Chancellor Helmut Kohl's meetings with other heads of state in terms of the potential electoral benefits to the CDU (Semetko and Schoenbach 1994). The readiness of reporters to mention the possible motives or electoral benefits associated with the leader's activities is one indicator of cross-national differences in "journalistic culture" (Semetko 1996).

One very popular form of access to election broadcasting is party leader debates. A debate is arguably the single most important unifying event of the campaign, if only because millions of electors share the experience. This is now a tradition in many countries as can be seen in Table 1.7.

Partisanship in the Printed Press

The printed press, its editorial independence, its relationship with political parties, and the extent to which newspapers and magazines express partisan sympathies are also crucial to an understanding of a country's media system.

Not bound by the rules and regulations concerning impartiality in broadcasting, the newspapers and magazines are free to express their partisan sympathies. In most countries, the print media sources are known for their political
leanings and could be described in simplistic terms on a left-right scale. In
Germany, for example, everyone knows that the elite *Frankfurter Allgemeine
Zeitung (FAZ)* and the high-circulation, tabloid style *BILD* are on the right,
whereas the *Sueedeutsche Zeitung* (published in Munich) and the prestigious
weekly magazine *Der Spiegel* are on the left. A less than astute observer
landing in Britain shortly before election day would have no trouble identifying the partisan sympathies of the national tabloids. The British press, as a
whole, is considerably more partisan than the U.S. press, with the tabloids
offering screamingly partisan news, often on the front page, in the run up to
election day. But the British press is not formally linked—through ownership—to political parties (Seymour-Ure 1974). In other European countries,
and particularly in Scandinavia, for example, political parties actually subsidize major newspapers (cf. Euromedia Research Group 1992). So partisanship
in the press may be expressed voluntarily or in response to the publisher's or
owner's wishes. Media mogul Rupert Murdoch, much beloved down under
for bringing the first national newspaper to Australia, is much maligned in
Britain because of his interference with the editorial independence of the
Times and the partisan news in the nation's highest circulation tabloid the *Sun*.
Murdoch was a staunch supporter of Mrs. Thatcher.

In countries facing dire economic circumstances, the role and influence of
the printed press is constrained. In many Latin American countries or Russia,
for example, where production costs increase as the general standard of living
declines, economic considerations are paramount. Many people simply cannot afford to purchase a daily newspaper. Most of the government, Communist
party-owned or -subsidized newspapers in the former Eastern bloc countries
could not remain commercially viable once the market became the criterion
for survival. In some democracies, the government controls the distribution
or subsidizes the cost of newsprint. In Mexico, for example, the government
can severely hamper the press simply by reducing the subsidies for newsprint.
In India, although readership is comparatively low, so are the costs of rural
colloquial newspapers, and these serve an important political function in
villages.

Other macrolevel system characteristics by which to compare nations
include legal regulations and the use of cable and satellite, as well as general
trends in viewership and readership. It is not possible to discuss all of these

here. It is worth noting, however, that the use of cable and satellite can be as much a consequence of the regulatory and political environment as the tastes and preferences of viewers. Most of the homes in Belgium, for example, have received cable since the 1970s due to government initiatives (de Bens 1986). In Britain, however, the Thatcher government's decision not to subsidize cable meant that it never caught on in the 1980s, although small household satellite dishes made greater inroads in the 1990s (Dutton, Blumler, and Kraemer 1987). Although cable may bring to mind an abundance of channels, it does not always mean this. In India, for example, one cable channel exists in most local media markets to play videotapes of movies.

Diversity of media ownership is another variable along which national media systems may be compared, but this is a vast topic deserving of a chapter in its own right. Suffice it to say that a number of media barons are now household names—Rupert Murdoch in Britain, Australia, and the United States; Leo Kirch in Germany; and Silvio Berlusconi in Italy and Spain, to name a few. The issues surrounding cross-media ownership and the extent of vertical and horizontal integration in the media and entertainment industries are the focus of frequent articles in the *Wall Street Journal Europe,* the *Financial Times,* and the *International Herald Tribune.*

Finally, transborder media may now exert an influence in national politics that can no longer be ignored by domestic political leaders. In some countries, this may prove to be a vital part of the democratization process. The bloodless revolution in East Germany in 1989 was at least in part attributed to the many viewers of West German television in East Germany (Hesse 1990). Transborder media also have an influence on foreign diplomacy as well as on public opinion about other countries and the preservation of national cultures.

Developments in Some Regional Media Systems

The literature on the media and elections ranges from simple descriptive accounts of regulation, media content, and media use to more elaborate models of media effects. Fletcher (1991) brings together in one edited volume case studies of the role of broadcasting in elections in France, Britain, Germany, Scandinavia, and the United States for purposes of making reforms to Canadian broadcast regulation and party finance. Fletcher (1992) and Johnston et al. (1992) show how the media can have important effects on

Canadian elections. Kaid and Holtz-Bacha's (1995b) edited volume provides studies of the content, use, and potential effect of television advertising in elections in a number of European countries as well as in the United States and Israel. The "Americanization" of modern campaigning is the focus of an insightful comparative volume edited by Swanson and Mancini (1996). As mentioned previously, although there is a substantial literature on media and elections in North America, Britain, and Germany, some of which has been mentioned above, systematic research on this topic in other countries is much less common. Developments in France and Italy, as well as in parts of Latin America and in Russia, point to why the role of the media in elections is important and deserving of empirical research (see also Mathes and Semetko 1991).

Western Europe

Despite the popular assumption about the importance of the media in French elections, there has been little systematic research into its effect on election campaigns. Instead, research has traditionally focused on ideology, social class, and religiosity. Whereas Converse and Dupeux (1962) were unable to compare French and U.S. electorates in terms of reliance of television for political information in their study of the 1958 French elections due to the comparatively small number of French households with television, today the media, and television especially, are important sources of information for French voters (Cayrol 1988; Missika and Bregman 1987; Gerstle 1992). A comparative study (Semetko and Borquez 1991) of the use and attention paid to the news media during the 1988 French and U.S. presidential elections found that attention to election news exercised an independent and significant influence on the ability to identify candidates' issue positions in both countries. This study also found that patterns of media use (whether one was highly attentive to the press or to television, or in the low-attention group) trigger the use of economic criteria in evaluations of Mitterrand and Chirac that reflected the prevailing leadership roles in economic management.

In Italy, where television was responsible for both the rise and the fall of Prime Minister Berlusconi, empirical research on media effects in elections nevertheless remains in its early stages (Mancini and Wolf 1990). The backdrop to one of the first studies of the content of the mass media in a national election, the general election campaign of 1983, was the increased commercialization of broadcasting in Italy in 1981, which resulted in hundreds of local channels, and the crisis of the mass political parties in terms of their declining membership as well as their shift to more "personalized" or leader-centered politics (Mazzoleni 1987). There is a long tradition of media subordination to political power in Italy both formally, with the political parties controlling the main public broadcasting organization RAI, and informally through close contacts with journalists (Mazzoleni and Roper 1995). More than a decade later, the crisis of the mass party in Italy continues, broadcasting continues to be intensely competitive, and the crisis of governance deepens.

Latin America

The Latin American experience suggests that the free enterprise system in the press and in broadcasting does not always go hand in hand with a news media that acts as a Fourth Estate or watchdog of the government (cf. Salwen and Garrison 1991; Fox 1988; Alisky 1981; Skidmore 1993). In many cases, privately owned television and newspapers have supported the government of the day. This has emerged in various ways in the different countries. Examples from Brazil and Mexico are illustrative.

Television has become the most important means of public communication in Brazil, where the rate of adult illiteracy is high and radio has never been a national medium. There is considerable evidence to support the position that privately owned Brazil's TV Globo, the fourth largest television network in the world, which dominates the country's broadcasting scene, has a remarkably close relationship with the state and has "manipulated its television newscasts by distorting, suppressing, and promoting information according to its own interests and those of the class fraction it represents" (de Lima 1988, 108). TV Globo's monopoly on broadcasting was ended in the early 1980s when the military themselves started to worry about the power the corporation wielded and how it might influence government policy. There was a challenge by some of the military within the government circle to break the monopoly, and three other channels were launched. SBT now has an audience share of 20 percent, Manchote has 6 percent, and Bandierantes has 5 percent, with TV Globo maintaining a minimum of 60 percent (Robinson and Rivero-Santos 1995).

In Brazil's 1989 presidential election campaign, TV Globo's main evening news program reflected the conservative political views of the owner, Roberto

Marinho. There was a "disproportionate amount of favorable coverage given to conservative candidate Fernando Collor de Mello in comparison with all other candidates and the weekly announcement (or the 'omission') of the poll estimates of what candidates were ahead and who would be the contenders in the second round" (de Lima 1993, 106). The reporting of opinion polls in the news also influenced the decisions of voters, and this influence was greater among those with less education (de Lima 1993, 108).

The vast majority of journalists in Latin America are poorly paid. Those covering the government in Mexico, however, have an opportunity to improve their standard of living by following the tradition of *embute,* an official bribe that has become part of the journalist-source relationship. Journalists who report on key sources in government are paid regularly by that source. As a political reporter, one adopts a ministry and is treated as a member of the family (Robinson and Rivero-Santos 1995). Although newspaper readership is low in Mexico—only about a million read a newspaper regularly—nearly all government employees read the press. Criticism is often between opposing elements within the PRI and government, and newspapers can send very subtle signals about counterarguments among government sparring partners.

One tradition held dear by nearly all journalists in Mexico is never to criticize the president while he is in office, for he is the emblem of the state. Criticism can mean different things to different people. For those in the office of President Carlos Salinas, the monthly publication of his downward-shifting approval rating in the elite-read magazine *Este Pais* was enough for them to encourage advertisers to end their contracts with the publication. According to Miguel Basanez, director of Market Opinion Research International (MORI) in Mexico City and one of the editors of *Este Pais*:

> The magazine simply dared to publish what U.S. media carry—a monthly tracking of the president's approval rating, based on a nationally representative random sample of Mexican electors using the identical question-and-response scale each month. The surveys were conducted by MORI-Mexico. The information on the president's public standing had not been published systematically before. Only selected questions which put the best possible light on the president up to that time had been released for publication by the president's office. By showing graphically the downward trend over time in the president's approval rating, *Este Pais* violated long-standing journalistic traditions. We then decided to go public with the news story about our advertisers wanting to pull out due to government pressure, and we published what was to be our last issue of the magazine. But this decision saved us. The public outcry was so great that we remain in print today. (Personal interview, January 14, 1995)

The development and use of opinion polling in Mexico has also had consequences for the electoral process. Whereas for many decades the final publication of election results would emerge only after some days following election day, presumably allowing for time to count votes and, as some political observers might add, time to *change* votes, the use of reliable exit polling in the 1994 presidential election meant that the results were known within hours after the polling booths closed.

Televisa, the privately owned television conglomerate, is the major force in the broadcast media industry in Mexico. It came into existence formally in 1973 with the merger of several Mexico City channels and more than 70 stations throughout the country. Through its owners, among whom is the son of a former president of Mexico, it is linked to the most "powerful political and economic interests" in the nation (Mahan 1985, 64). In the 1989 Mexican presidential election, Televisa's popular news program "24 Hours" devoted more than 80 percent of campaign news to the PRI candidate (Adler 1993, 155). The president of Televisa, Emilio Azcarraga, in the early stages of 1988, had surprised journalists and intellectuals with his open endorsement and declared, "Televisa is with the PRI" (Adler 1993, 154).

Apart from the popular perception that news on Televisa is largely the government's version of events, one of the most remarkable forms of overt cooperation between the television conglomerate and the state is in the making of the popular soap operas—*telenovelas.* Televisa cooperates with the Ministry of Public Education (SEP) to incorporate "the government's desired social themes into telenovelas" but in a way that does not "interfere with the realization of Televisa's own goals of providing entertainment that will attract the largest possible audiences (and thus enhance the value of the commercial time sold)" (Rogers and Dearing 1978, 69). This cooperation is of significant public relations value for the government.

In comparison with U.S. soap operas, telenovelas have "different themes (e.g., upward social mobility), contrasting purposes (e.g., educational and other goals in addition to entertainment), and a shorter duration" (Rogers and Antola 1985, 26). But they reach many more people in Latin America because they are shown many times daily. In Mexico, this presents the government with ample opportunity to encourage the airing of themes that could, for example, help to shape economic expectations or "socially desirable" responses to economic crises. In Brazil, too, the dominance of telenovelas in TV Globo's prime time and their enormous national audience make it possible for them to be a central player in the definition of political options for the country.

Russia

Developments in Soviet and post-Soviet Russia also point up the importance of broadcasting relative to the printed press. Mickiewicz's (1988) fascinating book, *Split Signals,* is devoted entirely to the subject of television as a medium of political communication in the Soviet Union during the 1980s. She argues that the evening news ("Vremya"), viewed daily in the 1970s and 1980s by more than 80 percent of the adult Soviet population, was extremely important particularly during the transition in leadership in the mid-1980s and with the introduction of *glasnost* because it became Mikhail Gorbachev's most powerful instrument for paving the way for major reforms. With glasnost, journalists began to abandon self-censorship and challenge the establishment. The Chernobyl nuclear accident marked a turning point for previously restrained Soviet news reporters.

By August 1990, a new media law was passed that marked the end of the Communist party's monopoly on ownership and control of all media. New political parties were formed and able to launch their own newspapers and journals. With the breakup of the Soviet Union, new television news programs were launched in the new republics on both state- and privately owned channels. The main competitor to state television in Russia is NTV, which stands for Independent Television, an independent, nongovernment commercial television station launched by journalists who chose to leave state television. The Yeltsin administration has clashed with the media on many occasions over the reporting of Chechnya and actually threatened to revoke NTV's broadcasting license because of "unverified," "unreliable," and "subjective" news reports in 1994 (Erlanger 1994).

What can we expect in the future? "Television electoral politics" in Russia, by emphasizing the personal, "could well retard the development of the very political parties that render the electoral system efficacious" (Mickiewicz and Richter 1996). Some informed observers predict the emergence of corporate fascism in the country. Russia, it seems, demonstrates that capitalism, in the form of a market economy, can exist without democracy (Freeland 1995). If the Latin American experience is any indicator, the path of corporatism is a likely one in which at least some part of the media is incorporated. Release from the economic misery may come in the form of entertainment programming. It may come as no surprise that the most popular television show in Russia today is an imported soap opera from Mexico—a telenovela.

General Media Effects

With some notable exceptions, the subject of media effects in U.S. election campaigns has received more attention from communication scholars than political scientists over the past three decades (cf. Patterson and McClure 1976; Patterson 1980; Bartels 1988). In recent years, as political communication research has grown to become a subfield in political science, the news media and their role in the electoral process have received greater attention from political scientists. Much of what we now know about the media in election campaigns comes from research conducted in the United States. There is a considerable amount of scholarship in Germany on media content, uses, and effects in elections, and a growing body of literature in Canada, Britain, Australia, and Scandinavia, but data remain limited for many other advanced industrial societies. The subject has only recently become the focus of scholarship in Latin America, largely because of the rise of television as a major source of political information, candidates' strategic use of the news media, and the growth of public opinion polling in these countries. In Russia, Eastern Europe, and the new republics, where television has become the new opiate of the people and the news media are the subject of much political debate, research on democratic elections and the media is still in its infancy.

Although it has proven difficult to isolate television exposure or attention to the medium as a significant variable in determining vote choice, there is no doubt that the predominance of television as a medium of communication in election campaigns has transformed the electoral process. Television personalizes politics. As Ian McAllister argues in chapter 11, in most of the political systems for which data are available, political leaders have become more important in determining election outcomes in the post-World War II period. Television has changed the nature of election campaigning (Seymour-Ure 1974). It has become the primary target of politicians' campaigning activities. The tone of election information transmitted on television may also have effects on public opinion. Some argue that the emphasis on the negative in U.S. presidential election campaign coverage over the past decades has resulted in a more cynical electorate (Patterson 1993). Whether it is the news that is primarily at fault or the negative ad campaigns sponsored by U.S. candidates remains unclear (Ansolabehere and Iyengar 1994). Television brings it all into the living room: the debates, the political advertisements, the daily news from the campaign trail, political discussion programs, and most recently, political talk shows.

Effects may be short term or long term. They may be cognitive (effects on political knowledge), attitudinal (effects on political opinions), or behavioral (effects on the vote decision). In recent years, a number of election studies have been concerned with media effects in one or another of these domains in national elections in Canada (Crête 1992; Macdermid 1992; Johnston et al. 1992), Britain (Miller et al. 1990; Curtice and Semetko 1994), France (Semetko and Borquez 1991), Germany (Baker, Dalton, and Hildebrandt 1981; Semetko and Schoenbach 1994; Pfetsch and Schmitt-Beck 1993; Schmitt-Beck and Schrott 1994), and the United States (Bartels 1988). Rather than review the specifics of each of these studies, I will discuss media effects more generally in the context of the methodological and theoretical approaches to one of the most important concepts—agenda-setting. This concept provides us with a way of looking at both questions of effects of news and information on public opinion and the influence of politicians on news content.

Agenda-Setting Effects

The idea that the press influences public opinion has been understood by politicians for centuries (Lippmann 1922). The notion of an all-powerful media—with direct effects injected as if by "hypodermic needle" was an important part of mass society theorists' explanation of the experience of Nazi Germany. The propaganda model of the 1920s later led social scientists in the United States to question the power of the media in democracy and the electoral process. But the early empirical evidence suggested only a limited ability of the media to influence the public's political attitudes and voting behavior (Lazarsfeld et al. 1948; Berelson, Lazarsfeld, and McPhee 1954; Katz and Lazarsfeld 1955). After more than a decade in which the hypodermic needle or "direct effects" model of media influence reigned, empirical research by political scientists and sociologists into media effects on the vote and partisan preferences in the United States brought the "reinforcement" model of media influence into fashion—for most people, exposure to news during the campaign did not change vote choice, it simply reinforced preexisting partisan preferences. By the 1970s and 1980s, as the party system weakened in the United States and the news media became major players in the presidential selection process, a broader view of media influence known as the "limited effects" model emerged (cf. Becker, McCombs, and McLeod 1975; McQuail 1994).

Cohen's (1963) study of the press and foreign policy was seminal for identifying the special importance of the media's role when "the world outside" is far away, when the news becomes our only experience of events and peoples abroad. Although Cohen did not mention agenda-setting, he reasserted the idea of media power in shaping public opinion. Agenda-setting brings scholarship back to the notion of a powerful media, but one that does not have electoral outcomes as its primary focal point. It is today one of the most important concepts in public opinion and media effects research (for reviews, see McCombs 1981a, 1981b; Becker 1982; Weaver 1984, 1991; Rogers and Dearing 1988; Swanson 1988; McCombs and Shaw 1993; Edelstein 1993; Kosicki 1993). Agenda-setting research has provided substantial support for the hypothesis that the issues that are most prominent in the news are also the issues that are most important in public opinion.

Many studies have drawn on two sources of data. One is content analysis of the news to establish the most important issues in the news. The other is measures of public opinion. The latter have included simple cross-sectional designs, time series of comparable cross-sectional surveys, and more elaborate panel studies, as well as, most recently, experimental approaches. Support for the agenda-setting hypothesis has been found using all of these methodological approaches, further strengthening the argument of a powerful news media. In the earliest study, McCombs and Shaw (1972) relied on a content analysis of news and a cross-sectional survey of undecided voters' opinions in a community during the 1968 U.S. presidential campaign. They concluded that the media set the campaign agenda for the public. The study was pioneering for providing evidence of a strong and significant correlation between the campaign agenda in the media and in public opinion and setting forth the hypothesis that agenda-setting is a process led by the news media (cf. Shaw and McCombs 1977).

Media power to influence public agendas may vary with a number of factors. One is the extent to which real-world indicators reinforce or diminish the media message. Another is the type of issue—"unobtrusive" issues may be more susceptible to agenda-setting (Zucker 1978). News about foreign affairs and foreign peoples, with whom viewers have little or no direct experience, is an example. Media influence may also vary with the type of public agenda. An individual's civic agenda (the most important issues or problems facing the community) may be quite different from an individual's personal agenda (the most important problems facing the person). When an individual's personal agenda is the focus of research, then there is considerably less support for the agenda-setting hypothesis (McLeod et al. 1974). But when the public lacks personal experience with an issue that might influence personal agendas, the opportunity for media influence is greater (Erbring, Goldenberg, and Miller 1980).

A year-long panel study of the 1976 U.S. presidential election designed specifically to test the agenda-setting hypothesis provided further evidence of the direction of the causal link between media agendas and public agendas. It also identified the relative strengths of television and the newspapers as influences on public opinion and established that agenda-setting effects varied over time, with the strongest during the spring and summer and the weakest during the final 12 weeks of the campaign, particularly with respect to unobtrusive issues such as foreign affairs, the environment, and government credibility (Weaver et al. 1981).

The next methodological innovation in agenda-setting research was to bring the public into the social scientists' laboratory. A series of sequential experiments, each lasting 1 week (which required pre- and postexperimental questionnaires), as well as assemblage experiments (which required only postquestionnaires) and an analysis of time-series data from national public opinion polls, taken together provided further substantial support for the agenda-setting hypothesis (Iyengar and Kinder 1987). This study was also innovative in its focus on television news as an agenda-setter in normal (nonelection) periods or routine news coverage.

The strength of the agenda-setting hypothesis is that it has been supported by evidence from more than 20 years of studies drawing on a range of methodological approaches (see McCombs 1992; McCombs and Shaw 1993). It has moved media effects scholarship away from the limited-effects model. It has helped us to view the role of the news media in the political process as influential in a variety of ways.

Expanding the Research Agenda

Unlike the European Community's long-standing debate over "wider or deeper" integration, agenda-setting research moved happily in both directions. It has become wider in that it no longer focuses simply on the connection between media agendas and public issue priorities; it now includes broader research questions. One of these concerns how the media agenda is formed. Another concerns the relationship between media agendas and policy agendas, thus moving the effects focus from mass to elite publics. It has also become deeper in that the traditional emphasis on media effects on public issue salience now extends beyond cognitions (knowledge and beliefs) and further into the domain of attitudes and opinions.

There have also been methodological developments. Structural equation models have been added to the list of methodological approaches to investigating the agenda-setting hypothesis (Huegel, Degenhardt, and Weiss 1989), linear and nonlinear models have been used to discuss the static and dynamic processes involved (Brosius and Kepplinger 1990, 1992, 1995), and depth interviews have been used to understand how people frame and interpret the variety of public issues in the news (Neuman, Just, and Crigler 1992; see also Graber 1988).

How the Media Agenda Is Formed

The question, "Who sets the agenda for the agenda-setters?" changes the focus of agenda-setting research from effects to agenda formation. It calls into question an implicit assumption of much of the agenda-setting-effects literature, by shifting the emphasis to the role played by external forces in shaping the news agenda. Is the news offering a unique agenda or is it simply transmitting the agendas of powerful sources? In a seminal study of the effect of public relations firms on the image of foreign countries in the *New York Times,* Mannheim and Albritton (1984) show that indeed, the hiring of such firms exerted a positive and significant influence on the image of foreign countries in one of the nation's most respected newspapers. If the visibility and tone of the news about a country in the *New York Times* can be manipulated by the hiring of a PR firm then, given the support for the agenda-setting hypothesis, it is likely that public opinion can also be manipulated. Another study of television news coverage of foreign countries in the U.S. media in 1989-1990 found that the more visible the country was in the news, the stronger the significant relationship between exposure to news and the likability of the country (Semetko et al. 1992). The influence that external actors have on developing news images is therefore an important subject of study.

Because politicians rely primarily on the news media to reach voters at election time, election campaigns provide a most interesting opportunity to address questions of influence on the media agenda and how it is formed. The election campaign agendas of top candidates and their parties in Britain and the United States were compared with television news and press agendas during elections in the 1980s in these two countries (Semetko et al. 1991).

The study found that politicians in Britain had considerably more opportunity to influence the campaign (news) agenda than their counterparts in the United States and that U.S. journalists exerted considerably more discretion in shaping the news agenda than their British counterparts.

Media Agenda-Setting,
Public Policy, and "Priming"

Policy agenda-setting research has a somewhat longer tradition in political science (see Rogers and Dearing 1988), but with some notable exceptions, too little attention has been paid to the role of the media (see, e.g., Cohen 1963; Downs 1972; Linsky 1986; Spitzer 1993). How the media agenda was formed during Watergate was the subject of a fascinating study by Lang and Lang (1983) in which politicians' agendas were linked with news agendas as well as public agendas. They refer to the process by which the public became aware of Watergate as something more than just a "caper" as "agenda-building." According to Graber (1993, 183): "In many instances the media manipulate the political scene by creating a climate for political action. This makes them major contributors to agenda building, the process whereby news stories influence how people perceive and evaluate issues and policies."

Page, Shapiro, and Dempsey (1987) provided some of the strongest evidence of a direct link between the media agenda-setting and public opinion, drawing on their analysis of 80 public policy issues over the 1970s and 1980s, and they gave added weight to the power of television as an agenda-setter. Network television coverage accounted for nearly half the aggregate changes in public issue preferences. In a subsequent study of foreign issues in the news over 15 years, the same authors found that television news was actually a significant predictor of the direction of public opinion on these issues (Page and Shapiro 1992).

Recent research suggests that Cohen's (1963, 13) comment—"[The press] may not be successful much of the time in telling people what to think, but it is stunningly successful in telling its readers what to think about"—is in need of modification. As McCombs and Shaw (1993, 63) note: "Whatever the attributes of an issue—or other topic—presented on the news agenda, the consequences for audience behavior are considerable. How a communicator frames an issue sets an agenda of attributes and can influence how we think about it. Agenda-setting is a process that can affect both what to think about and how to think about it." This represents a major development in the definition of agenda-setting. The effects of agenda-setting now go beyond merely learning and adopting the saliences attached to issues in the news. The effects now include shaping the direction of public opinion on an issue and altering the standards by which we evaluate our political leaders.

Other studies also provided evidence of the media's role in shaping the standards by which citizens evaluate political leaders and candidates (see, e.g., Weaver et al. 1981; Patterson and McClure 1976; Patterson 1980; Protess and McCombs 1991). This extension of effects is generally now referred to as "priming" (see Rogers and Dearing 1988). The term priming has been defined broadly by Fiske and Taylor (1984) as the effects of prior context on the interpretation and retrieval of information, and more narrowly by Iyengar and Kinder (1987) as changes in the standards used by the public to evaluate political leaders. The series of experiments conducted by Iyengar and Kinder provides impressive support for the priming hypothesis. Iyengar (1991) also shows that under some circumstances, the agenda of the news media can influence the standards by which people evaluate presidential performance. Krosnick and Kinder (1990) show that indeed, exposure to news about Attorney General Ed Meese's announcement concerning U.S. involvement in the Iran Contra affair directly and immediately led to changes in the issues used by the public in evaluating President Reagan's performance.

One of the earliest findings of agenda-setting research established variation in effects—not all of the people are influenced all of the time. One of the most important developments in agenda-setting research has been the identification of the contingent conditions under which it can occur. Two of the most commonly discussed are interest and knowledge. A number of studies have established that effects can be modified by the public's interest in information (see Weaver 1991). Those who are least susceptible to agenda-setting and hence priming are those who undertake the viewing experience with some independent store of knowledge that enables them to argue against what they see in the news. Krosnick and Kinder (1990) used a simple knowledge test (a count of the number of political elites a respondent was able to identify correctly) to partition their respondents into two groups—political "novices" (with low knowledge) and "experts" (with high knowledge)—and found that the novices are most susceptible to media influence. These studies thus suggest that shifts in public opinion about political leaders can be brought about by those who are least informed, the novices who are most likely to be influenced by the news.

Elections and Agenda-Setting
in Cross-National Perspective

Recent elections in Britain and Germany have been the subject of research on the effect of media agendas on public opinion during the campaigns, drawing on both content analysis and panel surveys, but the evidence failed to provide clear support for the agenda-setting hypothesis. William Miller and colleagues' (1990) study of the 1987 British general election, for example, found no significant agenda-setting effects over the 4-week campaign period. The issue agenda in television news was instead quite different from the public's issue agenda—although the public was interested in social and economic issues, television news about the election focused on social and national defense issues and at the same time the background (nonelection) news agenda on television concerned security and defense. Miller and his colleagues (1990, 232) described the television news agenda as having been profoundly biased in the direction of the Conservative's key issues and concluded that "television failed to set the public agenda and the public failed to set the media agenda." They continued: "It is a comforting conclusion, however, because we have uncovered massive partisan bias in British television news coverage and a massive gap between television's priorities and the public's" (1990, 232).

Media effects on public perceptions of issue salience have been found in a number of studies of German election campaigns. A study of the 1987 Bundestag election by Kepplinger and Brosius (1990) suggested that the issues covered heavily in the news media had not only an effect on public perceptions of issue salience but subsequently also on evaluations of political parties. A comparison of public, media, and political party agendas in the German 1990 election, however, showed little correspondence in the rank order of the topics in the news and the rank order of topics named by the public as important in the campaign; in fact, there was less correspondence between news agendas and public agendas than between party agendas and public agendas (Semetko and Schoenbach 1994, 93).

These studies provide important evidence to suggest that agenda-setting, as it was originally and narrowly defined in terms of media effects on issue salience, was not operating. But they also found evidence of other significant media effects, particularly in the domain of public evaluations of political parties and top candidates. German television news, for example, was largely devoid of any positive or negative evaluations of political parties or leaders during the final 8 weeks of the 1990 campaign, but there was at the same time a substantial visibility bonus accorded the incumbent chancellor and the parties of government, otherwise known as a *Regierungsbonus,* in the news (Semetko and Schoenbach 1994; Pfetsch and Schmitt-Beck 1993). As a result, there were significant changes in individuals' opinions about the parties and leaders, in the direction one would predict given the visibility gap between the government and opposition in the news. Agenda-setting therefore should not be taken as the sole or the primary indicator of a powerful news media. The absence of evidence to support the agenda-setting hypothesis in an election does not mean other important effects on opinions are entirely absent.

Debates and the Vote

Debates among party leaders have become key events in elections in many countries (see Table 1.7). They focus the campaign on individuals and enhance the importance of party leaders in parliamentary systems. Citizens are strongly interested in these events. They learn something about the candidates' issue stands as well as about their personal characteristics.

In Germany, political debates among the top candidates featured as key events from the 1972 to 1987 election campaigns. Baker, Norpoth, and Schoenbach (1981), in comparing the 1972 and 1976 debates, found that politicians who display a more positive style of debate are more likely to be perceived as the "winner" of that debate. And Baker and Norpoth's (1981) study of the 1972 debate found that electors did learn more about the candidates and parties from this event and that this had a particular effect on evaluations of the opposition party. Schrott's (1990) analysis of the electoral effect of the 1972, 1976, 1980, and 1983 debates suggests that debates do make an important difference to electoral outcomes. Perhaps concerned about the possible negative effect of debates, incumbent chancellor Helmut Kohl refused to participate in the 1990 Bundestag election campaign. There were no chancellor debates in 1990 or in 1994. Margaret Thatcher, too, as prime minister, was another modern political leader who resisted debates despite her obvious talents.

Ironically, as debates have become more of an institution in election campaigns, they may have less effect on election outcomes. Politicians have not only hired television debate coaches, but in most countries they have also moved up the timetable on the events so that debates now are held earlier in the race. Damage caused by a poor debate performance might then be overcome by election day (LeDuc 1990).

The reinforcement hypothesis was supported by some of the earliest studies of election campaigns in the United States (Lazarsfeld et al. 1948). There is evidence that the strength of partisanship is reinforced by the information obtained during a campaign (Norpoth and Baker 1980). In many European countries, where there is a strong sense of civic duty and voting is expected or in some cases mandatory, research on voter turnout has not revealed any significant media effects (Blumler 1983).

Conclusion

Studying the role and influence of the news media in elections is difficult enough in one society. To expand this to many countries requires much time, effort, and funding (cf. Swanson 1992). What was traditionally only a postelection cross-sectional survey needs to be expanded to include collection of data on media content and, ideally, panel instead of cross-sectional survey data. And this needs to be replicated cross-nationally. Although there is a long history of comparative survey research, cross-national comparative content analysis is relatively new. We need to have content analysis accompany election surveys and to use a set of media content indicators and variables central to an understanding of the dynamics of the information environment in campaigns. Another very useful source of information is journalists themselves, who, occasionally, will agree to interviews and newsroom observation (for a summary of studies of the BBC election newsroom since 1969, see Blumler and Gurevitch 1995; Semetko et al. 1991; Semetko, Scammell, and Nossiter 1994). How the news media cover election campaigns is an important basis for evaluating "media performance" over time and across countries (McQuail 1992).

In addition to the macrolevel characteristics discussed at the outset of this chapter, there are others external to the media system that should be taken into account when developing hypotheses concerning media influence in elections. The type of political and electoral systems are important, for example. Elections in presidential systems such as the United States or most Latin American countries would be more candidate driven and candidate centered, in contrast to parliamentary systems in which a broader range of party elites may be responsible for campaigning, whereas in proportional representation systems the party counts for more. But even in modern parliamentary systems, the emphasis of "news values" on personalities has meant greater visibility of party leaders and a potentially greater influence of party leaders on vote choice.

The party system—the range of political parties and their relative strength—is also important. Britain's stronger party system, for example, in comparison with the weaker party system in the United States, was "associated with less discretion on the part of journalists to set the campaign agenda and more opportunity for politicians to do so" (Semetko et al. 1991, 178; see also Blumler and Semetko 1987). But in countries with nonexistent or developing party systems, news values or journalistic preferences for personalities and conflict may actually serve to hinder the institutional development of parties and public attachment to them. Politicians in the democracies discussed in this chapter have clearly adapted their routines to the logic of the media, even though this central and institutional role for the media in elections has potentially unhealthy consequences for democracy (cf. Patterson 1993).

The majority of studies of the content, uses, and effects of the media in democracies have been bounded almost entirely by election campaigns. But there are more stable voters than vote-switchers, and most voters have made up their minds about how to vote before the campaign begins. In many democracies, the party of government strategically begins at least a year in advance of the election to use the media to set the stage for the forthcoming campaign. We therefore need to devote more attention to the contribution made by regular news sources to shaping partisan, leader, and issue preferences during nonelection or precampaign periods.

Leaders

IAN McALLISTER

The earliest classics of American voting behavior (Lazarsfeld et al. 1944; Berelson, Lazarsfeld, and McPhee 1954) devoted remarkably little attention to how candidates influenced electoral choices. Yet ever since publication of *The American Voter,* it has been accepted that perceptions of the personal attributes of presidential candidates form a central component in American voting behavior. Campbell et al. (1960) found that in presidential elections of the 1950s, most references to candidates dealt with their experience ("military record"), abilities and qualifications ("a good leader," "strong and decisive," "a good administrator"), and personal characteristics ("sense of duty," "integrity and ideals," "likability"). Such references were particularly common for the incumbent, President Dwight Eisenhower, who was much better known than his opponent Adlai Stevenson (Campbell et al. 1960, 54-9).

Building on this foundation, an extensive body of research has developed in the United States since the 1960s focusing on how far the character, leadership style, and personal qualities of presidential contenders shape the result in U.S. primary and general elections. A large literature has also developed on the nature and extent of the "personal vote" enjoyed by candidates for lower levels of office in the United States (for a review, see Cain, Ferejohn, and Fiorina 1987). What is less clearly established, however, is whether we can generalize from this research to voting behavior in other political systems. Only more recently have we started to look systematically at how far party leaders and legislative candidates influence the outcome in a range of parliamentary democracies such as Britain, Germany, and Canada. And it is not clear whether findings in the United States can be extended to voting behavior in presidential systems in emerging democracies such as Russia, the Philippines, and Mexico, or to established democracies with weaker presidencies such as Ireland, Austria, and France. Journalists and commentators often assume that leaders matter, and matter a great deal. Yet until recently, political scientists have largely downplayed the electoral effect of party leaders in Europe. The dominant theory in most parliamentary systems has been the responsible party government model: Party platforms, rather than personalities, do and should drive votes.

Yet, partly stimulated by new work in political communications, a scattered body of studies is becoming available on the effect of party leaders in parliamentary systems. This includes research in Germany (Klingemann and Taylor 1978; Semetko and Schoenbach 1994), Sweden (Esaiasson 1993), Ireland (Harrison and Marsh 1994), Australia (Bean and Mughan 1989), Canada (Brown et al. 1988; Clarke, Stewart, and Zuk 1986), and Britain (Nadeau, Niemi, and Amato 1996b; Crewe and King 1994; Norpoth 1992; Mishler, Hoskin, and Fitzgerald 1989; Clarke and Whiteley 1990; Hudson 1984; Butler and Stokes 1974; Graetz and McAllister 1987a). There is no consensus about the results, in part because of a multiplicity of measures and theories. Most of these studies suggest that public perceptions of leaders, if not decisive, often have a modest but significant influence on the vote. A comparative study of campaigning, by Swanson and Mancini (1996), theorizes that the process of modernization of political communications has produced an increasing personalization of politics. Some have gone further, claiming that television may have encouraged the "presidentialization" of politics, even in a strong parliamentary system like Britain (Mughan 1993). Yet increased coverage of party leaders in political communications does not necessarily mean that leaders have therefore become more important than parties or issues in voters' choices. This chapter aims to review the literature in the light of this debate to see what we know about the nature and strength of leadership effects on voting behavior in different countries. The first section outlines the institutional arrangements that set the context for elections and voting behavior in parliamentary and presidential systems and considers whether and how these matter to voting behavior. The middle section reviews studies about the effect of presidential candidates in primary and general elections in the United States. Last, the chapter draws together the more scattered body of evidence about the effect of party leaders in parliamentary systems.

Institutional Context
of Leadership Effects

Based on the premises of the "new institutionalism," we start from the assumption that leadership effects on voting behavior are likely to vary according to the institutional context. That is, the nature of the electoral choice matters: People choosing a presidential contender in a primary election, for example, will behave differently from voters selecting one party from a closed list in a parliamentary system. As March and Olsen (1989, 1) put it, "The organization of political life makes a difference." It is widely accepted that institutional arrangements largely determine the role and powers of political leaders. What is less clearly established is how the institutional context affects leadership effects in voting behavior.

Within established and newly emerging democracies, there is a major distinction in executive leadership between presidentialism and parliamentarism; other institutional forms exist, although they apply mainly to nondemocratic states (Shugart and Carey 1992; Stefan and Skach 1993). Lijphart (1992) suggests that the major distinctions among these systems are threefold:

1. In presidential systems, the head of government has a fixed term in office. In parliamentary systems, the head of government is dependent on the confidence of the legislature.

2. Presidents are *elected* (directly or via an electoral college), whereas prime ministers are *selected* by the legislature.

3. Presidential systems have one-person, noncollegial executives, whereas parliamentary systems have collective executives.

These generalizations serve as a broad definition of the two systems although, as discussed later, there are a number of qualifications that need to be made to each of them. There is a long-standing and heated debate about the virtues of each system (see Linz 1990). Presidentialism is said to have the advantages of executive stability, greater democracy, and more limited government, but the disadvantages of executive-legislative deadlock, temporal rigidity, and "winner-take-all" government. Parliamentarianism is said to reverse the pros and cons. The significance for electoral choice is that we would expect the individual character, record, and personal style of leaders to prove most influential in determining the popular vote in presidential systems. In contrast, we would expect parliamentary elections to reflect collective choices about parties—combining policies, teams of legislative candidates, and collective leadership—and the effects of the major party leader to be only indirect.

If countries are defined by the method of election or selection of the head of state, the democracies within this book divide roughly equally between presidential and parliamentary systems. In emerging democracies, which system was adopted was often influenced by their colonial origins and date of independence. Most West European democracies, as well as countries that were former British colonies, are parliamentary systems. In contrast, many nations influenced by the United States adopted presidentialism, including the former Spanish and Portuguese colonies in Latin America (Jones 1995), the Philippines, and South Korea. In Central and Eastern Europe, countries divided between presidential systems with direct elections, including Russia and Ukraine, and those where the legislature selects the president, such as Hungary and the Czech Republic.

Certain states are more difficult to classify. Countries with interrupted periods of democratic government have sometimes changed at different times from one system to the other. Bangladesh, for example, experienced several periods of constitutional change following the 1971 civil war with Pakistan that brought about independence. It is now a parliamentary system, although the military remains a dominant force in the country's politics. Other countries have adopted hybrid constitutions. Among the established democracies, Switzerland is perhaps the most difficult country of all to classify, because the executive is formed by a council elected by the cantons, with one council member serving annually as the president, in strict rotation. Moreover, Austria, Iceland, and Ireland are difficult cases. Duverger (1980), for example, has argued that because their presidents have weak powers, these countries are parliamentary democracies. France is also problematic because it involves "an alteration of parliamentary and presidential phases, depending on whether or not the president's party has a majority in the legislature" (Lijphart 1992, 8). At different periods in the history of the Fifth Republic, France could have been categorized as either a presidential or a parliamentary system, depending on the balance of political forces. Israel has a long tradition of parliamentary democracy but has recently adopted direct elections for the prime minister (Diskin and Diskin 1995).

As Blais and Massicotte (chap. 2 in this volume) demonstrate, presidents are popularly elected in 22 countries, either through a direct election, as in Austria or Poland, or through some form of electoral college, as in Argentina, Finland, and the United States. They thus conform to Verney's (1959, 75) tenth "proposition" concerning the nature of presidentialism: "The executive is responsible to the electorate." In 4 of the 17 countries with presidential systems—Ecuador, Ireland, South Korea, and Mexico—the president is ineligible to stand for reelection after one term. Most of the presidential systems considered here elect their presidents for either 4- or 5-year terms; two countries, France and Ireland, elect their presidents for 7-year terms.

Among the parliamentary systems, there is a distinction between those that have coalition forms of government, common throughout Western Europe (Budge and Keman 1990a; Laver and Schofield 1990), and those that have majoritarian arrangements. About half the parliamentary democracies under comparison have had mainly majoritarian government in the postwar years. The parliamentary systems divide equally between those that have a monarchical head of state (or a head of state appointed by the monarch in consultation with the government, as occurs in Australia, Canada, and New Zealand) and those that have some form of indirect election to choose their head of state. In almost all of the countries that apply indirect election, the head of state is selected by the legislature.

The adoption of a parliamentary or presidential system has systemic consequences in terms of the responsibility, accountability, and stability of government. Presidentialism generally encourages individual *responsibility*. Under presidentialism, executive authority resides with an individual who is elected to the position for a fixed period of time; even members of the president's own party may vote against whatever measures he or she proposes without undermining the day-to-day operation of the system or risking a split within the party. In contrast, under parliamentarism collective responsibility is much more likely to occur, so that the executive is both dependent on the confidence of members of the legislature and accountable to them. The operation of parliamentarism also encourages party government, so that party discipline becomes a primary factor in maintaining executive authority (Katz 1986; Linz 1990).

In terms of *accountability*, presidential systems elect their leaders for a fixed period of time. As a result, retaining office is not normally dependent on the day-to-day confidence of the legislature. A fixed term of office permits presidents considerable freedom to formulate policy and develop their political performance without the risk of a snap election. Even a deeply unpopular president remains in office, except for exceptional circumstances like impeachment. Directly elected presidents remain accountable to the public at a fixed date in the future, but they are less vulnerable to their party. These considerations are less important in systems such as Ireland's, where the president has only limited powers, a 7-year period of office and is, in any event, ineligible to stand for reelection. By contrast, it is a major consideration where the president does have extensive powers and a much shorter tenure in office. Moreover, presidential elections are a zero-sum game because there is only one winner, which makes it more difficult to sustain coalitions and allow power sharing.

Turning to *stability*, in parliamentary systems, the executive depends for its survival on the confidence of the legislature. Indeed, in most cases the prime minister is selected by parliament, although in practice this will be the leader of the majority party or, in coalition governments, the leader of the party with the most seats. The executive can therefore be removed at any time by the legislature, usually after a vote of no confidence. In practice, this means that a prime minister must make it a priority to retain the support of party colleagues. In majoritarian systems like Westminster, votes of confidence have rarely brought down the government, but in countries like Italy, frequent shifts in the coalitional basis has often produced unstable and short-lived administrations. In the postwar era, there have been 54 governments in Italy, although coalitions in countries like Germany and Switzerland have usually proved far more stable.

Institutional arrangements may also have important consequences for the context in which leaders contest democratic elections. In presidential systems, a national election focuses attention on the candidates who seek office. This is particularly marked in countries where the presidential and legislative elections are held separately. Primary elections to select nominees within parties have a similar effect. Single-member districts rather than closed-party lists also reinforce the emphasis on individual legislative candidates. These institutional arrangements can be expected to reinforce the focus on the candidates' personal characteristics.

Parliamentarism imposes a different set of institutional constraints on its actors. By its very nature, an election for a legislature focuses on parties with collective leadership. This is more likely to direct attention toward the whole package of party policies, platforms, and candidates, rather than personalities. Although the party leader will undoubtedly attract disproportionate attention, his or her colleagues are also likely to play a prominent role in the election campaign. In turn, it follows that partisan factors are likely to play a much larger role in the election, net of other things.

Yet some scholars contend that in recent decades parliamentary elections are becoming more like presidential contests. The increasing attention devoted to leaders in parliamentary systems has led to what has become known as the presidentialization thesis. Support for this argument is based on the premise that the institutional arrangements within a country have comparatively little influence on what leaders do and how they behave while in office. What matters are changes in the process of political communications and the nature of party organizations. Parliamentary systems were alleged to have become more presidential in style and character when prime ministers appeared to control their executives in much the same way as an elected president, that is, by assuming that the fate of the leader and the fate of the government are inextricably linked and that the leader has total control over the executive (Foley 1993; Weller 1985).

During the past half century, it is argued that political leaders have become increasingly central to electoral competition within democracies. Previously a phenomenon of presidential systems such as in France or the United States, some argue that the popular focus on leaders is now common in parliamentary systems, such as Australia or Britain, where parties once occupied center stage. In Mughan's phrase (1995), party leaders are now seen to have stronger "coattails": A popular leader can boost party fortunes. Impressionistic evidence signaling the extent of this change includes the substitution of leader images for party symbols during election campaigns; the tendency to label governments after the leader, rather than the party; and the unprecedented media interest in the personalities and private lives of major leaders.

This change has been variously described as "the rise of candidate-centered politics" in the United States (Wattenberg 1991) and the "presidentialization of politics" elsewhere (Mughan 1993). The most widely discussed explanation is the growth of television's role in campaigns in the postwar years (Glaser and Salmon 1991; Mughan 1995). It is suggested that the electronic media have forced a restructuring of political discussion in all democracies, establishing themselves as a crucial institution for the effective dissemination of political information throughout the electorate. Without the attention of the electronic media, a political party or a government will gain little or no popular visibility.

The changing political role of electronic media has in turn served to focus popular attention on a handful of major political leaders, who have come to symbolize partisan and ideological conflict. From the perspective of the electronic media, the concentration on leaders stems from the practical consideration of how to present information. In general, it is easier to communicate information through the projection of personalities than through the discussion of complex ideas or abstract policy issues. The drama of horse-race journalism (who's up, who's down) is more vivid than detailed debates about the European Monetary Union or the balance of trade deficit. But another explanation for the media's concentration on leaders relates to the psychology of democratic electorates. It is argued that voters are often more willing to associate political power and authority with a readily identifiable political personality than with an abstract institution or political ideal. For the ordinary citizen, it is easier to hold an individual accountable for his or her actions rather than an institution (Bean and Mughan 1989).

Two other factors are important in explaining this new focus on political leaders. The decline of party membership (Katz and Mair 1994), itself perhaps a consequence of the growth of the electronic media, has shifted voters' attentions from local to national election campaigns, and along with it, from local to national political leaders. Moreover, as Dalton (chap. 13 in this volume) discusses, extensive partisan and class dealignment in many established democracies has meant that voters have weaker (and in some cases nonexistent) loyalties to the major political parties and to the major social groups within the society. In the absence of partisan and social ties anchoring them to specific parties, voters are "thus set politically adrift and subject to volatile election swings" (Wattenberg 1991, 2). One consequence of this is the enhanced role of the leader in mobilizing that vote.

Yet the evidence to support the presidentialization part of the thesis is largely impressionistic. There is widespread agreement that in the postwar era, the modernization of political communications has increased the role of television as a source of voter information in every political system with a high penetration of viewers (Swanson and Mancini 1996; Butler and Ranney 1992). Evidence from the United States demonstrates how voters have increasingly come to rely on television as the major sources of news during presidential elections. In 1959 in a multiple-response question, more voters (57 percent) cited newspapers than television (51 percent) as the most important source of news; by 1994 almost three-quarters cited television, and only 38 percent cited newspapers. During this period, television has also increasingly been seen as the more credible source of news (Stanley and Niemi 1995a, 68).

Studies of campaign communications also demonstrate that in recent decades, leaders are gaining greater attention compared with the coverage of political issues, although the degree of "personalization" of television news varies substantially cross-nationally (Butler and Ranney 1992; Semetko 1996, forthcoming). One indicator is the use of party leadership debates during election campaigns. Once restricted to presidential systems such as the United States, the leader's debate is now common as well in many parliamentary systems such as Canada (Smith 1981). The televising of parliaments may also have increased the focus on party leaders, particularly on how they perform in dramatic debates. Viewers can form direct evaluations of their abilities and leadership styles. Beyond impressions, however, there is little firm evidence that party leaders in parliamentary systems behave—outside of election campaigns—in a way that is far removed from their predecessors in the days before the advent of the mass media. Moreover, it is not clear from the comparative evidence in parliamentary systems that the change in campaign coverage, which is widely documented, has necessarily led to the increasing importance of party leaders in determining votes. At present, the most appropriate evidence from existing studies is unproven. Let us consider the evidence for the effects of presidential candidates in the United States, where there is a wealth of research, with the more scattered and inconclusive results from studies of the effects of party leaders in parliamentary systems.

Presidential Candidate
Effects in the United States

In the United States, studies of presidential candidates and of how voters perceive them has progressed through three main stages in the postwar years. The first stage, which dominated the 1950s and 1960s, was to recognize the importance of voters' perceptions of the major candidates, but to view those perceptions as essentially irrational and therefore of little consequence as an influence on the vote—except in particular circumstances. This view persisted in spite of the findings that many voters said that they made up their minds based on their views of the leaders rather than of parties or policies. The classic voting studies, *The Voter Decides* (Campbell, Gurin, and Miller 1954) and *The American Voter* (Campbell et al. 1960), identified three influences on the vote of broadly equal importance—party, issues, and candidates. Although *The American Voter* focused on the personal factor as a major component in Eisenhower's reelection in 1956, this was treated as a special case.

The apparent importance of candidates led Stokes (1966) to examine the short-term factors that might influence presidential election outcomes. He suggested that short-term change, for example, during the course of an election campaign, could be traced substantially to changing voter perceptions of the major candidates. Later evidence suggests that this short-term, candidate-induced volatility appears to have increased (Miller and Miller 1975). However, during this period the predominant scholarly view remained that candidate images were largely projections of partisanship and that election outcomes were determined mainly by party identification. Although individual presidential candidates, such as Eisenhower, could inject some dynamism into presidential contests and thus generate electoral volatility, such events were rare; voting was anchored in the normal patterns of partisan voting.

The second stage in the treatment of leaders within models of electoral behavior emerged in the 1970s and 1980s, when research suggested that election outcomes could be—and regularly were—determined by voters' evaluations of the major candidates. No longer were elections decided by inherited party loyalties or by the party's policy program, but by how voters perceived and reacted to the major candidates. Evidence from the United States found that George McGovern's defeat in 1972 turned specifically on popular negative perceptions of him as a candidate (Popkin et al. 1976), as did Jimmy Carter's defeat in 1980 (Markus 1982), whereas Johnson's victory over Barry Goldwater in 1964 was attributed to his personal popularity (Nie, Verba, and Petrocik 1976, 307 ff.).

The renewed significance of presidential candidates in the scholarly literature, highlighted by the studies of the 1970s, has given rise to a third stage of electoral behavior research in the United States. This latest stage has aimed to identify the content of candidate images and to evaluate what aspects of these images influence how a voter will cast his or her ballot (Wattenberg 1991, 13-30). Most important, this approach has challenged earlier views of voter irrationality about leaders and argued that the way in which a voter accumulates information about a candidate—personal as well as political— is an essential tool that enables him or her to make judgments about the suitability of the competing candidates for elective office. This general view that voters make rational judgments about leaders is also linked to a more broadly based view in electoral behavior research that sees voters' opinions and behaviors as being grounded on rationality, whether it be in the field of leaders, issues, or parties (Page and Shapiro 1992; Rusk and Weisberg 1972).

The link between party identification and candidate image does, however, remain strong. The origins of popular feelings about leaders are usually traced to the socialization undergone by adolescents before they join the active electorate, which in turn is linked to partisanship (Greenstein 1965; Sigel 1968). Moreover, effects vary among different types of voters. Zaller (1992, 297-9) shows that the link between partisanship and candidate image varies by level of political awareness, with the less aware being least influenced by partisanship in their evaluations, the highly informed exhibiting most partisan influence.

We can shed some light on the postwar changes in how voters view the major candidate in the United States. Figure 11.1 uses data from the 1952 to 1992 American National Election Studies to show the proportion of voters who mention economic, partisan, and sociological factors when voting either for or against a presidential candidate over the 40-year period. In line with the decline in partisanship, the proportion of the American electorate that spontaneously evaluates the candidates along partisan lines has dropped from around one-third in 1952 to just 14 percent in 1992. Sociological factors have remained relatively constant, averaging just under 14 percent over the period and peaking at 25 percent in the 1984 presidential election.

The major change, however, has been in the proportion of respondents who mention economic factors in their evaluations of presidential candidates. The proportion more than doubled between 1968 and 1972, from 13 percent to 34 percent, then declined slightly in 1976. It rose again in 1980 and peaked in 1984, when no less than 60 percent of voter evaluations were economic in nature. The 1988 election was something of an exception, with a drop to 35 percent, the result of the election being based on many noneconomic issues such as Willie Horton's furlough, capital punishment, and the pollution of Boston harbor. However, the pattern was reestablished in 1992, when 57 percent of the evaluations were economic. In short, there has been a funda-

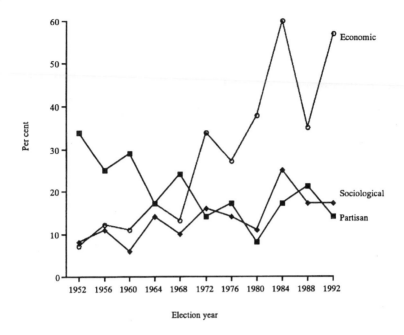

Figure 11.1. Voters' Evaluations of Presidential Election Candidates, 1952-1992

SOURCE: Wattenberg (1991: Figure 1.2, 1992) and Wattenberg (personal communication).

mental change in how American voters perceive presidential candidates, seeing them less in the context of partisanship and more in economic terms. This supports the argument that political leaders have become electorally important in their own right.

What qualities do American voters see in their political leaders? How are these perceptions shaped by agencies over which the voter has little control—such as the political parties and the mass media—as well as by the voter's own individual psychology? Perhaps most important of all, what leader qualities weigh more heavily in the voting decision? Examining these questions is fraught with difficulties, which helps to explain why there has been little attempt systematically to marry theory with the myriad of sometimes contradictory empirical results. One problem is that although leaders attempt to project certain images to the public, these are often not the images that voters receive. The disjuncture is caused by the exogenous factors that link the leader and the voter and mediate the images that flow between them. A second problem is that once a voter receives this image, it is again shaped by many factors, this time specific to the individual. These endogenous factors include educational attainment, level of political awareness and knowledge, partisanship, issue preferences, and not least, the voter's own personality. Again, each of these will play its role, separately and together, to shape the leader image that a voter will construct.

Two main explanations have been advanced to account for the sources of leader images, one focusing on the stimulus provided to the voter (an exogenous explanation), the other on how voters perceive or react to that stimulus (an endogenous explanation). Early communications studies suggested that images were a consequence of the stimuli or information presented by the leader (for reviews, see Blumler and McQuail 1969; Conover 1980). However, there was no direct link between the voter and the leader; all of the information was mediated by intervening individuals and groups. It follows from this, as Converse (1964), Page (1978), and others have implied, that leaders' images can be manipulated by public relations consultants to produce whatever they think the public wants to see and hear. This cynical view was based on the premise that voters' reactions to leaders were essentially irrational and that they were based on a leader's style or looks, rather than on his or her policies, experience, or expertise (Sullivan and Masters 1988). This view also emerged at the same time as the introduction of widespread opinion polling by the major political parties, thus—according to the cynics—enabling party strategists to identify the issues, traits, and styles that appealed most to voters, particularly those who might consider changing their vote.

The opposing view has been based on the "perceptual balance" approach, which focuses not on the stimuli provided to the voter but on how the voter perceives or reacts to such stimuli (Insko and Schopler 1972). This approach uses cognitive dissonance theory to argue that voters are driven by the need for consistency, so that contradictory information or stimuli must be revised to conform to whatever preexisting beliefs or values the individual possesses (Festinger 1957). Alternatively, new information may—much more rarely—result in a change in those beliefs or values. Cognitive dissonance theory implies that voters "are likely to engage in selective perception and distortion to maintain evaluative consistency among their beliefs. Thus, leader images should differ from voter to voter depending on the voter's particular beliefs" (Conover 1980, 92). This view emerged at the same time as the theory of party identification and led naturally to the conclusion that voters evaluated leaders through the perceptual filter of their partisanship.

There has been considerable debate about the relevance of these two theories. Early studies suggested that the "candidate image" theory was perhaps the most applicable, although the evidence has been by no means conclusive (McGrath and McGrath 1962; Sigel 1964; Blumler and McQuail 1969). Conover (1980, 93) suggests that both approaches have major short-comings. In the case of the candidate image thesis, she argues that it is undermined by the fact that candidate images often vary systematically from voter to voter, even though the information/stimuli that they have received about each candidate has been the same. Similarly, voters rarely form negative views of the opposing party's candidate, casting doubt on the notion that voters bring their perceptions of the candidates into line with their preexisting beliefs and values (Nimmo and Savage 1976).

What are the contents of leader images? One approach to this question has been to examine the emotional responses that leaders attract from voters, including such feelings as fear, hope, and pride. This "candidate trait" approach draws heavily on cognitive psychology (see, e.g., Lau and Sears 1986; Hamill, Lodge, and Blake 1985); one important contribution has been to show that the perceptions and emotions surrounding the economy are often more important determinants of voting than objective economic conditions (Lewis-Beck 1988). Studies have generally found an underlying pattern among these emotions, with favorable emotions correlating together, separately from un-favorable emotions (Abelson et al. 1982; see also Markus 1988). A related approach has examined the effect of facial displays and the emotions they elicit from voters. Using an experimental study based on 1984 presidential candidates, Sullivan and Masters (1988; see also Rosenberg et al. 1986; Ragsdale 1991) show that a reassuring or happy facial display by a candidate is more likely to alter voters' attitudes. Indeed, the authors found that such facial displays had a greater influence on the vote than cognitive variables such as party identification, issue agreement, or candidate traits.

An alternative approach to understanding the content of candidate images has been to focus on the public's evaluations of presidential character, in what is often called the candidate trait approach. Nimmo and Savage (1976) use such responses to make a basic distinction between stylistic images and political images. They argue that stylistic images are associated with candi-dates' mannerisms, personalities, and personal backgrounds, whereas political images are concerned primarily with leadership abilities, issue positions, and political backgrounds. In general, voters appear more likely to form stylistic rather than political impressions of candidates.

More recent research, however, has not made this distinction between stylistic and political images, but rather viewed all of the information that voters accumulate about a leader as part of a rational strategy to enable them to make an informed and balanced decision on election day. As Page (1978; see also Kinder et al. 1980; Kinder 1986; Miller, Wattenberg, and Malanchuk 1986; Popkin et al. 1976; Shabad and Andersen 1979) puts it, "Voters who pay personal attention to the personal characteristics of candidates should not be dismissed as irrational . . . these matters bear upon the utility outcome or benefits which voters can expect to get from alternative electoral outcomes" (p. 262). This approach, then, views voters' evaluations of candidate qualities as an essential component of democratic control. Moreover, because most voters will find it easier to evaluate personalities than policies, appraising leaders is arguably the central component of democratic selection within liberal democracies.

Many American studies have examined the dimensions of these candidate traits. One standard approach is to subject the batteries of items to factor analysis, to identify any underlying structure in the patterns of responses. For example, Kinder (1986) identifies four factors underlying candidate qualities: competence, leadership, integrity, and empathy. Miller et al. (1986) also see competence and integrity as major dimensions, but they also identify voters' comments that suggest a desire for reliability and charisma, as well as comments about the candidates' personal characteristics. Broadly similar patterns emerge in studies in Australia and Britain (Bean and Mughan 1989) and in Canada (Brown et al. 1988), using similar methodologies. Others have grouped voters' responses according to broad categories that emerge from open-ended questions. Page (1978), for example, identifies five categories of responses: incumbency and experience, knowledge, warmth and likability, strength, and candor.

This approach has been developed into what has been called "schema theory." Schema theory suggests mechanisms whereby voters use preexisting categories and frameworks to process and evaluate political information. The theory is based on the assumption that individuals do not have the time or the cognitive sophistication to make sense of the political world; they require shortcuts and simplifications (Nisbett and Ross 1980), particularly when they are required to vote. The schema approach argues that "individuals organize their thoughts about other people into broad pre-existing categories. These category 'prototypes' are then used in making judgments when only limited factual information is available" (Dalton and Wattenberg 1993, 209; see also

Conover and Feldman 1984). Research in the United States suggests that these schema change little from election to election or from candidate to candidate (Kinder et al. 1980; Kessel 1988). Similar findings have been reported in Australia and Britain, where Bean and Mughan (1989, 1176; see also Miller et al. 1990 on Britain) found that in both countries "prime ministerial candidates are judged against some kind of well-defined schema in the public mind."

Most important, American research has provided indications that these perceptions of presidential candidates play a role in determining election outcomes. In the United States, subtracting pro- and anticandidate comments in the 1964 presidential election suggested that Lyndon Johnson's victory over Barry Goldwater was substantially due to his personal popularity, at least relative to the comparatively unpopular Goldwater. Similarly, Nixon's victory over George McGovern has been ascribed to the latter's singular lack of popularity among voters (Nie et al. 1976; Miller and Levitin 1976; Page 1978). Other studies have shown that both the candidate trait and candidate affect factors have an influence on the vote. The most basic studies have calculated how trait and affect influence summary evaluations of the candidates, and how these in turn determine the vote (Markus 1982). Ragsdale's (1991) study examined the specific electoral influence of the emotion questions and concluded that emotions surpass issue opinions in their influence on the vote.

Party Leaders and Parliamentary Elections

Does the American literature on the importance of presidential candidates have any relevance for the influence of party leaders in parliamentary systems? As discussed earlier, given the institutional context, we would expect parliamentary elections to incorporate a much more complex interplay between parties, issues, and leaders. Although, as mentioned earlier, more studies have been carried out in a range of parliamentary systems, the most systematic evidence comes from Britain, where a series of studies has attempted to quantify the electoral effects of the major party leaders.

The earliest voting studies in Britain found that party leaders were generally associated with the images of the parties themselves, to the extent that they were almost indistinguishable (Milne and Mackenzie 1954, 1958). Yet

Butler and Stokes (1974, 367-8) found that the leaders had a significant effect on party fortunes during the 1960s, largely to the benefit of Labour. The authors interpreted this finding, like recent research, not in terms of an irrational concentration on personality for its own sake, but rather as evidence of voters' accumulating information about the "qualities which will affect the likelihood of his achieving goals which electors value." Butler and Stokes (1974, 367-8) concluded that although "attitudes towards the parties were a better guide to voting behavior than were attitudes towards the leaders it was also evident that leaders were set apart from parties sufficiently in the public mind to have demonstrable effects on the party balance when it becomes preponderantly positive or negative." Leaders gradually ceased to be viewed as mere projections of party identification, even in parliamentary systems, and became independent variables in their own right.

More recently, Graetz and McAllister (1987b) used the October 1974, 1979, and 1983 British election studies to estimate the relative effect on the vote of the major party leaders in each of the three general elections. Using summary (thermometer) scores of the party leaders, they found that leader evaluations had a major effect on defection and conversion between the parties, but that the net effect on the outcomes of the three elections was comparatively small. The most extreme effect was in 1983, when the Conservative's Margaret Thatcher, who was then benefiting from her success in the Falkland Islands War, faced Labour's unpopular Michael Foot; in that election, the relative standing of the leaders influenced the Conservative and Labour votes by about 4 percent, after a wide range of other factors had been taken into account. However, in the October 1974 and 1979 elections, when popular perceptions of the leaders were less polarized, their electoral effect was much smaller.

Bean and Mughan (1989, 1174) reach similar conclusions, this time comparing the popularity of the prime ministerial aspirants in Australia in 1987 and Britain in 1983. In the 1987 Australian federal election, they found that popular perceptions of Bob Hawke's qualities resulted in a net gain to the Australian Labor party (ALP) of just over 4 percent, compared to the Liberals' John Howard. In the 1993 Britain general election, Margaret Thatcher was worth just over 6.5 percent more votes when compared to Labour's Michael Foot. Although Foot's electoral liability to Labour was not sufficient to have altered the outcome, in Australia the difference between the two leaders "was sufficient on its own to tilt the outcome of the 1987 federal election in the ALP's favor" (Bean and Mughan, 1989, 1175). A major factor inhibiting each opposition leader's popularity, and its subsequent effect on the vote, was the lack of "effectiveness" in the eyes of many voters. This suggests that there may be a built-in incumbency advantage, which Wattenberg (1991, 1-2) sees as a major indicator of the growth of candidate-centered politics.

Other British studies have come to substantively similar, although often more impressionistic, conclusions. Miller et al. (1990) suggest that there were "large effects" for leaders on the result of the 1987 British general election. Controlling for party identification, they found that among Conservative identifiers, 94 percent of those who rated Thatcher ahead of any other leader actually voted Conservative, compared with 77 percent who rated her equal to another leader and 51 percent who rated another leader ahead of her (1990, 246-7). In another recent study Crewe and King (1994) suggest that the outcome of at least two postwar elections, those of 1964 and February 1974, may have turned on who the party leaders were. In other elections, Crewe and King found that the effects were far more limited, in part due to the serious problems of measurement of leadership effects with the limited number of items available in the British Election Studies. A variety of other studies, in Britain and elsewhere, also support the notion that leaders are an important component in the electorate's views of the government and of its voting behavior (e.g., Lafay 1991; Lanoue and Headrick 1994; Nadeau et al. 1996).

Conclusion

Political leaders possess an importance that transcends their electoral significance. In extreme cases, a leader can influence the stability of the political regime, so that leaders who possess high levels of charisma and widespread mass support may have more opportunity to downplay controversial issues and to implement radical or unpopular plans. Ronald Reagan's and Margaret Thatcher's ability to pursue radical policies owed much to their popularity during the earlier stages of their period in office (Cooper, Kornberg, and Mishler 1988). Conversely, less popular leaders may be reluctant to implement controversial policies and are more vulnerable to short-term, destabilizing political issues (Converse and Dupeux 1966).

What current research tells us about political leaders and democratic elections can be summarized as follows. Leaders have gained greater visibility in democratic countries in the postwar years, and as a result many believe that they have probably become more important in determining voting choice. The evidence outside of the United States remains scattered, but the available studies suggest that leaders are one of the factors—along with issues and parties—that need to be taken into account in explanations of voting behavior. Whether leadership effects have become more important as a result of changes in how information is presented to the electorate (such as through television) or as a consequence of more general changes in the political environment (such as the decline of parties or class dealignment) remains unknown. The U.S. literature suggests that voters use particular cues or frameworks to evaluate leaders and that in recent years economic performance has become more important in making these evaluations. In addition, voters' cues or frameworks for evaluating leaders may come from endogenous factors such as their own personality, as well as from exogenous factors such as the wider political environment. However, we do not know how or why these evaluations differ across individuals. Finally, we suspect that the electoral effects of leaders are relatively modest in parliamentary systems, but much larger, as we would expect, in presidential systems.

Early interpretations of how leaders were popularly elected suggested an irrational electorate, selecting aspirants for national office based on idiosyncratic criteria or on qualities that had been created for the election campaign by political consultants. This emerged as one of the principal justifications for the theory of democratic elitism, which sought to limit the powers and influence of democratic electorates (Bachrach 1967; Kariel 1970). More recently, doubt has been cast on this interpretation, and it has been argued that the information that voters collect about candidates—personal as well as political—is an essential part of the process by which voters ensure democratic control over their leaders (Page 1978). This more rational view of the electorate has important implications for our understanding of the changing role of leaders in the electoral equation and for representative democracy.

(12)

The Economy

HELMUT NORPOTH

When you make that decision [at the polls], you might ask yourself, "Are you better off now than you were four years ago?"

Ronald Reagan

Six days after posing that question in a televised debate, Ronald Reagan soundly defeated President Jimmy Carter in the 1980 election. The explanation seems clear. Most voters did not think they were better off economically and blamed it on failures of the incumbent government. If there is one explanation of elections that speaks for itself, as the saying goes, it is the economy. We all know that when economic times are good, governments thrive at election time; when times are bad, they stumble and fall. Or so it seems much of the time, and not just in the United States.

AUTHOR'S NOTE: The research was supported by National Science Foundation Grant SES-9307340. I am grateful to Sam Wilkin and Troy Flowers for assisting me with the collection and analysis of the 38-country data.

299

The economy is a concern that almost everywhere bonds electorates and governments as tightly as Siamese twins joined at the hip. Governments spend a lot of time trying to bend the economy to their will. During the past half century, the public sector has mutated into an economic giant, with more than half of the gross domestic product going through its hands in many Western democracies, especially the Scandinavian ones. The public's demand for an economy in good health is plain to any politician. No candidate for office should need a reminder that "it's the economy that matters" (a phrase used repeatedly by candidate Bill Clinton in 1992). Moreover, economic adversity is a disease that can kill infant democracies. The collapse of the Weimar Republic in Germany amid economic despair in the 1930s casts a long shadow over new democracies struggling with economic chaos these days.

Justifiably so, electoral analysts have paid the economy their compliments, especially for purposes of election forecasting and for tracking government popularity.[1] But as we shall see, the theoretical attempts to come to grips with the influence of the economy on political behavior span a diverse range and have spawned some long-running controversies. Although the big bulk of this research is of the single-country type, economic voting makes for an inviting target of comparative research as well.

The organization of this chapter is as follows. We begin by asking whether what economists call a "vote function" exists. Is the vote function—the relationship between economic conditions and vote outcomes—just good theory or also good fact? What is the evidence from cross-national studies? Next we explore the pathways of economic voting. In what shape does the economy register in the minds of individual voters and trigger an electoral response? That is a question that has embroiled the field in heated disputes.

Most studies, often implicitly, treat the economy as a consensus issue, synonymous with the undisputed goal of prosperity. But others maintain that the economy is a matter of conflicting policies. What economic course should the government steer to reach the port of prosperity while avoiding the shoals of recession and the gales of inflation? Do voters care enough and know enough to have a preference and cast their votes accordingly?

Common to much economic-voting research is also the premise of a reward-and-punishment calculus. Incumbents win reelection in good economic times, and the rascals are thrown out in bad times. One challenge to this orthodoxy is the proposition that people may be inclined to punish incumbents for economic failures but not to reward them for economic success stories. Another challenge has to do with the partisan twist of economic issues.

Based on their respective group support and political ideology, parties are said to have different electoral standings on key economic issues. An issue that helps (or hurts) a conservative party need not affect a liberal party.

One popular notion of economic voting that research has debunked is that economic voting means voting your pocketbook. Instead of their own personal well-being, voters are said to be concerned with the health of the overall economy. What do comparative studies show on this point? How compelling are the explanations for lack of pocketbook voting and the prevalence of "sociotropic" orientations?

In recent years, a major controversy has swirled around the question of whether it is the economic record of the past or the prospect in the time ahead that matters more to the general public. In other words, is the electorate's time perspective on the economy primarily retrospective or prospective?

In surveying the research on those questions, this chapter focuses on studies dealing with electoral choices proper, but it also draws on related work dealing with measures such as government popularity. We contrast evidence from cross-sectional, single-survey analysis with evidence from aggregate time-series analysis, though without getting bogged down in methodological disputes. All in all, although the economy makes for a compelling suspect in the trial of electoral analysis, the search for the murder weapon is not over yet.

The Vote Function

There is no country without an economy, although not every country lets its people vote in competitive elections. If economic well-being is a universal concern to people, then one should expect that economic conditions translate into vote choices in a regular, predictable form around the world wherever people exercise the suffrage. We should observe a vote function just like supply and demand functions. Paldam (1991) put this function to the test with a study of elections in 17 countries over a nearly 40-year period (1948-1985). The findings proved most discouraging. They showed that the vote function was highly unstable, "disappear[ing] in some countries and time periods" (Paldam 1991, 26).[2] Note that the countries examined were exclusively Western industrial, including the United States. Hence, the response of voters to Reagan's question in the 1980 election may not be typical for electorates everywhere. A further cross-national study with 19 countries and additional economic variables (inflation and unemployment) proved no more encouraging for the vote function (Powell and Whitten 1993). Whenever the net of countries is cast widely, the signs of economic effects on the vote seem faint at best. It is disturbing that something as compelling as the economy proves so elusive to pin down in cross-national research. Is this reason enough to abandon the economy as an important explanatory variable of voting?

It is telling that the authors of those negative findings invariably have not done so. They all agree that an understanding of the role of the economy in elections must recognize some key political circumstances. Economic voting, in other words, is contingent. Perhaps the critical contingency is the "clarity of responsibility" (Powell and Whitten 1993; see also Paldam 1991), coupled with what Lewis-Beck (1988, 108) calls the "alternatives for dissent." Clearly, the ideal political setting for casting an economic vote is a two-party system. When there is only one party in government, and only one party in opposition, voters are in a position to translate their economic judgments into partisan choices, as they apparently did in the 1980 U.S. presidential election, the distraction of John Anderson's third-party campaign notwithstanding. When, on the other hand, two or more parties share government responsibility, voters must first decide how to apportion blame and credit among the governing parties (Anderson 1995). And similarly, when two or more parties crowd the ranks of the opposition, voters face the problem of deciding which of them would best handle the economy if elected to office. These are daunting complications that may bedevil even the most sophisticated citizens at the polls. Unfortunately for the vote function, few countries in the world have stable two-party systems. Coalition governments and divided oppositions are far more prevalent conditions.

Evidence for economic voting, however, is not absent in countries with coalition governments, such as Germany (Kirchgässner 1991; Goergen and Norpoth 1992) or Italy (Bellucci 1991). In the German case of stable two-party coalitions (which last longer than the typical marriage these days), the dominant party in the coalition appears to be the primary target of economic voting (Anderson 1995). There are also signs that in countries with divided government—where different parties control the executive and legislative branches—economic voting can flourish so long as voters assign responsibility to only one of the branches (Tufte 1978). President Bush paid for economic sins in the 1992 election even though the opposition party controlled the Congress (Abramson, Aldrich, and Rohde 1994, 203-7). The case of France, however, under conditions of cohabitation—president and prime minister belonging to opposite parties—is more complicated (Lafay 1991).

To take a fresh look at the vote function, consider the plot of the vote against economic conditions for a set of countries that is much broader than commonly examined (Figure 12.1). The data set includes developing nations in addition to the usual suspects of the industrialized world, for a total of 38.[3] The vote variable is simply the percentage of the vote received in one election, not the change in the vote since the previous election (as used by Paldam 1991; Powell and Whitten 1993). More important, the vote pertains only to the major party in office, not the combined total of all incumbent parties (if there are more than one). It stands to reason that the typical minor party is not one whose appeal is grounded in consideration of the general economy. Electoral support for such parties derives from religious, ethnic, or other special issue cleavages. By contrast, the major party in government is the one that attracts most of the attention for such things as managing the economy and bears responsibility for what happens during the government's tenure. As it turns out, the plot in Figure 12.1 documents a significant correlation ($r = .33$) between the growth of real GDP (inflation-adjusted gross domestic product) and the vote received by the major party in office.[4] The relationship is such that for every percentage point that real GDP grows in the election year, the major incumbent party stands to gain roughly 1 ½ percent of the vote above its normal share.[5] This is evidence that a vote function exists in the universe of countries with competitive elections, regardless of party systems and institutional arrangements that conspire to dilute its thrust.[6] Economic voting is not contingent on political context, as assumed in some cross-national studies. With the vote function capturing a basic behavior of mass electorates, we turn now to an inquiry of how the economy registers in the minds of individual citizens. What are the aspects of economic life with which voters are most concerned?

Consensus and Conflict

Often when the economy registers as an important issue in opinion surveys, the matter of concern is not a particular policy of the government, but simply economic well-being. Butler and Stokes (1974) called the economy a classic example of a "valence issue." For the mass electorate, in other words, the economy refers to a universally desired goal to be achieved by all parties, not a matter of competing policy positions (a "position issue"). As Stigler (1973, 166) put it flippantly, "Prosperity is even more uncontroversial than motherhood now that overpopulation is feared." For any party to pursue anything less than the achievement of economic good times would be irrational and suicidal, given the voters' agreement on that goal.

For one reason or another, however, governments do not achieve that goal all the time. Unlike smallpox, recessions have not been eradicated (although depressions of the sort experienced in the 1920s may have). Contrary to some wishful thinking and overblown claims, economic policy has not succeeded in abolishing the business cycle. Perhaps voters should be realistic enough about that and not blame governments for failing to perform miracles. The valence-issue perspective does not require voters to be so kind. It lets them judge governments purely by outcomes. What matters is whether the commonly desired goal is reached, not how it is reached. According to this perspective, political parties and candidates compete for voter support not by taking stands for or against something but by making claims to be superior to their competitors in achieving a commonly desired goal.

In this battle of claims and counterclaims, however, the real economy need not be the central question anymore. The electoral battle over the economy has become one of credit-taking and blame-denial. What counts is how voters perceive the real economy and whose partisan claims about the economy they believe or are persuaded to believe as a result of campaigns and media coverage. Perhaps we should delegate the topic of economic voting to students of the mass media (Behr and Iyengar 1985; Haller and Norpoth 1995; Mutz 1994; and this volume, chap. 10). To be sure, the true state of the economy is not a trivial point in this competition, but neither does the economy per se resolve whether a party has achieved prosperity or failed to do so.

An important reason why that is so is that the economic package called prosperity contains a bundle of distinct goals where one may be achievable only at the expense of others. Foremost among those goals are full employment, stable prices, and economic growth. It seems impossible to maximize all those desirable goals simultaneously. Politics, like economics, entails making choices among alternatives with unfavorable trade-offs (Hibbs 1977, 1467). The commitment to "good times" does not dictate a single policy to policymakers.

Much of the debate over economic policy is a debate over trade-offs. How much price stability can be sacrificed in the attempt to secure full employment? Or how much unemployment can be tolerated in the attempt to curb inflation? The valence-model depicts the general public as oblivious to that dilemma, wishing for the best of all possible worlds. But an electorate harboring such a naive attitude is bound to be disappointed. And governments,

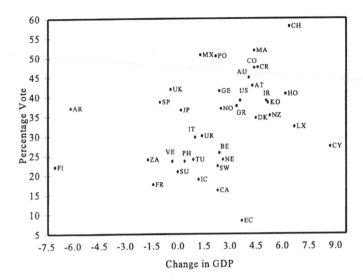

Figure 12.1. Major Incumbent Party Vote and Change in Real GDP
NOTE: See note 3 for the list of countries.

trying to meet unfulfillable expectations, face a poor, nasty, brutish, and above all, short life. Indeed, many prophesied such a gloomy fate for democracies in the age of the welfare state (e.g., Brittan 1977).

Quite to the contrary, the electoral experience of the 1980s has been that failure to achieve full employment has not driven governments from elective office. British voters, in particular, refrained from ousting the Conservatives under Margaret Thatcher in spite of unprecedented levels of unemployment, a highly salient issue (Norpoth 1992). If ever a government's failure to secure a universally desired goal should have sealed its electoral fate, this was the occasion. The ill feelings about Depression-level joblessness were not soothed by various attempts to excuse the governing party from blame. They threatened to inflict a major loss of electoral confidence that was offset, in good measure, by favorable perceptions of progress on the other big economic issue, inflation.

The trade-off dilemma also highlights the fact that no matter how uncontroversial the goal of economic prosperity is, there is plenty of controversy over policies to achieve that goal. To economists and policymakers, at least, the economy is primarily a position issue. Economic policy is the subject of sharp debate among the political parties. For many decades, parties of the left have championed some form of welfare state, whereas parties of the right have leaned more toward a free market orientation, although not in a dogmatic way. The positioning of parties on such a dimension is the centerpiece of spatial theories of electoral competition (Downs 1957).

The revival of conservatism in the age of Margaret Thatcher and Ronald Reagan stirred the political debate over economic policy in the 1970s and 1980s (Cooper et al. 1988; Norpoth 1992). Numerous disputes flared up over macroeconomic policy: Keynesian management versus monetarist control; fiscal versus monetary policy; control of the money supply versus control of interest rates; a deflationary versus an expansionist policy; lower taxes versus higher public spending; or more broadly, an economy guided by the invisible hand of the free market versus one steered by an interventionist state. In the Canadian election of 1988, free trade with the United States turned into a major electoral issue, as the Liberals aimed to unseat the Conservatives (Johnston et al. 1992). Electoral commentary often interprets voter choices as broad mandates for the policies advocated by the winning party and as rejections of those favored by the opposition.

Some of that interpretation undoubtedly misses the point in attributing the sophistication of policymakers to ordinary voters. There is ample evidence for the limited attention and comprehension of the average citizen for matters of politics and economics (e.g., Conover, Feldman, and Knight 1987). Yet the sputtering performance of the economies of industrial nations during the 1960s and 1970s raised profound doubts in the minds of ordinary voters about the economic wisdom of their governments. As Alt (1979, 12) has argued, "Harder economic times present a set of circumstances in which . . . individuals are also more likely to have an incentive to pay attention to . . . positions and preferences with regard to economic policy." Brute experience has a way of altering political and economic preferences (Friedman 1977, 31). Socialism in Europe and liberalism in the United States have sharply declined in popular esteem as economic doctrines. The issue of nationalization/privatization, in particular, was an electoral boon to Conservatives in Britain (Norpoth 1992, chap. 5; Särlvik and Crewe 1983, 189-92; Studlar, McAllister, and Ascui 1990).

Beyond the sharp imprint of policy issues like nationalization (or privatization since 1979), taxes, and union control, the Thatcher elections also reveal a marked ideological coloration. Mrs. Thatcher's plea for a market-oriented economy struck a highly responsive chord in the British electorate (Norpoth 1992). A widespread preference for free enterprise over socialism helped Mrs. Thatcher rout the Labour party and ultimately force it to abandon many of its positions on economic policy. The United States and most Western democracies followed this path of change, and soon after even the command-socialist countries of the Soviet bloc did (Duch 1995). Yet favorable ideological sentiments are no guarantee against electoral defeat. Election day is judgment day, an opportunity for the electorate to hand out rewards and mete out punishments for elected officials.

Rewards and Punishments

Elections, in V. O. Key's (1964, 568) immortal phrase, let voters play the "rational god of vengeance and reward."[7] Given the salience of economic issues, we can expect that voters pay close attention to the economy on judgment day. The standard model implicit in most studies of economic voting assumes a naive reward-and-punishment calculus. As Kramer (1971, 134) put it so succinctly in his pathbreaking article: "If the performance of the incumbent party is 'satisfactory' according to some simple standard, the voter votes to retain the incumbent governing party in office, while if the government's performance is not 'satisfactory,' the voter votes against the incumbent."

The vote decision, accordingly, derives from a simple calculation that allows the individual voter to make an exceedingly complex decision problem manageable. As Kiewiet and Rivers (1985, 208) have noted, the Kramer rule embodies three features. One, the political universe shrinks to only one political actor in the public mind, the incumbent party (president). Second, voters rely on "retrospective" judgments and need not sort out "promises of the novel and unknown" (Key 1966, 61); indeed, Kramer postulates a very short time frame, treating the electorate as highly myopic (see also Fair 1978; Tufte 1978). Third, voters are required only to determine whether they are satisfied with outcomes, not whether they agree or disagree with policies. In other words, voters are not assumed to make decisions that "maximize utility" but that "satisfice."

Thus, so long as the economic record of the governing party is judged to be satisfactory, the voter lets that party carry on, regardless of the economic policies that may have produced the record. Indeed, it is irrelevant whether the policies pursued by the governing party deserve the credit. If, on the other hand, the economic record is judged unsatisfactory, voters are willing to "throw the rascals out" of office. It does not matter whether government policies are at fault. Voters are not assumed to be familiar with the policies and policy positions of the opposition. It is apparent that the reward-and-punishment model treats the economy as a valence issue and hence raises some of the questions discussed above. In addition, it presumes a retrospective frame of mind, which ignores the possibility of future-oriented behavior, the subject of more intense discussion below. At this point, let us consider the incumbency focus and the assumption that the electorate is even-handed in doling out both "vengeance" and "reward" for economic deeds.

It makes good sense to assume that the public's attention is not evenly divided between the party in power and the party(ies) in opposition. What the government plans, does, and delivers commands the larger share of attention. The current economic record of the governing party is close at hand, far closer than the record of its predecessor. The public can scrutinize the government's record with some degree of certainty. By contrast, what the party out of power might have achieved had it been in power is a matter of guesswork and speculation. The total exclusion of the opposition party from the electoral calculus nonetheless goes too far. Some images of parties, almost stigma-like, linger in public awareness long after the event has passed into history. Even in opposition, the Republican party long paid for having been the party in power during the Great Depression.

Although no deeds go unpunished, a bad economy carries a longer electoral sentence than a good economy provides relief, as a hypothesis grounded in social psychology states (Katona 1975; Lau 1985). In other words, the electorate may be more inclined to act as a "god of vengeance" than as "god of reward"—unforgiving and ungrateful. The reasons for this kind of behavior seem quite plausible. Like Gresham's law, bad news drives good news out of circulation. Or, as the unattributed saying goes, good news is no news. The economy is likely to be in the news when it is ailing, not when it is healthy. Opinion polls register high importance ratings for the economy when inflation and unemployment are high, not when they are low. A good economic record is what the general public expects its government to deliver. Thus, when times are good, the public's attention is not likely to be riveted on the economy.

According to this hypothesis, the popular standing of the governing party suffers from bad economic performance but benefits much less, if at all, from good performance (Campbell et al. 1960, 554-5). This "negativity" effect has attracted considerable attention in the study of electoral behavior. Bloom and

Price (1975) have produced the most compelling evidence from longitudinal studies in favor of the asymmetry of economic effects for American elections. Voters in developing countries are not immune to this tendency (Pacek and Radcliffe 1995). Lau (1985) has explored the psychological processes underlying this asymmetry such as "figure-ground" perceptions and "cost" orientations.

Yet, for all the evidence, the negativity effect is profoundly unsettling. If it were true, it would be hard to imagine what incentives public officials have to secure a good economy. There would be no reward for it. All it would do is make voters look for bad deeds elsewhere to exact vengeance. Indeed, considerable counterevidence has accumulated. Mrs. Thatcher's reelection victories, especially the one in 1983, defy the negativity hypothesis. In a different vein, Ronald Reagan's landslide victory in 1984 is inexplicable without the electorate's favorable impressions about the U.S. economy. Good times do count for a lot in elections, especially when they come after a spell of economic malaise and misery. In a sweeping analysis of economic voting in five major European countries, Lewis-Beck (1988, 79) laid the negativity hypothesis to rest. "The electorates are 'even-handed' in their economic judgments, voting *for* governments that are liked, *against* governments that are disliked." Likewise, Kiewiet's study of American voters in presidential elections since 1956 showed that on average, favorable perceptions of the economy help the candidate of the incumbent party as much as unfavorable ones hurt (Kiewiet 1983, 49, 99). Fiorina and Shepsle (1989) make a persuasive case for the possibility that negative voting may be an artifact, with such behavior being concentrated among previous supporters of the incumbent party.

On the other hand, in time-series studies of political support for the incumbent party (or president), the impression of a negativity effect is sometimes hard to deny. American presidents along with leaders in many other countries pay for economic slumps (Mueller 1973; Hibbs and Fassbender 1981; also, more guardedly, Lanoue 1988). In Britain, the generally bad-news item of unemployment registered far more strongly in Thatcher approval ratings than did the generally good-news item of inflation (Norpoth 1987a, 1992, chap. 8). But in their decision on election day, British voters defied this negativity effect. Especially in the election of 1987, a groundswell of favorable opinion was evident about the governing party on matters of the overall economy (Norpoth 1992, chap. 7). Good economic news indeed paid off for the governing party in the run-up to the election while remaining in a dead spot of voter attention in the long haul between general elections. It was not the case that the economic conditions had changed so dramatically during those months, but that favorable perceptions of those conditions began to impinge on partisan choices more forcefully than before. With a general election imminent, voters are reminded that it is also time to play "god of reward" as well as of vengeance.

Parties and Economics

Whatever the precise calculus, it would be naive to assume that voters apply it in a partisan vacuum. We all know that even under the most dire circumstances, the governing party(ies) do not lose all their voting support, although the Conservatives in the last Canadian election came close. Although the proportion varies from country to country, many citizens are partisans, in the sense that they identity with a particular party and perceive the political and economic world through lenses tinted by partisan colors. An economic record that is "good enough" when the party of one's affection is in office may not be good enough when the opposition holds office. Partisanship means that one may use different yardsticks of evaluation, perceive the "facts" of economic life differently, and assign different priorities to conflicting economic goals. Partisanship makes it possible to concentrate on those aspects of the economy that allow one to feel satisfied or dissatisfied, depending on whether one's party is in power or out. This is not to deny that perceptions of economic reality may also feed back to voters' partisan ties. Just as the Democratic realignment of the 1930s is unthinkable without the Great Depression and the subsequent recovery during the New Deal, so were some of the changes in party identification in the 1980s spawned by major economic upheavals (Fiorina 1991; Alt 1979 for Britain).

But aside from serving as affective guides for voters, political parties are also major protagonists in the battle over economic policy. According to the "partisan theory" (Hibbs 1977, 1992; see also Weatherford 1978), political parties are rooted in different social classes, with the lower class forming the core constituency of left parties and the upper class the core constituency of the right parties. This class pressure compels political parties to embrace different economic ideologies and pursue different economic priorities. Class-based models argue that a party with a lower-class constituency is more likely to pursue a policy of full employment than one of price stability.

Pushed to the extreme, however, this theory faces some hard-to-explain facts. In the age of mass voting, parties of the right with an inherent minority constituency could never have survived without substantial appeal to the more numerous lower classes. By necessity, such an appeal would greatly water down the hypothesized differences between the parties; the more so, the more the traditional class foundation of partisan choice erodes. Especially in a two-party market, a party not keying on the median voter courts electoral extinction (Downs 1957). At best, partisan theory calls attention to some "empirically meaningful differences at the margin" (Hibbs 1992, 363).

Whether because of the lingering effect of social class or because of some noteworthy performance in the past, a given political party acquires a claim in the public's mind to a particular economic issue. For a long time, it was the Democratic party that was rated more favorably with respect to full employment, whereas the Republicans were preferred on price stability. In U.S. presidential elections, there is evidence of pro-Republican voting in response to the salience of inflation and pro-Democratic voting among voters for whom unemployment is more salient (Kiewiet 1983, 99). There are analogous findings for British voters regarding the Conservatives and the Labour party (Clarke et al. 1986; Mishler et al. 1989). And in Germany, as Rattinger (1986) has shown, unemployment does not hurt the Social Democrats electorally, and inflation hurts the Christian Democrats comparatively less in office than it benefits them in opposition. Given the class structure, unemployment was no particular cause of voting for Hitler in Weimar Germany, as Falter (1991) has demonstrated.

It is doubtful, however, that any party can forever cling to its issue priority, regardless of performance. The British Conservatives paid dearly for failing to curb inflation in the early 1970s. It was quite a gamble, in fact, for Mrs. Thatcher to stake her claim to office in 1979 on that issue, which then favored the Labour party in the public's view (Norpoth 1992, chap. 5). As far as inflation was concerned, Margaret Thatcher and her party had a lot to prove to a doubtful public. The fact that her government regained the public's confidence on inflation in the 1980s, after having lost it in the early 1970s, suggests that the British public may no longer assign unchanging priorities to the parties on economic issues. In a similar way, the Democratic party in the United States lost much of its economic reputation during the hapless stewardship of Jimmy Carter.

What is more, the logic of the issue-priority hypothesis tempts governing parties with perverse incentives (Kiewiet 1983, 12). A left government would be encouraged to let unemployment rise because concern over unemployment is supposed to raise the party's electoral stock. In like fashion, a right government should let inflation rise because concern with inflation is supposed to help its vote share. Few party strategists would be cynical enough to recommend such a scenario. Common sense tells us that this would be a foolish choice. The party following that recipe would quickly lose its priority issue. Nonetheless, it might take some time for public perceptions to adjust to that experience.

Personal and National Concerns

Ronald Reagan in 1980 was by no means the first candidate for office to pitch his campaign to voters' pocketbooks. Charles de Gaulle justified the two-round method of voting France adopted for its Fifth Republic in 1958 by saying that it allowed people to vote with their hearts first and then with their pocketbooks. Indeed, for many politicians as well as everyday observers of politics, economic voting means pocketbook voting. For the mass electorate, the economy is not like an issue of foreign policy. It is a doorstep issue. So does the economy claim its electoral due through each voter's pocketbook? If ever scholarly evidence has collided with common sense, this is a case in point. In studies of American voters, the pocketbook hypothesis has not fared very well (Kinder and Kiewiet 1979; Kiewiet 1983). Voters' perceptions of their own financial situations make only small and often insignificant contributions to partisan choices. The explanation offered for why personal economic interest fails to move U.S. voters at the polls is the pervasive "ethic of self-reliance" (Feldman and Conley 1991; Sniderman and Brody 1977). Americans see themselves, not government, as responsible for their own financial fortunes, in good times as in bad ones.

Such a culture-specific explanation invites a probe of pocketbook voting in societies not founded on rugged individualism. Lewis-Beck (1988) did just that with a comparative study of five European countries (Britain, France, Germany, Italy, and Spain). His verdict was unequivocal: "For legislative elections in these Western European countries, simple pocketbook evaluations have a negligible effect on individual vote choice" (Lewis-Beck 1988, 57). Hence, there is no need to resort to culture-specific explanations. One must wonder anyway about the strength of the ethic of self-reliance at a time when Americans gladly accept and even demand an ever-expanding panoply of benefits and entitlements from government, condemnations of welfare not-withstanding. How can rugged individuals take advantage of unemployment compensation, social security, Medicare, college loans, and so on? Not recognizing the government's hand in such programs is less a tribute to an ethic of self-reliance than to the human capacity for denial.

Indeed, evidence for pocketbook behavior is not entirely absent. Sanders (1993) maintains that given the British government's control over interest rates and the close linkage between those rates and home mortgages, the partisan choices of British voters are extremely sensitive to their personal financial situations. "The critical factor underpinning the Conservatives' victory [in the 1992 election] was the fact that enough people . . . were moved to vote according to their pocketbooks" (Sanders 1993, 212). In a sense, by raising or lowering interest rates, the British government raises and lowers a highly visible tax. Perhaps it should be expected that in such a clear case voters respond in kind. This would be consistent with the finding that U.S. voters who connect their own well-being with government policy also vote their pocketbooks (Feldman 1982).

For the most part, however, students of economic voting have placed more emphasis on perceptions of the national economy. This "sociotropic" hypothesis maintains that voters do not so much ask themselves, "What have you done for me lately," but, "What have you done for the nation's economy lately?" Even Ronald Reagan in his closing remarks during the 1980 debate appended his appeal to the pocketbook with the query, "Is there more or less unemployment in the country than there was four years ago?" The sociotropic hypothesis assumes that the linchpin of economic voting is the responsibility assigned to government for the shape of the macroeconomy (Feldman and Conley 1991). To put it simply, government is supposed to avoid depressions and secure full employment and stable prices, but not to make me or you richer or poorer. When both measures are included in a vote equation, the sociotropic side usually beats the pocketbook (Kiewiet 1983, 99; Lewis-Beck 1988, 62-5).

That evidence raises some puzzling questions nonetheless. There can be little doubt that sociotropic behavior makes more onerous demands of ordinary voters than does the pocketbook notion. Above all, why should anyone care more about everyone else's economic lot than about his or her own? Even the Bible does not ask us to love our neighbor *more* than ourselves. Turning to more mundane matters, it is no question that information about the macroeconomy is harder to come by than information, if that is even the right term, about one's pocketbook. And much of the economic news that is available may be hard to sort out. There is considerable room for error and bias in making sense of the economic world.

In a spirited challenge against the denial of pocketbook voting, Kramer (1983, 93) claims that "the evidence for sociotropic voting is artifactual." Given that much of what citizens perceive as their personal economic situation is not government induced, survey analysis relying on such perceptions is "hopelessly contaminated." Instead, he advises us to employ aggregate-level time-series evidence to flesh out the true relationship between the economy and electoral choice. He is correct to remind students of economic voting that "we are ultimately interested in how *real* economic outcomes affect *actual* voting decisions and not in economic rhetoric or perceptual imagery as such" (1983, 95).

Although that may be true, aggregate-level data on the real economy and elections do not speak for themselves. In the end, it is millions of individuals who make decisions based on how they perceive and evaluate, among other things, economic information. Data on individual perceptions may be flawed, contaminated, and biased, but to exclude them altogether from the analysis is to throw out the baby with the bathwater. To overcome the constraints of the aggregate level and avoid the pitfalls of the individual level, Markus (1988) employed an analytic strategy that combined data at both levels. His findings demonstrate pocketbook voting, but also note that personal economic circumstances vary too little across time at the aggregate level to account for electoral outcomes. Tantalizing though it may be, the case for pocketbook voting has proved maddeningly elusive.[8]

Past and Future

Most recently, the focus of economic-voting studies has shifted to the problem of expectations. Political science is feeling the reverberation of the "rational expectations" revolution that shook economics (Lucas and Sargent 1981). Just as in economics, so do advocates of the importance of expectations in political science wage a vigorous war against the established wisdom of the "retrospective" model (e.g., Kramer 1971). This is a matter of importance not only for the study of electoral behavior but for policy making as well. An electorate with an informed view of the future economy would be hard to fool by a government bent on manipulating the economy for short-term electoral gain by means of fiscal and monetary policy, as implied by proponents of the political-business cycle (Nordhaus 1975). On the other hand, if voters primarily rely on retrospective evaluations, governments retain enough latitude to bring about favorable conditions in the short run at the risk of a downturn later on.

In theory, the decision to vote for a particular party (or candidate) is a choice about the future: Whom (which party) does the voter want to govern the country in the years ahead? A rational voter ought to make a vote decision based on a comparison of future benefits. With respect to the economy, then, voters should ask themselves which party is most likely to deliver good times after the election, not what the parties have done lately.

Evidence for prospective voting has rapidly accumulated in recent years (Fiorina 1981; Kuklinski and West 1981; Lewis-Beck 1988; Sanders 1991). Chappell and Keech (1985, 1991) introduced a sophisticated-voter model that takes into account the future consequences of present economic policies. Others have gone as far as to depict voters as "bankers" rather than "peasants." When it comes to evaluating a president's performance in office, Americans are said to rely on "an informed view of the nation's economic prospects," not on a narrow view of their pocketbooks (MacKuen, Erikson, and Stimson 1992, 606).

The banker metaphor is meant to portray voters as highly sophisticated, knowledgeable, and farsighted rather than as naive, ignorant, and myopic. However flattering, this is a tall claim to live up to. How can voters predict with any confidence what the future will hold for the economy under one party or the other? Even a rational-choice proponent like Downs (1957) is not very sanguine about the capacity of ordinary citizens to appraise the future. Hence, he is willing to take a party's current performance as the best bet regarding its future performance. At that point, then, the introduction of expectations purchases little new insight into economic voting.

Others have shown that the economic forecasts of individual citizens are heavily swayed by various extraneous concerns, biases, and rationalizations (Conover et al. 1987). Far from sizing up the future with cool heads, people indulge their wishes and hopes as well as fears. Consumer expectations have a strong affective component, as argued by "psychological economics" (Katona 1975). Compared with assessments of current economic conditions, forecasts of the future exhibit a distinctive optimism bias, not just in the United States but also in Britain (Alt 1991, 247). As shown for the U.S. electorate, bad times quickly trigger a reaction that finds the public voicing a bright prognosis (Haller and Norpoth 1994, 646). At the same time, the public is in no hurry to abandon rosy forecasts when times are good. Examining the British case, Nadeau and Niemi (1995) show that the chain running from expert forecasts through media news to economic expectations in the mass public suffers from major distortions. As a result, it is "dubious, in the end, whether the impact of mass expectations on vote choices is in fact significantly driven by the diffusion of expert reports through the mass media" (Nadeau, Niemi, and Amato, 1996, 22).

The hypothesis that economic expectations guide voters' political judgments would seem especially dubious in the case of approval ratings of an incumbent president (or party). The approval question refers to current, not future, performance. It seems only fair and proper to grade an incumbent officeholder in light of recent economic conditions, not future ones. More important, economic expectations prove to be very sensitive to some of the same political events as does presidential approval (Jackman 1993; Suzuki 1992). When political interventions such as partisan change in the White House, wars, and scandals are specified in a time-series model of presidential approval (1960-1993), the effect of economic expectations vanishes (Norpoth forthcoming). At the same time, the effect of retrospective economic evaluations is substantial (Clarke and Stewart 1994; see also Beck 1991). It appears that the U.S. public evaluates the president far more in light of current economic circumstances than by way of an informed view of the future economy. Likewise, the popularity of political parties in a country like Germany does not meet the condition of rational expectations (Kirchgässner 1991).

But expressing approval is not the same as casting a vote on election day. One might expect that when citizens are asked to choose their future rulers they ponder the future state of the economy instead of current conditions. Hence, this might be another instance where the vote function differs from the popularity function; recall the divergence on the matter of a negativity effect, which appeared far more substantial in government popularity than in vote choices. On election day, the look ahead would seem most appropriate in sizing up the party(ies) out of power. What are they planning to accomplish? The question is especially pressing when voters are dissatisfied with the economy. Then voters should ask themselves not simply, "Am I better off now than I was four years ago?" but also, "Is the challenger going to make me better off?" Avoiding that question is not a safe way to cast one's vote. Voting for Hitler in 1930-1933, Germans learned that lesson the hard way.

Conclusion

Without a doubt, the economy is an important issue in many elections. That is palpably so when a country suffers an economic depression or runaway inflation. For the most part, the standard model has proved its worth: Voters key on retrospective assessments of the overall economy, hold the incumbent government responsible, and administer vengeance *and* reward at the polls. The evidence is weaker for claims that people vote their pocketbooks, take economic expectations into account, and punish bad deeds while letting good deeds go unrewarded. Yet, in an odd way, it is the exceptions to those rules that make economic voting intriguing.

Now and then, issues of economic policy have intruded on voters in critical ways, although for that to happen something had to go awry with the economy. Just as the Great Depression made voters call for government help, the stagflation of the 1960s and 1970s made them prepared to consider market remedies again. How else to fathom the electoral successes of conservative parties in the 1980s—often amid difficult economic times—and the trimming of the left parties' ideological sails?

How universal is economic voting? There are signs that the inclination to vote that way is hard-wired into the brain of citizens in democracies. But noneconomic circumstances, most notably the party system and the setup of political institutions, may frustrate voters in their attempts to vote the economy. Complex coalition alignments in government and divided oppositions would seem to discourage the expression of economic sentiments at the polls. Yet for all those obstacles, electorates in countries around the world, as shown by evidence above, find ways of administering vengeance and reward at the polls for the performance of the economy. Voters apparently accomplish that task by keying on the major party in office.

Finally, although important, how important is the economy for voters' decisions? Is it the singular factor that decides victory or defeat in elections? In some aggregate studies of voting or government support, the economy plays that role by default, simply because little else is specified besides economic variables. On the other hand, in studies of individual choice, the economic issue often drowns in a sea of voter responses to other topics and concerns. To be sure, the fit of the vote function is far from perfect. The economy does not claim the lion's share of the vote variance, but probably no other short-term factor does, either. To paraphrase Churchill's saying about democracy, the economy may be the worst explanation of voting, but it is still better than any other one, long-term predispositions aside.

Notes

1. The literature on this subject is so vast that one needs a review by now to keep up with reviews of the literature. For an up-to-date discussion of comparative research on the electoral influence of the economy, see Anderson (1995, chap. 3); Lewis-Beck (1988, chaps. 2, 3, and his painstaking inventory of findings in chap. 10); and Schneider and Frey (1988). For recent comparative research on economic voting, see Clarke et al. (1992) and the contributions to Eulau and Lewis-Beck (1985); Hibbs and Fassbender (1981); Monroe (1983); Norpoth, Lewis-Beck, and Lafay (1991); and Whiteley (1980). The economy is by far the most favored variable in election forecasting. See the readable discussion of forecasting models in Lewis-Beck and Rice (1992).

2. A technical reason for the weak findings very likely is the use of first differences. Paldam relates the change in the vote since the previous election, not the absolute vote in the given election, to changes in economic conditions. Such differencing is bound to attenuate the vote function. For a similar problem in studies of government support, see Norpoth and Yantek (1983).

3. The list of countries, with the year of the election in parentheses, is as follows: Argentina (1989), Australia (1993), Austria (1990), Belgium (1991), Canada (1993), Chile (1993), Colombia (1990), Costa Rica (1994), Cyprus (1988), Denmark (1994), Ecuador (1992), Finland (1991), France (1993), Germany (1994), Greece (1989), Honduras (1993), Iceland (1991), Ireland (1992), Italy (1992), Japan (1993), Korea (South; 1992), Luxembourg (1989), Malta (1992), Mexico (1988), the Netherlands (1994), New Zealand (1993), Norway (1993), the Philippines (1992), Portugal (1991), Spain (1993), Sweden (1994), Switzerland (1991), Turkey (1991), United Kingdom (1992), United States (1992), Uruguay (1989), Venezuela (1993), and Zambia (1991). For each country, we used only one election, namely, the most recent one for which economic data were also available. Countries that just started conducting competitive elections were excluded. The source of the electoral data is Keesing's Archive; the source of the GDP data is the World Bank. I am grateful to Sam Wilkin and Troy Flowers for assisting me with collecting and analyzing the data.

4. There is no significant correlation between this economic indicator and the combined vote of all incumbent parties in this 38-country data set. That finding is consistent with what other cross-national studies have found.

5. Several rather extreme cases among the 38 countries dilute a more substantial relationship. Limiting the analysis to cases within the range of plus/minus 2 standard deviations for both vote and GDP produces a correlation of .44.

6. What would also improve the fit of the vote function is a specification of the "normal vote" for the major governing party. No doubt that vote level varies from country to country. For a way of estimating the normal vote with aggregate data, see Tufte's (1978, chap. 5) moving-average method based on past election results.

7. Ironically, Key coined this phrase to describe a type of election, namely, U.S. midterm elections, lacking this particular characteristic.

8. It is symptomatic that a highly innovative paper by Rivers (1986) that aims to demonstrate a strong pocketbook effect remains unpublished.

(13)

Political Cleavages, Issues, and Electoral Change

RUSSELL J. DALTON

Electoral politics is the essence of democratic politics. Elections crystallize the political interests in a society and provide a mechanism for the public to decide between political options. Although elections are one of the essential and relatively constant features of democracies, the most striking conclusion that emerges from current electoral research is that the underlying bases of electoral choice have changed dramatically in the past generation.

This chapter provides an overview of the broad social and political changes that have transformed democratic electorates, and with them the nature of the electoral process in advanced industrial societies. One change involves the social and political cleavages that frame party competition in these systems. Political cleavages such as class and religion historically structured the content of political and electoral discourse in Western democracies, and thereby partisan alignments and voting choices (Lipset and Rokkan 1967; Lijphart 1981). Over the past generation, these traditional social cleavages have been transformed and weakened as predictors of electoral choice. We

319

consider how socioeconomic cleavages responded to the changing social context of advanced industrial democracies and how this has affected the nature of electoral politics. In addition, the development of new party systems in Eastern Europe poses an interesting comparison to the initial development of Western party systems. We will return to this point in the conclusion.

A second transformative force involves the changing bases of ideological conflict in many Western democracies. The publics in these societies have expanded their interests to include noneconomic, quality-of-life issues that represent a new postmaterial agenda. The growth of environmentalism, the emergence of a women's movement, and demands for increased involvement in the decisions affecting one's life have broadened the boundaries of contemporary politics (Inglehart 1977, 1990a). These new controversies have entered the political agenda and created new bases of partisan conflict. In addition, attention to these new issues has been paralleled by a general growth in issue-based voting, even for "old" issues, such as the size of the welfare state and the overall scope of government. The evolution of these new patterns of political competition is a distinguishing feature of contemporary electoral politics.

This chapter considers the implications of these changes for the nature of electoral behavior in the future. Today, a far smaller share of the electorate approaches each election with standing predispositions based on the broad social divisions that once structured electoral competition. Instead, citizens in advanced industrial democracies are using a new calculus to make their electoral decisions. We discuss the role of ideology and issue positions in this calculus and consider how the weight of different issues illustrates the changing nature of electoral competition in contemporary democracies.

The Declining Role of Social Cleavages

Modern electoral research began by observing that party competition and voting decisions were structured around the social divisions existing within a polity. In their seminal study, Seymour Martin Lipset and Stein Rokkan (1967) explained how ideological and partisan divisions sprang from the social cleavages existing in a nation. Differences between competing social groups provided the potential basis for political conflict, furnishing both a possible base of voting support and a set of political interests that parties vied to represent. Given their nature, such cleavages could be expected to persist over long periods of time. In one of the most often-cited conclusions of comparative politics, Lipset and Rokkan (1967, 50) stated "the party systems of the 1960s reflect, with but few significant exceptions, the cleavage structures of the 1920s." In other words, Lipset and Rokkan claimed that Western party systems were "frozen" around the cleavages existing during their formative periods.

Social cleavages were so powerful for several reasons. At the core, social cleavages represented the deep ideological divisions that existed within Western democratic societies. The class conflict reflected different ideologies on the nature of politics and economics, and the ideal relationship between these two social systems. Economic conservatives on the right stressed individual initiative, accepted social and economic inequality, and favored a limited role for government. Socialists and social democrats on the left advocated a more egalitarian society and attributed a larger role to government in finding political solutions for the inequalities produced by the social and economic systems. Similarly, the conflicts between Protestants and Catholics, or between the secular and religious, represented differences in basic value systems. For much of the past century, these social conflicts defined the primary ideological bases of politics in Western democracies and thus provided the framework for party competition.

In addition to these ideological elements, there were institutional reasons why social groups created a structure of party competition (Zuckerman 1982). Social groups enabled political parties to formalize a basis of support. Social groups could provide a political and an organizational basis for a party, furnishing members, funds, and the necessary votes at election times. Social democratic parties turned to labor for party workers and electoral support; Christian Democrats recruited their supporters at Sunday mass. For the groups themselves, close ties with a party guaranteed some representation within the legislative process and, it was hoped, the government. Moreover, this alliance pattern then provided an important reference structure in orienting citizens and political elites to the world of politics. Once this institutional framework was established, it produced a system of self-reinforcing political alliances.

Early survey research substantiated Lipset and Rokkan's claims on the importance of cleavage-based voting. Survey research found that social cleavages exerted a potent effect on voting, especially class and religious differences. Richard Rose and Derek Urwin's (1969, 1970) research on postwar party systems found striking stability in electoral results (see also Bartolini and Mair 1990).

Yet, as this theme of partisan stability became the conventional wisdom, dramatic changes began to affect these same party systems. The established parties were presented with new demands and new challenges, and the evidence of real partisan change became obvious. Within a decade, the dominant question changed from explaining the persistence of established patterns of electoral politics to explaining electoral change (Dalton et al. 1984; Crewe and Denver 1985).

The Class Cleavage

Social scientists have probably devoted more attention to the class cleavage than to any other social characteristic as a predictor of mass voting behavior. At a theoretical level, the class cleavage involves some of the most basic questions of power and politics that evolve from Marxian and capitalist views of political development. Empirically, the class cleavage represents the economic and material problems of industrial societies: providing for the economic security of all citizens and ensuring a just distribution of economic rewards. Issues such as unemployment, inflation, social services, tax policies, and government management of the economy reinforce class divisions. Consequently, Lipset (1981, 230, italics added) described the class cleavage as one of the most pervasive bases of party support:

> Even though many parties renounce the principle of class conflict or loyalty, an analysis of their appeals and their support suggests that they do represent the interests of different classes. On a world scale, the *principal generalization* which can be made is that parties are primarily based on either the lower classes or the middle and upper classes.

Similarly, Arend Lijphart's (1981) overview of modern party systems identified the class cleavage as a major dimension of ideological cleavage in virtually all democracies. Early empirical studies supported these conclusions (Rose 1974a).

As strong and persistent as class voting patterns were, they were not immutable. As the empirical evidence from the first wave of comparative electoral studies was being completed, this frozen cleavage began to defrost. Figure 13.1 displays the longitudinal trend in class voting for an illustrative set of advanced industrial democracies.[1] The general trend in the figure is obvious; class differences are declining. For example, the size of the class

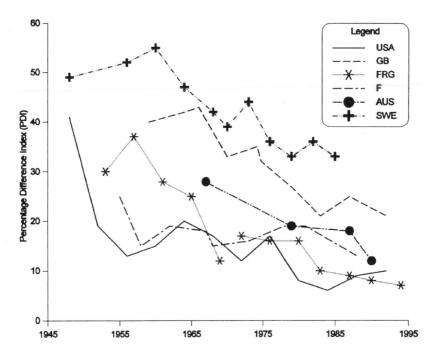

Figure 13.1. Trends in Class Voting

SOURCE: Australia (McAllister 1992, 134); Sweden (Inglehart 1990a, 260); other nations (Dalton 1996, chap. 8). Table entries are the Alford Class Voting index, that is, the percentage of the working class preferring a leftist party minus the percentage of the middle class voting for the left. American data are based on congressional elections, except for 1948, which is presidential vote.

voting index in Sweden, Britain, and Australia has decreased by almost half across post-World War II elections, and in Germany by more than two-thirds. Class voting patterns follow a less regular decline in American congressional elections; the erosion of class voting is more pronounced in presidential elections (Abramson et al. 1994, chap. 5; Stanley and Niemi 1995b).

Evidence from many other nations points to the same downward trajectory for the class cleavage. A decline in class voting is evident for Japan (Watanuki 1991), Scandinavia (Borre 1984), and a host of other nations (Inglehart 1990a; Lane and Errson 1991). Paul Nieuwbeerta (1995) recently completed a detailed study of class voting in 20 advanced industrial democracies. He finds a general erosion in class voting differences for these polities.

This evidence of a decline of the class cleavage has generated a series of new research controversies in the literature. Some scholars argue that the nature of class alignments in advanced industrial societies is changing and that in its new forms the effect of social class is as pervasive as in the past. John Goldthorpe (1980), for example, proposed a new categorization of social class, incorporating notions of job autonomy and authority relationships into traditional class criteria such as income level and manual labor. Some scholars have created an expanded list of class categories to incorporate new social contexts, such as the middle-class *salatariat* or affluent blue-collar worker (Robertson 1984; Heath, Jowell, and Curtice 1985, 1991; Pappi 1990). Other researchers have explored criteria other than employment as potential bases of socioeconomic cleavage, such as an education cleavage separating the information rich from the information poor, or conflicts between the public and private sectors (Dunleavy and Husbands 1985). Some of the most innovative recent research tries to define social position by lifestyle characteristics, distinguishing between industrial employees and Yuppies, for example (Gluchowski 1987; Hammond 1986; Delli Carpini and Sigelman 1986).

The reconceptualization of social class implies that social cues now function in more complex and differentiated ways than in the past. Yet the empirical reality remains: Even these complex class frameworks have only a modest value in explaining how citizens vote. Richard Rose and Ian McAllister (1986, 50-1) compared several of these alternative models to British voting behavior in the 1983 election and find that each explained only a very modest share of the vote. The comparative analyses of Mark Franklin and his colleagues (1992) also document a general erosion in the influence of social status measures on party choice.

The diminished electoral role of class position is reaffirmed by the data in Table 13.1, which document the current extent of class polarization in 18 advanced industrial democracies, using an expanded measure of social class.[2] The strongest correlations are for Scandinavian party systems (Norway, Denmark, Iceland, and Sweden), and the weakest correlations are for the United States, Canada, and Japan.[3] As Figure 13.1 suggests, these same national rankings may have applied a generation ago—but in all these nations class voting has weakened over time. Present levels of class voting in Sweden, for instance, are a shadow of prior class polarization. In cross-national terms, the overall effect of social class is now quite modest (average Cramér's $V = .15$). Class-based voting, as conceived of from Marx to Lipset and Rokkan, currently has limited influence in structuring voting choices.

TABLE 13.1   Cross-National Levels of Cleavage Voting, 1990-1991

Country	Social Class	Religious Denomination	Church Attendance	Rural/ Urban	Region
Austria	.20	.15	.26	.16	.17
Belgium	.16	.18	.30	.25	.33
Britain	.18	.11	.12	.12	.21
Canada	.10	.14	.12	.09	.18
Denmark	.21	.13	.29	.15	—
Finland	.16	.23	.27	—	—
France	.15	.14	.22	.13	.12
Germany (West)	.13	.14	.22	.08	.09
Iceland	.19	.11	.17	—	—
Ireland	.14	.14	.16	.14	—
Italy	.15	.21	.27	.12	.16
Japan	.11	.14	.15	.07	.10
Netherlands	.18	.29	.37	.16	.14
Norway	.22	.14	.27	.15	—
Portugal	.11	.22	.22	.10	.17
Spain	.15	.14	.25	.13	—
Sweden	.16	.15	.20	.12	—
United States	.10	.09	.08	.10	.10
Average	.15	.15	.22	.13	.16

SOURCE: 1990-1991 World Values Survey. Entries are Cramér's *V* correlating social characteristics with the party preference of the respondent. Respondents without a party preference are not included in the analyses.

The Religious Cleavage

The other major basis for social division in Western party systems has been the religious cleavage in its various forms. As was true with the class cleavage, conflicts over religion defined the structure of elite conflict and the political alliances that existed in the late 19th century. The political parties formed with the extension of mass suffrage often allied themselves with specific religious interests—Catholic or Protestant, religious or secular (Lipset and Rokkan 1967). Indeed, parties often proclaimed their religious identity by calling themselves Christian or Christian Democratic parties.

Early empirical research on mass voting behavior underscored the continuing importance of the religious cleavage. Richard Rose and Derek Urwin

(1969, 12) examined the social bases of party support in 16 Western democracies. Their often-cited conclusion maintains "religious divisions, not class, are the main social bases of parties in the Western world today." Additional evidence comes from Arend Lijphart's (1979) comparison of the religious, class, and linguistic cleavages in four democracies where all three cleavages existed. He found that religion was the strongest influence on voting choice. Numerous other cross-national and longitudinal studies have documented the persisting importance of the religious cleavage.

Despite this evidence of a strong relationship between religious values and partisan preferences, the religious cleavage has followed the same pattern of decline as for the class cleavage. Social modernization disrupted religious alignments in the same way that social-class lines have blurred. Changing lifestyles and religious beliefs decreased involvement in church activities and diminished the church as a focus of social activities. Most Western democracies have experienced a steady decline in religious involvement over the past 50 years (Ashford and Timms 1992; Franklin et al. 1992, chap. 1). In the Catholic nations of Europe, for instance, frequent church attendance has decreased by nearly half since the 1950s. Predominantly Protestant countries, such as the United States and the nations of northern Europe, began with lower levels of church involvement, but have followed the same downward trend. By definition, this secularization trend means that fewer voters are integrated into religious networks and exposed to the religious cues that can guide the vote.

Also paralleling the class cleavage, conflict between secular and religious forces apparently has moderated since World War II. Socialists in many European nations reached a rapprochement with religious groups, especially with the Catholic church in countries with a large Catholic population. The churches also sought to normalize political relations if church interests could be guaranteed as part of the process.

Measuring the present effect of religious cues on voting behavior is more complicated than the analyses of the class cleavage. The class composition of most advanced industrial democracies is similar, but their religious composition is quite varied. Some nations, like Britain or the Scandinavian nations, are predominantly Protestant; the nations of Mediterranean Europe are predominantly Catholic; other nations, such as Germany, Holland, and the United States, are characterized by religiously divided publics; and the Japanese case is the most distinct because of its non-Western religious traditions. In addition to the diverse religious composition of these nations, the partisan tendencies of religious denominations also vary cross-nationally (Lipset and Rokkan 1967). In some nations, Catholics have allied with conservative parties; in other nations they are part of a left alliance. This means that the voting cues provided by religious affiliation may differ across national boundaries, in contrast to the consistent working-class/middle-class pattern of the class cleavage.

The special nature of religious cleavages means that it is more difficult to document the cross-temporal and cross-national trends in ways that are comparable to class voting statistics. Table 13.1 describes the current effect of religious denomination and church attendance on partisan preferences.[4] Where religious voting patterns are uniformly weak, as in the United States, Canada, Japan, and Britain, this reflects an ongoing characteristic of the party system rather than the recent erosion in religious voting (Dalton et al. 1984; Franklin et al. 1992). Significant voting differences between religious denominations have persisted in the Netherlands even as this society has secularized. However, the overall cross-national level of denominational-based voting is fairly modest (average Cramér's $V = .155$).

Table 13.1 shows that the secular/religious divide (average Cramér's $V = .22$) has a greater influence on party preferences than does religious denomination. In Catholic and Protestant nations, this taps the degree of involvement in a religious network and adherence to religious values. The available longitudinal data suggest that secular and religious differences in voting preferences have not followed the same dramatic downward trend as the class cleavage. Despite the paucity of explicitly religious issues and the lack of religious themes in most campaigns, religious attachments often are a strong predictor of party choice.

Christian fundamentalism appears to be a growing cleavage in elections in the United States. Employing television and other means of mass communication, evangelical leaders have mobilized people on the basis of policy issues dealing with matters of morality and traditional family values (e.g., abortion, school prayer, and pornography). Miller and Wattenberg (1984) isolate a fundamentalist subset of the electorate who form a group of such size and voting cohesion that they constitute a significant part of the Republican coalition, as witnessed by their prominence during the 1992 Republican national convention. Still, longitudinal electoral studies fail to find a significant growth in the relationship between religion and vote choice; the effect of the fundamentalist revival is dwarfed by the ebb and flow of other electoral forces (Wald 1987; Abramson et al. 1994, chap. 5).

Although the partisan division between religiously-defined voter groups has persisted, the actual importance of religion as a basis of voting behavior has declined in another sense. Comparisons of voting patterns between religious denominations ignore the compositional change in contemporary electorates because of secularization trends. Voting differences between religious and secular voters have remained fairly constant for the past generation, but secularization is steadily increasing the absolute number of nonreligious citizens. Individuals who attend church regularly (like individuals who are embedded in traditional social class networks) are still well integrated into a religious network and maintain distinct voting patterns, but there are fewer of these individuals today. By definition, the growing number of secular voters are not basing their party preferences on religious cues. Thus, the changing composition of the electorate is lessening the partisan significance of religious cues by decreasing the number of individuals for whom these cues are relevant.

Other Social Divisions

The decline of social-based voting is most apparent for the class and religious cleavages, but a similar erosion of influence has occurred for most other sociological characteristics. In most advanced industrial democracies, urban/rural residence displays only modest differences in voting patterns. The average correlation between the size of place and partisan preference is only .13 (Table 13.1). Furthermore, other studies show that these differences have narrowed as the forces of modernization decreased the gap between urban and rural lifestyles.

Regional differences have occasionally flared up as a basis of political division. Britain, Belgium, Canada, and now the unified Germany have seen regional interests polarize over the past generation. In other societies, such as Spain and Italy, sharp regional differences from the past have persisted to the present. In most nations, however, region exerts only a minor influence on voting preferences (Rose 1982; Clarke et al. 1979). Table 13.1 reaffirms this point; the average correlation between region and party preferences is .16.

One possible exception to the rule of declining social cleavages involves race and ethnicity, such as the link between blacks and the Democratic party in the United States (Tate 1993; Carmines and Stimson 1989) or the voting patterns of minority immigrant populations in Europe. Ethnicity has the potential to be a highly polarized cleavage, because it may involve sharp social differences and strong feelings of in-group identity. Yet, to the extent that most societies remain ethnically homogeneous or nearly so, the effect of ethnicity as an overall predictor of vote choice is limited.[5]

When all the evidence is assembled, one of the most widely repeated findings of modern electoral research is the declining value of the sociological model of voting behavior. Mark Franklin and his colleagues (1992) have compiled the most comprehensive evidence supporting this conclusion. They tracked the ability of a set of social characteristics (including social class, education, income, religiosity, region, and gender) to explain partisan preferences. Across 14 Western democracies, they find a marked and fairly consistent erosion in the voting effect of social structure. The rate and timing of this decline varies across nations, but the end-product is the same. In party systems like the United States and Canada, where social-group-based voting was initially weak, the decline has occurred slowly. In other electoral systems, such as Germany, the Netherlands, and several Scandinavian nations, where sharp social divisions once structured the vote, the decline has been steady and dramatic. They conclude with the new "conventional wisdom" of comparative electoral research: "One thing that has by now become quite apparent is that almost all of the countries we have studied show a decline . . . in the ability of social cleavages to structure individual voting choice" (Franklin et al. 1992, 385).

Explaining the Decline in
Cleavage-Based Voting

Although the evidence of the decline in cleavage-based voting is generally accepted, scholars disagree on how to interpret this finding. Perhaps the most far-reaching explanation has been offered by Mark Franklin and his colleagues (1992, chap. 15). They argue that the goal of democratic politics is to resolve political divisions that exist within societies. To the extent that social cleavages reflect broad-based and long-standing social and economic divisions within advanced industrial democracies, then the declining electoral relevance of these cleavages signals success in resolving these political divisions. A consensus on the welfare state, for instance, presumably

resolved old political conflicts between socioeconomic groups, as an equali-
zation of living conditions may have eroded urban/rural differences, and so
forth.[6]

This interpretation is linked to the "end of ideology" literature, which
argued that advanced industrial democracies have moved away from ideological politics in the post-World War II era (Kirchheimer 1966; Beer 1978).
Analysts argued that parties wanted to broaden their electoral appeals, which
led the parties to adopt moderate programs that would attract centrist voters.
Socialist parties shed their Marxist programs and adopted more moderate
domestic and foreign policy goals. Conservative parties tempered their views
and accepted the basic social programs proposed by the left. Socialist parties
vied for the votes of the new middle class, and conservative parties sought
votes from the working class. Historical analyses of party programs show a
general convergence of party positions on socioeconomic issues during the
past half century (Thomas 1980; Robertson 1976; Budge, Robertson, and
Hearl 1987). With smaller class-related differences in the parties platforms, it
seemed only natural that class and religious cues would become less important
in guiding voting behavior.

Although this is an appealing explanation, especially as Western democracies bask in their new-found self-esteem with the collapse of the Soviet
empire, it suffers from the same problem as the earlier end-of-ideology thesis.
Although Western democracies have made real progress in meeting their
long-term social goals, social and political divisions have *not* ended. Recur-
ring global recessions periodically renewed the focus on economic problems
in most Western industrial countries, and problems of persisting poverty, the
homeless, and mounting crime rates are still with us. Similarly, current
political debates over abortion, homosexual rights, and other moral issues
reflect the value differences underlying the religious cleavage.

Furthermore, partisan contrasts on these political controversies have not
necessarily ended. A recent survey of political experts documents a clear
awareness of the continuing party differences on the socioeconomic issues
that underlie the class and religious cleavages (Laver and Hunt 1992). Evidence from Germany indicates that the partisan clarity of class cues actually
has increased over the same period that class voting has diminished (Dalton
1992). Recent surveys of the German and American publics show that the
public still clearly perceives the partisan leanings of unions, business associations, and religious groups (Dalton 1996, chap. 7). In short, it does not appear

that citizens are unclear about the class positions of the parties—rather, these cues are less relevant to today's voters.

I favor an explanation that links the decline in the sociological model to the declining relevance of institutional structures and fixed social characteristics for contemporary electoral politics. Social cues may still be a potent influence on voting behavior for people who are integrated into traditional class or religious networks and who share the values of these milieu, but today there are far fewer people who fit within such clearly defined social categories. This partially reflects a fragmentation of life spaces. Fewer people are integrated into stable and bounded social structures, such as the working-class milieu and religious networks that originally furnished the basis of the class and religious cleavages (also see Putnam 1995). Lifestyles have become more individualized and diverse.

This change in lifestyles has also led to greater diversity within the established political parties. For instance, Robert Huckfeldt and Carole Kohfeld (1989) described how the constituency of the U.S. Democratic party is now split along class, racial, and value lines. It is a monumental task to unite such diverse constituencies at election time, and even more difficult to sustain agreement during the governing process. A similar fragmentation of constituencies has affected both social democratic and conservative parties in Europe (Kitschelt 1993a).

Once these processes of social change began to blur the lines of political cleavage, on which many of the established parties were based, the parties were forced to respond to these developments. Adam Przeworski and John Sprague (1985) showed that the numerical demise of the working class forced social democratic parties to soften their class image and look to new sources of support in the middle class. Similarly, attempts to broaden the sources of political support are occurring among conservative parties as they observe their past social bases of support eroding. In other words, the parties are contributing to the demise of cleavage voting by their need to compensate for the changing social bases of advanced industrial societies.

In summary, it is not that cleavages have become entirely irrelevant. They still shape the partisan loyalties of many voters. Yet many other voters now find themselves without a clear location in the class, religious, or other social groupings. The fragmentation of party images further erodes the value of social cues in guiding behavior. Thus, social change is weakening the structure of political cleavages that once framed party competition and provided voters with a simple framework for making their electoral decisions.

Emergence of New Bases
of Political Cleavage

The weakening of party bonds based on traditional cleavages such as class and religion creates the potential for new political cleavages to develop. Indeed, as the old cleavages began to weaken, a new set of postmaterial controversies emerged onto the agenda of advanced industrial societies (Inglehart 1977, 1990a). Environmental protection, women's rights, and quality-of-life issues now attract the attention of a significant number of contemporary voters. These issues expanded the boundary of politics to include areas that were once the prerogative of markets or individual choice.

On the one hand, these new issues benefited from the weakening of traditional party bonds. With fewer citizens bound to the parties by social bonds or party attachments, voters could potentially be mobilized by new issues and innovative programs. A more fluid electorate created the potential for new issues of all forms to influence voting choice. On the other hand, postmaterial issues had characteristics that contributed to the decline of social-cleavage-based alignments (Knutsen 1987). The new issues tended to cut across established cleavage lines, thereby weakening traditional social bonds. For instance, some members of the middle class were drawn to the political program of environmentalists. In addition, the public demanded more opportunities to participate in the decisions affecting their lives and pressed for a further democratization of society and politics. These participatory trends worked to erode the parties' oligarchic control of political representation. Furthermore, New Politics issues attract the attention of the same social groups that are weakly integrated into traditional social cleavages: the young, the new middle class, the better educated, and the nonreligious.

At first, these new issues were simply added to the political agenda of advanced industrial societies, representing a set of discrete concerns. Gradually, however, the advocates of these issues began to articulate a more encompassing view of politics. Environmental issues were framed in terms of a conceptualization of a sustainable society; gender issues and minority programs were part of a larger image of human rights; empowerment became a symbol for expanding participation opportunities. Political alliances also developed between the social groups and citizen interest lobbies that developed to represent these issues.

As these issues have become interlinked, they have formed a new dimension of political cleavage that runs orthogonal to the traditional left/right framework underlying the class and religious cleavages (Inglehart 1984, 1990a; Weisberg and Rusk 1970).[7] The old left pitted support for social programs, working-class interests, and the influence of labor unions against an old right that was identified with limited governmental support for middle-class interests and the influence of the business sector. Now there was also a new left that supported a sustainable society and libertarian values, and a new right representing conservative social values and advocacy of more structured life choices (Betz 1994). These political orientations also have their partisan representatives. The new left is represented by Green and left-Libertarian parties, such as the German and French Greens, the Dutch PSP (part of the current Green alliance in Dutch politics), or the Danish SF. The representatives of the new right include the French National Front, the German Republikaner, and the Austrian Freedom party.

Survey research indicates that this new left/new right framework is reshaping the left/right identities of at least some voters. People can use left/right as a reference structure to evaluate political stimuli and guide their political behavior, even if they do not possess a sophisticated abstract framework or theoretical dogma. Furthermore, left/right orientations tap public perceptions of the major lines of political conflict in a society (Inglehart 1979; Fuchs and Klingemann 1989). When citizens reorient their left/right framework to reflect their new values and issue interests, a potential new base of political cleavage is established. A change in the content of left/right orientations therefore involves a more fundamental transformation of mass politics than a simple change in issue interests, because it affects how citizens evaluate politics and orient themselves to the political process.

To illustrate the changing political orientations of contemporary publics, Table 13.2 displays the correlations between left/right attitudes and three broad issue areas: the government's role in the economy (class issues), attitudes toward abortion (religious issues), and postmaterial values.[8] Despite some claims of the end of economic conflict, we find evidence that the traditional economic issues of the welfare state are still alive and present among Western publics. The average relationship between economic attitudes and left/right orientations is fairly strong (Pearson's r is .32, and in several Scandinavian nations the relationship exceeds .50). The development of advanced industrial societies has not, as of yet, brought an end to the issues formed in the industrial era. When political parties and social groups reinforce these divisions, they can still strongly structure the public's political orientations.

TABLE 13.2 Issue Correlates of Left/Right Attitudes, 1990-1991

Country	Economic Issues	Abortion Attitudes	Postmaterial Values
Austria	.06	.03	.03
Belgium	.23	.11	.18
Britain	.36	.02	.30
Canada	.19	.12	.21
Denmark	.50	.09	.39
Finland	.54	.05	.16
France	.41	.11	.27
Germany (West)	.35	.20	.38
Iceland	.52	.03	.19
Ireland	.15	.15	.16
Italy	.28	.17	.24
Japan	.19	.06	.23
Netherlands	.43	.22	.39
Norway	.44	.05	.25
Portugal	.13	.02	.18
Spain	.36	.37	.25
Sweden	.52	.04	.24
United States	.15	.18	.22
Average	.32	.11	.24

SOURCE: 1990-1991 World Values Survey. Entries are Pearson's r correlating issues with the party preference of the respondent. Respondents without a party preference are not included in the analyses.

We chose abortion as an example of a religious issue, and Table 13.2 indicates that this issue has relevance only in a subset of nations. In religiously divided nations (Germany, the Netherlands, and the United States) and in predominantly Catholic nations (Ireland, Italy, and Spain), this issue is still part of voters' core political identity. In most Protestant nations, however, abortion has been removed from the political agenda or no longer captures public interest. The average correlation with left/right attitudes is quite weak (.11).

The final column of Table 13.3 indicates that the postmaterial agenda has substantial importance in shaping political identities. Inglehart's postmaterial value measure is strongly related to left/right attitudes in most nations, and in at least five nations it exceeds the effect of economic issues. To the extent that environmental attitudes, the women's movement, and other postmaterial issues represent a new political agenda, this signifies a major change in the content of electoral politics compared to earlier periods.

In summary, the issues of political controversy are not fading away in advanced industrial democracies. We are not reaching an end of ideology. Instead, empirical research suggests just the opposite. Concerns with non-economic and quality-of-life issues have not replaced traditional economic issues, but rather have been added to the political framework of contemporary democracies.

A New Electoral Behavior

It is at this point in the research process that scholars often call on Gramsci's ghost: The old order is passing, but the form of the new order is not yet apparent. We should be able to say more. Our knowledge about the mechanisms of electoral choice and the dynamics of public opinion should provide a basis for describing the new electoral order.

One immediate implication is that the decline of long-term partisan predispositions based on social position should shift the basis of electoral behavior to short-term factors, such as candidate image and issue opinions. Another possibility is that performance-based voting increases, such as judging the government by the performance of the economy (see Norpoth, chap. 12 in this volume). There is evidence that the new electoral order includes a shift toward candidate-centered politics. Martin Wattenberg (1991) has documented the growing importance of candidate image in Americans' electoral choices, and comparable data are available for other Western democracies (Bean and Mughan 1989; Kaase 1994). This is an important development that has potentially far-reaching implications for the nature of contemporary electoral politics, but it lies outside of this chapter's coverage (see chap. 11 in this volume).

The decline in long-term forces shaping the vote also has increased the potential for issue voting. In fact, Franklin (1985) showed that the decreasing influence of long-term forces on British voting decisions was counterbalanced by an increased effect of issues on the vote (see also Baker et al. 1981, chap. 10; van der Eijk and Niemöller 1983). In reviewing the evidence from their comparative study of voting behavior, Mark Franklin (1992, 400) supports this point, concluding: "If all the issues of importance to voters had been measured and given their due weight, then the rise of issue voting would have compensated more or less precisely for the decline in cleavage politics."

There is, of course, a long and very distinguished literature that discusses the capability of modern electorates to fulfill the requirements of rational issue voting. We will not engage in this discussion because it is a point that has been addressed elsewhere (Dalton and Wattenberg 1993). Even if we place the question of the rationality of issue voting aside, it seems that issue voting per se should increase to fill in some of the decline in the ability of stable social characteristics to guide electoral choice.

However, one problem hampering the comparative study of issue voting, either across time or across nations, is the variability of issues across elections and across voters. One campaign might emphasize economic conflicts, and the next might stress questions of candidate competence. Furthermore, elections are seldom dominated by a single issue. Thus, the effect of any one issue often appears modest because not all the informed voters will be interested in all issues. Instead, the contemporary electorates are comprised of partially overlapping issue publics.

Although the issues of each specific election campaign are different, we use two methods to assess the general effect of policy preferences on voting behavior (Table 13.3). The first method examines the overall relationship between left/right attitudes and the vote. As we have just argued, such ideological positions summarize the voters' preferences on the various issues that concern them. In addition, we correlated each of the issue items from Table 13.2 with party preferences to assess the weight of each at one specific time point. Obviously, this is only a single snapshot of the ebb and flow of issues across specific elections. But snapshots can still illuminate the general cross-national pattern that might transcend specific elections.

The correlation between left/right attitudes and party preferences is much higher than for social characteristics (average Cramér's V is .27). The strength of these correlations is partially because left/right attitudes are more psychologically proximate to the voting choice (and thus is an intervening variable) and partially because the effect of social cleavages has weakened, which allows for attitudinal factors to increase in importance. Only in a few nations—notably in two cases where social cleavages are also weak (the United States and Canada)—does the correlation fall below .20.

There are two possible explanations of how issues have maintained (or even increased) their effect on vote choice in contemporary democracies. To an extent, we think both explanations are partially correct. First, even though

TABLE 13.3 Correlation Between Attitudes and Party Preference, 1990-1991

Country	Left/Right	Economic Issues	Abortion Attitudes	Postmaterial Values
Austria	.23	.10	.14	.21
Belgium	.21	.17	.17	.13
Britain	.24	.21	.07	.16
Canada	.15	.13	.09	.14
Denmark	.29	.29	.18	.21
Finland	.33	.25	.19	.25
France	.36	.24	.13	.16
Germany (West)	.24	.16	.12	.18
Iceland	.34	.24	.12	.20
Ireland	.24	.15	.14	.12
Italy	.30	.15	.20	.15
Japan	.24	.15	.10	.21
Netherlands	.31	.24	.20	.22
Norway	.26	.22	.19	.16
Portugal	.30	.15	.14	.13
Spain	.31	.19	.22	.18
Sweden	.29	.19	.22	.14
United States	.13	.15	.06	.11
Average	.27	.19	.14	.17

SOURCE: 1990-1991 World Values Survey. Entries are Cramér's *V* correlating left/right attitudes and the issues from Table 13.2 with the party preference of the respondent. Respondents without a party preference are not included in the analyses.

the social bases of political cleavage have diminished in importance, the issues derived from these cleavages are still influencing voting choices. For instance, economic issues are strongly related to party preferences in many nations. Often, the effect of economic issues is strongest when social groups and the parties remain oriented toward this dimension, such as in Scandinavia, Britain, and Australia. But even in nations where class divisions are weak, such as the United States, Canada, and Japan, economic issues have a significant effect on party preferences. Similarly, the abortion issue is significantly related to partisanship in Mediterranean Europe and in several nations with a religiously divided electorate (such as Belgium). Despite the long-term erosion of the group bases of both issue conflicts, these long-standing political controversies remain a significant influence on the vote in many advanced industrial democracies.

Second, postmaterial issues have been added to the electoral equation. Table 13.3 indicates that postmaterialism is related to partisanship (average correlation is .17) at almost the same level as economic issues (average .19). In several nations—Germany, Austria, and Japan—postmaterial values is the strongest single correlate of partisanship. Research has noted that the development of a new basis of partisan cleavage is a long and difficult process (Dalton et al. 1984, chap. 15). Groups must organize to represent New Politics voters and mobilize their support. The parties also must develop clear policy images on these issues. Initially, many established parties were hesitant to identify themselves with these issues because the stakes are still unclear and many parties are internally divided on the issues (Rohrschneider 1993; Dalton 1994, chap. 9). Yet the data presented in Table 13.3, and the longitudinal trends that are available, suggest that the postmaterial issues *are* being integrated in the calculus of issue voting. Indeed, the additional influence of these new issue interests may explain the general increase in issue voting over time.

Conclusion

If party systems were ever frozen (Bartolini and Mair 1990), it is clear that they are no lower so. Contemporary electoral politics is now characterized by a greater fluidity in the vote, greater volatility in electoral outcomes, and even a growing turnover in the number and types of parties being represented. The gathering winds of electoral change that first appeared in the early 1980s have now grown in force.

We have traced these changes to two broad trends in the electoral politics of advanced industrial societies. First, there has been an erosion in the ability of social cleavages (and the social characteristics derived from these cleavage) to explain electoral choice. The weakening of class and religious alignments has been accompanied by an apparent erosion in long-term partisan commitments and enduring feelings of party identification (Dalton 1996, chap. 9; Schmitt and Holmberg 1995; Holmberg 1994; cf. van Deth and Janssen 1994 for an opposing view). Second, concomitant with this trend has been the growth of short-term factors, such as issues and candidate images, as a basis of electoral choice. Indeed, we should consider these as complementary trends and not just coincidental; the erosion of social cleavages created more "free-floating" voters who might be mobilized on the basis of candidate images or issue appeals, and the changing nature of citizen issue interests spurred the erosion of fixed social cleavages.

For the emerging democracies in Central and Eastern Europe and Asia, there is an apparent similarity to the portrait of voting choice we have just described. Emerging party systems are unlikely to be based on stable group-based cleavages, especially when the democratic transition has occurred quite rapidly.[9] Similarly, new electorates are also unlikely to hold long-term party attachments that might guide their behavior. Thus, the patterns of electoral choice in many new democracies may be based on the same short-term factors—candidate images and issue positions—that have recently gained prominence in the electoral politics of advanced industrial democracies.

These similarities are only superficial, however. They do not reach below the surface of the electoral process. Advanced industrial democracies are experiencing an evolution in the patterns of electoral choice that flow from the breakdown of long-standing alignments and party attachments, the development of a more sophisticated electorate, and efforts to move beyond the restrictions of representative democracy. The new electoral forces in Western democracies also are developing within an electoral setting in which traditional group-based and partisan cues still exert a significant, albeit diminishing, influence.

Newly democratic party systems face the task of developing the basic structure of electoral choice—the political frameworks that Lipset and Rokkan examined historically for the West. This presents the unique opportunity to study this process scientifically: to examine how new party attachments take root, the relationships between social groups and parties are formed, party images are created, these images are transmitted to new voters, and citizens learn the process of electoral choice and representative democracy. The venerable Lipset and Rokkan framework may provide a valuable starting point for this research, and the Michigan model of party identification may provide a framework for studying how new political identities may form. However, now we can study these processes with the scientific tools of empirical research. In addition, the creation of party systems in the world of global television, greater knowledge about electoral politics (from the elite and public levels), and fundamentally different electorates is unlikely to follow the pattern of Western Europe in the 1920s.

If we return to the case of advanced industrial democracies, our findings lead to several predictions about the changing nature of electoral behavior in these democracies. An increased weight of short-term factors as predictors of voting choice means that electoral volatility is likely to be a continuing characteristic of contemporary electoral systems. For a time, issues and candidate images may create an equilibrium that endures across a set of elections. By their very nature, these factors are more labile and susceptible to exogenous forces. Thus, some U.S. commentators foresaw a new democratic era following Clinton's victory in 1992, and then a new era of Republic ascendancy in 1994. John Major and Helmut Kohl appeared to face certain defeat in 1992 and 1994, respectively, only to emerge from these elections with their majorities intact. Rather than the failures of survey research, one might cite these cases as illustrations of the inherent volatility of contemporary electoral politics. As electoral research has developed in its scientific skill, the phenomenon we are trying to predict has become less predictable. Elsewhere I have argued that the issue-based cleavages we are describing are intrinsically less stable than the group-based cleavages of the past (Dalton et al. 1984, chap. 14; Dalton 1991).

The shift to issue and candidate voting is likely to increase the evaluative content of elections. Parties will be judged by their leadership and the policies they advocate. On the one hand, this might be a welcomed trend because it suggests an increase in democratic responsiveness, or implies that electorates are developing some of the characteristics identified with theories of rational democratic choice. Issues and candidates, not party identifications and life-long social traits, are becoming more important as predictors of voting. On the other hand, we cannot be certain that the content of these evaluations will necessarily be more rational. Some voters will be drawn to candidates or issue positions for well-reasoned principles; others might be drawn by superficial media campaigns and oversimplified electioneering. Indeed, the political framework of the group-based party systems provided a method for ensuring electoral responsiveness and accountability that is lacking in an electorate with only short-term considerations (Kirchheimer 1966).

The proliferation of issue interests also raises questions about how to develop coherent government programs in a fragmented political context. At one level, this involves the potential tension between the economic issues of the traditional left/right cleavage and the new political themes of postmaterialism. The tensions between old left and new left have created considerable instability in many Western party systems over the past two decades; now this is being amplified by heightened tensions between old right/new right constituencies. The ultimate resolution of these ideological divisions remains one of the major research questions facing political scientists.

More generally, governments that function in a multidimensional political space with shifting emphases on each dimension face major difficulties in finding any political equilibrium. The fixed system of cleavage structures and party alignments solved this paradox by constraining electoral choice. Modern governments thus should face increasing difficulty in generating a political consensus in favor of any policy in this new context of electoral politics. For instance, even if Americans agree to make the federal budget deficit a priority, they cannot agree how to resolve this problem.

In the end, the degree of change in electoral politics will be dependent on the choices that parties and candidates make in responding to these new electoral forces. How democracies choose will determine whether these new forces of electoral change ultimately enrich or weaken the democratic process.

Notes

1. The figure presents the Alford index of class voting. To maximize the comparability of these analyses, we focus on the left/right voting patterns of the working class versus the combined middle class (old and new). The Alford index measures class voting as the simple difference between the percentage of the working class voting for the left and the percentage of the middle class voting left. The partisan measure is based on a question about voting choice: "If there were a general election tomorrow, which party would you vote for?"

2. The source of these data are the 1990-1991 World Values Survey. The World Values Survey was conducted in more than 40 nations under the direction of the European Values Group. These data are available from the Inter-university Consortium for Political and Social Research at the University of Michigan. We based the class measure on the occupation of the head of the household coded into five categories: old middle class, new middle class, working class, agriculture, and other occupation.

3. One important anomaly to note involves class voting in eastern Germany. The Alford index for the 1990 and 1994 federal elections shows a *reversal* of the normal class alignment. That is, the eastern middle class supports parties of the left, and the eastern working class supports the conservative CDU (Dalton and Bürklin 1996). This may be a general legacy of post-Communist party systems in Eastern Europe.

4. Religious denomination used the codes as provided in the World Values Survey; church attendance was collapsed to (1) weekly or more often, (2) monthly or several times a year, (3) less often, and (4) never or no religion.

5. The Cramér's V correlations for ethnicity were United States = .14, Canada = .12.

6. Supporting this position, Nieuwbeerta (1995) finds that the strength of class polarization in voting is inversely related to the extent of the welfare state in a nation.

7. We should note that compared to the structured ideologies that underlie the class cleavage or religious values, the postmaterial framework is still diffuse and imprecise. One can speak of an

ecologist ideology, but the literature and the movement disagree on the exact principles and goals of the environmental movement. Thus, it is probably inaccurate to speak of a postmaterial ideology. This said, the individual issues advocated by postmaterial groups are being interconnected by social movements and their partisan supporters.

8. The economic measure is a simple additive combination of positions on four issue dimensions: income inequality, government ownership of economic enterprises, state responsibility for individual well-being, and government responsibility for providing jobs. The abortion issue measures support for abortion under four different conditions. The postmaterial values index is based on Inglehart's 12-item battery.

9. The exception may be the party systems of Latin America and East Asia (Taiwan and South Korea), which might be able to integrate existing social cleavages because of the different nature of these democratic transitions (e.g., Remmer 1991; Chu 1992).

(14)

Elections and
Democratic Governance

LAWRENCE LeDUC

Elections may have meaningful consequences. To believe otherwise would undermine some of the most fundamental tenets of liberal democracy. But what are some of these consequences? They are not always the ones that would seem most desirable to democratic theorists or most obvious to students of elections. The path from electoral democracy to democratic governance is not a smooth one, as voters in the new South Africa or in the restored democracies of Central and Eastern Europe or Latin America have quickly learned. Even in countries with a long and well-established tradition of democratic elections, the electoral process can sometimes lead to deadlock, uncertainty, or unanticipated policy changes. The election that seemed set to refashion and revitalize Italian democracy in the spring of 1994 led instead to renewed political instability 6 months later. And Japan had three different coalition governments, including one led by an opposition party, within a year following its dramatic 1993 election. Although elections are one of the core institutions in what we think of as democratic politics, they may reveal either a little or a lot about the process of government that flows from them. The linkage between electoral politics and the actual process of policy making is often complicated and indirect (Castles 1994).

But in spite of these uncertainties and inconsistencies, it is clear that in a democracy elections do decide many important matters. At the most fundamental level, they establish the norms by which political power can be wielded in a society. Sartori (1967) argues that elections are the one democratic institution through which it is established that legitimate political power flows only from below. By setting limits within which power can be legitimately exercised, elections help to determine *how* a country is governed. At the same time, they determine *who* will exercise that power, although in most democratic countries elected officials share power in varying degrees with bureaucracies and with many nonelected state agencies. And elections provide at least a rough guide to the economic, social, and foreign policies that will be put in place after the election, that is, to *what* a government in power actually does. Although the actual consequences of an election may not always be the most obvious ones, this "how," "who," and "what" would seem to lie at the very roots of the concept of democracy as it has become established in Western political thought.

Political theorists have always differed widely in their expectations regarding the consequences of the electoral process, as discussed in other chapters in this volume. Schumpeter (1942) envisioned elections as a competition between individuals or groups (parties) for the support of the voters. Once the election was over, it was basically up to the winners to get on with the process of government. Others would demand more. Writers such as Bachrach (1967) or Ginsberg (1982) would not be persuaded that an election can, in itself, produce real democracy. Elections that are held under conditions of restricted freedom of the press, limited participation, or severely constrained choice invariably raise basic questions of democratic legitimacy. And should not elections in a democracy imply that the individuals or groups who compete for votes present a specific program or set of policy alternatives? The people, after all, should know what they are voting for, and the policy commitments of parties or candidates should amount to more than the proverbial campaign "promises." In other words, getting elected is only a starting point for democratic governance. The conditions under which the rulers of a country are elected, and the manner in which they govern, are also an important part of our understanding of what it means to be a democracy.

The concept of democratic elections perhaps of necessity combines both normative and empirical elements. In this chapter, we will consider the effect of an election on the formation of a government, the various linkages between the outcome of an election and public policy, the role played by political parties in that process, both in elections and in government, and the possible consequences of an election for the future of party systems in particular countries. In each of these areas, one finds a diverse empirical literature, but also some contention regarding the effects that elections might be expected to have on processes of government more generally. That elections do have consequences might be taken as an assumption. But the question of what those consequences are, and how precisely they can be measured, requires some further exploration.

Who Governs?

In a democracy, the power of governing might be expected to fall to the winners of an election. But political reality is much more complicated than this, and the variations on the theme of "who governs?" among the countries examined here are extensive. The vast majority of elections are for legislative offices, and legislators are elected to represent rather than to govern. In fewer than half of the nations considered here is the chief executive power vested in an official who is directly elected—generally a president. But in these cases, of which the United States, France, and Mexico are perhaps among the more prominent examples, the president is required to share power with separately elected legislative bodies, whose terms of office do not necessarily coincide with the president's own. And, in virtually all of the countries considered here, substantial governing authority is also vested in nonelected bureaucracies and agencies, sometimes, as with the U.S. Federal Reserve Board, appointed for terms of office far longer than the normal electoral term or, as with British Permanent Secretaries, enjoying the effective political immunity of tenure in the civil service. Whereas elections can shift the balance of power among the various groups and individuals who share in the process of government, such shifts are not always as decisive as they sometimes appear on the day after an election.

Lijphart (1984, 1989) attempted a classification that arranged democracies along two dimensions measuring the extent to which power is concentrated or dispersed in various systems, and other institutional variables that affect the degree of centralization of authority. Although he found that there were differences of degree among a number of nations, his basic distinction was between *majoritarian* democracies, which tend to concentrate greater power in the hands of an electoral majority, and *consensual* ones, which require the construction of coalitions or otherwise limit or constrain the power of a winning party or candidate. In his scheme, the purest examples of majoritarian systems are those organized along the lines of the British "Westminster" model. In these cases, elections tend to produce a "winner take all" type of result, in which a single victorious party is generally able to name the cabinet and implement its legislative program. At the other extreme are more purely consensual democracies such as Switzerland, in which elections have much less effect on the process of government because most important political decisions are arrived at either through negotiation in a broadly based coalition or by referendum. The rather fundamental cultural difference between the British "adversarial" style of politics and the Continental model based on coalitions or "consociational" norms and behavior has been identified by other political scientists as well (Finer 1975; Blondel and Müller-Rommel 1993). But, as Lijphart (1989) notes, most countries are not pure types. The United States, for example, has electoral institutions that are essentially majoritarian but governmental processes that are consensual. Denmark and Israel, on the other hand, have electoral systems that necessitate coalition building but place few constraints on the political authority exercised by a governing coalition once it is formed.

In Figure 14.1, we attempt a somewhat simplified version of Lijphart's classification, emphasizing basic institutional variables. Here, a distinction is also made for presidential systems, in which the existence of a separately elected chief executive generally requires a more consensual style of governance.[1] But even within each of the three broad groupings shown here, there is considerable variation. Canada, which follows the Westminster model, has sometimes had "minority" governments, in which the governing party did not control a majority of the seats in Parliament but was nevertheless not required to form a coalition. And Israel, as already noted, tends to produce coalition governments that, once formed, are as powerful as any that operate under a more majoritarian institutional framework.

In the relatively small number of countries that conform most closely to the Westminster model, the party that is victorious in an election may be able

Majoritarian   **Consensus**

← ── →

Majority/minority parliamentary	*Presidential*	*Coalition*
Australia[a]	Argentina	Belgium
Austria	Bolivia	Czech Republic
Bangladesh	Brazil	Denmark
Canada	Bulgaria	Finland[e]
Germany[a]	Chile	Hungary
Greece	Colombia	Israel
India	Costa Rica	Ireland[b]
Nepal	Ecuador	Italy
New Zealand	France	Japan[b]
Norway[a]	Madagascar	Netherlands
Pakistan	Malawi	Poland
Portugal	Mali	Switzerland
South Africa	Mexico	Thailand
Spain	Mozambique	Turkey[b]
Sweden[a]	Philippines	
United Kingdom	Russia	
	South Korea	
	Taiwan[c]	
	Ukraine	
	United States	
	Uruguay[d]	
	Venezuela	
	Zambia	

Figure 14.1. Institutional Characteristics of Government Formation

a. May involve coalitions, but the makeup of the coalition is generally known prior to the election.
b. Classification based on outcome of most recent election.
c. Direct election of president commencing in 1996.
d. Simultaneous presidential and legislative elections.
e. Sometimes also classified as "semipresidential."

to govern alone. In a few additional cases, such as Germany and Australia, coalition agreements between parties are put in place before the election campaign begins, thereby signaling to voters in advance the composition of possible alternative governments. But in many other instances, the process of constructing a governing coalition can begin only after the votes have been counted. Governments in countries such as Belgium, Hungary, and Thailand will typically be formed by negotiation between one of the larger parties and several smaller ones. Such a process can take weeks, and the result is not always the one that the voters might have anticipated beforehand (Dodd 1976; Strøm 1990). When Sylvio Berlusconi became prime minister following the 1994 Italian election, it was as the head of a three-party coalition in which his Forza Italia was the smallest of the three parties that combined to form the government. Similarly, the defeat of the Social Democrats in the 1991 Swedish election eventually produced, after protracted negotiations, a four-party coalition led by Conservative Carl Bildt.

The classification shown in Figure 14.1 is not necessarily definitive, because a particular country may shift from the majoritarian grouping to the coalition category abruptly, depending on a particular election result. In the Swedish example already mentioned, power has generally alternated between the Social Democrats governing alone or with the support of one or more minor parties and a "bourgeois" coalition, whose exact composition cannot be determined until after the election, when the electoral strength of the various parties composing it is known. The Eastern European countries are particularly difficult to classify according to these criteria because most have had several quite different types of governments during their still relatively brief experience with democratic elections. Poland, for example, had an elected president in Lech Walensa who, because of his personal prestige, enjoyed perhaps greater political influence than the formal powers of his office provided. But Poland also had a series of relatively unstable coalition governments during the period following the 1991 elections. New elections in 1993 produced a more decisive result, in part because of changes in the electoral law that eliminated many of the smaller parties. Even an established democracy such as Japan would have been classified very differently prior to its 1993 election, before which the Liberal Democratic Party (LDP) had governed alone or in stable coalitions with various minor parties. But Japan has now clearly moved either temporarily or permanently into the grouping where the election is only the first step in the often long and complex process of forming a government.

Electoral Agendas and Policy Mandates

The question of how an election outcome translates into specific policy consequences likewise generates a range of possible answers. Parties that are successful in winning office will often claim a "mandate" to carry forward the policy proposals that they advanced during the campaign. Following the Canadian election of 1988, the winning Progressive-Conservatives claimed that they had secured a popular mandate for the Canada-U.S. North American Free Trade Agreement (NAFTA) and proceeded to a quick ratification of the treaty immediately following the election. Although they had won only 43 percent of the vote, there were few challengers to their claim, in spite of the fact that evidence from various public opinion polls indicated that the Canadian public continued to have serious doubts about the proposed agreement (LeDuc 1990). In parliamentary systems such as those of Canada, Britain, and New Zealand, where one party or a stable coalition controls a majority of the legislative seats, few constraints exist on the ability of a government to implement its policies. An American president, in contrast, or the head of a multiparty coalition government in the Netherlands, may find it considerably more difficult to interpret an electoral mandate.

In their comprehensive study of the linkages between the content of the manifestos that parties use to represent their issue stances in election campaigns and the policies that they follow when in government, Klingemann, Hofferbert, and Budge (1994) note that elections may influence policy in two ways, through the *agenda* and through the *mandate*. Political parties often hold policy conferences prior to an election, specifically intended to set out the party's position on a variety of issues. American parties establish platform committees at their quadrennial conventions for the purposes of putting together a program in support of the presidential nominee. The Republicans heavily promoted their "Contract With America" package of legislative and constitutional proposals during the 1994 congressional election campaign, and the Liberal party in Canada focused its successful 1993 campaign around its "Red Book" of policy proposals. In most democratic political systems, there is little to bind a party or candidate to such policy commitments except the potential sanction of the next election. Nevertheless, Klingemann et al. found in their study of 10 democracies that manifesto positions did predict to a considerable degree the policies that parties would tend to follow in government. This was true in spite of some of the institutional differences among countries noted earlier.

The linkage that Klingemann et al. found between party programs and policy priorities tended to be policy specific rather than broadly ideological. But elections can sometimes also result in more wide-ranging changes in policy direction as well as in specific choices between parties and programs.

Did the electorate truly signal a new neo-conservative direction for economic and social policy in the United States following the election of Ronald Reagan in 1980, or did British voters endorse the policy initiatives that later became known as "Thatcherism"? These are fundamental questions that have interested many analysts of politics in those two countries over the past decade (Miller and Shanks 1982; Crewe and Searing 1988).

Students of elections have long recognized that the message that voters, both individually and collectively, send with their votes may be either *prospective* in the sense that Klingemann et al. intend, that is, linked to the policies that a party proposes to follow if elected, or *retrospective,* based on its past performance in office (Key 1966; Fiorina 1981). Not infrequently, an election campaign itself can involve a contest between these two, quite different, approaches as followed by one or more parties. The 1993 Australian election campaign, for example, began with competing evaluations of the record compiled by the Labor government, which had held office since 1981. But the new Labor prime minister, Paul Keating, was ultimately successful during the course of that campaign in shifting the electorate's attention to the controversial "Fightback!" package of economic proposals put forward by the Liberal/National opposition (Bean and Marks 1993). Thus, what might have been an election mandate based on a retrospective evaluation of the Labor record became instead a prospective rejection by the voters of the opposition parties' policy initiatives. It was no accident that Keating seized the opportunity to make the opposition's "Fightback!" proposals a major campaign issue. For not only did it focus the attention of the voters on such controversial items as a proposed new sales tax, it also served to divert attention from a retrospective evaluation of Labor's 12 years in office.

The 1993 Australian example is one in which the main opposition parties believed that it was in their interest to present fairly specific alternative policies to the electorate. But often voters are asked to pass a retrospective judgment on the record of the party in power rather than to consider particular alternative policies or projects. Opposition parties that can get by with simply attacking the record of the governing party may try to avoid putting forward too many of their own proposals. And governing parties sometimes have a strong interest in diverting the attention of the voter to matters such as "leadership" rather than allowing the campaign to become a kind of referendum on their performance in office. Canadian elections, for example, have frequently involved a struggle between these competing campaign strategies, resulting in electoral mandates that are at best ambiguous (Clarke et al. 1995).

Klingemann et al. found that the program-to-policy linkage in Australia was weak and that in Canada it was applicable only to certain parties and issues. Nevertheless, these 2 countries fell in the middle of the 10 studied in the manifestos project. In Sweden and France, the overall link between party program and policy outcome was considerably stronger, and in Belgium and the Netherlands, it was weaker (Klingemann et al. 1994).

The 1980 presidential election in the United States also provides a useful illustration of the tensions between these differing interpretations of electoral mandates. Ronald Reagan's victory over Jimmy Carter could be (and was) readily interpreted either as an endorsement of the new policy directions proposed by Reagan, or as a rejection of those associated with Carter during his term of office. When Reagan asked, at the end of his televised debate with Carter, "Are you better off than you were four years ago?" he was clearly seeking a retrospective mandate. Yet within days of his victory, the election was being widely interpreted as "a profound and general turn toward conservatism."[2] Although academic analyses can provide at least partial answers to questions that arise regarding the policy implications of a particular election, governments will nevertheless form their own interpretations and act accordingly. A political party that truly believes that it has secured a popular mandate for its policies is more likely to try to carry them out.

Dahl (1990) considered the concept of a policy mandate emanating from U.S. presidential elections a myth, but nevertheless concluded that presidents will often claim an electoral mandate as part of a strategy to fulfill their own policy goals. More generally, the concept of a mandate is almost by its very nature politically self-serving, and often it cannot be discovered in the results of a specific election. In countries where the voter casts one ballot for a parliamentary representative, that single vote may have embedded within it several quite different messages. And systems that permit a simultaneous direct vote for other offices such as a president or members of an upper house can sometimes generate inconsistent and possibly conflicting messages. Even politicians who are determined to carry through on their commitments may encounter difficulty in discerning a specific electoral message and translating it into effective public policy. Parties or candidates may find, on taking office, that their proposals require substantial modification. Or significant political, bureaucratic, or economic barriers may be discovered that effectively delay or alter the implementation of policies to which a party seemed irrevocably committed only a few weeks or months before.

There are also instances in which the full public policy significance of an electoral change does not become clear until after a new government has taken office. Few New Zealand voters, for example, could have anticipated the sweeping restructuring of the economy that followed Labour's victory in the 1984 election. This example is particularly striking because the revolutionary policy changes in New Zealand, which came to be known as "Rogernomics" (after Finance Minister Roger Douglas), ran completely counter to the Keynesian economic principles and social democratic political philosophy that had long been associated with Labour (Vowles and Aimer 1993). In voting for Labour over a National government that had held office for 9 years, voters may have opted for change. But neither the direction nor the wide-ranging character of the policy innovations that took place over the following 3 years were anticipated. New Zealand's dramatic swing to the right, both in its politics and in its social and economic policies, began not in the 1984 election campaign, but afterward. It would be another 3 years before voters would have the opportunity to render a verdict on Labour's controversial program.

Political Parties and Public Policy

There are several quite different aspects of the linkage between elections and public policy that have long been of interest to political scientists. Klingemann et al. (1994) were concerned primarily with the extent to which party positions as represented by election manifestos were successfully translated into policies by parties when in power. Attempting to measure in this way whether parties actually do what they *say* they will do speaks to classic questions regarding responsible party government (Birch 1964; Katz 1987). The concern of Kelley (1983) or Clarke et al. (1995) with the idea of electoral mandates, on the other hand, is more addressed to interpreting the message of an election and attempting to determine whether parties in government do what the electorate *wants* them to. This aspect of the election-government linkage speaks more to the classic questions of popular sovereignty (Schattschneider 1960; Barber 1984), also a fundamental concern of democratic polities.

But there is yet another side to this linkage that has also been the subject of a substantial political science literature—namely, the extent to which parties can be readily differentiated on the basis of their commitment to particular policies (Epstein 1967; Rose 1984a). Clearly, if multiple parties attempt to occupy the same policy space, in or out of government, or parties try to hide their true positions during an election campaign, the linkage between elections and policy outcomes will be weakened. Thus, determining whether parties themselves "make a difference" in government has also been a long-standing concern of political scientists.

To make a difference, parties must be different. Beginning with Downs (1957), there have been many attempts to investigate the extent to which parties actively compete with each other or present clearly defined images to their electorates in various policy areas (Laver and Hunt 1992). These distinctions may be clearest in the case of parties that firmly locate themselves on either the left or right of the ideological spectrum, or parties that tend to be identified with the interests of a particular group or region. But they need not be confined to these alone. As Budge and Farlie (1983) note, parties may come to "own" particular issues or policy positions in the minds of voters simply because they have been consistently identified with these over a substantial period of time. To the extent that voters are able to perceive differences between parties on a range of policy-related matters, the choices made between parties in elections may translate themselves into real policies if and when those parties assume a role in government. Thus, by comparing different periods of party government in a particular political system, or by comparing a number of countries with different party configurations, we might be able to discern whether the electoral differences between parties eventually become differences in public policy.

Following the latter approach, Jackman (1975) concluded that the effect of the strength of socialist parties on the distribution of income across 15 countries was minimal, and where it existed tended to favor middle-income groups rather than the poorest. Cameron (1978), on the other hand, found in a study of 18 OECD countries that the participation of social democratic parties in government was positively correlated with patterns of public expenditure. Obviously, both of these studies, along with others that employ correlation techniques and use aggregate data, differ considerably in methods and measures. For the most part, however, these studies are not concerned with the specific positions that parties take on issues in an election campaign, but rather with the presence and strength of a particular type of party (generally, a left party) in the system and its possible effects on the overall direction of public policy over time. And, as the above-noted differences suggest, their findings have not been entirely conclusive in regard to the longer-term effects of such parties on public policy.

Castles (1982) and his colleagues, however, did find relationships between a number of political variables relating to party strength and position and major policy areas such as total government expenditure, macroeconomic policy, welfare spending, and wage policies. Their analysis supports the view that partisan control of government is one of the more important factors accounting for differences in patterns of public expenditure among the 18 countries studied.[3] However, the differences found are for the most part broadly ideological rather than party/policy specific. The patterns that they disclose are related less to what happens in particular election campaigns than to the presence or absence of "party political structures that institutionalize class and interest political cleavages and make them continuingly policy-relevant" (Castles 1982, 88). On the basis of their findings, we might expect that the effect of parties will be greatest in those countries where left and right are more clearly delineated or where class cleavages are more sharply politicized. The existence of corporatist political arrangements (Luebbert 1986) or a consensual approach to policy making (Lijphart 1989) may, however, intervene to reduce or moderate the effects of partisan electoral changes on policy outcomes. On the other hand, where particular institutional arrangements enhance the role of "veto players" in the policy process, even small changes in electoral outcomes can have significant consequences for the policy process (Tsebelis 1995).

The Election/Policy Cycle

The studies mentioned above attempted to measure the effect of parties on public policy over periods of time substantially greater than one electoral term. But there may also be policy cycles of much shorter duration that are driven at least in part by what happens in an election campaign. When it possesses the institutional and policy levers needed to do so, a governing party may try to manage economic policy in a way that is most advantageous to its reelection prospects (Tufte 1978). (A more detailed discussion of this question, particularly as it relates to the economy, may be found in this volume, chap. 12.)

An attempt to coordinate electoral and policy cycles can be viewed in two different ways—from the perspective of policy making or as an element of election timing. In the first instance, governments may be inclined to pursue more contractionary monetary and fiscal policies during the early part of their term, either because these are perceived as necessary or because they can afford to take the political risks that such policies often entail. But later in the cycle, more expansionary policies may be preferred. A governing party that can face the electorate during a period of economic growth often enhances its electoral prospects. In Britain, for example, the so-called U-turn in monetary policy began about a year in advance of the 1987 election, and two reductions in tax rates also took place during the same period (Miller et al. 1990). But British governments possess a degree of control over both fiscal and monetary policy that many others do not. In the United States, Congress exercises considerable authority over the budgetary process, whereas the Federal Reserve Board, which oversees monetary policy, has substantial independence from both Congress and the president. And the American election timetable is fixed by law, thereby also denying to the president the ability to time elections to his party's advantage. But in many other countries, it is often possible to adjust the electoral timetable to take advantage of favorable economic circumstances or to lessen the effect of unfavorable ones.

The American and French systems provide a contrasting illustration of the implications that overlapping terms of office may have for the policy process. Following the national elections that by law occur every 2 years in the United States, the president and Congress will make accommodations to the election result. Reagan's election as president in 1980 created a new political climate in which the still Democrat-controlled House of Representatives could readily be persuaded that Reagan had a mandate to carry forward his policies, whether any such mandate really existed (Miller and Shanks 1982). Similarly, the election of a Republican Congress in the 1994 midterm elections effectively rearranged much of the policy agenda of President Clinton's remaining 2 years of his term of office. In the French case, President Mitterrand dissolved the National Assembly following his election in 1981 and ordered new legislative elections in which his party secured a decisive majority. This produced for a short period of time a legislative majority supportive of the president's policy initiatives (Hall 1986). But a swing against the Socialists in the 1986 Assembly elections eventually forced Mitterrand to share power with a Gaullist prime minister, Jacques Chirac. Because presidential systems vary widely in the degree of authority vested in the president independently of the legislative bodies, it is difficult to generalize about the nature of the policy process under these types of arrangements. However, what these systems do have in common is some degree of power sharing, ranging from the American concept of checks and balances to the more powerful presidential authorities of France,

Mexico, and South Korea (Rose and Sulieman 1980). A presidential system such as Russia's, in part because of the untested character of many of its new political institutions, sometimes seems to exhibit elements of both weakness and strength in presidential leadership.

In countries where coalition formation following an election is necessary to form a government, the policy process necessarily proceeds in a very different fashion. Normally, a bargain must be struck that includes not only the partisan composition of the government but also its policy agenda (Luebbert 1986; Budge and Keman 1990a). Such a process invariably involves compromise. Thus, a party that campaigned successfully on its commitments to certain policies during an election may find itself forced to moderate or even bargain away some of those commitments so it can participate in a governing coalition. Even the largest party in such a grouping cannot generally win all of its demands. For example, after a protracted period of interparty bargaining following the 1988 election in Israel, the two largest parties opted for a "grand coalition" in which the position of prime minister rotated between the Labour leader Shimon Peres and the Likud leader Yitzhak Shamir over a 4-year period. Although unusual, this arrangement represented a viable alternative to either of the two larger parties acceding to the policy demands of the small religious parties as the price of their participation in a coalition with one of the two larger parties (Diskin 1991).

Such a bargain, once agreed, will sometimes define the pattern of government over a 4- or 5-year cycle, as in the Israeli example, or it may come apart, thereby necessitating the construction of a new coalition agreement or even new elections. In 1994, the Irish government's connections to a controversial judicial matter precipitated the resignation of the prime minister, Albert Reynolds, and the collapse of the governing coalition headed by the largest party in the Dail, Fianna Fáil. The subsequent coalition, led by Fine Gael, was thus implicitly beginning a new policy cycle midway through what would have otherwise been a normal electoral term. Similarly, the policy initiatives that might have been expected to take place in Italy following the 1994 election were derailed by the collapse of the Berlusconi government only 7 months later. The new "nonparty" government headed by Lamberto Dini was politically too weak to set out a new policy agenda and was able to govern only until a timetable for new elections could be agreed on. Thus, although an election is certainly capable of putting an end to a period of political uncertainty or instability, it can also be the event that itself precipitates such a period.

The policy cycle generally followed in those cases where a single majority party or a stable coalition has the ability to exercise control of government for a full term of office is very different. Under these conditions, a winning party will generally act to implement its perceived policy mandate very quickly and often wants to be seen by the public to be delivering on its campaign commitments. Following its victory in the 1993 Canadian election, the Liberal government of Jean Chrétien moved quickly to scale back purchases of new military equipment made by its predecessor and ended a controversial airport privatization plan, both items that the Liberals had criticized during the campaign. The Liberals also moved swiftly to implement a public works program, which had been a central part of their campaign document, and also to replace the governor of the Bank of Canada, whose monetary policies had been a target of opposition criticism during the campaign. However, a party in this position, possessing a large majority of parliamentary seats, has considerable freedom to shift its priorities when it chooses to do so and to be quite selective in interpreting its electoral mandate. Chrétien's government also signed NAFTA, which it had criticized during the campaign, and proceeded to adopt as its own many of the fiscal policies followed by the previous government. Predictably, critics were soon calling the new government to task for "reneging on its promises" or engaging in policy "flip-flops." But by the time of the next election 4 or 5 years later, such criticisms are generally long forgotten.

A governing party in a majority or stable coalition situation has in fact several years of what might be called "policy freedom." Not needing to worry about maintaining a fragile coalition, and freed of immediate concern about the potential electoral consequences of its policies, a governing party in this position is often able to rearrange its policy agenda or even to set an entirely new one (Rose 1984a). The first year or two in office is, in a strategic sense, the ideal time for a governing party to push through unpopular measures such as tax increases or cutbacks in public expenditures.

Such a pattern of policy making has been commonplace in Canada, which has exactly this type of majoritarian parliamentary system, not normally involving coalition bargaining or interim elections. Canadian and British prime ministers have generally been quick to realize that their period of greatest freedom to pursue new or controversial policy objectives occurs in the first 2 years after an election. Pierre Trudeau initiated the controversial National Energy Program following his return to power in the 1980 election, and Margaret Thatcher's government increased the value added tax (VAT) shortly after her election in 1979. In neither instance had these initiatives been discussed in any detail during the preceding election campaign. It is not surprising that the popularity of a new government that pursues such a course often declines sharply. But the real political costs of such temporary unpopularity are relatively low, as evidenced by the long and successful political careers enjoyed by these two leaders. Roger Douglas, the New Zealand finance minister who initiated the sweeping changes in economic policy following the 1984 election advises potential reformers to move quickly in implementing major policy changes.[4] Failure to do so creates the risk that both the political will and the freedom to move decisively will gradually dissipate.

A governing party in a majoritarian parliamentary system can risk temporary unpopularity to further its policy objectives. But by the end of the third year in office (in systems where a 4-year term is the norm), most governing parties begin to engage in the early steps of planning the next election campaign. The overall effect of such strategic maneuvers is to lengthen considerably the period of time devoted to what can rightly be called campaigning. The period of a year or more in which a governing party devotes its attention toward improving its reelection prospects can be thought of as the "long campaign" (Miller et al. 1990). The election-related activities of this long campaign period are often subtle and blend easily into the day-to-day activities of government.

The reason why such policy, economic, and political cycles are played out again and again over an electoral term is that governing parties will almost always try to structure the political agenda in such a way as to maximize their chances of reelection. In many parliamentary systems, one of the most potent political options possessed by the prime minister and his or her advisers is the prerogative of calling an election—a power explicitly denied to American presidents. The political benefits associated with this simple function extend far beyond the power to merely choose the election date. Rather, they accrue from the ability of a governing party to fight an election on its own terms and to arrange the policy agenda in such a way as to give itself every possible electoral advantage. Fixed timetables remove part (but certainly not all) of this advantage. And reduced authority over key areas of policy making may remove more. But the countries surveyed here include a wide range of examples, in which governing parties will often be able to adapt many, if not all, of the elements of a typical election/policy cycle.

Short-Term and
Long-Term Consequences

Concepts such as an electoral mandate or policy cycle are relatively short term in nature, and they help to explain how governments might behave in the period immediately following an election or during the long campaign period leading up to one. But elections can often have consequences ranging well beyond the life of a government. Such longer-term implications are found in the effect of an election on the party system itself, on the functioning of key political institutions, or on the basic philosophy of government. The 1932 election of Franklin Roosevelt, for example, established the "New Deal" party alignment, shifted the direction of government, and altered Americans' perceptions of the presidency (Andersen 1979). Yet such important changes would not have been immediately evident in the postelection debate over what type of mandate Roosevelt had received. They would become apparent only many years later, as people began to realize that the political landscape had been permanently altered. The question of cause and effect becomes frustratingly complex in attempting to discern the long-term consequences of elections, because a given election may simply reflect powerful social forces that are also manifested in other ways. But the election, as a major political event, can sometimes also coalesce or even set in motion such forces. It is possible that something like the New Deal party system in the United States might have come into being without the election of Roosevelt. V. O. Key (1955), for example, argued persuasively that fundamentally new patterns of party support caused by the forces of social change led by immigration or the economic transformation associated with industrialization were already visible in American politics in the results of the 1928 election. Nevertheless, it is the 1932 election that is commonly associated with realignment of the U.S. party system because it represented in a variety of ways a higher level of change than that normally associated with the replacement of one government by another (Burnham 1970).

A similar debate has taken place among American scholars regarding the extent to which the 1980 election of Reagan represented the beginnings of a new conservative political alignment. The 1994 Republican congressional victory would seem to strengthen the claims of those who argue that such a new alignment is now well established in American politics. But whether the 1980 election itself was a key element in such a shift, or whether it was more a harbinger of larger forces that were already coming into place, will continue to be a matter of debate (Norpoth 1987b; Ladd 1985, 1995). And, of course, there are others who maintain that neither of these two elections is reflective of a truly fundamental ideological shift, but only of the increased volatility or "dealignment" of American party politics that has been increasingly evident in recent years. Under this interpretation, the 1980 election may also be part of a significant longer-term trend, but one of a quite different character and significance (Wattenberg 1984; Shafer 1991).

Although American presidential elections often generate this type of specu-lation concerning their longer-term importance, there is nothing inherently unique to the United States in the application of concepts such as realignment or dealignment, or the idea of a "critical" election. In many other countries, particular elections will over time be recognized as ones in which a funda-mental shift of political alignments occurred, regardless of whether such shifts were a direct consequence of the election itself. The election of the 1945 Labour government in Britain, for example, is generally recognized as such a case, because it established the fundamental pattern of postwar British politics and solidified the party system of the next 30 years. Similarly, the 1957 and 1958 elections in Canada ended decades of Liberal party dominance and fundamentally altered the regional alignments of the Canadian parties. The election of de Gaulle in 1958, which legitimized the institutions of the French Fifth Republic; the establishment of the SPD/FDP coalition under Willy Brandt following the 1969 West German election; Indira Ghandi's defeat in the 1977 elections in India; or the coming to power for the first time of the Likud Bloc under Menachem Begin in the 1973 Israeli election might also serve as examples of elections that fundamentally altered political align-ments in their respective countries (see also Lewin, Jansson, and Sörbom 1972). Whether they were major political events in themselves or part of a larger process of social or political transformation is somewhat beside the point. Whatever the source of the changes taking place, it was the election that served as their focal point. And the changes that such critical elections put in place are never easily reversed.

These examples of elections that had such a transformative quality to be called critical are deliberately dramatic ones. Although the benefit of histori-cal hindsight reveals more clearly the nature of the fundamental political changes that they represented, all would have been recognized even at the time as major political events. There are many other cases where elections bring about changes of long-term significance but where the immediate results are not nearly so dramatic. The rise of Green parties in a number of European countries, notably Germany, during the 1980s had considerable significance for the maintenance of established political alignments as well as implications for public policy, even though such parties were not contenders for power. The consolidation of the Dutch Protestant (CHU, ARP) and Catholic (KVP) religious parties into a single Christian Democratic party (CDA) in 1977 actually took place over a period of several elections, but it was also part of a larger process of social and political change in the Netherlands commonly referred to as "deconfessionalization" (Miller and Stouthard 1975; Irwin and Dittrich 1984). Protest parties have also sometimes succeeded in bringing about changes in party systems, sometimes across a period of more than one election. The sudden surge of the antitax Progress party in the 1973 election destabilized the Danish party system and shattered familiar patterns of coalition politics in Denmark. Such an election is sometimes referred to as a "political earthquake," whose aftershocks continue to reverberate for a number of years or even several elections afterward (Pedersen 1988). But the longer-term consequences of such events can vary greatly depending on the staying power of new parties or issues, their effects on public policy, and other institutional variables such as the structure of electoral systems. The dramatic 19 percent of the popular vote obtained by independent candidate Ross Perot in the 1992 U.S. presidential election is unlikely to have direct long-term partisan consequences because of the enormous difficulties that third parties face under American electoral rules. Yet its indirect consequences in further eroding established patterns of party support could ultimately be quite substantial. The February 1974, British election returned Labour to power, but it also ushered in Britain's "decade of dealignment" (Särlvik and Crewe 1983). The eventual political consequences of "the election that everyone lost" (King 1975) would not become clear until many years later.

Conclusion

Elections in modern democracies are called on to perform many functions in addition to the most obvious one of selecting those people who will exercise responsibility for the government of the country. They are the principal mechanism by which citizens hold governments accountable, both retrospectively for their policies and more generally for the manner in which they govern. Much of the research in the field indicates that the choices that citizens make in an election do have effects on public policy, either over the course of a government's term in office or over longer periods. But, as Rose (1984a) notes, a great deal of what happens to a party in office will be determined by factors beyond its control and often not related to the election at all. And this observation was applied to Britain, the case that perhaps comes closest to the archetype of majoritarian politics and responsible party government. Institutional arrangements that disrupt the linkages between the electoral process and the policy process can further alter the relationship between what the voter decides and what governments do.

Elections are not a panacea, important as they are to Western concepts of democracy. Canadian voters have proven in recent years to be very adept at "throwing the rascals out" when they have become dissatisfied with the party in power, yet they continue to believe in alarming numbers that governments are "out of touch" and "unresponsive" (Blais and Gidengil 1991; Clarke et al. 1995). These concerns are shared in varying degrees by citizens of many other long-established democracies (Dalton 1988). For newly emerging democracies, such patterns represent a clear signal that elections alone cannot provide a solution to their problems. Their effect on public policy is sometimes less than desired or different than expected, easily leading to frustration among citizens, politicians, and analysts alike. An election is generally positioned at the beginning of the process of democratic governance, or at a midpoint of an ongoing cycle. It is not an end in itself. Yet even voters who are deeply disillusioned with government tend to have positive perceptions of the electoral process, and they are for the most part not unrealistic in understanding its limits (LeDuc 1992). Elections remain a cornerstone of democracy, an institution that can take many forms, but without which it is all but impossible to imagine a functioning democratic political system.

Notes

1. This classification does not include as "presidential" those countries such as Austria, Finland, and Ireland, in which a president is directly elected but in which the effective head of government is a prime minister or chancellor. But, as noted, the actual political powers of an elected president, even in these cases, can vary widely.

2. Anthony Lewis, "Tidal Wave," *New York Times,* November 6, 1980, as quoted in Kelley (1983, 183).

3. The countries covered were Australia, Austria, Belgium, Canada, Denmark, Finland, France, Germany, Ireland, Italy, Japan, the Netherlands, New Zealand, Norway, Sweden, Switzerland, the United Kingdom, and the United States (Castles 1982, 59).

4. Roger Douglas, "The Politics of Successful Structural Reform," from a paper by the former finance minister, cited in Vowles and Aimer (1993, 77).

Bibliography

Abelson, Robert P., Donald R. Kinder, Mark D. Peters, and Susan T. Fiske. 1982. "Affective and Semantic Components in Political Person Perception." *Journal of Personality and Social Psychology* 42:619-30.

Abramowitz, Alan. 1978. "The Impact of a Presidential Debate on Voter Rationality." *American Journal of Political Science* 22:680-90.

Abramson, Jeffrey B., F. Christopher Arterton, and Gary R. Orren. 1988. *The Electronic Commonwealth: The Impact of New Media Technologies on Democratic Politics.* New York: Basic Books.

Abramson, Paul R., John H. Aldrich, Phil Paolino, and David Rohde. 1992. "Sophisticated Voting in the 1988 Presidential Primaries." *American Political Science Review* 86:55-70.

Abramson, Paul R., John H. Aldrich, and David W. Rohde. 1994. *Change and Continuity in the 1992 Elections.* Washington, DC: CQ Press.

Abramson, Paul R., and Ronald Inglehart. 1995. *Value Change in Comparative Perspective.* Ann Arbor: University of Michigan Press.

Adler, Ilya. 1993. "The Mexican Case: The Media in the 1988 Presidential Election." In *Television, Politics and the Transition to Democracy in Latin America,* ed. Thomas A. Skidmore. Baltimore: Johns Hopkins University Press.

Agranoff, Robert. 1976a. *The Management of Election Campaigns.* Boston: Holbrook.

———, ed. 1976b. *The New Style in Election Campaigns,* 2nd ed. Boston: Holbrook.

Aguiar, Roberto. 1994. "The Cost of Election Campaigns in Brazil." In *Comparative Political Finance Among the Democracies,* ed. Herbert E. Alexander and Rei Shiratori. Boulder, CO: Westview.

Alexander, Herbert E., and Rei Shiratori, eds. 1994. *Comparative Political Finance Among the Democracies.* Boulder, CO: Westview.

Alisky, Martin. 1969. *Uruguay: A Contemporary Survey.* New York: Praeger.

———. 1981. *Latin American Media: Guidance and Censorship.* Ames: Iowa State University Press.

Allison, Graham T. 1971. *Essence of Decision: Explaining the Cuban Missile Crisis.* Boston: Little, Brown.

Almond, Gabriel A., G. Bingham Powell, and Robert J. Mundt. 1993. *Comparative Politics: A Theoretical Framework.* New York: HarperCollins.

Almond, Gabriel, and Sidney Verba. 1963. *The Civic Culture.* Princeton, NJ: Princeton University Press.

Alt, James E. 1979. *The Politics of Economic Decline.* Cambridge: Cambridge University Press.

———. 1991. "Ambiguous Intervention: The Role of Government Action in Public Evaluation of the Economy." In *Economics and Politics: The Calculus of Support,* ed. Helmut Norpoth, Michael S. Lewis-Beck, and Jean-Dominique Lafay. Ann Arbor: University of Michigan Press.

Andersen, Kristi. 1979. *Creation of a Democratic Majority: 1928-1936.* Chicago: University of Chicago Press.

Anderson, Christopher. 1995. *Blaming the Government: Citizens and the Economy in Five European Democracies.* Armonk, NY: M. E. Sharpe.

Angell, Alan, Maria D'Alva Kinzo, and Diego Urbaneja. 1992. "Latin America." In *Electioneering: A Comparative Study of Continuity and Change,* ed. David Butler and Austin Ranney. Oxford: Clarendon.

Ansolabehere, Stephen, and Shanto Iyengar. 1994 "Riding the Waves and Claiming Ownership Over Issues: The Joint Effects of Advertising and News Coverage in Campaigns." *Public Opinion Quarterly* 58:335-57.

Appleton, Andrew, and Amy Mazur. 1993. "France." In *Gender and Party Politics,* ed. Joni Lovenduski and Pippa Norris. London: Sage.

Arter, David. 1984. *The Nordic Parliaments.* London: C. Hurst.

Asher, Herbert. 1992. *Presidential Elections and American Politics,* 5th ed. Pacific Grove, CA: Brooks-Cole.

Ashford, Sheena, and Noel Timms. 1992. *What Europe Thinks: A Study of Western European Values.* Brookfield, VT: Dartmouth.

Avril, Pierre. 1994. "Regulation of Political Finance in France." In *Comparative Political Finance Among the Democracies,* ed. Herbert E. Alexander and Rei Shiratori. Boulder, CO: Westview.

Ayres, B. Drummond, Jr. 1995. "Easier Voter Registration Doesn't Raise Participation." *New York Times,* December 3.

Bachrach, Peter. 1967. *The Theory of Democratic Elitism: A Critique.* Boston: Little, Brown.

Bachrach, Peter, and Morton Baratz. 1963. "Decisions and Nondecisions: An Analytical Framework." *American Political Science Review* 57:641-51.

Bagehot, Walter. 1966. *The English Constitution.* Ithaca, NY: Cornell University Press.

Baker, Gordon E. 1986. "Whatever Happened to the Reapportionment Revolution in the United States?" In *Electoral Laws and Their Political Consequences,* ed. Bernard Grofman and Arend Lijphart. New York: Agathon.

Baker, Kendall, Russell Dalton, and Kai Hildebrandt. 1981. *Germany Transformed: Political Culture and the New Politics.* Cambridge, MA: Harvard University Press.

Baker, Kendall L., and Helmut Norpoth. 1981. "Candidates on Television: The 1972 Electoral Debates in West Germany." *Public Opinion Quarterly* 45:329-45.

Baker, Kendall L., Helmut Norpoth, and Klaus Schoenbach. 1981. "Fernsehdebatten der Spitzenpolitiker im Bundestagswahlkamph 1972 und 1976." *Publizistik* 26:530-44.

Bakvis, Herman. 1988. "The Canadian Paradox: Party System Stability in the Face of a Weakly Aligned Electorate." In *Parties and Party Systems in Liberal Democracies,* ed. Steven B. Wolinetz. London: Routledge.

————, ed. 1991. *Representation, Integration and Political Parties in Canada.* Toronto: Dundurn.

Balinski, Michel L., and H. Peyton Young. 1982. *Fair Representation: Meeting the Ideal of One Man One Vote.* New Haven, CT: Yale University Press.

Banks, Arthur S. 1995. *Political Handbook of the World 1995.* New York: CSA.

Banks, Arthur S., and Robert B. Textor 1963. *A Cross-Polity Survey.* Cambridge: MIT Press.

Barber, Benjamin. 1984. *Strong Democracy: Participatory Politics for a New Age.* Berkeley: University of California Press.

Barnes, Samuel, Max Kaase, et al. 1979. *Political Action: Mass Participation in Five Western Democracies.* Beverly Hills, CA: Sage.

Bartels, Larry M. 1988. *Presidential Primaries and the Dynamics of Public Choice.* Princeton, NJ: Princeton University Press.

————. 1992. "The Impact of Electioneering in the United States." In *Electioneering: A Comparative Study of Continuity and Change,* ed. David Butler and Austin Ranney. Oxford: Clarendon.

Barthélemy, Joseph. 1912. *L'organisation du suffrage et l'expérience belge.* Paris: M Jiard et É. Brière.

Bartolini, Stefano. 1984. "Institutional Constraints and Party Competition in the French Party System." *West European Politics* 7:103-27.

Bartolini, Stefano, and Roberto D'Alimonte. 1995. "Il Sistema Partitico: Una Transizione Difficile." In *Maggioritario Ma Non Troppo,* ed. Stefano Bartolini and Roberto D'Alimonte. Bologna: Il Mulino.

Bartolini, Stefano, and Peter Mair. 1990. *Identity, Competition and Electoral Availability: The Stabilisation of European Electorates, 1885-1985.* Cambridge: Cambridge University Press.

Bashevkin, Sylvia. 1994a. "Confronting Neo-Conservatism: Anglo-American Women's Movements Under Thatcher, Reagan and Mulroney." *International Political Science Review* 15:275-96.

————. 1994b. "Facing a Renewed Right: American Feminism and the Reagan/Bush Challenge." *Canadian Journal of Political Science* 27:669-98.

————. 1996. "Tough Times in Review: The British Women's Movement During the Thatcher Years." *Comparative Political Studies* 28:525-52.

Bauer, Raymond A., Ithiel de Sola Pool, and Lewis Anthony Dexter. 1963. *American Business and Public Policy.* New York: Atherton.

Bean, Clive, and David Butler. 1991. "Uniformity in Australian Electoral Patterns: The 1990 Federal Election in Perspective." *Australian Journal of Political Science* 26:127-36.

Bean, Clive, and Gary Marks. 1993. "The Australian Federal Election of 1993." *Electoral Studies* 12:253-6.

Bean, Clive, and Anthony Mughan. 1989. "Leadership Effects in Parliamentary Elections in Australia and Britain." *American Political Science Review* 83:1165-79.

Beck, Nathaniel. 1991. "The Economy and Presidential Approval: An Information Theoretic Perspective." In *Economics and Politics: The Calculus of Support,* ed. Helmut Norpoth, Michael S. Lewis-Beck, and Jean-Dominique Lafay. Ann Arbor: University of Michigan Press.

Becker, Lee B. 1982. "The Mass Media and Citizens Assessment of Issue Importance: A Reflection on Agenda Setting Research." In *Mass Communications Review Yearbook 3,* ed. D. Charles Whitney, Ellen Wartella, and S. Windahl. Newbury Park, CA: Sage.

Becker, Lee B., Max McCombs, and Jack McLeod. 1975. "The Development of Political Cognitions." In *Political Communication: Issues and Strategies for Research,* ed. Steven H. Chaffee. Beverly Hills, CA: Sage.

Beer, Samuel H. 1978. *The British Political System.* New York: Random House.

———. 1982. *Modern British Politics: Parties and Pressure Groups in the Collectivist Age.* New York: Norton.

Beetham, David. 1994. *Defining and Measuring Democracy.* London: Sage.

Behr, Roy, and Shanto Iyengar. 1985. "Television News, Real-World Cues, and Changes in the Public Agenda." *Public Opinion Quarterly* 49:38-57.

Bell, Daniel. 1988. *The End of Ideology.* Cambridge, MA: Harvard University Press.

Bellucci, Paolo. 1991. "Italian Economic Voting: A Deviant Case or Making a Case for a Better Theory?" In *Economics and Politics: The Calculus of Support,* ed. Helmut Norpoth, Michael S. Lewis-Beck, and Jean-Dominique Lafay. Ann Arbor: University of Michigan Press.

Benjamin, G. 1982. "Innovations in Telecommunications and Politics." In *The Communication Revolution in Politics,* ed. G. Benjamin. New York: Academy of Political Science.

Bens de, Else. 1986. "Cable Penetration and Competition Among Belgian and Foreign Stations." *European Journal of Communication* 1:477-92.

Berelson, Bernard, Paul F. Lazarsfeld, and William N. McPhee. 1954. *Voting: A Study of Opinion Formation in a Presidential Campaign.* Chicago: University of Chicago Press.

Bernays, Edward, ed. 1955. *The Engineering of Consent.* Norman: University of Oklahoma Press.

Betz, Hans-Georg. 1994. *Radical Right-Wing Populism in Western Europe.* Houndmills: Macmillan; New York: St. Martin's.

Bhambhri, C. P. 1994. *Indian Politics Since Independence.* Delhi: Shipra.

Bille, Lars. 1990. "Denmark: The Oscillating Party System." In *Understanding Party System Change in Western Europe,* ed. Peter Mair and Gordon Smith. London: Cass.

Bille, Lars, Jørgen Elklit, and Mikael V. Jakobsen. 1992. "Denmark: The 1990 Campaign." In *Electoral Strategies and Political Marketing,* ed. Shaun Bowler and David M. Farrell. Houndmills: Macmillan.

Birch, Anthony H. 1964. *Representative and Responsible Government.* London: Allen and Unwin.

———. 1993. *The Concepts and Theories of Modern Democracy.* London: Routledge.

Black, Jerome H. 1978. "The Multicandidate Calculus of Voting: Application to Canadian Federal Elections." *American Journal of Political Science* 22:609-38.

———. 1984. "Revisiting the Effects of Canvassing on Voting Behaviour." *Canadian Journal of Political Science* 17:351-74.

Blais, André. 1988. "The Classification of Electoral Systems." *European Journal of Political Research* 16:99-110.

———. 1991. "The Debate Over Electoral Systems." *International Political Science Review* 12:239-60.

———. 1993. "Rethinking Our Electoral System: The Case for Majority Run-Off Elections." *Inroads* 2:124-31.

Blais, André, and Ken Carty. 1987. "The Impact of Electoral Formulae on the Creation of Majority Governments." *Electoral Studies* 5:209-18.

———. 1991. "The Psychological Impact of Electoral Laws: Measuring Duverger's Elusive Factor." *British Journal of Political Science* 21:79-93.

Blais, André, and Stéphane Dion. 1990. "Electoral Systems and the Consolidation of New Democracies." In *Democratic Transition and Consolidation in Southern Europe, Latin America and Southeast Asia,* ed. Diane Ethier. London: Macmillan.

Blais, André, and Elisabeth Gidengil. 1991. *Making Representative Democracy Work: The Views of Canadians.* Toronto: Dundurn.

Blais, André, and Louis Massicotte. Forthcoming. "Electoral Formulas: A Macroscopic Perspective." *European Journal of Political Research.*

———. 1996. "Electing Heads of States." Université de Montréal. Typescript.

Blais, André, and Richard Nadeau. 1996. "Measuring Strategic Voting: A Two-Step Procedure." *Electoral Studies* 15:39-52.

Blaustein, A. P., and Gilbert P. Flanz. n.d. *Constitutions of the Countries of the World.* Dobbs Ferry, NY: Oceana.

Blondel, Jean. 1968. "Party Systems and Patterns of Government in Western Democracies." *Canadian Journal of Political Science* 1:180-203.

———. 1985. *Government Ministers in the Contemporary World.* London: Sage.

———. 1987. *Political Leadership.* London: Sage.

Blondel, Jean, and Ferdinand Müller-Rommel, eds. 1993. *Governing Together: The Extent and Limits of Joint Decision Making in Western European Cabinets.* New York: St. Martin's.

Blondel, Jean, and Jean-Louis Thiebault, eds. 1991. *The Profession of Government Minister in Western Europe.* New York: St. Martin's.

Bloom, Howard S., and H. Douglas Price. 1975. "Voter Response to Short-Run Economic Conditions: The Asymmetric Effect of Prosperity and Recession." *American Political Science Review* 69:1240-54.

Blumer, Herbert. 1951. *Principles of Sociology.* New York: Barnes & Noble.

Blumler, Jay G. 1983. "Communication and Turnout." In *Communicating to Voters: Television in the First European Parliamentary Elections,* ed. Jay G. Blumler. Beverly Hills, CA: Sage.

Blumler, Jay G., Malcolm Brynin, and T. J. Nossiter. 1986. "Broadcasting Finance in Transition." *European Journal of Communication* 1:343-64.

Blumler, Jay G., and Michael Gurevitch. 1995. *The Crisis of Public Communication.* London: Routledge.

Blumler, Jay G., and Dennis McQuail. 1969. *Television in Politics.* Chicago: University of Chicago Press.

Blumler, Jay G., and T. J. Nossiter, eds. 1990. *Broadcasting Finance in Transition.* Oxford: Oxford University Press.

Blumler Jay G., and Holli A. Semetko. 1987. "Mass Media and Legislative Campaigns in a Unitary Parliamentary Democracy: The Case of Britain." *Legislative Studies Quarterly* 12:415-44.

Bochel, John Main, and David Denver. 1971. "Canvassing, Turnout and Party Support: An Experiment." *British Journal of Political Science* 1:257-69.

———. 1972. "The Impact of the Campaign on the Results of Local Government Elections." *British Journal of Political Science* 2:239-60.

Bogdanor, Vernon, and David Butler, eds. 1983. *Democracy and Elections.* Cambridge: Cambridge University Press.

Boissevain, Jeremy. 1965. *Saints and Fireworks: Religion and Politics in Rural Malta.* London: Athlone.

Boll, Bernhard, and Thomas Poguntke. 1992. "Germany: The 1990 All-German Election Campaign." In *Electoral Strategies and Political Marketing,* ed. Shaun Bowler and David M. Farrell. Houndmills: Macmillan.

Bollen, Kenneth. 1980. "Issues in the Comparative Measurement of Political Democracy." *American Sociological Review* 45:370-90.

———. 1993. "Liberal Democracy: Validity and Method Factors in Cross-National Measures." *American Journal of Political Science* 37:1207-30.

Borre, Ole. 1984. "Critical Electoral Change in Scandinavia." In *Electoral Change in Advanced Industrial Democracies,* ed. Russell Dalton, Scott Flanagan, and Paul Beck. Princeton, NJ: Princeton University Press.

Bowler, Shaun. 1990. "Voter Perceptions and Party Strategies: An Empirical Approach." *Comparative Politics* 23:61-83.

Bowler, Shaun, and David M. Farrell. 1992a. "Conclusion: The Contemporary Election Campaign." In *Electoral Strategies and Political Marketing,* ed. Shaun Bowler and David M. Farrell. New York: St. Martin's.

———, eds. 1992b. *Electoral Strategies and Political Marketing.* New York: St. Martin's.

Boyd, Richard W. 1981. "The Decline of U.S. Voter Turnout: Structural Explanations." *American Politics Quarterly* 9:133-59.

Boyer, J. Patrick. 1983. *Election Law in Canada.* Toronto: Butterworths.

Brady, Henry E., and Richard Johnston. 1987. "What's the Primary Message: Horse Race or Issue Journalism." In *Media and Momentum,* ed. Gary R. Orren and Nelson W. Polsby. Chatham, NJ: Chatham House.

Brams, Steven J., and Peter C. Fishburn. 1982. *Approval Voting.* Boston: Birkhauser.

———. 1988. "Does Approval Voting Elect the Lowest Denominator?" *PS: Political Science and Politics* 21:277-84.

Brants, Kees, and Karen Siune. 1992. "Public Broadcasting in a State of Flux." In *Dynamics of Media Politics: Broadcasting and Electronic Media in Western Europe,* ed. Karen Suine and Wolfgang Truetzschler. London: Sage.

Braunthal, Gerald. 1983. *The West German Social Democrats, 1969-1982.* Boulder, CO: Westview.

Braybrooke, David. 1968. *Three Tests for Democracy: Personal Rights, Human Welfare, Collective Preference.* New York: Random House.

Brittan, Samuel. 1977. *The Economic Consequences of Democracy.* London: Temple Smith.

Brosius, Hans Berndt, and Hans Mathias Kepplinger. 1990. "The Agenda-Setting Function of Television: Static and Dynamic Views." *Communication Research* 17:183-211.

———. 1992. "Linear and Non-Linear Models of Agenda-Setting on Television." *Journal of Broadcasting and Electronic Media* 36:5-24.

———. 1995. "Killer and Victim Issues: Issue Competition in the Agenda-Setting Process of German Television." *International Journal of Public Opinion Research* 7:211-31.

Broughton, David. 1995. *Public Opinion Polling and Politics in Britain.* Hempstead: Harvester Wheatsheaf.

Brown, Steven D., Ronald D. Lambert, Barry J. Kay, and James E. Curtis. 1988. "In the Eye of the Beholder: Leader Images in Canada." *Canadian Journal of Political Science* 21:729-55.

Budge, Ian, and Dennis Farlie. 1983. *Explaining and Predicting Elections.* London: Allen and Unwin.

Budge, Ian, and Hans Keman. 1990a. *Parties and Democracy: Coalition Formation and Government Functioning in Twenty States.* Oxford: Oxford University Press.

———. 1990b. *Comparative Federalism and Federation.* London: Harvester Wheatsheaf.

Budge, Ian, David Robertson, and D. Hearl. 1987. *Ideology, Strategy and Party Change.* Cambridge: Cambridge University Press.

Burnham, Walter Dean. 1965. "The Changing Shape of the American Political Universe." *American Political Science Review* 59:7-28.

———. 1970. *Critical Elections and the Mainsprings of American Politics.* New York: Norton.

Burrell, Barbara. 1993. "Party Decline, Party Transformation and Gender Politics: The USA." In *Gender and Party Politics,* ed. Joni Lovenduski and Pippa Norris. London: Sage.

———. 1994. *A Woman's Place Is in the House.* Ann Arbor: University of Michigan Press.

Butler, David, and Gareth Butler. 1986. *British Political Facts 1900-1985.* Houndmills: Macmillan.

Butler, David, and Dennis Kavanagh. 1988. *The British General Election of 1987.* London: Macmillan.

———. 1992. *The British General Election of 1992.* London: Macmillan.

Butler, David, and Uwe Kitzinger. 1976. *The 1975 Referendum.* London: Macmillan.

Butler, David, Howard Penniman, and Austin Ranney, eds. 1981. *Democracy at the Polls.* Washington, DC: American Enterprise Institute.

Butler, David, and Austin Ranney, eds. 1992. *Electioneering: A Comparative Study of Continuity and Change.* Oxford: Clarendon.

————, eds. 1994. *Referendums Around the World: The Growing Use of Direct Democracy.* Washington, DC: American Enterprise Institute.

Butler, David, and Donald E. Stokes. 1974. *Political Change in Britain,* 2nd ed. London: Macmillan.

Cain, Bruce E. 1978. "Strategic Voting in Britain." *American Journal of Political Science* 22:639-55.

Cain, Bruce E., John A. Ferejohn, and Morris P. Fiorina. 1987. *The Personal Vote: Constituency Service and Electoral Independence.* Cambridge, MA: Harvard University Press.

Cairns, Alan C. 1968. "The Electoral System and the Party System in Canada, 1921-1965." *Canadian Journal of Political Science* 1:55-80.

Cameron, David. 1978. "The Expansion of the Public Economy: A Comparative Analysis." *American Political Science Review* 72:1243-61.

Camp, Roderick A. 1993. *Politics in Mexico.* New York: Oxford University Press.

Campbell, Angus, Philip E. Converse, Donald E. Stokes, and Warren E. Miller. 1960. *The American Voter.* New York: John Wiley.

Campbell, Angus, Gerald Gurin, and Warren E. Miller. 1954. *The Voter Decides.* Evanston, IL: Row, Peterson.

Cansino, César, et al. 1995. "Party Government: The Search for a Theory." *International Political Science Review* 16:169-83.

Capdevielle, Jacques, Elisabeth Dupoirier, and Colette Yamal. 1988. "Tableau des électorats en mars 1978." In *France de gauche, vote à droite?* ed. Jacques Capedevielle et al. Paris: Fondation Nationale des Sciences Politiques.

Carmines, Edward, and James Stimson. 1989. *Issue Evolution: Race and the Transformation of American Politics.* Princeton, NJ: Princeton University Press.

Carter, R. F. 1962. "Some Effects of the Debates." In *The Great Debates,* ed. Sidney Kraus. Bloomington: Indiana University Press.

Carty, R. K. 1994. "Canada." *European Journal of Political Research* 26:255-68.

Caspi, Dan. 1996. "American-Style Electioneering in Israel: Americanization Versus Modernization." In *Politics, Media and Modern Democracy: An International Study of Innovations in Electoral Campaigning and Their Consequences,* ed. David L. Swanson and Paolo Mancini. New York: Praeger.

Castles, Francis G. 1967. *Pressure Groups and Political Culture: A Comparative Study.* London: Routledge and Kegan Paul.

————, ed. 1982. *The Impact of Parties.* London: Sage.

————. 1994. "The Policy Consequences of Proportional Representation." *Political Science* 46:161-71.

Castles, Francis, and Rudolf Wildenmann, eds. 1986. *Visions and Realities of Party Government.* Berlin: de Gruyter.

Caviedes, César N. 1991. *Elections in Chile: The Road Towards Redemocratization.* Boulder, CO: Rienner.

Cawson, Alan, ed. 1985. *Organized Interests and the State.* London: Sage.

Cayrol, Roland. 1988. "The Electoral Campaign and the Decision-Making Process of French Voters. In *France at the Polls, 1981 and 1986: Three National Elections,* ed. H. R. Penniman. Washington, DC: American Enterprise Institute.

Central Intelligence Agency. 1994. *The World Factbook 1994.* Washington, DC: Central Intelligence Agency.

Chaffee, Steven H., and Jack Dennis. 1979. "Presidential Debates: An Empirical Assessment." In *The Past and Future of Presidential Debates,* ed. Austin Ranney. Washington, DC: American Enterprise Institute.

Chagall, David. 1981. *The New King-Makers.* New York: Harcourt Brace Jovanovich.

Chappell, Henry W., Jr., and William R. Keech. 1985. "A New View of Political Accountability for Economic Performance." *American Political Science Review* 79:10-27.

———. 1991. "Explaining Aggregate Evaluations of Economic Performance." In *Economics and Politics: The Calculus of Support,* ed. Helmut Norpoth, Michael S. Lewis-Beck, and Jean-Dominique Lafay. Ann Arbor: University of Michigan Press.

Chartrand, Robert. 1972. *Computers and Political Campaigning.* New York: Spartan.

Chu, Yun-han. 1992. *Crafting Democracy in Taiwan.* Taipei: Institute for National Policy Research.

Clarke, Harold, et al. 1992. *Controversies in Political Economy: Canada, Great Britain, the United States.* Boulder, CO: Westview.

Clarke, Harold D., Jane Jenson, Lawrence LeDuc, and Jon H. Pammett. 1979. *Political Choice in Canada.* Toronto: McGraw-Hill Ryerson; New York: McGraw-Hill.

———. 1995. *Absent Mandate: Canadian Electoral Politics in an Era of Restructuring,* 3rd ed. Toronto: Gage.

Clarke, Harold D., and Marianne C. Stewart. 1994. "Prospections, Retrospections and Rationality: The 'Bankers' Model of Presidential Approval Reconsidered." *American Journal of Political Science* 38:1104-23.

Clarke, Harold D., Marianne C. Stewart, and Gary Zuk. 1986. "Politics, Economics, and Party Popularity in Britain, 1979-1983." *Electoral Studies* 5:123-41.

Clarke, Harold D., and Paul Whiteley. 1990. "Perceptions of Macroeconomic Performance, Government Support and Conservative Party Strategy in Britain, 1983-1987." *European Journal of Political Research* 18:97-120.

Clogg, Richard. 1987. *Parties and Elections in Greece: The Search for Legitimacy.* London: C. Hurst.

Clubb, Jerome, William Flanigan, and Nancy Zingale. 1980. *Partisan Realignment.* Beverly Hills, CA: Sage.

Cohan, Al, R. McKinlay, and Anthony Mughan. 1975. "The Used Vote and Electoral Outcomes: The Irish General Election of 1973." *British Journal of Political Science* 5:363-83.

Cohen, Akiba A., and Gadi Wolfsfeld. 1995. "Overcoming Adversity and Diversity: The Utility of Television Political Advertising in Israel." In *Political Advertising in Western Democracies,* ed. Lynda Lee Kaid and Christina Holtz-Bacha. Thousand Oaks, CA: Sage.

Cohen, Bernard C. 1963. *The Press and Foreign Policy.* Princeton, NJ: Princeton University Press.

Cohen, Jacob, and Patricia Cohen. 1983. *Applied Multiple Regression/Correlation Analysis for the Behavioral Sciences,* 2nd ed. Hillsdale, NJ: Lawrence Erlbaum.

Coleman, William D. 1987. "Federalism and Interest Group Organization." In *Federalism and the Role of the State,* ed. Herman Bakvis and William M. Chandler. Toronto: University of Toronto Press.

———. 1988. *Business and Politics: A Study of Collective Action.* Kingston: McGill-Queen's University Press.

———. 1990. "The Banking Policy Community and Financial Change." In *Policy Communities and Public Policy in Canada,* ed. William D. Coleman and Grace Skogstad. Toronto: Copp Clark Pitman.

Conover, Pamela Johnston. 1980. "The Perception of Political Figures: An Application of Attribution Theory." In *The Electorate Reconsidered*, ed. John C. Pierce and John L. Sullivan. London: Sage.

Conover, Pamela Johnston, and Stanley Feldman. 1984. "How People Organize the Political World." *American Journal of Political Science* 28:95-126.

Conover, Pamela Johnston, Stanley Feldman, and Kathleen Knight. 1987. "The Personal Underpinnings of Economic Forecasts." *American Journal of Political Science* 31:559-83.

Converse, Philip E. 1964. "The Nature of Belief Systems in Mass Publics." In *Ideology and Discontent*, ed. David E. Apter. New York: Free Press.

———. 1974. "Comment on Burnham's 'Theory and Voting Research.' " *American Political Science Review* 68:1024-7.

Converse, Philip E., and Georges Dupeux. 1962. "Politicization of the Electorate in France and the United States." *Public Opinion Quarterly* 26:1-23.

———. 1966. "DeGaulle and Eisenhower: The Public Image of the Victorious General." In *Elections and the Political Order*, Angus Campbell, Philip E. Converse, Warren E. Miller, and Donald E. Stokes. New York: John Wiley.

Conway, M. Margaret, David W. Ahern, and Gertrude A. Steuernagel. 1995. *Women and Public Policy*. Washington, DC: CQ Press.

Cooper, Barry, Allan Kornberg, and William Mishler, eds. 1988. *The Resurgence of Conservatism in Anglo-American Democracies*. Durham, NC: Duke University Press.

Copeland, Gary W. 1983. "Activating Voters in Congressional Elections." *Political Behavior* 5:391-401.

Coppedge, Michael. 1992. "Deinstitutionalization of Latin American Party Systems." Presented at the 17th International Congress of the Latin American Studies Association, Los Angeles.

———. 1994. *Strong Parties and Lame Ducks: Presidential Partyarchy and Factionalism in Venezuela*. Stanford, CA: Stanford University Press.

Cotteret, Jean-Marie, and Claude Emeri. 1994. *Les systèmes électoraux*. Paris: Presses Universitaires de France.

Cox, Gary. 1995. "The Politics of Electoral Coalition. University of California, San Diego. Typescript.

Covell, Maureen. 1991. "Parties as Institutions of National Governance." In *Representation, Integration and Political Parties in Canada*, ed. Herman Bakvis. Toronto: Dundurn.

Crête, Jean. 1992. "Television, Advertising and Canadian Elections." In *Media and Voters in Canadian Election Campaigns*, ed. Frederick J. Fletcher. Toronto: Dundurn.

Crewe, Ivor. 1981. "Electoral Participation." In *Democracy at the Polls*, ed. David Butler, Howard Penniman, and Austin Ranney. Washington, DC: American Enterprise Institute.

Crewe, Ivor, and David Denver, eds. 1985. *Electoral Change in Western Democracies: Patterns and Sources of Electoral Volatility*. London: Croom-Helm; New York: St. Martin's.

Crewe, Ivor, and B. Gosschalk. 1995. *Political Communications: The General Election Campaign of 1992*. Cambridge: Cambridge University Press.

Crewe, Ivor, and Martin Harrop. 1989. *Political Communications: The British General Election Campaign of 1987*. Cambridge: Cambridge University Press.

Crewe, Ivor, and Anthony King. 1994. "Did Major Win? Did Kinnock Lose? Leadership Effects in the 1992 Election." In *Labour's Last Chance?* ed. Anthony Heath, Roger Jowell, and John Curtice. Aldershot: Dartmouth University Press.

Crewe, Ivor, and Donald Searing. 1988. "Ideological Change in the British Conservative Party." *American Political Science Review* 82:371-84.

Curtice, John, and Holli Semetko. 1994. "Does It Matter What the Papers Say?" In *Labour's Last Chance?* ed. Anthony Heath, Roger Jowell, and John Curtice. Aldershot: Dartmouth University Press.

Curtis, Gerald L. 1971. *Election Campaigning Japanese Style.* New York: Columbia University Press.

——. 1988. *The Japanese Way of Politics.* New York: Columbia University Press.

——. 1992. "Japan." In *Electioneering: A Comparative Study of Continuity and Change,* ed. David Butler and Austin Ranney. Oxford: Clarendon.

Czudnowski, Moshe M. 1975. "Political Recruitment." In *Micropolitical Theory,* Vol. 2 of *Handbook of Political Science,* ed. Fred Greenstein and Nelson W. Polsby. Reading, MA: Addison-Wesley.

Daalder, Hans. 1983. "The Comparative Study of European Parties and Party Systems: An Overview." In *Western European Party Systems: Continuity and Change,* ed. Hans Daalder and Peter Mair. London: Sage.

Dahl, Robert A. 1961. *Who Governs? Democracy and Power in an American City.* New Haven, CT: Yale University Press.

——. 1966. "Patterns of Opposition." In *Political Oppositions in Western Democracies,* ed. Robert A. Dahl. New Haven, CT: Yale University Press.

——. 1970. *Polyarchy.* New Haven, CT: Yale University Press.

——. 1982. *Dilemmas of Pluralist Democracy.* New Haven, CT: Yale University Press.

Dahlerup, Drude. 1988. "From a Small to a Large Minority: Women in Scandinavian Politics." *Scandinavian Political Studies* 11:275-98.

Dalton, Russell. 1988, 1996. *Citizen Politics in Western Democracies.* Chatham, NJ: Chatham House.

——. 1991. "The Dynamics of Party System Change." In *Eurobarometer: The Dynamics of European Public Opinion,* ed. Karlheinz Reif and Ronald Inglehart. London: Macmillan.

——. 1992. "Two German Electorates?" In *Developments in German Politics,* Gordon Smith et al. London: Macmillan.

——. 1993a. "Strategies of Partisan Influence: West European Environmental Groups." In *The Politics of Social Protest,* ed. J. Craig Jenkins and Bert Klandermans. Minneapolis: University of Minnesota Press.

——, ed. 1993b. *Citizens, Protest, and Democracy.* Special issue of *Annals of the American Academy of Political and Social Science,* Vol. 528. Newbury Park, CA: Sage.

——. 1994. *The Green Rainbow: Environmental Groups in Western Europe.* New Haven, CT: Yale University Press.

Dalton, Russell, and Wilhelm Bürklin. 1996. "The Two Electorates." In *Germans Divided,* ed. Russell Dalton. New York and Oxford: Berg.

Dalton, Russell, Scott Flanagan, and Paul Allen Beck, eds. 1984. *Electoral Change in Advanced Industrial Democracies.* Princeton, NJ: Princeton University Press.

Dalton, Russell J., and Manfred Kuechler, eds. 1990. *Challenging the Political Order: New Social and Political Movements in Western Democracies.* New York: Oxford University Press.

Dalton, Russell J., and Martin P. Wattenberg. 1993. "The Not So Simple Act of Voting." In *The State of the Discipline,* ed. Ada W. Finifter. Washington, DC: American Political Science Association.

Davidson, Chandler, and Bernard Grofman, eds. 1994. *Quiet Revolution in the South.* Princeton, NJ: Princeton University Press.

Davis, D. K. 1979. "Influence on Vote Decisions." In *The Great Debates: Carter vs. Ford, 1976,* ed. Sidney Kraus. Bloomington: Indiana University Press.

de Guchteneire, Paul, Lawrence LeDuc, and Richard G. Niemi. 1985. "A Compendium of Survey Studies of Elections Around the World." *Electoral Studies* 4:159-74.

———. 1991. "A Compendium of Survey Studies of Elections Around the World, Update 1." *Electoral Studies* 10:231-43.

de Lima, Vinicio A. 1988. "The State, Television and Political Power in Brazil." *Critical Studies in Mass Communication* 5:108-28.

———. 1993. "Brazilian Television in the 1989 Presidential Campaign: Constructing a President." In *Television, Politics and the Transition to Democracy in Latin America,* ed. Thomas A. Skidmore. Baltimore: Johns Hopkins University Press.

Del Castillo, Pilar. 1989. "Financing of Spanish Political Parties." In *Comparative Political Finance in the 1980s,* ed. Herbert E. Alexander. Cambridge: Cambridge University Press.

Delli Carpini, Michael X., and Lee Sigelman. 1986. "Do Yuppies Matter? Competing Explanations of Their Political Distinctiveness." *Public Opinion Quarterly* 50:502-18.

Denver, David, and Gordon Hands. 1993. "Measuring the Intensity and Effectiveness of Constituency Campaigning in the 1992 General Election." In *British Elections and Parties Yearbook, 1993,* ed. David Denver, Pippa Norris, David Broughton, and Colin Rallings. Hemel: Harvester Wheatsheaf.

Deth, Jan van, and J. Janssen. 1994. "Party Attachments and Political Fragmentation in Europe." *European Journal of Political Research* 25:87-109.

Diamond, Larry, Juan J. Linz, and Seymour Martin Lipset. 1995. *Politics in Developing Countries: Comparing Experiences With Democracy.* Boulder, CO: Rienner.

Diamond, Larry, and Marc F. Plattner, eds. 1993. *The Global Resurgence of Democracy.* Baltimore: Johns Hopkins University Press.

Diez-Nicolas, Juan, and Holli A. Semetko. 1995. "La Televisión y las Elecciones de 1993." In *Communicación Política,* ed. Alejandro Muñoz-Alonso and Juan Ignacio Rospir. Madrid: Editorial Universitas.

Dionne, E. J. 1976. "What Technology Has Not Changed: Continuity and Localism in British Politics." In *Changing Campaign Techniques: Elections and Values in Contemporary Democracies,* ed. Louis Maisel. Beverly Hills, CA: Sage.

Diskin, Abraham. 1991. *Elections and Voters in Israel.* New York: Praeger.

Diskin, Hanna, and Abraham Diskin. 1995. "The Politics of Electoral Reform in Israel." *International Political Science Review* 16:31-46.

Dodd, Lawrence C. 1976. *Coalitions in Parliamentary Government.* Princeton, NJ: Princeton University Press.

Dodson, Debra, and Susan J. Carroll. 1991. *Reshaping the Agenda: Women in State Legislatures.* New Brunswick, NJ: Center for American Women in Politics.

Dominelli, Lena, and Gudrún Jónsdóttir. 1988. "Feminist Political Organization in Iceland." *Feminist Review* 30:36-60.

Downs, Anthony. 1957. *An Economic Theory of Democracy.* New York: Harper and Row.

———. 1972. "Up and Down With Ecology—The 'Issue Attention' Cycle." *Public Interest* 12:38-50.

Dragnich, Alex N., and Jorgen Rasmussen. 1982. *Major European Governments,* 6th ed. Homewood, IL: Dorsey.

Duch, Raymond M. 1995. "Economic Chaos and the Fragility of Democratic Transition in Former Communist Regimes." *Journal of Politics* 57:121-58.

Dunleavy, Patrick, and Christopher Husbands. 1985. *British Democracy at the Crossroads.* London: Allen and Unwin.

Dunleavy, Patrick, and Helen Margetts. 1995. "Understanding the Dynamics of Electoral Reform." *International Political Science Review* 16:9-30.

Dutton, William H., Jay G. Blumler, and Kenneth L. Kraemer. 1987. *Wired Cities: Shaping the Future of Communications.* Boston: GK Hall.

Duverger, Maurice. 1951, 1954, 1959. *Les Partis Politiques.* Paris: Colin; *Political Parties.* London: Methuen; 2nd ed. New York: John Wiley.

———. 1980. "A New Political System Model: Semi-Presidential Government." *European Journal of Political Research* 8:165-87.

Eckstein, Harry. 1960. *Pressure Group Politics: The Case of the British Medical Association.* London: Allen and Unwin.

Edelstein, Alex. 1993. "Thinking About the Criterion Variable in Agenda-Setting Research." *Journal of Communication* 43:85-99.

Ehrenhalt, Alan. 1992. *The United States of Ambition.* New York: Times Books.

Ehrmann, Henry, and Martin A. Schain. 1992. *Politics in France,* 5th ed. New York: Harper-Collins.

Eijk, Cees van der, Mark Franklin, et al. 1996. *Choosing Europe? The European Electorate and National Politics in the Face of the Union.* Ann Arbor: University of Michigan Press.

Eijk, Cees van der, Mark Franklin, and Michael Marsh. 1996. "What Voters Teach Us About Europe-Wide Elections; What Europe-Wide Elections Teach Us About Voters." *Electoral Studies* 15.

Eijk, Cees van der, and B. Niemöller. 1983. *Electoral Change in the Netherlands.* Amsterdam: CT Press.

Elder, Niel, Alistair Thomas, and David Arter. 1988. *The Consensual Democracies? The Government and Politics of the Scandinavian States.* Oxford: Basil Blackwell.

Elklit, J. 1991. "Sub-National Election Campaigns: The Danish Local Elections of November 1989." *Scandinavian Political Studies* 14:219-39.

Epstein, Leon. 1967. *Political Parties in Western Democracies.* New Brunswick, NJ: Transaction Books.

Epstein, Leon. 1980. *Political Parties in Western Democracies,* 2nd ed. New Brunswick, NJ: Transaction Books.

Erbring, Lutz, Edie N. Goldenberg, and Arthur H. Miller. 1980. "Front-Page News and Real-World Clues: A New Look at Agenda-Setting by the Media." *American Journal of Political Science* 24:16-49.

Erickson, Lynda. 1993. "Making Her Way In: Women, Parties, and Candidacies in Canada." In *Gender and Party Politics,* ed. Joni Lovenduski and Pippa Norris. London: Sage.

Erikson, Robert. 1989. "The Puzzle of Low Voter Turnout in the United States." In *Perspectives on American and Texas Politics,* ed. Donald Lutz and Kent Tudlin, 2nd ed. Dubuque, IA: Kendal/Hunt.

Erlanger, Steven. 1994. "Russians Watch First War on Uncensored TV, to Yeltsin's Alarm." *New York Times,* December 20, A14.

Esaiasson, Peter. 1992. "Scandinavia." In *Electioneering: A Comparative Study of Continuity and Change,* ed. David Butler and Austin Ranney. Oxford: Clarendon.

———. 1993. "Traits and Evaluations of Candidates in Presidential and Parliamentary Elections." Presented at the annual meeting of the Midwest American Political Science Association, Chicago.

Esberey, Joy, and Grace Skogstad. 1991. "Organized Interests." In *Introductory Readings in Canadian Government and Politics,* ed. Robert M. Krause and R. H. Wagenberg. Toronto: Copp Clark Pitman.

Eulau, Heinz, and Michael S. Lewis-Beck, eds. 1985. *Economic Conditions and Electoral Outcomes: The United States and Western Europe.* New York: Agathon.

Eulau, Heinz, and John C. Wahlke. 1978. *The Politics of Representation.* London: Sage.

Euromedia Research Group. 1992. *Dynamics of Media Politics: Broadcasting and Electronic Media in Western Europe.* London: Sage.

Europa World Year Book. 1994. London: Europa Publications.

European Journal of Communication. 1992. Special issue titled "Media and the Law: The Changing Landscape of Western Europe." 7.

Evans, Robert R., ed. 1973. *Social Movements: A Reader and Source Book.* Chicago: Rand McNally.

Fair, Ray C. 1978. "The Effect of Economic Events on Votes for President." *Review of Economics and Statistics* 60:159-73.

Falter, Jürgen W. 1991. *Hitler's Wähler.* Munich: Beck.

Farrell, D. M. 1986. "The Strategy to Market Fine Gael in 1981." *Irish Political Studies* 1:1-14.

———. 1987. "Campaign Strategies: The Selling of the Parties." In *How Ireland Voted: The Irish General Election 1987,* ed. Michael Laver, Peter Mair, and Richard Sinnott. Dublin: Poolbeg.

———. 1990. "Campaign Strategies and Media Coverage." In *How Ireland Voted 1989,* ed. Michael Gallagher and Richard Sinnott. Galway: Centre for the Study of Irish Elections.

———. 1993. "Campaign Strategies." In *How Ireland Voted 1992,* ed. Michael Gallagher and Michael Laver. Dublin: Folens.

———. Forthcoming. "The Transition of Irish Election Campaigning From the Traditional to the Modern." In *Government, Politics and the Media in Ireland,* ed. Tom Garvin, Maurice Manning, and Richard Sinnott.

Farrell, David M., and Martin Wortmann. 1987. "Party Strategies in the Electoral Market: Political Marketing in West Germany, Britain and Ireland." *European Journal of Political Research* 15:297-318.

Feldman, Stanley. 1982. "Economic Self-Interest and Political Behavior." *American Journal of Political Science* 26:446-66.

Feldman, Stanley, and Patricia Conley. 1991. "Explaining Explanations of Changing Economic Conditions." In *Economics and Politics: The Calculus of Support,* ed. Helmut Norpoth, Michael S. Lewis-Beck, and Jean-Dominique Lafay. Ann Arbor: University of Michigan Press.

Festinger, Leon. 1957. *A Theory of Cognitive Dissonance.* Evanston, IL: Row, Peterson.

Finer, Samuel E. 1975. *Adversary Politics and Electoral Reform.* London: Wigram.

Fiorina, Morris. 1981. *Retrospective Voting in American National Elections.* New Haven, CT: Yale University Press.

———. 1991. "Elections and the Economy in the 1980s: Short- and Long-Term Effects." In *Politics and Economics in the Eighties,* ed. A. Alesina and G. Carliner. Chicago: University of Chicago Press.

Fiorina, Morris, and Kenneth Shepsle. 1989. "Is Negative Voting an Artifact?" *American Journal of Political Science* 33:423-39.

Fishkin, James. 1991. *Democracy and Deliberation.* New Haven, CT: Yale University Press.

Fisichella, Dominico. 1984. "The Double-Ballot as a Weapon Against Anti-System Parties." In *Choosing an Electoral System: Issues and Alternatives,* ed. Arend Lijphart and Bernard Grofman. New York: Praeger.

Fiske, S. T., and S. E. Taylor. 1984. *Social Cognition.* Reading, MA: Addison-Wesley.

Fitzgibbon, Russell H. 1956. *Uruguay: Portrait of a Democracy.* London: Allen and Unwin.

Fletcher, Frederick J., ed. 1991. *Media, Elections, and Democracy.* Toronto: Dundurn.

———, ed. 1992. *Media and Voters in Canadian Election Campaigns.* Toronto: Dundurn.

Foley, Michael. 1993. *The Rise of the British Presidency.* Manchester: Manchester University Press.

Fowler, Linda. 1993. *Candidates, Congress and the American Democracy.* Ann Arbor: University of Michigan Press.

Fowler, Linda, and Robert D. McClure. 1989. *Political Ambition: Who Decides to Run for Congress.* New Haven, CT: Yale University Press.

Fox, Elizabeth, ed. 1988. *Media and Politics in Latin America: The Struggle for Democracy.* Newbury Park, CA: Sage.

Fox, Paul, and Graham White, eds. 1991. *Politics: Canada,* 7th ed. Toronto: McGraw-Hill.

Franklin, Mark. 1985. *The Decline of Class Voting in Britain: Changes in the Basis of Electoral Choice, 1964-1983.* Oxford: Oxford University Press.

Franklin, Mark N., and Thomas T. Mackie. 1983. "Familiarity and Inertia in the Formation of Governing Coalitions in Parliamentary Democracies." *British Journal of Political Science* 13:275-98.

Franklin, Mark, Thomas T. Mackie, Henry Valen, et al. 1992. *Electoral Change: Responses to Evolving Social and Attitudinal Structures in Western Countries.* Cambridge: Cambridge University Press.

Franklin, Mark, Cees van der Eijk, and Erik Oppenhuis. 1995. "The Motivational Basis of Electoral Participation: European Elections Provide a Critical Test." Presented at the European Consortium for Political Research Joint Sessions Workshops, Bordeaux.

Franklin, Mark, Richard G. Niemi, and Guy Whitten. 1994. "Two Faces of Tactical Voting." *British Journal of Political Science* 24:549-57.

Freeland, Chrystia. 1995. "Capitalism Exposes the Poverty Gap." Financial Times Survey: Russia. *Financial Times,* April 10.

Frendreis, John P., James L. Gibson, and Laura L. Vertz. 1990. "The Electoral Relevance of Local Party Organizations." *American Political Science Review* 84:225-35.

Friedman, Milton. 1977. "Inflation and Unemployment: The 1976 Alfred Nobel Memorial Lecture." Institute of Economic Affairs, London.

Frizzell, A., et al. 1989. *The Canadian General Election of 1988.* Ottawa: Carleton University Press.

Fuchs, Dieter, and Hans-Dieter Klingemann. 1989. "The Left-Right Schema." In *Continuities in Political Action,* M. Kent Jennings, Jan van Deth, et al. Berlin: de Gruyter.

Fuchs, Peter, and Hans-Dieter Klingemann. 1995. "Citizens and the State: A Relationship Transformed." In *Citizens and the State,* ed. Hans-Dieter Klingemann and Dieter Fuchs. Oxford: Oxford University Press.

Fukai, Shigeko N., and Haruhiro Fukui. 1992. "Elite Recruitment and Political Leadership." *PS: Political Science and Politics* 25:25-36.

Gallagher, Michael, Michael Laver, and Peter Mair. 1995. *Representative Government in Modern Europe,* 2nd ed. New York: McGraw-Hill.

Gallagher, Michael, and Michael Marsh, eds. 1988. *Candidate Selection in Comparative Perspective.* London: Sage.

Garramone, Gina M. 1985. "Effects of Negative Political Advertising: The Roles of Sponsor and Rebuttal." *Journal of Broadcasting and Electronic Media* 29:147-59.

Gelb, Joyce. 1989. *Feminism and Politics: A Comparative Perspective.* Berkeley: University of California Press.

Gerstle, Jacques. 1992. "Election Communication in France." In *Media, Elections and Democracy,* ed. Frederick H. Fletcher. Toronto: Dundurn.

Giles, Michael, and Marilyn Dantico. 1982. "Political Participation and the Neighborhood Social Context." *American Journal of Political Science* 26:144-50.

Ginsberg, Benjamin. 1982. *The Consequences of Consent.* Reading, MA: Addison-Wesley.

Glaser, Theodore, and Charles Salmon. 1991. *Public Opinion and the Communication of Consent.* New York: Guilford.

Gluchowski, Peter. 1987. Lebensstile und Wandel der Wählerschaft in der Bundesrepublik Deutschland. *Aus Politik und Zeitgeschichte,* March 21, 18-32.

Godwin, R. Kenneth. 1988. *One Billion Dollars of Influence: The Direct Marketing of Politics.* Chatham, NJ: Chatham House.

Goergen, Christian, and Helmut Norpoth. 1992. "Government Turnover and Economic Accountability." *Electoral Studies* 10:191-207.

Goldthorpe, John. 1980. *Social Mobility and Class Structure in Modern Britain.* Oxford: Clarendon.

Gosnell, Harold F. 1927. *Getting Out the Vote: An Experiment in the Stimulation of Voting.* Chicago: University of Chicago Press.

Grabendorff, Wolf. 1992. "The Party Internationals and Democracy in Central America." In *Political Parties and Democracy in Central America,* ed. Louis W. Goodman, William M. LeoGrande, and Johanna Mendelson. Boulder, CO: Westview.

Graber, Doris A. 1988. *Processing the News.* New York: Longman.

———. 1993. *Mass Media and American Politics.* Washington DC: CQ Press.

Graetz, Brian, and Ian McAllister. 1987a. "Popular Evaluations of Party Leaders in the Anglo-American Democracies." In *Political Elites in the Anglo-American Democracies,* ed. Harold D. Clarke and Moshe M. Czudnowski. DeKalb: Northern Illinois University Press.

———. 1987b. "Party Leaders and Election Outcomes in Britain, 1974-83." *Comparative Political Studies* 19:484-507.

Greenstein, Fred I. 1965. *Children and Politics.* New Haven, CT: Yale University Press.

Grumm, John. 1958. "Theories of Electoral Systems." *Midwest Journal of Political Science* 2:357-76.

Guadagnini, Marila. 1993. "A Partitocrazia Without Women: The Case of the Italian Party System." In *Gender and Party Politics,* ed. Joni Lovenduski and Pippa Norris. London: Sage.

Gundle, Stephen. 1992. "Italy." In *Electioneering: A Comparative Study of Continuity and Change,* ed. David Butler and Austin Ranney. Oxford: Clarendon.

Gunther, Richard. 1989. "Electoral Laws, Party Systems, and Elites: The Case of Spain." *American Political Science Review* 83:835-59.

Gunther, Richard, P. Nikiforos Diamandouros, and Hans-Jurgen Puhle. 1995. *Southern Europe in Comparative Perspective.* Baltimore: Johns Hopkins University Press.

Haavio-Mannila, Elina, et al. 1985. *Unfinished Democracy: Women in Nordic Politics.* New York: Pergamon.

Haddow, Rodney. 1991. "The Poverty Policy Community in Canada's Liberal Welfare State." In *Policy Communities and Public Policy in Canada,* ed. William D. Coleman and Grace Skogstad. Toronto: Copp Clark Pitman.

Hall, Peter. 1986. *Governing the Economy.* London: Polity.

Haller, H. Brandon, and Helmut Norpoth. 1994. "Let the Good Times Roll: The Economic Expectations of American Voters." *American Journal of Political Science* 38:625-50.

———. 1995. "News and Opinion: The Economy and the American Voter." Presented at the annual meeting of the Midwest Political Science Association, Chicago.

Hamill, Ruth, Milton Lodge, and Frederick Blake. 1985. "The Breadth, Depth, and Utility of Class, Partisan and Ideological Schemata." *American Journal of Political Science* 29:850-70.

Hammond, John. 1986. Yuppies. *Public Opinion Quarterly* 50:487-501.

Hardin, Russell. 1982. *Collective Action.* Baltimore: Johns Hopkins University Press.

Harrison, Michael J., and Michael Marsh. 1994. "What Can He Do for Us? Leader Effects on Party Fortunes in Ireland." *Electoral Studies* 13:289-312.

Harrop, Martin, and William L. Miller. 1987. *Elections and Voters: A Comparative Introduction.* Houndmills: Macmillan.

Harvey, Neil. 1990. "Peasant Strategies and Corporatism in Chiapas." In *Popular Movements and Political Change in Mexico,* ed. Joe Foweraker and Ann L. Craig. Boulder, CO: Rienner.

Heath, Anthony, Roger Jowell, and John Curtice. 1985. *How Britain Votes.* New York: Pergamon.

———. 1991. *Understanding Political Change: The British Voter 1964-1987.* New York: Pergamon.

Heberle, Rudolf. 1951. *Social Movements: An Introduction to Political Sociology.* New York: Appleton-Century-Crofts.

Helander, Voitto. 1995. "Legislative Recruitment in Finland." Presented at the ECPR Joint Sessions, Bordeaux.

Herrnson, Paul. 1986. "Do Parties Make a Difference? The Role of Party Organization in Congressional Elections." *Journal of Politics* 48:589-615.

Hesse, Kurt. 1990. "Cross-Border Mass Communication From West to East Germany." *European Journal of Communication* 5:355-71.

Hibbs, Douglas A., Jr. 1977. "Political Parties and Macroeconomic Policy." *American Political Science Review* 71:1467-87.

———. 1992. "Partisan Theory After Fifteen Years." *European Journal of Political Economy* 8:361-73.

Hibbs, Douglas A., Jr., and Heino Fassbender, eds. 1981. *Contemporary Political Economy.* Amsterdam: North-Holland.

Hiebert, Ray, Robert Jones, John d'Arc Lorenz, and Ernest Lotito, eds. 1975. *The Political Image Merchants: Strategies for the Seventies.* Washington, DC: Acropolis.

Hillman, Richard S. 1994. *Democracy and the Privileged: Crisis and Transition in Venezuela.* Boulder, CO: Rienner.

Hirczy, Wolfgang. 1992. *Electoral Participation.* Ann Arbor, MI: University Microfilms (University of Houston Ph.D. Dissertation).

———. 1995. "Explaining Near-Universal Turnout: The Case of Malta." *European Journal of Political Research* 27:255-72.

Hirschman, Albert O. 1970. *Exit, Voice, and Loyalty: Responses to Decline in Firms, Organizations, and States.* Cambridge, MA: Harvard University Press.

Holbrook, Thomas M. 1996. *The Sound and the Fury: The Impact of Campaigns in Contemporary Presidential Elections.* Thousand Oaks, CA: Sage.

Holmberg, Sören. 1994. "Party Identification Compared Across the Atlantic." In *Elections at Home and Abroad,* ed. M. Kent Jennings and Thomas Mann. Ann Arbor: University of Michigan Press.

Howell, Susan E., and William S. Oiler. 1981. "Campaign Activities and Local Election Outcomes." *Social Science Quarterly* 62:151-60.

Hrebenar, Ronald J. 1992. *The Japanese Party System.* Boulder, CO: Westview.

Huckfeldt, R. Robert. 1979. "Political Participation and the Neighborhood Social Context." *American Journal of Political Science* 23:579-92.

———. 1986. *Politics in Context: Assimilation and Conflict in Urban Neighborhoods.* New York: Agathon.

Huckfeldt, Robert, and Carol Kohfeld. 1989. *Race and the Decline of Class in American Politics.* Urbana: University of Illinois Press.

Huckfeldt, Robert, and John Sprague. 1992. "Political Parties and Electoral Mobilization: Political Structure, Social Structure, and the Party Canvass." *American Political Science Review* 86:70-86.

Hudson, John. 1984. "Prime Ministerial Popularity in the UK: 1960-81. *Political Studies* 32:86-97.

Huegel, R., W. Degenhardt, and H. Weiss. 1989. "Structural Equation Models for the Analysis of the Agenda-Setting Process." *European Journal of Communication* 4:191-210.

Hunter, Floyd. 1953. *Community Power Structure.* New York: Doubleday.

Huntington, Samuel. 1991. *The Third Wave: Democratization in the Late Twentieth Century.* Cambridge, MA: Harvard University Press.

Ignazi, Piero. 1992. "The Silent Counter-Revolution: Hypotheses on the Emergence of Extreme Right-Wing Parties in Europe." *European Journal of Political Research* 22:3-34.

————. 1994. *L'Estrema Destra in Europa.* Bologna: Il Mulino.

Ikenberry, G. John, David A. Lake, and Michael Mastanduno. 1988. "Introduction: Approaches to Explaining American Foreign Economic Policy." In *The State and American Foreign Economic Policy,* ed. G. John Ikenberry, David A. Lake, and Michael Mastanduno. Ithaca, NY: Cornell University Press.

Inglehart, Ronald. 1977. *Silent Revolution: Changing Values and Political Styles Among Western Publics.* Ann Arbor: University of Michigan Press.

————. 1979. "Political Action." In *Political Action,* Samuel Barnes, Max Kaase, et al. Beverly Hills, CA: Sage.

————. 1984. "Changing Cleavage Alignments in Western Democracies." In *Electoral Change in Advanced Industrial Democracies,* ed. Russell Dalton, Scott Flanagan, and Paul Beck. Princeton, NJ: Princeton University Press.

————. 1990a. *Culture Shift in Advanced Industrial Society.* Princeton, NJ: Princeton University Press.

————. 1990b. "Values, Ideology, and Cognitive Mobilization in New Social Movements." In *Challenging the Political Order,* ed. Russell J. Dalton and Manfred Kuechler. New York: Oxford University Press.

Inkeles, Alex. 1991. *On Measuring Democracy.* New Brunswick, NJ: Transaction.

Insko, C. A., and J. Schopler. 1972. *Experimental Social Psychology.* New York: Academic Press.

Inter-Parliamentary Union. 1986. *Parliaments of the World: A Comparative Reference Compendium,* 2nd ed. Hants: Gower.

————. 1990-1992. *Chronicle of Parliamentary Elections and Developments.* Geneva: Inter-Parliamentary Union.

————. 1992. *Women and Political Power.* Geneva: Inter-Parliamentary Union.

————. 1993. *Electoral Systems: A World-Wide Comparative Study.* Geneva: Inter-Parliamentary Union.

————. 1994a. *Chronicle of Elections.* Geneva: Inter-Parliamentary Union.

————. 1994b. *Distribution of Seats Between Men and Women in the 178 National Parliaments Existing as at 30 June 1994.* Geneva: Inter-Parliamentary Union.

Irwin, Galen, and Karl Dittrich. 1984. "And the Walls Came Tumbling Down: Party Dealignment in the Netherlands." In *Electoral Change in Advanced Industrial Democracies,* ed. Russell Dalton, Scott Flanagan, and Paul Allen Beck. Princeton, NJ: Princeton University Press.

Iyengar, Shanto. 1991. *Is Anyone Responsible?* Chicago: University of Chicago Press.

Iyengar, Shanto, and Donald R. Kinder. 1987. *News That Matters: Agenda-Setting and Priming in a Television Age.* Chicago: University of Chicago Press.

Jackman, Robert. 1975. *Politics and Social Equality: A Comparative Analysis.* New York: John Wiley.

————. 1987. "Political Institutions and Voter Turnout in the Industrial Democracies." *American Political Science Review* 81:405-23.

Jackman, Robert, and Ross A. Miller. 1975. "Voter Turnout in the Industrial Democracies During the 1980s." *Comparative Political Studies* 27:467-92.

Jackman, Simon. 1993. "Economic Expectations, Realizations, and Presidential Approval."
    Presented at the annual meeting of the Midwest Political Science Association, Chicago.

Jackson, Brooks. 1990. *Broken Promise: Why the Federal Election Commission Failed.* Winchester, MA: Unwin Hyman.

Jackson, Robert, Doreen Jackson, and Nicholas Baxter-Moore. 1986. *Politics in Canada: Culture, Institutions, Behavior and Public Policy.* Toronto: Prentice Hall.

Jacobson, Gary. 1978. "The Effects of Campaign Spending in Congressional Elections." *American Political Science Review* 72:469-91.

———. 1980. *Money in Congressional Elections.* New Haven, CT: Yale University Press.

Jasiewicz, Krzysztof. 1994. "Poland." *European Journal of Political Research* 26:397-408.

Jenson, Jane. 1985. "Struggling for Identity: The Women's Movement and the State in Western Europe." In *Women and Politics in Western Europe,* ed. Sylvia Bashevkin. London: Cass.

Johnson-Parker, Karen, and Tony Parker. 1994. "Telephone Contact Basics." *Campaigns and Elections* 15(7): 38.

Johnston, Richard, André Blais, Henry E. Brady, and Jean Crête. 1992. *Letting the People Decide: Dynamics of a Canadian Election.* Stanford, CA: Stanford University Press.

Johnston, Ron J., and Charles J. Pattie. 1995. "The Impact of Spending on Party Constituency Campaigns at Recent British General Elections." *Party Politics* 1:261-73.

Jones, Mark P. 1995. "A Guide to the Electoral Systems of the Americas." *Electoral Studies* 14:5-22.

Jowell, Roger, Sharon Witherspoon, and Lindsay Brook, eds. 1989. *British Social Attitudes: Special International Report.* Aldershot: Gower.

Jupp, James. 1982. *Party Politics: Australia 1966-81.* Sydney: Allen and Unwin.

Kaase, Max. 1994. "Is There Personalization of Politics: Candidates and Voting Behavior in Germany." *International Political Science Review* 15:211-30.

Kaid, Lynda Lee. 1981. "Political Advertising." In *The Handbook of Political Communication,* ed. Dan Nimmo and K. R. Sanders. Beverly Hills, CA: Sage.

Kaid, Lynda Lee, and J. Boydston. 1987. "An Experimental Study of the Effectiveness of Negative Political Advertisements." *Communication Quarterly* 35:193-201.

Kaid, Lynda Lee, and Christina Holtz-Bacha. 1995a. "Political Advertising Across Cultures: Comparing Content, Styles and Effects." In *Political Advertising in Western Democracies: Parties and Candidates on Television,* ed. Lynda Lee Kaid and Christina Holtz-Bacha. Thousand Oaks, CA: Sage.

———. 1995b. *Political Advertising in Western Democracies: Parties and Candidates on Television.* Thousand Oaks, CA: Sage.

Karatnycky, Adam. 1995. "Democracies on the Rise: Democracies at Risk." *Freedom Review* 26:5-10.

Kariel, Henry S., ed. 1970. *Frontiers of Democratic Theory.* New York: Random House.

Karvonen, Lauri. 1991. "The Study of Election Campaigns: An Introduction." *Scandinavian Political Studies* 14:195-203.

Karvonen, Lauri, and Per Selle. 1995. *Women in Nordic Politics.* Aldershot: Dartmouth University Press.

Katona, George. 1975. *Psychological Economics.* New York: Elsevier.

Katz, Daniel, and Henry Valen. 1964. *Political Parties in Norway: A Community Study.* Oslo: Universitetsförlaget.

Katz, Elihu, and J. J. Feldman. 1962. "The Debates in the Light of Research: A Survey of Surveys." In *The Great Debates,* ed. Sidney Kraus. Bloomington: Indiana University Press.

Katz, Elihu, and Paul Lazarsfeld. 1955. *Personal Influence.* New York: Free Press.

Katz, Richard S. 1980. *A Theory of Parties and Electoral Systems.* Baltimore: Johns Hopkins University Press.

———. 1986. "Party Government: A Rationalistic Conception." In *The Future of Party Government,* ed. Frances G. Castles and Rudolf Wildemanns. Berlin: de Gruyter.

———, ed. 1987. *Party Government: European and American Experiences.* Berlin: de Gruyter.

———. 1990. "Party as Linkage: A Vestigial Function?" *European Journal of Political Research* 18:143-61.

———. 1997. *Democracy and Elections.* New York: Oxford University Press.

Katz, Richard S., and Robin Kolodny. 1994. "Party Organization as an Empty Vessel: Parties in American Politics." In *How Parties Organize: Change and Adaptation in Party Organizations in Western Democracies,* ed. Richard S. Katz and Peter Mair. London: Sage.

Katz, Richard S., and Peter Mair, eds. 1992. *Party Organizations: A Data Handbook on Party Organizations in Western Democracies, 1960-90.* London: Sage.

———. 1993. "The Evolution of Party Organizations in Europe: The Three Faces of Party Organization." *American Review of Politics* 14:593-618.

———, eds. 1994. *How Parties Organize: Change and Adaptation in Party Organizations in Western Democracies.* London: Sage.

———. 1995. "Changing Models of Party Organization and Party Democracy: The Emergence of the Cartel Party." *Party Politics* 1:5-28.

Katz, Richard S., Peter Mair, et al. 1992. "The Membership of Political Parties in European Democracies, 1960-1990." *European Journal of Political Research* 22:329-45.

Katzenstein, Peter J. 1986. *Small States in World Markets: Industrial Policy in Europe.* Ithaca, NY: Cornell University Press.

Kavanagh, Dennis. 1981. "Opinion Polls." In *Democracy at the Polls,* ed. David Butler, Howard Penniman, and Austin Ranney. Washington, DC: American Enterprise Institute.

———. 1992. "The Political Class and Its Culture." *Parliamentary Affairs* 45:18-32.

———. 1995. *Election Campaigning.* Oxford: Basil Blackwell.

Kazee, Thomas, ed. 1994. *Who Runs for Congress?* Washington, DC: CQ Press.

Kelley, Stanley. 1983. *Interpreting Elections.* Princeton, NJ: Princeton University Press.

Kelly, Mary. 1983. "Influences on Broadcasting Policies for Election Coverage." In *Communicating to Voters,* ed. Jay G. Blumler. Beverly Hills, CA: Sage.

Kenny, Christopher. 1992. "Political Participation and Effects From the Social Environment." *American Journal of Political Science* 36:259-67.

Kepplinger, Hans Mathias, and Hans-Berndt Brosius. 1990. "Der Einfluss der Parteibindung und der Fernsehberichterstattung auf die Wahlabsichten der Bevölkerung." In *Wahlen und Wähler: Analysen aus Anlass der Bundestagswahl 1987,* ed. Max Kaase and Hans-Dieter Klingemann. Opladen: Westdeutscher Verlag.

Kessel, John H. 1988. *Presidential Campaign Politics,* 3rd ed. Chicago: Dorsey.

Key, V. O., Jr. 1955. "A Theory of Critical Elections." *Journal of Politics* 17:3-18.

———. 1964. *Politics, Parties, and Pressure Groups,* 5th ed. New York: Thomas Y. Crowell.

———. 1966. *The Responsible Electorate.* Cambridge, MA: Harvard University Press.

Kiewiet, D. Roderick. 1983. *Macroeconomics and Micropolitics.* Chicago: University of Chicago Press.

Kiewiet, D. Roderick, and Douglas Rivers. 1985. "A Retrospective on Retrospective Voting." In *Economic Conditions and Electoral Outcomes,* ed. Heinz Eulau and Michael Lewis-Beck. New York: Agathon.

Kinder, Donald R. 1986. "Presidential Character Revisited." In *Political Cognition,* ed. Richard R. Lau and David O. Sears. Hillsdale, NJ: Lawrence Erlbaum.

Kinder, Donald R., and D. Roderick Kiewiet. 1979. "Economic Discontent and Political Behavior: The Role of Personal Grievances and Collective Economic Judgments in Congressional Voting." *American Journal of Political Science* 23:495-527.

Kinder, Donald R., Mark D. Peters, Robert P. Abelson, and Susan T. Fiske. 1980. "Presidential Prototypes." *Political Behavior* 2:315-37.

King, Anthony. 1975. "The Election That Everyone Lost." In *Britain at the Polls: 1974*, ed. Howard Penniman. Washington, DC: American Enterprise Institute.

———, ed. 1992. *Britain at the Polls: 1992*. Chatham, NJ: Chatham House.

Kirchgässner, Gebhard. 1991. "Economic Conditions and the Popularity of West German Parties: Before and After the 1982 Government Change." In *Economics and Politics: The Calculus of Support*, ed. Helmut Norpoth, Michael S. Lewis-Beck, and Jean-Dominique Lafay. Ann Arbor: University of Michigan Press.

Kirchheimer, Otto. 1966. "The Transformation of Western European Party Systems." In *Political Parties and Political Development*, ed. Joseph LaPalombara and Myron Weiner. Princeton, NJ: Princeton University Press.

Kitschelt, Herbert. 1989. *The Logics of Party Formation: Ecological Politics in Belgium and West Germany*. Ithaca, NY: Cornell University Press.

———. 1990. "New Social Movements and the Decline of Party Organization." In *Challenging the Political Order*, ed. Russell J. Dalton and Manfred Kuechler. New York: Oxford University Press.

———. 1993a. *The Transformation of European Social Democracy*. Cambridge: Cambridge University Press.

———. 1993b. "Social Movements, Political Parties, and Democratic Theory." *Annals of the American Academy of Political and Social Science* 528:13-29.

Klingemann, Hans-Dieter, Richard I. Hofferbert, and Ian Budge. 1994. *Parties, Policies, and Democracy*. Boulder, CO: Westview.

Klingemann, Hans-Dieter, and Charles Taylor. 1978. "Partisanship, Candidates and Issues: Attitudinal Components of the Vote in West Germany Federal Elections." In *Elections and Parties*, ed. Max Kaase and Klaus von Beyme. London: Sage.

Klugman, Barbara. 1994. "Women in Politics Under Apartheid: A Challenge to the New South Africa." In *Women and Politics Worldwide*, ed. Barbara J. Nelson and Najma Chowdhury. New Haven, CT: Yale University Press.

Knutsen, Oddbjorn. 1987. The Impact of Structural and Ideological Cleavages on West European Democracies. *British Journal of Political Science* 18:323-52.

Kolinsky, Eva. 1993. "Party Change and Women's Representation in Unified Germany." In *Gender and Party Politics*, ed. Joni Lovenduski and Pippa Norris. London: Sage.

Koncz, Katalin. 1994. "Hungarian Women's Political Participation in the Transition to Democracy." In *Women and Politics Worldwide*, ed. Barbara J. Nelson and Najma Chowdhury. New Haven, CT: Yale University Press.

Koole, Ruud. 1989. "The 'Modesty' of Dutch Party Finance." In *Comparative Political Finance in the 1980s*, ed. Herbert E. Alexander. New York: Cambridge University Press.

Kosicki, Gerald. 1993. "Problems and Opportunities in Agenda-Setting Research." *Journal of Communication*. 43:69-76.

Kramer, Gerald H. 1971. "Short-Term Fluctuations in U.S. Voting Behavior." *American Political Science Review* 65:131-43.

———. 1983. "The Ecological Fallacy Revisited: Aggregate- Versus Individual-Level Findings on Economics and Elections and Sociotropic Voting." *American Political Science Review* 77:92-111.

Krasner, Stephen. 1978. *Defending the National Interest.* Princeton, NJ: Princeton University Press.

Kraus, Sidney, and R. G. Smith. 1962. "Issues and Images." In *The Great Debates,* ed. Sidney Kraus. Bloomington: Indiana University Press.

Krosnick, John, and Donald Kinder. 1990. "Altering the Foundations of Support for the President Through Priming." *American Political Science Review* 84:499-512.

Kuklinski, James H., Robert C. Luskin, and John M. Bolland. 1991. "Where's the Schema? Going Beyond the 'S' Word in Political Psychology." *American Political Science Review* 85:1341-55.

Kuklinski, James, and Darrel West. 1981. "Economic Expectations and Voting Behavior in the United States Senate and House Elections." *American Political Science Review* 75:436-47.

Laakso, M., and Rein Taagepera. 1978. "Effective Number of Parties: A Measure With Application to West Europe." *Comparative Political Studies* 12:3-27.

Lachapelle, Guy. 1991. *Polls and the Media in Canadian Elections.* Vol. 16 of *Research Studies of Canadian Royal Commission on Elections.* Toronto: Dundurn.

Ladd, Everett C. 1985. "On Mandates, Realignments, and the 1984 Presidential Election." *Political Studies Quarterly* 100:1-25.

———. 1995. "The 1994 Congressional Elections: The Realignment Continues." *Political Studies Quarterly* 110:1-24.

Lafay, Jean-Dominique. 1991. "Political Dyarchy and Popularity Functions: Lessons From the 1986 French Experience." In *Economics and Politics: The Calculus of Support,* ed. Helmut Norpoth, Michael S. Lewis-Beck, and Jean-Dominique Lafay. Ann Arbor: University of Michigan Press.

Lakeman, Enid. 1974. *How Democracies Vote: A Study of Electoral Systems.* London: Faber and Faber.

Landes, Ronald G. 1983. *The Canadian Polity.* Toronto: Prentice Hall.

Lane, Jan-Erik, and Svante Errson. 1991. *Politics and Society in Western Europe,* 2nd ed. Newbury Park, CA: Sage.

Lang, Gladys E., and Kurt Lang. 1983. *The Battle of Public Opinion: The President, the Press, and the Polls During Watergate.* New York: Columbia University Press.

Lanoue, David. 1988. *From Camelot to the Teflon President: Economics and Presidential Popularity.* Westport, CT: Greenwood.

———. 1991. "The 'Turning Point': Viewers' Reactions to the Second 1988 Presidential Debate." *American Politics Quarterly* 19:80-95.

Lanoue, David J., and Barbara Headrick. 1994. "Primer Ministers, Parties and the Public." *Public Opinion Quarterly* 58:191-209.

Lanoue, David J., and P. Schrott. 1989. "The Effects of Primary Season Debates on Public Opinion." *Political Behavior* 11:289-306.

LaPalombara, Joseph G. 1987. *Democracy, Italian Style.* New Haven, CT: Yale University Press.

Lau, Richard R. 1985. "Two Explanations for Negativity Effects in Political Behavior." *American Journal of Political Science* 29:119-38.

Lau, Richard R., and David O. Sears, eds. 1986. *Political Cognition.* Hillsdale, NJ: Lawrence Erlbaum.

Laver, Michael. 1989. "Party Competition and Party System Change." *Journal of Theoretical Politics* 1:301-24.

Laver, Michael, and Audrey Arkins. 1990. "Coalition and Fianna Fáil." In *How Ireland Voted 1989,* ed. Michael Gallagher and Richard Sinnott. Galway: PSAI.

Laver, Michael, and W. Ben Hunt. 1992. *Policy and Party Competition.* New York: Routledge.

Laver, Michael, and Norman Schofield. 1990. *Multiparty Government: The Politics of Coalition in Europe.* Oxford: Oxford University Press.

Laver, Michael, and Kenneth A. Shepsle. 1990. "Government Coalitions and Intraparty Politics." *British Journal of Political Science* 20:489-507.

———, eds. 1994. *Cabinet Ministers and Parliamentary Government.* Cambridge: Cambridge University Press.

Lavrakas, P. J., and J. K. Holley. 1991. *Polling and Presidential Election Coverage.* Newbury Park, CA: Sage.

Law Library of Congress. 1979. *Government Financing of National Elections, Political Parties, and Campaign Spending in Various Foreign Countries.* Washington, DC: Law Library of Congress.

Lawson, Kay, and Peter Merkl, eds. 1988. *When Parties Fail.* Princeton, NJ: Princeton University Press.

Lawson, Kay, and Colette Ysmal. 1992. "France: The 1988 Presidential Campaign." In *Electoral Strategies and Political Marketing,* ed. Shaun Bowler and David M. Farrell. Houndmills: Macmillan.

Lazarsfeld, Paul, Bernard Berelson, and Helen Gaudet. 1944, 1948. *The People's Choice.* New York: Duell, Sloan, and Pearce; 2nd ed., New York: Columbia University Press.

LeDuc, Lawrence. 1990. "Party Strategies and the Use of Televised Campaign Debates." *European Journal of Political Research* 18:121-41.

———. 1991. "Voting For Free Trade?" In *Politics: Canada,* 7th ed., ed. Paul Fox and Graham White. Toronto: McGraw-Hill.

———. 1992. "Public Perceptions of the Electoral Process." In *British Elections and Parties Yearbook, 1992,* ed. David Denver, Pippa Norris, David Broughton, and Colin Rallings. London: Harvester Wheatsheaf.

Lee, Manwoo. 1990. *The Odyssey of Korean Democracy: Korean Politics, 1987-1990.* New York: Praeger.

Legavre, Jean-Baptiste. 1990. "La 'bataille des comités de soutien' ou la droite en campagne." *Revue Française de Science Politique* 40:793-808.

Leighley, Jan. 1990. "Social Interaction and Contextual Influences on Political Participation." *American Politics Quarterly* 18:459-75.

Levush, Ruth, et al. 1991. *Campaign Finances of National Elections in Foreign Countries.* Washington, DC: Law Library of Congress.

Lewin, Leif, Bo Jansson, and Dag Sörbom. 1972. *The Swedish Electorate, 1887-1968.* Stockholm: Almqvist & Wiksell.

Lewis-Beck, Michael S. 1988. *Economics and Elections: The Major Western Democracies.* Ann Arbor: University of Michigan Press.

Lewis-Beck, Michael S., and Tom W. Rice. 1992. *Forecasting Elections.* Washington, DC: CQ Press.

Lijphart, Arend. 1977. *Democracy in Plural Societies.* New Haven, CT: Yale University Press.

———. 1979. "Religious Vs. Linguistic Vs. Class Voting." *American Political Science Review* 73:442-58.

———. 1981. "Political Parties." In *Democracy at the Polls: A Comparative Study of Competitive National Elections,* ed. David Butler, Howard Penniman, and Austin Ranney. Washington, DC: American Enterprise Institute.

———. 1984. *Democracies: Patterns of Majoritarian and Consensus Government in Twenty-One Countries.* New Haven, CT: Yale University Press.

———. 1989. "Democratic Political Systems: Types, Cases, Causes and Consequences." *Journal of Theoretical Politics* 1:33-48.

———. 1992. *Parliamentary Versus Presidential Government.* Oxford: Oxford University Press.

———. 1994a. "Democracies: Forms, Performance, and Constitutional Engineering." *European Journal of Political Research* 25:1-17.

———. 1994b. *Electoral Systems and Party Systems: A Study of Twenty-Seven Democracies, 1945-1990.* Oxford: Oxford University Press.

Lijphart, Arend, Rafael Lopez Pintor, and Yasumori Sone. 1986. "The Limited Vote and the Single Nontransferable Vote: Lessons From Japanese and Spanish Examples." In *Electoral Laws and Their Political Consequences,* ed. Bernard Grofman and Arend Lijphart. New York: Agathon.

Lindblom, Charles. 1977. *Politics and Markets.* New York: Basic Books.

Lindon, Denis. 1976. *Marketing Politique et Social.* Paris: Dalloz.

Linsky, Martin. 1986. *Impact: How the Press Affects Federal Policymaking.* New York: Norton.

Linz, Juan. 1990. "The Perils of Presidentialism." *Journal of Democracy* 1:51-69.

Lippmann, Walter. 1922. *Public Opinion.* New York: Free Press.

Lipset, Seymour Martin. 1981. *Political Man: The Social Bases of Politics.* Baltimore: Johns Hopkins University Press.

Lipset, Seymour Martin, and Stein Rokkan. 1967. "Cleavage Structures, Party Systems, and Voter Alignments: An Introduction." In *Party Systems and Voter Alignments,* ed. Seymour Martin Lipset and Stein Rokkan. New York: Free Press.

Loewenberg, Gerhard, and Samuel C. Patterson. 1979. *Comparing Legislatures.* Boston: Little, Brown.

Lopez-Escobar, Estaban. 1992. "Spanish Media Law: Changes in the Landscape." *European Journal of Communication* 7:241-60.

Lopez-Escobar, Estaban, and Angel Faus-Belau. 1985. "Broadcasting in Spain: A History of Heavy-Handed State Control." In *Broadcasting and Politics in Western Europe,* ed. Raymond Kuhn. London: Frank Cass.

Lovenduski, Joni. 1993. "Introduction: The Dynamics of Gender and Party." In *Gender and Party Politics,* ed. Joni Lovenduski and Pippa Norris. London: Sage.

Lovenduski, Joni, and Pippa Norris, eds. 1993. *Gender and Party Politics.* London: Sage.

Lovenduski, Joni, and Vicky Randall. 1993. *Contemporary Feminist Politics: Women and Power in Britain.* Oxford: Oxford University Press.

Lucas, Robert E., Jr., and Thomas J. Sargent. 1981. *Rational Expectations and Econometric Practice.* Minneapolis: University of Minnesota Press.

Luebbert, Geoffrey. 1986. *Comparative Democracy: Policy Making and Governing Coalitions in Europe and Israel.* New York: Columbia University Press.

Luntz, Frank I. 1988. *Candidates, Consultants and Campaigns: The Style and Substance of American Electioneering.* Oxford: Basil Blackwell.

Macdermid, R. H. 1992. "Media Usage and Political Behaviour." In *Media and Voters in Canadian Election Campaigns,* ed. Frederick J. Fletcher. Toronto: Dundurn.

MacDonald, Ronald H., and J. Mark Ruhl. 1989. *Party Politics and Elections in Latin America.* Boulder, CO: Westview.

MacIvor, Heather. 1995. "Do Canadian Parties Form a Cartel?" Unpublished manuscript.

Mackie, Thomas T., and Richard Rose. 1991. *The International Almanac of Electoral History,* 3rd ed. Houndmills: Macmillan; Washington, DC: CQ Press.

MacKuen, Michael B., Robert S. Erikson, and James A. Stimson. 1992. "Peasants or Bankers? The American Electorate and the U.S. Economy." *American Political Science Review* 86:597-611.

Mahan, Elizabeth. 1985. "Mexican Broadcasting: Reassessing the Industry-State Relationship." *Journal of Communication* 35:60-75.

Mainwaring, Scott. 1990. "Presidentialism in Latin America." *Latin American Research Review* 25:157-79.

Mainwaring, Scott, and Matthew Shugart. 1994. "Electoral Rules, Institutional Engineering, and Party Discipline." Presented at the conference on Political Parties: Changing Roles in Contemporary Democracies, Madrid.

Mair, Peter. 1987. *The Changing Irish Party System: Organization, Ideology and Electoral Competition.* London: Pinter.

————. 1989. "The Problem of Party System Change." *Journal of Theoretical Politics* 1:251-76.

————, ed. 1990. *The West European Party System.* Oxford: Oxford University Press.

————. 1991. "The Electoral Universe of Small Parties in Postwar Western Europe." In *Small Parties in Western Europe: Comparative and National Perspectives,* ed. Ferdinand Müller-Rommel and Geoffrey Pridham. London: Sage.

————. 1993. "Fianna Fáil, Labour and the Irish Party System." In *How Ireland Voted 1992,* ed. Michael Gallagher and Michael Laver. Dublin: Folens/PSAI.

————. 1995. "Political Parties, Popular Legitimacy, and Public Privilege." *West European Politics* 18:40-57.

Mair, Peter, and Gordon Smith, eds. 1990. *Understanding Party System Change in Western Europe.* London: Cass.

Mancini, Paolo, and Mauro Wolf. 1990. "Mass Media Research in Italy: Culture and Politics." *European Journal of Communication* 5:187-205.

Mann, Thomas, and Gary Orren. 1992. *Media Polls in American Politics.* Washington, DC: Brookings Institution.

Mannelli, Gilberto Tinacci, and Enrico Cheli. 1986. *L'immagine del potere: Comportmaneti, atteggiamenti e strategie d'immagine dei leader politici italiani.* Milano: Franco Angeli Libri.

Mannheim, Jarol B., and Robert B. Albritton. 1984. "Changing National Images: International Public Relations and Media Agenda-Setting." *American Political Science Review* 78:641-57.

Manor, James. 1992. "India." In *Electioneering: A Comparative Study of Continuity and Change,* ed. David Butler and Austin Ranney. Oxford: Clarendon.

March, James G., and Johan P. Olsen. 1989. *Rediscovering Institutions: The Organizational Basis of Politics.* New York: Free Press.

Market Research Society. 1994. *The Opinion Polls and the 1992 General Election.* London: Market Research Society.

Markus, Gregory B. 1982. "Political Attitudes During an Election Year: A Report on the 1980 NES Panel Study." *American Political Science Review* 76:538-60.

————. 1988. "The Impact of Personal and National Economic Conditions on the Presidential Vote: A Pooled Cross-Sectional Analysis." *American Journal of Political Science* 32:137-54.

Martz, John D. 1990. "Electoral Campaigning and Latin American Democratization: The Grancolombian Experience." *Journal of InterAmerican Studies and World Affairs* 32:17-43.

Martz, John D., and David J. Myers. 1994. "Technological Elites and Political Parties: The Venezuelan Professional Community." *Latin American Research Review* 29:7-27.

Massicotte, Louis, and André Bernard. 1985. *Le scrutin au Québec: Un miroir déformant.* Montréal: Hurtubise HMH.

Matas, Robert. 1995. "Greenpeace Making Waves." *Globe and Mail,* July 11.

Mathes, Rainer, and Holli A. Semetko. 1991. "Foreword: A Comparative Perspective on Television and Election Campaigns." *Political Communication and Persuasion* 8:139-44.

Mauser, Gary 1983. *Political Marketing: An Approach to Campaign Strategy.* New York: Praeger.

Mazzoleni, Gianpietro. 1987. "Media Logic and Party Logic in Campaign Coverage: The Italian General Election of 1983." *European Journal of Communication* 2:81-103.

Mazzoleni, Gianpietro, and Cheryl Roper. 1995. "The Presentation of Italian Candidates and Parties in Television Advertising." In *Political Advertising in Western Democracies,* ed. Lynda Lee Kaid and Christina Holtz-Bacha. Thousand Oaks, CA: Sage.

McAdam, Doug. 1988. *Freedom Summer.* New York: Oxford University Press.

McAllister, Ian. 1992. *Political Behaviour: Citizens, Parties and Elites in Australia.* Melbourne: Longman Cheshire.

McCombs, Maxwell. 1981a. "The Agenda Setting Approach." In *Handbook of Political Communications,* ed. Daniel D. Nimmo and Keith R. Sanders. Beverly Hills, CA: Sage.

———. 1981b. "Setting the Agenda for Agenda Setting Research: An Assessment of the Priority Ideas and Problems." In *Mass Communication Review Yearbook 2,* ed. G. Cleveland Wilhoit and Harold de Bock. Beverly Hills, CA: Sage.

———, ed. 1992. "Foreword." *Journalism Quarterly* 69:837-46.

McCombs, Maxwell, and Donald Shaw. 1972. "The Agenda-Setting Function of the Mass Media." *Public Opinion Quarterly* 36:176-87.

———. 1993. "The Evolution of Agenda-Setting: Twenty-Five Years in the Marketplace of Ideas." *Journal of Communication* 43:58-67.

McDonald, Ronald H., and J. Mark Ruhl. 1989. *Party Politics and Elections in Latin America.* Boulder, CO: Westview.

McGrath, J. E., and M. F. McGrath. 1962. "Effects of Partisanship on Perceptions of Political Figures." *Political Opinion Quarterly* 26:236-48.

McLaughlin, Barry. 1969. *Studies in Social Movements.* New York: Free Press.

McLeod, Jack M., J. A. Durall, D. A. Ziemke, and C. R. Bybee. 1974. "Another Look at the Agenda-Setting Function of the Press." *Communication Research* 1:131-66.

McQuail, Denis. 1992. *Media Performance.* London: Sage.

———. 1994. *Mass Communication Theory.* London: Sage.

McRoberts, Kenneth. 1988. *Quebec: Social Change and Political Crisis,* 3rd ed. Toronto: McClelland and Stewart.

Meisel, John. 1991. "Decline of Party in Canada." In *Party Politics in Canada,* ed. Hugh G. Thorburn. Scarborough, Ontario: Prentice Hall.

Melucci, Alberto. 1988. "Getting Involved: Identity and Mobilization in Social Movements." In *From Structure to Action,* ed. Bert Klandermans, Hanspeter Kriesi, and Sidney Tarrow. Greenwich, CT: JAI.

Mezey, Michael L. 1979. *Comparative Legislatures.* Durham, NC: Duke University Press.

Michels, Robert. 1962 [1911]. *Political Parties: A Sociological Study of the Oligarchical Tendencies of Modern Democracies.* New York: Free Press.

Mickiewicz, Ellen. 1988. *Split Signals: Television and Politics in the Soviet Union.* New York: Oxford University Press.

Mickiewicz, Ellen, and Andrei Richter. 1996. "Television, Campaigning and Election in the Soviet Union and Post-Soviet Russia." In *Politics, Media and Modern Democracy: An International Study of Innovations in Electoral Campaigning and Their Consequences,* ed. David L. Swanson and Paolo Mancini. New York: Praeger.

Milbrath, Lester, and M. L. Goel. 1977. *Political Participation: How and Why Do People Get Involved in Politics?* 2nd ed. New York: University Press of America.

Millard, Frances. 1994. "Poland." In *Political Parties of Eastern Europe, Russia and the Successor States,* ed. Bogdan Szajkowski. Harlow: Longman.

Miller, Arthur E., and Warren E. Miller. 1975. "Issues, Candidates and Partisan Divisions in the 1972 American Presidential Election." *British Journal of Political Science* 5:393-434.

Miller, Arthur, and Martin Wattenberg. 1984. "Politics and the Pulpit: Religiosity and the 1980 Elections." *Public Opinion Quarterly* 48:301-17.

Miller, Arthur E., Martin P. Wattenberg, and Oksana Malanchuk. 1986. "Schematic Assessments of Presidential Candidates." *American Political Science Review* 80:521-40.

Miller, Warren E., and Teresa E. Levitin. 1976. *Leadership and Change.* Cambridge, MA: Winthrop.

Miller, Warren, and Merrill Shanks. 1982. "Policy Directions and Presidential Leadership: Alternative Interpretations of the 1980 Presidential Election." *British Journal of Political Science* 12:357-74.

Miller, Warren, and Philip Stouthard. 1975. "Confessional Attachment and Electoral Behavior in The Netherlands." *European Journal of Political Research* 3:219-58.

Miller, William L., Harold Clarke, Martin Harrop, Lawrence LeDuc, and Paul Whiteley. 1990. *How Voters Change: The 1987 British Election Campaign in Perspective.* Oxford: Clarendon.

Mills, C. Wright. 1956. *The Power Elite.* New York: Oxford University Press.

Milne, Robert S., and Hugh C. Mackenzie. 1954. *Straight Fight.* London: Hansard Society.

———. 1958. *Marginal Seat.* London: Hansard Society.

Ministerio del Interior de España. 1992. *Legislatión Electoral de Iberoamérica.* Madrid: Ministerio del Interior.

Mirchandani, G.G. 1977. *320 Million Judges: Analysis of 1977 Lok Sabha and State Elections in India.* New Delhi: Abhinav.

Mishler, William, Marilyn Hoskin, and Roy Fitzgerald. 1989. "British Parties in the Balance: A Time Series Analysis of Long-Term Trends in Labour and Conservative Support." *British Journal of Political Science* 19:211-36.

Missika, Jean-Louis, and D. Bregman. 1987. "On Framing the Campaign: Mass Media Roles in Negotiating the Meaning of the Vote." *European Journal of Communication* 2:289-309.

Mitchell, Glenn, and Christopher Wlezien. 1995. "The Impact of Legal Constraints on Voter Registration, Turnout, and the Composition of the American Electorate." *Political Behavior* 17:179-202

Moe, Terry M. 1980. *The Organization of Interests.* Chicago: University of Chicago Press.

Molinar, Juan. 1991. "Counting the Number of Parties: An Alternative Index." *American Political Science Review* 85:1383-91.

Molteno, Robert, and Ian Scott. 1974. "The 1968 General Election and the Political System." In *Politics in Zambia,* ed. William Tordoff. Manchester: Manchester University Press.

Monroe, Kristen R., ed. 1983. *The Political Process and Economic Change.* New York: Agathon.

Moodie, Graeme C., and Gerald Studdert-Kennedy. 1970. *Opinions, Publics and Pressure Groups.* London: Allen and Unwin.

Mudde, C. E. 1995. "Right-Wing Extremism Analyzed." *European Journal of Political Research* 27:203-24.

Mueller, John. 1973. *War, Presidents and Public Opinion.* New York: John Wiley.

Mughan, Anthony. 1993. "Party Leaders and Presidentialism in the 1992 British Election: A Postwar Perspective." In *British Elections and Parties Yearbook, 1993,* ed. David Denver, Pippa Norris, David Broughton, and Colin Rallings. London: Harvester Wheatsheaf.

———. 1995. "Television and Presidentialism: Australian and U.S. Legislative Elections Compared." *Political Communication* 12:327-42.

———. Forthcoming. *Party Leaders and the Presidentialization of British Politics.*

Müller, Wolfgang C., and Fritz Plasser. 1992. "Austria: The 1990 Campaign." In *Electoral Strategies and Political Marketing,* ed. Shaun Bowler and David M. Farrell. Houndmills: Macmillan.

Müller-Rommel, Ferdinand. 1989. *The New Politics: The Rise and Success of Green Parties and Alternative Lists.* Boulder, CO: Westview.

Mutz, Diana C. 1994. "Contextualizing Personal Experience: The Role of Mass Media." *Journal of Politics* 56:689-714.

Nadeau, Richard, Richard G. Niemi, and Timothy Amato. 1996a. "Prospective and Comparative or Retrospective and Individual? Party Leaders and Party Support in Great Britain." *British Journal of Political Science* 26:245-58.

————. 1996b. "Elite Economic Forecasts, Economic News, Mass Economic Expectations, and Voting Intentions in Great Britain." Mimeo.

Napolitan, Joe. 1972. *The Election Game.* New York: Doubleday.

————. 1995. "AAPC and IAPC: Looking at the Differences." *Campaigns and Elections* 16:67.

Negrine, Ralph, and Stylianos Papathanassopoulos. 1996. "The 'Americanization' of Political Communication: A Critique." *Harvard International Journal of Press/Politics* 1(2):45-62.

Nelson, Barbara J., and Najma Chowdhury, eds. 1994. *Women and Politics Worldwide.* New Haven, CT: Yale University Press.

Neuman, W. Russell, Marion Just, and Ann N. Crigler. 1992. *Common Knowledge: News and the Construction of Political Meaning.* Chicago: University of Chicago Press.

Newman, Bruce I. 1994. *The Marketing of the President: Political Marketing as Campaign Strategy.* Thousand Oaks, CA: Sage.

Nie, Norman H., Sidney Verba, and John R. Petrocik. 1976. *The Changing American Voter.* Cambridge, MA: Harvard University Press.

Niemi, Richard G. 1984. "The Problem of Strategic Behavior Under Approval Voting." *American Political Science Review* 78:952-58.

Niemi, Richard G., Lynda W. Powell, and Patricia L. Bicknell. 1986. "The Effects of Congruity Between Community and District on Salience of U.S. House Candidates." *Legislative Studies Quarterly* 11:187-203.

Niemi, Richard G., and Herbert F. Weisberg. 1993. *Controversies in Voting Behavior,* 3rd ed. Washington, DC: CQ Press.

Nienstedt, John. 1994. "How to Hire Phone Centers." *Campaigns and Elections* 15(10): 54-5.

Nieuwbeerta, Paul. 1995. *The Democratic Class Struggle in Twenty Countries, 1945-1990.* Amsterdam: Thesis Publishers.

Nimmo, Dan. 1970. *The Political Persuaders: The Techniques of Modern Election Campaigns.* Englewood Cliffs, NJ: Prentice Hall.

Nimmo, Dan, and Robert L. Savage. 1976. *Candidates and Their Images.* Pacific Palisades, CA: Goodyear.

Nisbett, Richard E., and Lee Ross. 1980. *Human Inference.* Englewood Cliffs, NJ: Prentice Hall.

Noelle-Neumann, Elisabeth. 1980. *Die Schweigespirale.* Frankfort: Ulbster; *The Spiral of Silence.* Chicago: University of Chicago Press.

Nohlen, Dieter. 1993. *Enciclopedia Electoral Latino-Americana y del Caribe.* San José: Instituto Interamericano de Derechos Humanos.

Nordhaus, William D. 1975. "The Political Business Cycle." *Review of Economic Studies* 42:169-90.

Norgren, Jill. 1988. "In Search of a National Child-Care Policy." In *Women, Power and Policy,* ed. Ellen Boneparth and Emily Stoper. New York: Pergamon.

Norpoth, Helmut. 1987a. "Guns and Butter and Government Popularity in Britain." *American Political Science Review* 81:949-59.

————. 1987b. "Under Way and Here to Stay: Party Realignment in the 1980s." *Public Opinion Quarterly* 51:376-91.

————. 1992. *Confidence Regained: Economics, Mrs. Thatcher, and the British Voter.* Ann Arbor: University of Michigan Press.

————. Forthcoming. "Presidents and the Prospective Voter." *Journal of Politics.*

Norpoth, Helmut, and Kendall L. Baker. 1980. "Mass Media Use and Electoral Choice in West Germany." *Comparative Politics* 13:1-14.

Norpoth, Helmut, Michael S. Lewis-Beck, and Jean-Dominique Lafay, ed. 1991. *Economics and Politics: The Calculus of Support.* Ann Arbor: University of Michigan Press.

Norpoth, Helmut, and Thom Yantek. 1983. "Macroeconomic Conditions and Fluctuations of Presidential Popularity: The Question of Lagged Effects." *American Journal of Political Science* 27:785-807.

Norris, Pippa. 1985. "Women's Legislative Participation in Western Europe." *West European Politics* 8:90-101.

————. 1996a. *Electoral Change in Britain Since 1945.* Oxford: Blackwell.

————. 1996b. "Women Politicians: Transforming Westminster?" *Parliamentary Affairs* 49(1): 89-102

————. 1996c. *Women, Media, and Politics.* New York: Oxford University Press.

Norris, Pippa, and Joni Lovenduski. 1993. " 'If Only More Candidates Came Forward': Supply-Side Explanations of Candidate Selection in Britain." *British Journal of Political Science* 23:373-408.

————. 1995. *Political Recruitment: Gender, Race and Class in the British Parliament.* Cambridge: Cambridge University Press.

Oberschall, Anthony. 1973. *Social Conflict and Social Movements.* Englewood Cliffs, NJ: Prentice Hall.

Offe, Claus. 1981. "Challenging the Boundaries of Institutional Politics: Social Movements since the 1960s." In *Organizing Interests in Western Europe,* ed. Suzanne D. Berger. Cambridge: Cambridge University Press.

Olson, David M. 1993. "Political Parties and Party Systems in Regime Transformation: Inner Transition in the New Democracies of Central Europe." *American Review of Politics* 14:619-58.

Olson, Mancur. 1965. *The Logic of Collective Action.* Cambridge, MA: Harvard University Press.

Oppenhuis, Erik. 1995. Voting Behavior in the European Community: A Comparative Analysis of Electoral Participation and Party Choice. Ph.D. dissertation, University of Amsterdam.

Ordeshook, Peter C., and Olga V. Shvetsova. 1994. "Ethnic Heterogeneity, District Magnitude and the Number of Parties." *American Journal of Political Science* 38:100-23.

O'Shaughnessy, N. J. 1990. *The Phenomenon of Political Marketing.* Houndmills: Macmillan.

Ostrogorski, M. I. 1964 [1902]. *Democracy and the Organization of Political Parties.* Garden City, NY: Anchor Books.

Pacek, Alexander, and Benjamin Radcliffe. 1995. "The Political Economy of Competitive Elections in the Developing World." *American Journal of Political Science* 39:745-59.

Page, Benjamin I. 1978. *Choices and Echoes in Presidential Elections.* Chicago: University of Chicago Press.

Page, Benjamin I., and Robert Y. Shapiro. 1992. *The Rational Public.* Chicago: University of Chicago Press.

Page, Benjamin I., Robert Y. Shapiro, and Glenn R. Dempsey. 1987. "What Moves Public Opinion?" *American Political Science Review* 81:23-43.

Paldam, Martin. 1991. "How Robust Is the Vote Function? A Study of Seventeen Nations Over Four Decades." In *Economics and Politics: The Calculus of Support,* ed. Helmut Norpoth, Michael S. Lewis-Beck, and Jean-Dominique Lafay. Ann Arbor: University of Michigan Press.

Paletz, David L., Karol Jakubowicz, Pavao Novosel, eds. 1995. *Glasnost and After: Media and Change in Central and Eastern Europe.* Cresskill, NJ: Hampton.

Paletz, David L., and Richard J. Vinegar. 1977-78. "Presidents on Television: The Effects of Instant Analysis." *Public Opinion Quarterly* 41:488-97.

Palmer, Norman D. 1971. *The Indian Political System,* 2nd ed. Boston: Houghton Mifflin.

Panebianco, Angelo. 1988. *Political Parties: Organization and Power.* Cambridge: Cambridge University Press.

Panitch, Leo. 1977. "The Development of Corporatism in Liberal Democracies." *Comparative Political Studies* 10:61-90.

Panitch, Leo, and Donald Swartz. 1993. *The Assault on Trade Union Freedoms.* Toronto: Garamond.

Pappi, Franz Urban. 1990. Klassenstruktur und Wählerverhalten im sozialen Wandel. In *Wahlen und Wähler: Analysen aus Anlass der Bundestagswahl 1987,* ed. Max Kaase and Han-Dieter Klingemann. Opladen: Westdeutscher Verlag.

Parodi, Jean-Luc. 1978. "Note sur une règle peu connue du deuxième tour en régime majoritaire bipolaire." *Revue française de science politique* 28:21-7.

Parry, Geriant, George Moiser, and Niel Day. 1990. *Political Participation and Democracy in Britain.* New York: Cambridge University Press.

Pateman, Carole. 1970. *Participation and Democratic Theory.* Cambridge: Cambridge University Press.

Patterson, Thomas E. 1980. *The Mass Media Election.* New York: Praeger.

———. 1993. *Out of Order.* New York: Knopf.

Patterson, Thomas, and Robert McClure. 1976. *The Unseeing Eye: The Myth of Television Power in National Elections.* New York: Putnam.

Pattie, Charles J., Paul F. Whiteley, Ron J. Johnston, and Patrick Seyd. 1994. "Measuring Local Campaign Effects: Labour Party Constituency Campaigning at the 1987 General Election." *Political Studies* 42:469-79.

Pedersen, Mogens N. 1983. "Changing Patterns of Electoral Volatility in European Party Systems: Explorations in Explanation." In *Western European Party Systems: Continuity and Change,* ed. Hans Daalder and Peter Mair. London: Sage.

Pedersen, Mogens N. 1987. "The Danish 'Working Multiparty System': Breakdown or Adaptation?" In *Party Systems in Denmark, Austria, Switzerland, the Netherlands and Belgium,* ed. Hans Daalder. London: Pinter.

———. 1988. "The Defeat of All Parties: The Danish Folketing Election of 1973." In *When Parties Fail: Emerging Alternative Organizations,* ed. Kay Lawson and Peter H. Merkl. Princeton, NJ: Princeton University Press.

Penniman, Howard, ed. 1975. *Britain at the Polls: 1974.* Washington, DC: American Enterprise Institute.

———, ed. 1980a. *New Zealand at the Polls: The General Election of 1978.* Washington, DC: American Enterprise Institute.

———, ed. 1980b. *Venezuela at the Polls: The National Elections of 1978.* Washington, DC: American Enterprise Institute.

———. 1981. "Campaign Styles and Methods." In *Democracy at the Polls,* ed. David Butler, Howard R. Penniman, and Austin Ranney. Washington, DC: American Enterprise Institute.

———, ed. 1983a. *Australia at the Polls: The National Elections of 1980 and 1983.* Washington, DC: American Enterprise Institute.

———, ed. 1983b. *Switzerland at the Polls: The National Elections of 1979.* Washington, DC: American Enterprise Institute.

Petracca, Mark P. 1992. "The Rediscovery of Interest Group Politics." In *The Politics of Interests,* ed. Mark P. Petracca. Boulder, CO: Westview.

Pfetsch, Barbara, and Rüdiger Schmitt-Beck. 1993. "Amerikanisierung von Wahlkämpfen? Kommunikationsstrategien und Massenmedien im Politischen Mobilisierungsprozess." In *Politik und Medien-der Aktuelle Forschungsstand zum Verhältnis von Politik, Medien und Rezipienten,* ed. Michael Jaeckel and Peter Winterhoff-Spurk. Berlin: Vistas.

Phillips, Susan D. 1989. "Rock-a-Bye, Brian: The National Strategy on Child Care." In *How Ottawa Spends, 1989-90,* ed. Katherine A. Graham. Ottawa: Carleton University Press.

Pinto-Duschinsky, Michael. 1991. "Foreign Political Aid: The German Political Foundations and Their U.S. Counterparts." *International Affairs* 67:33-63.

Pitkin, Hanna. 1967. *The Concept of Representation.* Berkeley: University of California Press.

Piven, Frances Fox, and Richard A. Cloward. 1977. *Poor People's Movements.* New York: Vintage.

Poguntke, Thomas. 1989. "The 'New Politics Dimension' in European Green Parties." In *New Politics in Western Europe: The Rise and Success of Green Parties and Alternative Lists,* ed. Ferdinand Müller-Rommel. Boulder, CO: Westview.

Pollack, Barry, and Marcelo Pollack. 1993. "Overview: The Vulnerability of Democracy." *Parliamentary Affairs* 46:447-57.

Popkin, Samuel, John W. Gorman, Charles Phillips, and Jeffrey A. Smith. 1976. "What Have You Done for Me Lately? Towards an Investment Theory of Voting." *American Political Science Review* 70:779-805.

Powell, G. Bingham, Jr. 1980. "Voting Turnout in Thirty Democracies: Partisan, Legal and Socio-Economic Influences." In *Electoral Participation: A Comparative Perspective,* ed. Richard Rose. London: Sage.

————. 1982. *Contemporary Democracies: Participation, Stability and Violence.* Cambridge, MA: Harvard University Press.

————. 1986. "American Voter Turnout in Comparative Perspective." *American Political Science Review* 80:17-43.

————. 1989. "Constitutional Design and Citizen Electoral Control." *Journal of Theoretical Politics* 1:107-30.

Powell, G. Bingham, Jr., and Guy D. Whitten. 1993. "A Cross-National Analysis of Economic Voting: Taking Account of the Political Context." *American Journal of Political Science* 37:391-414.

Powell, Walter W., and Paul J. Dimaggio, eds. 1991. *The New Institutionalism in Organizational Analysis.* Chicago: University of Chicago Press.

Praag, Philip van. 1992. "The Netherlands: The 1989 Campaign." In *Electoral Strategies and Political Marketing,* ed. Shaun Bowler and David M. Farrell. Houndmills: Macmillan.

Pridham, Geoffrey. 1988. "The SDP in Britain: Protest Movement or New Political Tendency?" In *When Parties Fail,* ed. Kay Lawson and Peter Merkl. Princeton, NJ: Princeton University Press.

Pross, A. Paul. 1986. *Group Politics and Public Policy.* Toronto: Oxford University Press.

Protess, David, and Maxwell McCombs. 1991. *Agenda-Setting: Readings on Media, Public Opinion and Policymaking.* Hillsdale, NJ: Lawrence Erlbaum.

Przeworski, Adam, and John Sprague. 1985. *Paper Stones: A History of Electoral Socialism.* Chicago: University of Chicago Press.

Putnam, Robert D. 1976. *The Comparative Study of Political Elites.* Englewood Cliffs, NJ: Prentice Hall.

———. 1993. *Making Democracy Work: Civic Traditions in Modern Italy.* Princeton, NJ: Princeton University Press.

———. 1995. "Bowling Alone: America's Declining Social Capital." *Journal of Democracy* 6:65-78.

Rae, Douglas W. 1967. *The Political Consequences of Electoral Laws.* New Haven, CT: Yale University Press.

Ragsdale, Lyn. 1985. "Legislative Elections." In *Handbook of Legislative Research,* ed. Gerhard Loewenberg, Samuel C. Patterson, and Malcolm E. Jewell. Cambridge, MA: Harvard University Press.

———. 1991. "Strong Feelings: Emotional Responses to Presidents." *Political Behavior* 13:33-65.

Ramsdell, Daniel B. 1992. *The Japanese Diet.* Lanham, MD: University Press of America.

Randall, Vicky, ed. 1988. *Political Parties in the Third World.* London: Sage.

Ranney, Austin. 1965. *Pathways to Parliament: Candidate Selection in Britain.* London: Macmillan.

———. 1981. "Candidate Selection." In *Democracy at the Polls,* ed. David Butler, Howard Penniman, and Austin Ranney. Washington, DC: American Enterprise Institute.

Rattinger, Hans. 1986. "Collective and Individual Economic Judgments and Voting in West Germany, 1961-1984." *European Journal of Political Research* 14:393-419.

Reagan, Ronald. 1990. *An American Life.* New York: Simon & Schuster.

Reif, Karlheinz. 1985. "Ten Second-Order Elections." In *Ten European Elections,* ed. Karlheinz Reif. Aldershot: Gower.

Reif, Karlheinz, and Ronald Inglehart, eds. 1991. *Euro-Barometer: The Dynamics of European Opinion.* London: Macmillan.

Reif, Karlheinz, and Hermann Schmitt. 1980. "Nine Second-Order National Elections: A Conceptual Framework for the Analysis of European Election Results." *European Journal of Political Research* 8:3-44.

Remmer, Karen. 1991. "The Political Economy of Elections in Latin America." *American Political Science Review* 87:393-407.

Richardson, Jeremy J., ed. 1993. *Pressure Groups.* New York: Oxford University Press.

Riker, William H. 1982. *Liberalism Against Populism.* San Francisco: Freeman.

———. 1986. "Duverger's Law Revisited." In *Electoral Laws and Their Political Consequences,* ed. Bernard Grofman and Arend Lijphart. New York: Agathon.

Rivers, Douglas. 1986. "Microeconomics and Macropolitics: A Solution to the Kramer Problem." Mimeo.

Robertson, David. 1976. *A Theory of Party Competition.* New York: John Wiley.

———. 1984. *Class and the British Electorate.* Oxford: Basil Blackwell.

Robinson, David, and Angelo Rivero-Santos. 1995. Lecture on Politics and the News Media in Latin America: Comparisons of Brazil, Chile, Mexico and Venezuela. Syracuse University, April 19.

Robinson, Robert. 1989. "Coalitions and Political Parties in Sub-National Government: The Case of Spain." In *Political Parties and Coalitions in European Local Government,* ed. C. Mellors and B. Pijnenburg. London: Routledge.

Rochon, Thomas R. 1990. "The West European Peace Movement and the Theory of New Social Movements." In *Challenging the Political Order,* ed. Russell J. Dalton and Manfred Kuechler. New York: Oxford University Press.

Rogers, Everett M., and Livia Antola. 1985. "Telenovelas: A Latin American Success Story." *Journal of Communication* 35:24-35.

Rogers, Everett M., and J. W. Dearing. 1978. "Agenda-Setting Research: Where Has It Been, Where Is It Going?" *Communication Yearbook 2.* Beverly Hills, CA: Sage.

Rohme, N. 1985. "National Restrictions on the Conduct and Release of Public Opinion Polls." *European Research,* January.

———. 1992. "The State of the Art of Public Opinion Polling Worldwide." *Marketing and Research Today* 20:264.

Rohrschneider, Robert. 1993. "New Party Versus Old Left Realignments." *Journal of Politics* 55:682-701.

Rokkan, Stein. 1966. "Norway: Numerical Democracy and Corporate Pluralism." In *Political Oppositions in Western Democracies,* ed. Robert A. Dahl. New Haven, CT: Yale University Press.

———. 1968. "The Growth and Structuring of Mass Politics in Smaller European Democracies." *Comparative Studies in Society and History* 10:173-210.

Rose, Richard. 1967. *Influencing Voters: A Study of Campaign Rationality.* New York: St Martin's.

———. 1974. *The Problem of Party Government.* London: Macmillan.

———. 1982. *The Territorial Dimension in Politics.* Chatham, NJ: Chatham House.

———. 1984a. *Do Parties Make a Difference?* 2nd ed. Chatham, NJ: Chatham House.

———. 1984b. "Electoral Systems: A Question of Degree or of Principle?" In *Choosing an Electoral System: Issues and Alternatives,* ed. Arend Lijphart and Bernard Grofman. New York: Praeger.

Rose, Richard, and Phillip L. Davies. 1994. *Inheritance in Public Policy: Change Without Choice in Britain.* New Haven, CT: Yale University Press.

Rose, Richard, and Ian McAllister. 1986. *Voters Begin to Choose: From Closed-Class to Open Elections in Britain.* Beverly Hills, CA: Sage.

Rose, Richard, and Ezra Sulieman, eds. 1980. *Presidents and Prime Ministers.* Washington, DC: American Enterprise Institute.

Rose, Richard, and Derek Urwin. 1969. "Social Cohesion, Political Parties and Strains in Regimes." *Comparative Political Studies* 2:7-67.

———. 1970. "Persistence and Change in Western Party Systems Since 1945." *Political Studies* 18:287-319.

Rosenberg, Shawn W., Lisa Bohan, Patrick McCafferty, and Kevin Harris. 1986. "The Image and the Vote: The Effect of Candidate Presentation on Voter Preference." *American Journal of Political Science* 30:108-27.

Rosenstone, Steven J., and John Mark Hansen. 1993. *Mobilization, Participation, and Democracy in America.* New York: Macmillan.

Rospir, Juan I. 1996. "Political Communication and Electoral Campaigns in the Young Spanish Democracy" In *Politics, Media and Modern Democracy: An International Study of Innovations in Electoral Campaigning and Their Consequences,* ed. David L. Swanson and Paolo Mancini. New York: Praeger.

Rule, Wilma. 1987. "Electoral Systems, Contextual Factors, and Women's Opportunity for Election to Parliament in Twenty-Three Democracies." *Western Political Quarterly* 33:477-98.

———. 1992. "Multimember Legislative Districts: Minority and Anglo Women's and Men's Recruitment Opportunity." In *United States Electoral Systems: Their Impact on Women and Minorities,* ed. Wilma Rule and Joseph F. Zimmerman. New York: Praeger.

———. 1994. "Women's Underrepresentation and Electoral Systems." *PS: Political Science and Politics* 27:689-93.

Rule, Wilma, and Pippa Norris. 1992. "Anglo and Minority Women's Underrepresentation in Congress: Is the Electoral System the Culprit?" In *United States Electoral Systems: Their Impact on Women and Minorities,* ed. Wilma Rule and Joseph F. Zimmerman. New York: Praeger.

Rule, Wilma, and Joseph F. Zimmerman, eds. 1992. *U.S. Electoral Systems: Their Impact on Minorities and Women.* Westport, CT: Greenwood.

Rush, Michael. 1969. *The Selection of Parliamentary Candidates.* London: Nelson.

Rusk, Jerrold G. 1974. "Comment: The American Electoral Universe: Speculation and Evidence." *American Political Science Review* 68:1028-49.

Rusk, Jerrold G., and Herbert F. Weisberg. 1972. "Perceptions of Presidential Candidates: Implications for Electoral Change." *Midwest Journal of Political Science* 16:388-410.

Sabato, Larry J. 1981. *The Rise of Political Consultants: New Ways of Winning Elections.* New York: Basic Books.

———, ed. 1989. *Campaigns and Elections: A Reader in Modern American Politics.* Glenview, IL: Scott Foresman.

———. 1993. *Feeding Frenzy: How Attack Journalism Has Transformed American Politics.* New York: Free Press.

Salwen, Michael B., and Bruce Garrison. 1991. *Latin American Journalism.* Hillsdale, NJ: Lawrence Erlbaum.

Sanders, David. 1991. "Government Popularity and the Next Election." *Political Quarterly* 62:235-61.

———. 1993. "Why the Conservatives Won—Again." In *Britain at the Polls 1992,* ed. Anthony King. Chatham, NJ: Chatham House.

Sankoff, David, and Koula Mellos. 1972. "The Swing Ratio and Game Theory." *American Political Science Review* 66:551-54.

———. 1973. "La régionalisation électorale et l'amplification des proportions." *Canadian Journal of Political Science* 6:380-98.

Särlvik, Bo, and Ivor Crewe. 1983. *Decade of Dealignment.* Cambridge: Cambridge University Press.

Sartori, Giovanni. 1966. "European Political Parties: The Case of Polarized Pluralism." In *Political Parties and Political Development,* ed. Joseph LaPalombara and Myron Weiner. Princeton, NJ: Princeton University Press.

———. 1967. *Democratic Theory.* New York: Praeger.

———. 1970. "The Typology of Party Systems: Proposals for Improvement." In *Mass Politics: Studies in Political Sociology,* ed. Erik Allardt and Stein Rokkan. New York: Free Press.

———. 1976. *Parties and Party Systems: A Framework for Analysis.* Cambridge: Cambridge University Press.

———. 1994. *Comparative Constitutional Engineering: An Inquiry Into Structures, Incentives and Outcomes.* Houndmills: Macmillan.

Sawer, Marian. 1994. "Locked Out or Locked In? Women and Politics in Australia." In *Women and Politics Worldwide,* ed. Barbara J. Nelson and Najma Chowdhury. New Haven, CT: Yale University Press.

Scammell, Margaret, and Holli A. Semetko. 1995. "Political Advertising on Television: The British Experience." In *Political Advertising in Western Democracies: Parties and Candidates on Television,* ed. Lynda Lee Kaid and Christina Holtz-Bacha. Thousand Oaks, CA: Sage.

Scarrow, Susan E. 1996. *Parties and Their Members: Organizing for Victory in Britain and Germany.* Oxford: Oxford University Press.

Schattschneider, E. E. 1942. *Party Government.* New York: Holt, Rinehart & Winston.

———. 1960. *The Semi-Sovereign People: A Realist's View of Democracy in America.* New York: Holt, Rinehart & Winston.

Schlesinger, Joseph. 1966. *Ambition and Politics: Political Careers in the United States.* Chicago: Rand McNally.

———. 1991. *Political Parties and the Winning of Office.* Ann Arbor: University of Michigan Press.

Schlozman, Kay Lehman, and John L. Tierney. 1986. *Organized Interests and American Democracy.* New York: Harper and Row.

Schmitt, Hermann, and Sören Holmberg. 1995. "Political Parties in Decline?" In *Citizens and the State,* ed. Hans-Dieter Klingemann and Dieter Fuchs. Oxford: Oxford University Press.

Schmitt-Beck, Rüdiger, and Peter Schrott. 1994. "Dealignment durch Massenmedien? Zur These der Abschwächung von Parteibindungen als Folge der Medienexpansion." In *Wahlen und Wähler: Analysen aus Anlass der Bundestagswahl 1990,* ed. Hans-Dieter Klingemann and Max Kaase. Opladen: Westdeutscher Verlag.

Schmitter, Philippe C. 1979. "Still the Century of Corporatism?" In *Trends Toward Corporatist Intermediation,* ed. Philippe C. Schmitter and Gerhard Lehmbruch. Beverly Hills, CA: Sage.

———. 1981. "Interest Intermediation and Regime Governability in Contemporary Western Europe and North America." In *Organizing Interests in Western Europe,* ed. Suzanne D. Berger. Cambridge: Cambridge University Press.

Schneider, Friedrich, and Bruno S. Frey. 1988. "Politico-Economic Models of Macroeconomic Policy: A Review of Empirical Evidence." In *Political Business Cycles,* ed. Thomas D. Willett. Durham, NC: Duke University Press.

Schoenbach, Klaus. 1987. "The Role of Mass Media in West German Election Campaigns." *Legislative Studies Quarterly* 12:373-94.

Schrott, Peter. 1989. "West German Televised Debates From 1972 to 1987." Presented at the annual meeting of the American Political Science Association, Atlanta.

———. 1990. "Electoral Consequences of 'Winning' Televised Campaign Debates." *Public Opinion Quarterly* 54:567-85.

Schumpeter, Joseph. 1942. *Capitalism, Socialism and Democracy.* New York: Harper.

Sears, David O., and Steven H. Chaffee. 1979. "Uses and Effect of the 1976 Debates: An Overview of Empirical Studies." In *The Great Debates: Carter Vs. Ford, 1976,* ed. Sidney Kraus. Bloomington: Indiana University Press.

Seidle, F. Leslie, ed. 1991. *Comparative Issues in Party and Election Finance.* Toronto: Dundurn.

Semetko, Holli A. 1996. "Political Balance on Television: Campaigns in the U.S., Britain, and Germany." *Harvard International Journal of Press/Politics* 1(1):51-71.

Semetko, Holli A., Jay G. Blumler, Michael Gurevitch, and David H. Weaver. 1991. *The Formation of Campaign Agendas: A Comparative Analysis of Party and Media Roles in Recent American and British Elections.* Hillsdale, NJ: Lawrence Erlbaum.

Semetko, Holli A., and Julio Borquez. 1991. "Audiences for Election Communication." In *Mediated Politics in Two Cultures: Presidential Campaigning in the United States and France,* ed. Lynda Lee Kaid, Jacques Gerstle, and Keith R. Sanders. New York: Praeger.

Semetko, Holli A., Joanne Bay Brzinski, David Weaver, and Lars Willnat. 1992. "TV News and U.S. Public Opinion About Foreign Countries: The Impact of Exposure and Attention." *International Journal of Public Opinion Research* 4:18-36.

Semetko, Holli A., Margaret Scammell, and T. J. Nossiter. 1994. "The Media's Coverage of the Campaign." In *Labour's Last Chance?* ed. Anthony Heath, Roger Jowell, and John Curtice. Aldershot: Dartmouth University Press.

Semetko, Holli A., and Klaus Schoenbach. 1994. *Germany's 'Unity' Election: Voters and the Media.* Cresskill, NJ: Hampton.

———. 1995. "The Media and the Campaign in the New Germany." In *Germany's New Politics: Politics and Issues in the 1990s,* ed. David Conradt, Gerald R. Kleinfeld, George K. Romoser, and Christian Soe. Oxford: Berghahn.

Seyd, Patrick, and Paul Whiteley. 1992. *Labour's Grass Roots: The Politics of Party Membership.* Oxford: Clarendon.

———. 1994. "The Influence of Local Campaigning on the Conservative Vote in the 1992 General Election." In *British Elections and Parties Yearbook, 1994,* ed. David Broughton, David M. Farrell, David Denver, and Colin Rallings. London: Cass.

Seymour-Ure, Colin. 1974. *The Political Impact of Mass Media.* London: Constable.

Shabad, Goldie, and Kristi Andersen. 1979. "Candidate Evaluations by Men and Women." *Public Opinion Quarterly* 43:19-35.

Shadegg, Stephen. 1964. *How to Win an Election: The Art of Political Victory.* New York: Taplinger.

———. 1972. *The New How to Win an Election.* New York: Taplinger.

Shafer, Byron, ed. 1991. *The End of Realignment?: Interpreting American Electoral Eras.* Madison: University of Wisconsin Press.

Shaw, Donald, and Maxwell E. McCombs. 1977. *The Emergence of American Political Issues: The Agenda-Setting Function of the Press.* St. Paul, MN: West.

Shugart, Matthew Soberg. 1995. "The Electoral Cycle and Institutional Sources of Divided Presidential Government." *American Political Science Review* 89:327-43.

Shugart, Matthew S., and John. M. Carey. 1992. *Presidents and Assemblies: Constitutional Design and Electoral Dynamics.* Cambridge: Cambridge University Press.

Siemienska, Renata. 1994. "Polish Women as the Object and Subject of Politics During and After the Communist Period." In *Women and Politics Worldwide,* ed. Barbara J. Nelson and Najma Chowdhury. New Haven, CT: Yale University Press.

Sigel, Roberta. 1964. "Effect of Partisanship on the Perception of Political Candidates." *Public Opinion Quarterly* 28:483-96.

———. 1968. "Image of the President: Some Insights Into the Political Views of Schoolchildren." *American Political Science Review* 62:216-26.

Sisk, Timothy D. 1994. "Electoral System Choice in South Africa: Implications for Intergroup Moderation." Presented at the International Political Science Association 16th World Congress, Berlin.

Skidmore, Thomas A. 1993. "Politics and the Media in a Democratizing Latin America." In *Television, Politics and the Transition to Democracy in Latin America,* ed. Thomas A. Skidmore. Baltimore: Johns Hopkins University Press.

Skocpol, Theda. 1979. *States and Social Revolutions: A Comparative Analysis of France, Russia, and China.* Cambridge: Cambridge University Press.

———. 1985. "Bringing the State Back In: Strategies of Analysis in Current Research." In *Bringing the State Back In,* ed. Peter B. Evans, Dietrich Rueschemeyer, and Theda Skocpol. Cambridge: Cambridge University Press.

Smith, Anthony. 1979. *Television and Political Life: Studies in Six European Countries.* London: Macmillan.

———. 1981. "Mass Communications." In *Democracy at the Polls,* ed. David Butler, Howard R. Penniman, and Austin Ranney. Washington, DC: American Enterprise Institute.

Smith, Eric R. A. N. 1989. *The Unchanging American Voter.* Berkeley: University of California Press.

Smith, Tom W. 1990. "The First Straw: A Study of the Origins of Opinion Polls." *Public Opinion Quarterly* 54:21-36.

Smolka, Richard G. 1992. *The Book of the States, 1992-93.* Lexington, KY: Council of State Governments.

Sniderman, Paul M., and Richard A. Brody. 1977. "Coping: The Ethic of Self-Reliance." *American Journal of Political Science* 21:501-22.

Southall, Roger. 1994. "South Africa's 1994 Election in an African Perspective." *Africa Insight* 24:86-98.

Spafford, Duff. 1970. "The Electoral System of Canada." *American Political Science Review* 64:168-76.

Spencer, Herbert. 1851. *Social Statics.* London: Gregg International.

Spitz, Elaine. 1984. *Majority Rule.* Chatham, NJ: Chatham House.

Spitzer, Robert. 1993. *Media and Public Policy.* Westport, CT: Praeger.

Staggenborg, Suzanne. 1991. *The Pro-Choice Movement: Organization and Activism in the Abortion Conflict.* New York: Oxford University Press.

Stanley, Harold W., and Richard G. Niemi. 1994, 1995a. *Vital Statistics on American Politics,* 4th ed.; 5th ed. Washington, DC: CQ Press.

———. 1995b. "The Demise of the New Deal Coalition: Partisanship and Group Support, 1952-1992." In *Democracy's Feast: Elections in America,* ed. Herbert F. Weisberg. Chatham, NJ: Chatham House.

Statera, Gianni. 1986. *La Politica Spettacolo: Politici e Mass Media Nell'era Dell'immagine.* Milan: Mondadori.

The Statesman's Year Book: 1995-96. 1995. London: Macmillan.

Stefan, Alfred, and Cindy Skach. 1993. "Constitutional Frameworks and Democratic Consolidation: Parliamentarism Versus Presidentialism." *World Politics* 46:1-22.

Steinberg, Arnold. 1976a. *The Political Campaign Handbook: Media, Scheduling and Advance.* Lexington, MA: D. C. Heath.

———. 1976b. *Political Campaign Management: A Systems Approach.* Lexington, MA: D. C. Heath.

Stigler, George. 1973. "General Economic Conditions and National Elections." *American Economic Review* 62:540-52.

Stockwin, J. A. 1982. *Japan: Divided Politics in a Growth Economy.* London: Weidenfeld and Nicolson.

Stokes, Donald E. 1966. "Some Dynamic Elements of Contests for the Presidency." *American Political Science Review* 60:19-28.

Story, Dale. 1992. *The Mexican Ruling Party: Stability and Authority.* New York: Praeger.

Strøm, Kaare. 1990. *Minority Government and Majority Rule.* Cambridge: Cambridge University Press.

Studlar, Donley T., Ian McAllister, and Alvaro Ascui. 1990. "Privatization and the British Electorate: Microeconomic Policies, Macroeconomic Evaluations and Party Support." *American Journal of Political Science* 34:1077-101.

Sullivan, Denis G., and Roger G. Masters. 1988. "Happy Warriors: Leaders' Facial Displays, Viewers' Emotions, and Political Support." *American Journal of Political Science* 32:345-68.

Sundberg, Jan, and Stefan Högnabba. 1992. "Finland: The 1991 Campaign." In *Electoral Strategies and Political Marketing,* ed. Shaun Bowler and David M. Farrell. Houndmills: Macmillan.

Suzuki, Motoshi. 1992. "Political Business Cycles in the Public Mind." *American Political Science Review* 86:989-96.

Swanson, David L. 1988. "Feeling the Elephant: Some Observations on Agenda-Setting Research." *Communication Yearbook 11.* Newbury Park, CA: Sage.

———. 1992. "Managing Theoretical Diversity in Cross-National Studies of Political Communication." In *Comparatively Speaking: Communication and Culture Across Space and Time,* ed. Jay G. Blumler, Jack M. McLeod, and Karl Erik Rosengren. Newbury Park, CA: Sage.

Swanson, David, and Paolo Mancini. 1996. *Politics, Media and Modern Democracy.* New York: Praeger.

Szyliowicz, Joseph S. 1966. *Political Change in Rural Turkey: Erdemli.* The Hague: Mouton.

Taagepera, Rein. 1986. "Reformulating the Cube Law for Proportional Representation Elections." *American Political Science Review* 80:489-504.

Taagepera, Rein, and Matthew Soberg Shugart. 1989. *Seats and Votes: The Effects and Determinants of Electoral Systems.* New Haven, CT: Yale University Press.

Tarrow, Sidney. 1983. *Struggling to Reform: Social Movements and Policy Change During Cycles of Protest.* Ithaca, NY: Cornell University Center for International Studies.

———. 1991. *Struggle, Politics, and Reform: Collective Action, Social Movements, and Cycles of Protest.* Ithaca, NY: Cornell University Center for International Studies.

Tate, Katherine. 1993. *From Politics to Protest.* Cambridge, MA: Harvard University Press.

Taylor, Charles. 1992. "Multiculturalism and the Politics of Recognition." In *Multiculturalism and the Politics of Recognition,* ed. Amy Gutmann. Princeton, NJ: Princeton University Press.

Taylor, Humphrey. 1995. "Horses for Courses: How Different Countries Measure Opinion in Very Different Ways." *Public Perspective* 6(2): 3-7.

Taylor, Peter J., and R. J. Johnston. 1979. *Geography of Elections.* New York: Penguin.

Teixeira, Ruy. 1992. *The Disappearing American Voter.* Washington, DC: Brookings Institution.

Thatcher, Margaret. 1993. *The Downing Street Years.* New York: HarperCollins.

Thayer, Nathaniel. 1969. *How the Conservatives Rule Japan.* Princeton, NJ: Princeton University Press.

Thomas, John. 1980. "Ideological Trends in Western Political Parties." In *Western European Party Systems,* ed. Peter Merkl. New York: Free Press.

Thomas, Sue. 1994. *How Women Legislate.* Oxford: Oxford University Press.

Thomassen, Jacques. 1994. "The Intellectual History of Election Studies." *European Journal of Political Research* 25:241-2.

Tingston, Herbert. 1937. *Political Behavior.* London: King.

Topf, Richard. 1995. "Electoral Participation." In *Citizens and the State,* ed. Hans-Dieter Klingemann and Dieter Fuchs. Oxford: Oxford University Press.

Truman, David B. 1951. *The Governmental Process: Political Interests and Public Opinion.* New York: Knopf.

Tsebelis, George. 1990. "Elite Interaction and Constitutional Building in Consociational Democracies." *Journal of Theoretical Politics* 2:5-29.

———. 1995. "Decision Making in Political Systems: Veto Players in Presidentism, Parliamentarism, Multicameralism and Multipartism." *British Journal of Political Science* 25:289-325.

Tufte, Edward R. 1978. *Political Control of the Economy.* Princeton, NJ: Princeton University Press.

Tuohy, Carolyn. 1990. "Institutions and Interests in the Occupational Health Arena: The Case of Québec." In *Policy Communities and Public Policy in Canada,* ed. William D. Coleman and Grace Skogstad. Toronto: Copp Clark Pitman.

United Nations. 1994. *UNESCO Statistical Yearbook 1994.* New York: United Nations.

United Nations Department of Public Information. 1992. *World Media Handbook 1992-4.* New York: United Nations.

Valen, Henry. 1988. "Norway: Decentralization and Group Representation." In *Candidate Selection in Comparative Perspective,* ed. Michael Gallagher and Michael Marsh. London: Sage.

Van den Bergh, George. 1995. *Unity in Diversity: A Systematic Critical Analysis of All Electoral Systems.* London: B. T. Batsford.

Verba, Sidney, and Norman H. Nie. 1972. *Participation in America: Political Democracy and Social Equality.* New York: Harper and Row.

Verba, Sidney, Norman H. Nie, and Jae-on Kim. 1978. *Participation and Political Equality.* Cambridge: Cambridge University Press.

Verba, Sidney, Kay Schlozman, and Henry Brady. 1995. *Voice and Equality: Civic Voluntarism in American Politics.* Cambridge, MA: Harvard University Press.

Verney, Douglas V. 1959. *The Analysis of Political Systems.* London: Routledge and Kegan Paul.

Vickers, Jill, Pauline Rankin, and Christine Appelle. 1993. *Politics as if Women Mattered: A Political Analysis of the National Action Committee on the Status of Women.* Toronto: University of Toronto Press.

Vig, Norman, and Steven Schier, eds. 1985. *Political Economy in Western Democracies.* New York: Holmes and Meier.

Von Berme, Klaus. 1983. *The Political System of the Federal Republic of Germany.* New York: St. Martin's.

Voronina, Olga A. 1994. "Soviet Women and Politics: On the Brink of Change." In *Women and Politics Worldwide,* ed. Barbara J. Nelson and Najma Chowdhury. New Haven, CT: Yale University Press.

Vowles, Jack, and Peter Aimer. 1993. *Voters' Vengeance: The 1990 Election in New Zealand and the Fate of the Fourth Labour Government.* Auckland: Auckland University Press.

Wald, Kenneth. 1987. *Religion and Politics in America.* New York: St. Martin's.

Walker, Jack L. 1991. *Mobilizing Interest Groups in America.* Ann Arbor: University of Michigan Press.

Wangen, Edgar. 1983. *Polit-Marketing: Das Marketing-Management der Politischen Parteien.* Opladen: Westdeutsher Verlag.

Ware, Alan, ed. 1987. *Political Parties: Electoral Change and Structural Response.* Oxford: Basil Blackwell.

———. 1996. *Political Parties and Party Systems.* Oxford: Oxford University Press.

Watanuki, Joji. 1991. "Social Structure and Voting Behavior." In *The Japanese Voter,* Scott Flanagan et al. New Haven, CT: Yale University Press.

Wattenberg, Martin. 1984. *The Decline of American Political Parties.* Cambridge, MA: Harvard University Press.

———. 1991. *The Rise of Candidate-Centered Politics: Presidential Elections of the 1980s.* Cambridge, MA: Harvard University Press.

Wearing, Joseph, ed. 1991. *The Ballot and Its Message.* Toronto: Copp Clark Pitman.

Weatherford, Stephen M. 1978. "Economic Conditions and Electoral Outcomes: Class Differences in the Political Response to Recession." *American Journal of Political Science* 22:917-38.

Weaver, David. 1991. "Issue Salience and Public Opinion: Are There Consequences of Agenda-Setting?" *International Journal of Public Opinion Research* 3:53-68.

———. 1984. "Media Agenda-Setting and Public Opinion: Is There a Link?" *Communication Yearbook 8.* Beverly Hills, CA: Sage.

Weaver, David H., Doris A. Graber, Maxwell E. McCombs, and C. E. Eyal. 1981. *Media Agenda-Setting in a Presidential Election: Issues, Images, and Interest.* New York: Praeger.

Weaver, R. Kent, and Bert A. Rockman, eds. 1992. *Do Institutions Matter?* Washington, DC: Brookings Institution.

Webb, Paul. 1992. "Britain: The 1987 Campaign." In *Electoral Strategies and Political Marketing,* ed. Shaun Bowler and David M. Farrell. Houndmills: Macmillan.

Weir, Blair T. 1985. "The American Tradition of the Experimental Treatment of Elections: A Review Essay." *Electoral Studies* 4:125-33.

Weisberg, Herbert, and Jerold Rusk. 1970. "Dimensions of Candidate Evaluation." *American Political Science Review* 64:1167-85.

Welch, Susan, and Rebecca Herrick. 1992. "The Impact of At-Large Elections on the Representation of Minority Women." In *United States Electoral Systems: Their Impact on Women and Minorities,* ed. Wilma Rule and Joseph F. Zimmerman. New York: Praeger.

Welch, Susan, and Donley T. Studlar. 1990. "Multimember Districts and the Representation of Women: Evidence From Britain and the United States." *Journal of Politics* 52:391-413.

Weller, Patrick. 1985. *First Among Equals: Prime Ministers in Westminster Systems.* Sydney: Allen and Unwin.

White, Theodore. 1961. *The Making of the President, 1960.* New York: Atheneum.

Whiteley, Paul F., ed. 1980. *Models of Political Economy.* Beverly Hills, CA: Sage.

Wiarda, Howard J. 1974. "Corporatism and Development in the Iberic-Latin World." In *The New Corporatism,* ed. Fredrick B. Pike and Thomas Stritch. Notre Dame, IN: University of Notre Dame Press.

Wilkinson, Paul. 1971. *Social Movement.* London: Pall Mall.

Williams, Robert J. 1981. "Candidate Selection." In *Canada at the Polls, 1979, 1980,* ed. Howard R. Penniman. Washington, DC: American Enterprise Institute.

Williams, Shirley, and Lascher, Edward L. 1993. *Ambition and Beyond: Career Paths of American Politicians.* Berkeley: University of California Press.

Wilson, Frank L. 1983. "French Interest Group Politics: Pluralist or Neocorporatist?" *American Political Science Review* 77:895-910.

Wilson, Graham K. 1990. *Interest Groups.* Oxford: Basil Blackwell.

———. 1992. "American Interest Groups in Comparative Perspective." In *The Politics of Interests,* ed. Mark P. Petracca. Boulder, CO: Westview.

Wolchik, Sharon L. 1994. "Women's Issues in Czechoslovakia in the Communist and Postcommunist Periods." In *Women and Politics Worldwide,* ed. Barbara J. Nelson and Najma Chowdhury. New Haven, CT: Yale University Press.

Wolfinger, Raymond and Steven Rosenstone. 1980. *Who Votes?* New Haven, CT: Yale University Press.

Wolinetz, Steven B., ed. 1988. *Parties and Party Systems in Liberal Democracies.* London: Routledge.

Woo, Lillian C. 1980. *The Campaign Organizer's Manual.* Durham, NC: Carolina Academic Press.

Wootton, Graham. 1970. *Interest Groups.* Englewood Cliffs, NJ: Prentice Hall.

Worcester, Robert. 1983. *Political Opinion Polling.* London: Macmillan.

———. 1994. *British Public Opinion Since 1945.* Oxford: Basil Blackwell.

Wright, William. 1971a. *A Comparative Study of Party Organization.* Columbus, OH: Charles Merrill.

———. 1971b. "Comparative Party Models: Rational-Efficient and Party Democracy." In *A Comparative Study of Party Organization,* ed. William Wright. Columbus, OH: Charles Merrill.

Young, Lisa. 1996. "Women's Movements and Political Parties: A Canadian-American Comparison." *Party Politics* 2:229-50.

Zaller, John R. 1992. *The Nature and Origin of Mass Opinion.* Cambridge: Cambridge University Press.

Zermano, Sergio. 1990. "Crisis, Neoliberalism, and Disorder." In *Popular Movements and Political Change in Mexico,* ed. Joe Foweraker and Ann L. Craig. Boulder, CO: Rienner.

Zolo, Danilo. 1992. *Democracy and Complexity.* Cambridge, MA: Polity.

Zucker, Harold G. 1978. "The Variable Nature of New Media Influence." *Communication Yearbook 2.* Beverly Hills, CA: Sage.

Zuckerman, Alan. 1982. "New Approaches to Political Cleavage." *Comparative Politics* 15:131-44.

Author Index

Subject Index

Abortion, 137, 141, 159, 334, 337
Additional member system, 6
Africa, 2, 171
Age:
    of members of parliaments, 187, 193
    and voting turnout, 220, 224
Agenda setting. *See* Media, effects
Alignment, party, 97, 324, 359-361
Alternative vote. *See* Electoral systems
American Association of Political
    Consultants, 178
Anderson, John, 302
Approval voting, 55, 82n
Argentina, 2, 54
    leaders, 284
    representation, 198
Asia, 2, 339, 342n
Association of Public Opinion Pollsters, 252
Australia, 3, 5, 346, 350-351
    campaign finance, 128, 132
    election campaigns, 173
    electoral system, 55, 65, 82n20
    interest groups, 141, 151
    leaders, 284, 296
    Liberal party, 240
    media, 256, 263, 269
    polls, 239, 247

    representation, 186, 200
Austria, 3, 338, 362n
    Austrian People's party (ÖVP), 92, 105,
      178
    Austrian Socialist party (SPÖ), 92, 105
    candidate recruitment, 205-206
    election campaigns, 173
    electoral system, 60, 101, 105, 114
    FPÖ, 105, 114
    interest groups, 151
    leaders, 281, 283, 284
    Liberal party, 89
    media, 256, 262
    participation, 230, 235n
    party membership, 114, 121
    party organization, 129, 130, 131
    representation, 187-188, 199

Ballots. *See* Electoral systems
Bangladesh, 283
Barre, Raymond, 165
Begin, Menachem, 259, 360
Belgium, 3, 328, 346, 351
    Christian People's party, 105
    election campaigns, 174
    electoral system, 59, 60, 64, 80n

415

About the Contributors

Sylvia Bashevkin is Professor of Political Science at the University of Toronto. Her publications include *Toeing the Lines: Women and Party Politics in English Canada* (2nd ed., 1993); *True Patriot Love: The Politics of Canadian Nationalism* (1991); *Canadian Political Behaviour* (1985); and *Women and Politics in Western Europe* (1985). In 1993-94, she served as President of the Canadian Political Science Association. Her comparative study of organized feminism in the Thatcher, Reagan, and Mulroney years will be published in a forthcoming book entitled *On the Defensive: Women in Conservative Times.*

André Blais is Professor in the Department of Political Science and Associate Fellow at the Centre de Recherche et de Developement en Economique at the Université de Montréal. He has published *Governments, Parties and Public Sector Employees: Canada, United States, Britain and France* (forthcoming); *The Challenge of Direct Democracy* (forthcoming); *Representative Democracy: The Views of Canadians* (1992); *Letting the People Decide: Dynamics of a Canadian Election* (1992); *The Budget Maximizing Bureaucrat: Appraisals and Evidence* (1991); and *Industrial Policy* (1986). He has also taught at the University of Ottawa and Université Laval.

David Butler is Emeritus Fellow of Nuffield College, Oxford. He has been associated with the Nuffield British general election studies since 1945 and has been author or coauthor of each one since 1951. He has written widely on British, American, and Australian politics, producing 3 dozen books. His most recent publications include *British Political Facts, 1900-94* (1995); *The British General Election of 1992* (1992); *Referendums Around the World* (1994); and *British Politics and European Elections 1994* (1995). He is well known for his election commentaries on BBC television and radio.

Russell J. Dalton is Professor in the Department of Politics and Society at the University of California, Irvine. His publications include *The Green Rainbow* (1994); *Citizen Politics in Western Democracies* (2nd ed., 1996); *Germany Transformed* (1981); and *Electoral Change in Advanced Industrial Democracies* (1984).

David M. Farrell is Jean Monnet Lecturer in European Politics, University of Manchester. He has taught at University College Dublin and the University of Wales, Cardiff. His main research interests are in parties, campaigns, and elections in Western Europe. He is coeditor of *Electoral Strategies and Political Marketing* (1992) and of the journal *Party Politics,* and is the author of *Comparing Electoral Systems* (1996).

Mark Franklin is Professor of Political Science at the University of Houston and visiting Professor of Government, University of Strathclyde. His publications include *Electoral Change: Responses to Evolving Social and Attitudinal Structures in Western Countries* (1992); *The Decline of Class Voting in Britain* (1985); and *Choosing Europe? The European Electorate and National Politics in the Face of the Union* (1996). In recent years, his research interests have focused on comparative electoral behavior within the European Union.

Richard S. Katz is Professor of Political Science at the Johns Hopkins University. He has published *How Parties Organize* (Sage 1994); *Party Organizations: A Data Handbook* (Sage 1992); *A Theory of Parties and Electoral Systems* (1980); *Party Governments: European and American Experience* (1987); and *The Patron State: Government and the Arts in Europe, North America, and Japan* (1987). He has worked on elections and political parties in Europe and America and taught at Queens College of the City University of New York and at the State University of New York at Buffalo.

Lawrence LeDuc is Professor of Political Science at the University of Toronto. He has published *Political Choice in Canada* (1980); *Absent Mandate: The Politics of Discontent in Canada* (1984, 1991); and *How Voters Change: The 1987 British Election Campaign in Perspective* (1990). He has held visiting fellowships at the University of Essex, Florida State University, and the University of Amsterdam.

Peter Mair is Professor of Comparative Politics at the University of Leiden, the Netherlands and Director of the Netherlands Graduate School for Political Science and International Relations. His books include *The Changing Irish Party System* (1987); *Identity, Competition, and Electoral Availability: The Stabilisation of European Electorates, 1885-1985* (1990); *Representative Government in Modern Europe* (2nd ed., 1995); *The West European Party System* (1990); *Party Organisations: A Data Handbook* (1992); and *How Parties Organize* (1994). He is coeditor of the *European Journal of Political Research*. He previously taught at the University of Manchester and the European University Institute in Florence.

Louis Massicotte is Assistant Professor of Political Science at the Université de Montréal. He is coauthor of *Le Scrutin au Québec: Un Miroir Déformant* (1985). His articles on legislatures, party discipline, by-elections, and electoral systems have been published in the *Canadian Journal of Political Science, Canadian Public Administration,* and *Recherches Sociographiques.* He has been active in the field of democratic development in 13 countries and was formerly a research officer in the Library of Parliament and Chief, Policy and Strategic Planning at Elections Canada.

Ian McAllister is Professor of Government at Manchester University. His publications include *The Loyalties of Voters: A Lifetime Learning Model* (1990); *Political Behaviour: Citizens, Parties and Elites in Australia* (1992); and *Russia Votes* (1996). He has previously taught at the University of New South Wales, Australia and held research positions at the Australian National University and the University of Strathclyde.

Richard G. Niemi is Professor of Political Science at the University of Rochester. He is coauthor or coeditor of *Vital Statistics in American Politics* (5th ed., 1995); *Controversies in Voting Behavior* (3rd ed., 1993); *Classics in Voting Behavior* (1993); and *Minority Representation and the Quest for Voting Equality* (1992), among other books. He has written on voting behavior, political socialization, and legislative districting. He has held visiting positions at the University of Lund, the University of Iowa, and in Japan.

Helmut Norpoth is Professor of Political Science at the State University of New York at Stony Brook. He has published *Confidence Regained: Economics, Mrs. Thatcher, and the British Voter* (1992); *Politics and Government in*

Europe Today (1990); *Economics and Politics: The Calculus of Support* (1991); and *Analysis of Variance* (2nd ed., 1987). His research covers electoral behavior in the United States, Britain, and Germany. He has taught at the Universities of Texas, Arizona, and Cologne.

Pippa Norris teaches at the Kennedy School of Government, Harvard University, and is Associate Director (Research) of the Joan Shorenstein Center on the Press, Politics and Public Policy. Her books include *Electoral Change Since 1945* (1996); *Women, Politics and Media* (1996); *Women and Politics in Britain* (1996); *Political Representation: Gender, Class and Race in the British Parliament* (1995); *Different Roles, Different Voices* (1994); *Gender and Party Politics* (Sage 1993); *British Elections and Parties Yearbook* (1991-1994); *British By-elections: The Volatile Electorate* (1990); and *Politics and Sexual Equality: The Comparative Position of Women in Western Democracies* (1987). She edits the *Harvard International Journal of Press/Politics.* She has taught at Edinburgh University, with visiting positions at the University of California, Berkeley, and Columbia University.

Holli A. Semetko is currently Professor and Chair of Audience Research and Public Opinion at the University of Amsterdam, on leave from Syracuse University. She has published *Germany's Unity Election: Voters and the Media* (1994) and *The Formation of Campaign Agendas: A Comparative Analysis of Party and Media Roles in Recent American and British Elections* (1991). She is currently writing *Campaigning on Television: News and Elections in Comparative Perspective.*